Henry Kingsley

**Madlle. Mathilde**

A Novel

Henry Kingsley

**Madile. Mathilde**
*A Novel*

ISBN/EAN: 9783337228378

Printed in Europe, USA, Canada, Australia, Japan

Cover: Foto ©ninafisch / pixelio.de

More available books at **www.hansebooks.com**

*Handy-Volume Series.*

Nº· IX.

———

# Madlle. Mathilde.

BY

HENRY KINGSLEY.

TO

## MY WIFE

AND

## MISS THACKERAY,

IN MEMORY

OF THE PLEASANT SUMMER DAYS DURING WHICH THE
BETTER PARTS OF IT WERE WRITTEN.

# PREFACE.

WHEN asked to write the first story which has ever appeared in the "Gentleman's Magazine" in a course of 137 years, I was extremely diffident, feeling somewhat like a modest young curate, who has to return thanks for the clergy before a large audience principally composed of dissenters; I was not reassured by being told, before I began, that a large number of the subscribers strongly objected to the arrangement; and I am glad to hear that the opposition has ceased, but it made me as careful as I could be, and it accounts for many little notes which I was forced to give as authority, and some of which we have thought worth retaining even for the general reader.

The longest one, not by my hand, was retained through a mistake of my own as to its length. It is, however, valuable and interesting, and so the reader may be consoled as Mr. Swiveller was by Mr. Brass, when he complained that one leg of his stool was longer than the others, "He has got a piece of timber in for his money."

The choice of a story was extremely difficult, till in consultation one said, "Tell them the story we heard at St.

Malo, and of which we have so often spoken since." The thing was done.

To make the plot go squarely, to turn it from a simple narrative to a dramatically-written fiction, I had to take a few little liberties. Mathilde of this story was not the cousin but the *married sister* of the heroic André. Adèle, again, was the younger and unmarried sister, and was by no means the weak little creature which one sees in Adèle; she was of very singular personal beauty, and of great courage and resolution.

The real Mathilde did all that she is represented as doing here, but something more besides, so weird and odd, that I have omitted it from the story as being likely to be thought improbable even for fiction. When the conspiracy, which I have described as being in the house of Madame, in the Rue de Jesouil, at Dinan, was surprised by the Revolutionists, the list of the conspirators was on Adèle's person, and there was no fire. Mathilde took it from her, and before the Revolutionists could reach them, had *eaten and swallowed it*. These Desilles must have been a strange family.

My authority for Marat's having lectured in England is M. Lamartine.

# CONTENTS.

| CHAPTER | | PAGE |
|---|---|---|
| I. | A CHAPTER WHICH WILL HAVE TO BE WRITTEN SEVERAL TIMES AGAIN: EACH TIME IN DARKER INK . . . . . . . . . | 1 |
| II. | SOME NECESSARY GOSSIP AND CONVERSATION . . | 6 |
| III. | MORE NECESSARY GOSSIP . . . . . . | 11 |
| IV. | GOSSIP STILL, PRINCIPALLY ABOUT MADEMOISELLE ADÈLE . . . . . . . . . | 20 |
| V. | LOUIS AND ANDRÉ TALK OVER THE STATE OF PUBLIC AFFAIRS . . . . . . . . | 25 |
| VI. | AND FINDING THEM UNSATISFACTORY, DISCUSS THE D'ISIGNYS . . . . . . . | 31 |
| VII. | WHICH ENDS IN ANDRÉ GOING TO CHURCH . . | 38 |
| VIII. | AND THE AUTHOR, HAVING TO TAKE UP THE THREAD OF THE STORY— . . . . . | 43 |
| IX. | LANDS THE READER ONCE MORE AT SHEEPSDEN . | 52 |
| X. | MONSIEUR D'ISIGNY RETURNS . . . . | 55 |
| XI. | "IPHIGENIA IN AULIS" . . . . . . | 58 |
| XII. | NEWS FROM FRANCE FOR M. D'ISIGNY . . . | 64 |
| XIII. | ADÈLE'S PENANCE . . . . . . . | 75 |
| XIV. | MATHILDE WALKS OUT WITH HER FATHER . . | 80 |
| XV. | FATHER MARTIN'S ADVICE . . . . . | 88 |
| XVI. | THE FRENCH REVOLUTION IN THE STOUR VALLEY . | 90 |

## CONTENTS.

| CHAPTER | | PAGE |
|---|---|---|
| XVII. | THE FIRST SACRIFICE | 103 |
| XVIII. | ASHURST AND SHEEPSDEN | 110 |
| XIX. | M. D'ISIGNY'S EXPLOSION | 114 |
| XX. | NEWS FROM FRANCE | 123 |
| XXI. | SIR LIONEL FINDS HIMSELF AGAIN IN THE MARKET | 126 |
| XXII. | THE FOUNTAINS OF THE GREAT DEEP ARE BROKEN UP | 135 |
| XXIII. | SIR LIONEL COMES TO SHEEPSDEN | 142 |
| XXIV. | LA GARAYE | 158 |
| XXV. | A GROUP OF OUR GRANDFATHERS | 168 |
| XXVI. | THE FOOLISH REASONS FOR MATHILDE AND SIR LIONEL GETTING IN LOVE | 173 |
| XXVII. | ONE OF THE SADDEST CHAPTERS IN THE WHOLE STORY | 176 |
| XXVIII. | ANDRÉ, LIONEL, AND MATHILDE | 179 |
| XXIX. | BARBOT'S FIRST REVENGE | 187 |
| XXX. | SILENCE THAT DREADFUL BELL | 196 |
| XXXI. | M. D'ISIGNY MEETS STRANGE COMPANY | 200 |
| XXXII. | LA GARAYE AGAIN | 207 |
| XXXIII. | EXPLANATIONS | 217 |
| XXXIV. | THE SHEEPSDEN LETTER-BAG | 222 |
| XXXV. | MONTAUBAN | 233 |
| XXXVI. | MEDEA | 242 |
| XXXVII. | MONTAUBAN, WITH A, AS YET DISTANT, VIEW OF NANTES | 248 |
| XXXVIII. | MONTAUBAN, WITH NEWS OF ANDRÉ DESILLES | 255 |
| XXXIX. | CORRESPONDENCE | 261 |
| XL. | NANCI | 265 |
| XLI. | MADAME APPEARS IN STRANGE COMPANY | 277 |
| XLII. | MADAME'S PLOT PROSPERS | 287 |
| XLIII. | AN ACCOUNT OF THE PIETY AND VIRTUE OF MADAME D'ISIGNY | 289 |

## CONTENTS.

| CHAPTER | | PAGE |
|---|---|---|
| XLIV. | IN WHICH MADAME BECOMES ONCE MORE ENRAGED | 293 |
| XLV. | PARIS | 299 |
| XLVI. | IPHIGENIA IN TAURIS | 306 |
| XLVII. | THE JOURNEY | 313 |
| XLVIII. | THE LAST OF ST. MALO | 317 |
| XLIX. | MA SŒUR | 323 |
| L. | THE LAST NIGHT | 326 |
| LI. | À LA LOIRE | 329 |
| LII. | THE THUNDERBOLT | 332 |
| LIII. | THE JOURNEY | 336 |
| LIV. | THE ABBAYE | 342 |
| LV. | WILLIAM'S WATCH | 346 |
| LVI. | THE PRISON MICE | 355 |
| LVII. | "BUT DANTON HE HAS SLEPT" | 361 |
| LVIII. | ADIEU | 364 |
| LIX. | MADAME'S JOURNEY | 371 |
| LX. | TOGETHER ONCE MORE | 380 |
| LXI. | CONCIERGERIE | 386 |
| LXII. | THE ALTAR | 390 |
| LXIII. | SHEEPSDEN ONCE MORE | 393 |
| LXIV. | A CHAPTER WHICH I HOPE THE READER WILL BE SORRY TO READ, FOR IT IS THE LAST | 396 |

# MADLLE. MATHILDE.

## CHAPTER I.

A CHAPTER WHICH WILL HAVE TO BE WRITTEN SEVERAL TIMES AGAIN: EACH TIME IN DARKER INK.

T was quite impossible, so Mademoiselle Mathilde D'Isigny concluded, that any reasonable being could dream of going out on such an afternoon. It was not to be thought of. Nevertheless, she began thinking at once about her sabots and her red umbrella.

A wild revolutionary-looking nimbus, urged on by a still wilder wind, which seemed, from its direction, to have started from America, had met the rapidly-heated and rapidly-cooled strata of chalk in the valley of the Stour in Dorsetshire. The nimbus, chased by the furious headlong American wind, met the chalk downs while they were cooled by a long winter's frost, and at once dissolved itself into cataracts of water; into cataracts more steady, more persistent, and, in the end, more dangerous, than any which ever came from the wildest and noisiest summer thunderstorm.

It was quite impossible that any reasonable woman could go out on such an afternoon; still the sabots and the red umbrella dwelt on her mind, for it might under certain circumstances become necessary, although impossible.

No summer thunderstorm, in its very worst behaviour, had ever done worse by one than this. You could in a way calculate on those summer thunderstorms. The worst of them came from south-east, then changed to south-west, and the moment the wind got north of west it was all over. But here was a tearing wild wind, straight from godless, or, to say the least, "uncatholic" America, which persisted and deluged and drenched one, and, if one went in and got dry, was perfectly ready to deluge one again. Was there ever such an ill-conditioned, inexorable wind and rain as this?

Toilers in fields might stand such weather for their own purposes; but it was quite evident that no lady could be expected, under any circumstances, to go out in it. Given even the sabots and the red umbrella, it was quite impossible.

For the vast Atlantic, set in motion, doubtless, by the pestilent republicanism of America, had broke loose, and was pouring its torrents on the unsympathetic chalk hills of Dorsetshire; hills which absorb the deluge of rain, and in their way utilize it; but which never "scour" down in a revolutionary manner. On these English hills there are what we dwellers on the chalk call "swilly holes," down which your revolutionary rain channel pours, and, having reconsidered itself, comes up again gently in the meadows and other low lands, which, however, from time to time require draining.

But the meadows in 1789 were not drained, and, therefore, the furious, persistent downfall of rain deserved the epithet which we gave it just now, of "dangerous." It meant flood; and, in those low-lying meadows, between unexpandable hills, flood meant temporary disaster. Stored stacks of hay were carried off, though the next year's crop was improved by the silt left by the flood; lambs were drowned, but the breed of sheep was improved in the end by Mr. Coke's finer sorts, brought from Norfolk; boats, such as careless people had left afloat in such strange times as 1789, were dashed against bridges and broken; which, in the long run, must have been good for the boatbuilders.

Mademoiselle Mathilde may or may not have thought of these things; but one thing is certain, she came to the conclusion that no lady could possibly be expected to go out in such weather. And almost immediately afterwards she rang the bell, and told the middle-aged woman who answered it to bring her cloak with the hood, and her sabots, and her red umbrella; and, in short, began to make preparations for going out into the very weather which she had just before voted impossible.

"I have seen neither my sabots nor my umbrella for some days, Mrs. Bone," she said, "and should expect penance after confession for my carelessness; but that does not excuse my servant. I hope that the sabots have not been mislaid, and that my umbrella was properly dried before it was put by. If such has not been the case, I shall find it necessary to rebuke Anne," their foolish little maid. "I value those things very much. I got those sabots a bargain at Pontorson Fair; and I bought that red umbrella, the colour of which you object to, from old Barbot at Dol, and I beat him down from eleven livres to nine. These things, if lost, can never be replaced."

Some people said that Mademoiselle Mathilde was decidedly plain. Some said that she must have been rather pretty when she was younger. Others, again, said that what little beauty she had wore well, and that she did not show her age, which was twenty-four. Others, again, said that she had a cold, hard, and somewhat stupid face. Others said that her face wanted expression until she was roused. But Mrs. Bone, the middle-aged woman before mentioned, declared until far on into this century that Mademoiselle's face was that of an angel. And Sir Joshua Reynolds, of all people, almost forgot his manners one evening, after having been introduced to her; (at least, so one reads in the "D'Isigny Mémoires," written by the sobered Adèle, not so long ago). French mémoires are French mémoires; and Adèle's are much as others. Sir Joshua is represented as saying to Boswell, "I can't make that face out; I never saw one exactly like it before." He then, according to Adèle's Mémoires, pushed himself through the press up to her, bowing; and, after a little light and easy conversation, asked her would she favour him with a sitting, to which she answered,—

"Most assuredly no. My sister Adèle plays the ornamental rôle in our family. Paint her, milord, if you wish to paint a D'Isigny."

Now, with all due deference to Mrs. Bone and Sir Joshua Reynolds, Mathilde was not a *pretty* woman; any face more utterly unlike his lovely "Kitty Fisher" cannot be imagined; and I very much doubt if she ever had been. The face was very aquiline—strongly Norman; a face which you find not only in the Pays de Caux, but also about Coutances and

Avranches everywhere. A face which is, for a few years, almost always beautiful; a face which still remains here and there among the British aristocracy; a face, however, which often, after a very few years, gets peaked, and sharp, and hawk-like; —if I dare say such a thing, ugly, hard, and avaricious.

Hers was this kind of face, but with a difference.

The beauty of the real Norman face consists in its exquisite form in early womanhood. The Norman women, like the Jewish women, discount their beauty in about two years of unapproachable splendour; at this time the features of Norman beauty are, as the penny novelist would say, "exquisitely chiselled." Whether he knows what he means or no, he is perfectly right; their features *are* beautifully chiselled; but it does not last, this chiselling. The hard old Scandinavian muscle asserts itself; and the result is often a British dowager of that extreme type with which John Leech and Richard Doyle between them have made the general public familiar.

Mathilde had escaped all this. The form of her face was certainly Norman and hawk-like; but it was also, in largeness of mouth, and a certain breadth in the *upper* jaw, Anglo-Teutonic; and the softer, tenderer, Teutonic muscles in her face refused to become "ropy" and prononcés, like those in the face of the Dowager-Marchioness of Thingaby and the Comtesse de Chose. She was always what she had been, both in personal appearance and in character. She had escaped the "chiselling" phase of beauty, and at the same time had escaped the first, fierce, impatient phase of Norman womanhood. She was a woman who could *wait:* she had got that habit from her Anglo-Teutonic mother. Her sister Adèle always told her that she could never make up her mind; and she always told her sister that she leaped at conclusions without any sound basis. They were both right in a way.

A few more words about her, before we see her through the medium of incident. There was a strong suspicion of beauty about her. Everyone called her plain, and yet Sir Joshua Reynolds would have painted her. Her figure was almost deformed, and her gait was very clumsy. She was very broad though not fat; and above her shoulders was that half Norman, half Teutonic head, which gave rise to so many theories as to what was inside it. A short clumsy woman, with such a head as I have mentioned. I have no further portrait. I know the portrait of her great cousin, fourth, as I remember, from Lamennais, nearly opposite that of Jacques Cartier, with Chateaubriand, painted in apparent imitation of David's Marat, looking in from the end of the room. She may have been like him. But I distrust that portrait. I fear it was painted under the later empire.

Adèle, in her Mémoires, says that Mathilde was the very image of her cousin; but I distrust both Adèle and the portrait; and so we must make out a portrait of Mademoiselle Mathilde D'Isigny for ourselves, or go without one. Even the great Emerald Portrait, they tell us, is a forgery of the third century. But their deeds live after them, when their place knoweth them no more.

She never knew her own mind, said her sister Adèle. A "*thin* thing" like her sister Adèle, might easily believe so. Mathilde spent her life in violently protesting against doing anything whatever, in a real Teutonic manner, and in doing such things as were fit to be done, such as were *right* after all: which is all we ask from any one. Not an obstructive woman, or she would not have found herself where she did at last. She did not want a reason for everything.

So we begin our little journey with her. She began by declaring in the most positive manner that no respectable woman could go out in such weather, and immediately afterwards ordered her sabots and her umbrella, and *went* out in it, because some wretched old hind, down in the village of Stourminster Osborne, was dying. The Romanists were then, as they are now, *au fait* with the machinery of charity; and Mademoiselle Mathilde was a Romanist, and so she went to the old man.

So she passed out of the shelter of the porch and faced the furious weather, protesting and a little petulant; yet she faced it. Protesting in her inmost heart against the weather, but not uttering her protest to Mrs. Bone. Petulant to a very little degree at finding that her common-sense resolution to stay at home was overridden by her sentimental desire to make the death of the old man down by the river more easy and more comfortable. She went out into the driving wild weather. She knew that she was "protesting" against the weather God had sent, and she knew she was petulant towards Mrs. Bone. But she could confess the matter about the weather, and give Mrs. Bone her prayers, a *novena*, if necessary. Nevertheless, human nature is human nature, and the bill about the confession and the prayers was not yet presented. So she was still a little bit cross.

The priceless sabots were there, but they had not been properly dried ; and expensive sabots like these were subject to the dry rot, and these in particular could never be replaced to *her*. (She had forgotten that she had told Mrs. Bone that she had picked them up a bargain at Pontorson ; she wanted to be sentimental about them.) The red umbrella had been improperly dried, and there was never such an umbrella before. The horn handle, too, had come off ; innumerable little complaints, about which the Teutonic Bone cared as much as a horse did for a house-fly, knowing Mademoiselle's worth.

Still Mrs. Bone was glad when Mademoiselle had fairly got out into the rain, under her great red umbrella, and she, Bone, could get back to the fire and see about the dinner.

Her opinion of Mademoiselle's character was strangely like, and yet strangely different from, that of Mademoiselle Adèle's.

"She says one thing and does another, William," said Mrs. Bone to the quiet young man who was sitting by the fire, shelling kidney-beans ; "but she is worth the whole lot of us put together."

"Worth developing," says a critic. I answer, Mademoiselle Mathilde is already developed. The circumstances around her will develop ; but she will remain the same.

---

## CHAPTER II.

### SOME NECESSARY GOSSIP AND CONVERSATION.

THE wild furious weather from the south-west, which swept up the valley of the Stour, into which weather Mademoiselle Mathilde had trusted herself, did not produce any great effect on the ordinary inmates of the old Grange from which she had issued. It took the full fury of that weather : it was a very draughty, early seventeenth-century old place, with large stone-framed windows filled with latticed panes ; and yet no one complained of the draughts to-day, for the wind was south-west and warm. Mademoiselle Adèle did not, at all events; and if she did not complain, you might be pretty sure that no one within twenty miles was dissatisfied.

Sheepsden was nestled among elms, in a deep hollow, half-way up the side of one of the chalk hills which form the valley of the Stour, and overlooking the low-lying meadows. The most comfortable room in it was not a very comfortable room in the ordinary way of speaking, taking into consideration modern ideas of comfort. It was large and draughty; it was hall, kitchen, and eating-room all in one; and opened, through the porch from which Mademoiselle Mathilde had just passed, on to the wild weather; yet, even in these dark early spring days, when the weather was an enemy, and not a friend as it was in summer, this room was really the most comfortable in the house. There were no fauteuils or easy chairs; yet these French people, these D'Isignys, who had kept the house on their own hands while they let all the farms, had made it, in their way, most comfortable.

The room was naturally what Mrs. Bone called "whistling cold." The great antre of a fireplace, pile it as high as you would with blazing logs, never cast its warmth over one-fifth of it, until M. D'Isigny had brought French ingenuity to bear upon it. He had caused to be made two great folding-screens, which, starting from each side of the fire-place, overlapped each other in the middle, leaving a passage between which might be closed by a curtain. These two screens inclosed a large space, which was well warmed by the heat of the fire, and in which space the family, servants and all, principally lived: reading, writing, singing, working, eating, drinking, and even cooking. Yet they were wonderfully comfortable.

Next to the fire, on the right-hand side as you looked at it, was the writing-table, and the shaded lamp of M. D'Isigny himself. On the same side, but further from the fire, was a longer table, the fireside half of which was the drawing-room table, sacred to the ladies; while the half farthest from the fire represented the dining-room table, and was devoted to the meals of the D'Isignys. Altogether on the other side of the fireplace, was another table parallel to it, which was the servants' table—the half next the fire being given up to cooking purposes, and the cooler half to the meals, the lighter work, and recreations of these few domestics. In this charmed circle of warmth and cheerfulness, the whole of the family lived nine-tenths of their strict innocent life.

Only two days before the day we speak of, Adèle had objected, for the very first time, to this arrangement about the servants, and had dared (for she made Mathilde tremble at her audacity sometimes) to go as far as to say to her father that she should not care if the servants were French, but that she did not like to consort with English boors. Mathilde trembled as she heard this fearful indiscretion of Adèle's. She knew that her father would punish her for it in some way, and Adèle was so fearfully indiscreet and rebellious whilst undergoing " punition." Her father's manner on this occasion did not re-assure her experienced judgment. He was sedate, calm, and explanatory: and when he took that line his punishments were generally severe. He leant calmly against the high mantel-piece, which, high as it was, was just of the height to support his great shoulders, and confronted his two daughters. Mathilde folded her hands, and looked patiently and submissively at him; Adèle drooped her head, and was ready for tears and recantation even before he had begun, with the beautifully modulated voice of the old French gentleman, still to be heard occasionally, to give his reasons.

"The great cause which has led to these illimitable troubles, now threatening to become incalculable disasters in France, has been a want of confidence between classes. Had classes in France confided in one another, and studied one another's habits and wants more, there might have been some chance of a general and confidential consultation; and the present hideous state of affairs, growing more hideous every day, might have been averted. A revolution is impossible here: not because of the better being of the peasantry, but because the aristocracy are deservedly in better *rapport* with the peasantry than in France. No one agrees with me in this view of the matter, not even Sir Lionel Somers; but I hold it, and intend that our servants should live with us. If Sir Lionel Somers objects to the arrangements, he may cease his visits. A D'Isigny of the thirteenth century, need not, I hope, go on his knees to ask for the society of an English baronet of the seventeenth, whose title was only got by the most extraordinary—I will go as far as that, *extraordinary*—use of the Divine Right which the world has ever seen."

At this dreadful allusion to James I.'s baronetcies, which were a pet grievance of her father's, and which caused him to ride a considerably high horse with Sir Lionel, Mathilde gave herself up for lost. "Bread and water on fast days, and haricots without gravy on flesh days; and I doubt we shall not get out of it with that. I wish I was at Avranches; I'd go pilgrimage barefoot to Mount St. Michael. It is only four leagues, and when you pass Louis it is not bad walking across the sands. I'd do it gladly to save Adèle, for she is so indiscreet under these impositions; and there is eight pounds of prime beef in the house, besides dripping. And this will be a month's *maigre* for us. It must go to the poor, that is all. I wonder how much he knows? I wish we had a priest. Since he has taken to doing the priest business himself, things are getting perfectly intolerable. No priest would set us such penances."

He very soon let Adèle and Mathilde know how much he knew.

"I may be crotchety, and I may be an old fool, though I am not so old. But I have my opinions and my will in spite of Sir Lionel Somers, who might have done better, as my future son-in-law, than incite my daughter Adèle to rebellion. There is another reason, young ladies, why more than ever I intend to live in presence of my servants. I wish you to hear every word which the servants dare to say in your presence; a process which will, by curbing their tongues, elevate them to something like your level; and I wish the servants to hear every word which *you* say, which will curb *your* tongues, and make you careful about scandalous talk."

Mathilde put in a mental protest against her being classed with Adèle in this respect, as well she might, but she said nothing; only thought to herself, "now comes our penance."

"Therefore," said Monsieur D'Isigny, "I forbid either of you, from this moment, to address one word of French to me, or to one another." He acted on his determination on the instant, as he always did. "For ze future, my daughtare, we sall all spek ze English for everlasting everaremore, until we sall learn our obediences and our dutys. Ze servants sall laugh at our English, without doubt. That is good disciplines for our vanity. But we sall all spek English till we learn our obediences. Have you reply, you two?"

Adèle had nothing to say. Sir Lionel Somers had certainly been ridiculing her father, and she had listened and laughed. She was glad to get out of it under the penance of speaking the hated English for a limited time. Mathilde, however, had something to say. She was dreadfully afraid of her father, his word was law to her; yet the woman always said what was in her, and said it now, in perfectly beautiful English,—a strange contrast to her father's English,—perhaps with a slight and pretty French accent.

"Adèle is as near blameless as possible in this matter, sir. Your discipline is, I think, a good one: we should talk more English. Adèle's English and your own are absolutely ridiculous; mine is not good, but it is better than yours. Adèle, I say, is blameless in this matter, or nearly so. The lover you have chosen for her made jokes, and she laughed at them, but rebuked him at the same time. The fault lies at my door entirely. I could have stopped them, but I did not."

"And why not, daughter?"

"Because what he said was in the main true. He said that you were *sujet aux lubies*."

"That is French," said M. D'Isigny.

"I beg pardon; but it is true, you know."

"I did not know it. It is possibly in consequence of the conduct of my daughters," replied M. D'Isigny, whose bad English we are not going to reproduce. "I do not say that my English is good, and you will even allow that your own might be improved. But read for me in your English the tragedy of *King Lear*, and put it to your heart. Lear had three daughters: I have but two—my Regan and Goneril; but where is my Cordelia?"

After which bitter sarcasm M. D'Isigny mounted his horse, and went off for Silchester.

"He will make himself so utterly ridiculous with that English of his," thought Mathilde, when he was gone, and she was helping Mrs. Bone with the cooking, "that he will lose half his prestige. I wish there were a priest nearer than Lulworth; I'd go barefoot to him twenty miles. My father has assumed a kind of amateur priesthood, and one gets neither confession nor absolution—only penance. Father Martin, dear old man, would never have condemned us to talk English till further orders. I must and will talk French. I shall talk French to Mrs. Bone, who don't understand it, and get out of it in that way."

## CHAPTER III.

### MORE NECESSARY GOSSIP.

SO Monsieur D'Isigny, in redingote, buckskin breeches, top-boots, and three-cornered hat, covering a close-cropped head (a *chevelure*, which, like everything else he did, gave extreme offence to both parties, both to the new party and the old), had ridden away on a splendid, large-boned brown horse, through the bad weather, on the day before our opening. He was in the very best temper possible. He had done his duty, and that was quite enough for him. He was bound on an antiquarian journey to Silchester. We will make his further acquaintance on his return.

"He beant much like a frog-eating Frenchman," said an old stone-breaker by the road-side to an old shepherd, who was leaning over a gate as he passed.

"No, a beant," said the shepherd. "He's a straight upstanding old chap, for a Frenchman," replied he. "He'd give good account of Sir Lionel, or of any gentleman in these parts, for the matter of that."

He never condescended for one moment to let his household know the possible or probable period of his return, although he always expected, under penalties, that his daughters should be at home to receive him. It was part of his discipline. He used to quote to them the text, "Let thy master when he cometh find thee watching." So, on the next day after his departure, Mathilde not only faced the furious weather, in going to see the dying old man by the river, but also the chance of some extra penance for herself. Still, as I impressed on you by reiteration in the first chapter, she went in defiance of both duty and inclination.

There are some women who are so entirely loveable, beautiful, fragile, illogical, childish—to sum up all, irresistible—in favour of whom the very sternest man, if he has anything of the man in him, gives up a few, more or less, of his pet crotchets. These are generally silly women, who appeal to his pity, like a starving bird in a frost. Adèle was such a woman; Mathilde was not.

Mathilde would have liked a quiet little bower of a room upstairs, with a few flowers and birds, for there were plenty of rooms for the purpose; but she proposed it to her father, and seeing, from his cold, steady look, that he entirely disapproved of it, abandoned the idea at once. Adèle, on the other hand, had made such a bower without consulting her father at all, and he had never looked coldly on her. He would have paid Mathilde the respect of despising her had she insisted on any such frivolity. Adèle, as he put it to himself, was too light and childish to be despised; her character was not formed, and she must be treated as a child. He never allowed to himself the fact, that in spite of her waywardness, and, what is more, her foolishness, he loved her more deeply than any human being, and that, if she only went the right way to work, she could do what she liked with him. He paid Mathilde, whom in his way he respected, the compliment of showing her by a very cool, calm stare, that she would fall in his opinion if she forgot herself so far as to mention the subject of a boudoir again. She did not. His look was law, and she gave the idea up; and so she knitted and stitched down with the servants, while Adèle had her little bower aloft.

This bower of Adèle's was a heaven to Mathilde; yet she seldom went there. She knew that her father disapproved of it, though he let child Adèle do as she liked. "He disapproved of my having a *boudoir;* it would be rather mean to traverse his intentions by using Adèle's." Honest enough, like herself; but, then, the excuses she made to Adèle for not going there! "Holy Mary," she said to herself once, "what fearful lies one has to tell to enable one to do one's duty; no confession or absolution to be got either."

On this wild spring day, she had told one of the most astounding of all the fictions which weighed so on her conscience. Adèle had asked her to come up into her room and sit with her. She had fenced off Adèle's proposal as usual, until Adèle had got petulant, and taxed her with pride and jealousy, in her silly way; upon which Mathilde had told her that her reason was that Adèle's room was too great a pleasure to indulge in during Lent. After which shocking and transparent fib Adèle had gone off in a huff, and Mathilde began trying to remember as much as she could of what the last priest she had seen had told her about the allotted periods in purgatory. For she had told a terrible falsehood, and she lived to tell another,—if a falsehood could ever be anything but evil,—the greatest and most glorious which was ever told in the history of the world.

After Adèle had gone upstairs, she had sat by the fire sewing. But a lad had come in and told her that Dick Halfacre was worse, and she had gone out.

She never thought that, even according to the faith of her own Church, a good deed can (under circumstances) balance an evil one. She went out from sheer Christian goodwill to help as far as she could a dying old Protestant hind. Lonely and lost for want of the spiritual direction to which she had accustomed herself, she went unwillingly on her errand of mercy with her last lie lying heavy on her heart.

God help women like this: with spiritual experiences far deeper than those of most priests, yet yearning for the outward and visible ceremonials of their faith. Mathilde would have poured out the whole of her noble soul to the first Catholic priest, young or old, wise or foolish, that she could find.

There were two people left before the fire-place, after her departure, whom we must notice. They were engaged in cooking, or in preparing things for cooking. French people, as far as I have observed, begin their preparations for the day's dinner the moment they get out of bed; English people, on the other hand, put it off to the last minute, and then begin to fry and boil in a frantic manner. Whether this English habit of putting off everything till you are forced to do it can be so widely applied as to touch such matters as Reform bills and ironclad squadrons, is no part of our business here; but everyone knows a good dinner from a bad one, and ordinary French dinners have always been better than ours, principally, I believe, because they begin at them earlier. The two people, to whom I am about to call your attention, were busy in preparing dinner;

but it was not to-day's dinner, it was the day after to-morrow's dinner. They were shelling haricots, which require at least a day's soaking.

Yet they were both English among English; a man and a woman. William, "the general young man," groom, gardener, footman, what you will; and Mrs. Bone, the "general" woman, housekeeper, lady's maid, cook, still-room maid, whatever you please to call her. I wish to introduce you to these two people, and I wish you to know William first; because if you will do me the honour to follow me, I will lead William, and you, and Mathilde into a very strange place, possibly the very strangest of which we have ever heard. My promise is great, but I think I can perform it.

"Solid," "a very 'solid' young man," said his brother and sister peasants, in their Dorsetshire way of speaking. Undoubtedly a very "solid" young man, indeed. Not what you would call a *very* handsome young man, but with a fine, frank, square face, and a good, bold eye; with a finely shaped head well set on, and a carriage as fine as Westall's the model.

He could neither read nor write, as yet, but he was learning from Mathilde and Mrs Bone. A very taciturn young man—so much so, that Adèle, of the "Mémoires," christened him "William the Silent," and told it to her father as a good little joke. In reply to which he got down his "Hamlet" (he was great in Shakspeare), and read aloud the great passage which follows the Soliloquy; in which "nicknaming God's creatures" appears among the catalogue of crimes charged generally against women. "I am sure I don't jig, and amble, and lisp," said Adèle, as soon as M. D'Isigny had shut the book, and gone coldly upstairs to bed, "and *you* know, Mathilde, that I don't paint."

William was certainly silent with his social superiors, perhaps not so silent with his social equals. He would obey and follow a "gentleman," but had an instinctive eye for a snob, whether that snob was a duke or a grocer. He came of the poor, or half-poor, agricultural class; of a class which had watched, with their *own* eyes, and not with those of a newspaper, all the faults of the land-holding families (and great they were), and which could trust them still. The class of farmers who would toast "a bloody war and a bad harvest" had not come yet, but was coming. The squire or lord in those times was to a certain extent representing, in his free-handed hospitality and charity, the old religious houses, whose lands in very many instances he had taken possession of two hundred and fifty years before. The memory, nay, even the knowledge of that usurpation was gone from among the peasants, though there still remained among the older of them a belief that the lay occupiers of church lands would never have an heir in direct succession, and they quoted startling precedents for their belief. Still the need of the old hospitality and charity was left; and those of the agricultural class who had from their superior activity and good looks been thrown against the landowners, liked them and trusted them.

William's family, from its traditional good looks, good temper, and activity, had always gone to service. He had had his doubts about taking service with a Frenchman; but as M. D'Isigny was much the finest gentleman he had ever seen, he came to him, and stayed with him. For M. D'Isigny had a stronger claim on his admiration than that of being "a true gentleman:" M. D'Isigny had the quality of bravery.

William, like most Englishmen of good nerve and physique, in those days as in these, had what a man might call loosely the *empeiric* courage, as a birth-gift: he would face a new danger carelessly and well. But in the matter of *apeiric* courage, when he was called on to face a danger which he had never faced before, but of which he had heard a bad name from his neighbours, he was perhaps a little deficient; until a certain accident cured him, and at the same time gave him a confidence in M. D'Isigny which lasted until his death.

He had been a week or so with M. D'Isigny, and M. D'Isigny and he were in the yard together, Monsieur giving him some orders, when they heard a noise in the village below, as of men shouting a single sentence continuously.

"And what may be the matter there, for instance?" said M. D'Isigny.

"I expect," said William, "that they are a-giving old Tom Blowers rough music."

"Rough music? As how then?"

"When a man ill-treats his wife, or a wife ill-treats her husband, they generally, in these parts, gives 'em rough music.

Blows harvest horns, and beats on the bottom of kettles, and hollers," replied William.

"But I have not been ill-treating my wife, and this is not the road to Dinan, at which place Madame D'Isigny resides at present; and the music seems to be coming in this direction; and it is also all what you call 'hollering.' What are they saying?"

"'Mad dog,' by the Lord!" said William, running across the yard and catching up a ladder. "Here, sir, up into the loft with you."

William, like all English peasants of those days, had an utter blind terror of mad dogs. They used then to smother people with feather beds who were afflicted with hydrophobia. A woman told me herself that her mother had assisted at one of these immolations. Hydrophobia was a real terror and scourge in those days: an inexorable fact so horrible that all ordinary laws of morality and charity were set aside on its appearance. William never dreamt of facing the dog itself, and ran for a ladder.

He himself had got up a safe number of rungs, when he noticed that M. D'Isigny was not following, but was standing his ground with his hammer-headed whip in his hand. William came down two rungs at once.

"It is death, Monsieur," he said. "It is a horrible death."

"But we must kill the dog first," said M. D'Isigny, "and die ourselves afterwards. Get some kind of fork and help me."

William was roused now. He dashed into a stable for a pitchfork, as the dog, the kind of dog which the Americans call a "yallah dog," what we call a tall under-bred tinker's lurcher, came into the yard, at a slowish trot, with his ears down, and his tail between his legs, evidently in the last stage of hydrophobia, with half the hamlet behind him, carrying pitchforks and staves, crying out, "Mad dog! mad dog!" D'Isigny saw the dog tear at the posts of the yard-gate as he trotted in, but held his own; and looking at the dog, began to bethink himself of a certain M. Marat, a Swiss, who had been here giving lectures at Stourminster Marshall, on Comparative Anatomy, as we call it now, some few years before.

William was behind him now. "Be steady, sir," said he.

"I'll be steady," said M. D'Isigny.

The dog, more dangerous than the most terrible serpent—for the snake's poison is quickest and most merciful—ran towards M. D'Isigny, while the villagers stood aghast. The dog was a gipsy's dog; which had lain in the straw with the pretty children, and had been fondled by them; now it was a terrible devil. The same thing happens sometimes among human beings. Horrible! unutterable! The brute dashed at M. D'Isigny with a rattling, gasping snarl, but it never quite reached him. A terrible blow from the hammer-head of his whip, caught the poor wretch under the ear, and laid him convulsively struggling on the ground; where another blow of the same dexterous and inexorable sort killed him.

William's mouth was dry, and his tongue parched, but he made no remark any more than did M. D'Isigny. From this moment, however, there began a confidence and respect in the two men towards one another. Quite undemonstrative, but which never getting disturbed grew firmer and firmer as years went on.

So much about the servant, William. Why so much about him? Because this is a story of the past, and for good or for evil, men exactly like him are, by education and change of social habits, as extinct as the Dodo. His brothers won Aboukir and Trafalgar for us, though they were liable to be flogged, and *were* flogged for looking " saucy " at a ten-year old midshipman who had joined his ship yesterday. They also mutinied at the Nore, and did other very decided things. A class of men which could be *led* anywhere, and driven into most places; the very class which gave to Britain the undoubted command of the seas. William being a good representative of this class, I have said just so much about him as being a man worth preserving, and because we shall have to go far a-field with him. When I began speaking of him, I used the old Hants-Dorset word, "solid;" and repeating it once more, I leave him to tell his own story.

Mrs. Bone, who was his companion in shelling haricots, was a delicate-featured woman of about forty-five, who must once have been very handsome. Delicate-featured as she was, she was the most patient and diligent of drudges; always in good humour, always ready and willing to do anything, from lugging coals or wood up into Adèle's room, or sitting up all night with

C

her when she chose to be ill, "*pour s'amuser.*" She is also worthy of notice, because she belonged to a class which existed then, and exists, I regret to say, now,—to the class of widows without provision, who having had some poor house of their own, and having brought up a family, find themselves obliged to return to drudgery, just as old age begins to look them in the face, to keep themselves from the workhouse.

William and she were extremely confidential. Both Stourminster Osborne people, and that town being the Omphalos of the earth to both of them, they had a never-ending fund of conversation about its inhabitants. People who have had the privilege of hearing two old folks, who are in society, talking about who *she* was, and who was *his* father, tell one that the two old folks seemed immensely delighted by their conversation. Mrs. Bone and William delighted one another in this way, or rather Mrs. Bone delighted William, for she knew three generations to his one. Had they been in a different rank in life, he would probably have said, in the slang of that time, as far as I can judge, that she was "a deuced agreeable woman, who knew the world and people amazingly well;" but, although he *thought* the equivalent to this, he never expressed it. His appreciation of it was shown by his calling her "mother," and by his chivalrous devotion to her; his great diligence in easing her of every bit of hard work which he could; and his habit of buying for her little bits of finery—handkerchiefs, which she would have died sooner than wear, and twopenny brooches at fairtime, all of which she put by "for his sake," as if she was his sweetheart.

He had a sweetheart, of course—everyone had in those days—a beef-faced young lady, whom Shakspeare one hundred odd years before had christened "Audrey;" but all his attentions to her were confined to walking out with her along Lovers'-lane, up on to the Down after afternoon church; she carrying her prayer-book in a carefully unused pocket-handkerchief, not saying anything which has come down to our time; and he grinning and growling to her at intervals. I suppose they both liked it, or they would not have done it; but it never led to anything, and so we may dismiss it.

Mrs. Bone had the benefit of his *petits soins*, and on one occasion at least he got into trouble about her. He strongly objected to her carrying baskets of sea-coal (as he called them) up to Mademoiselle Adèle's bower; and on this occasion, finding the coalscuttle (a wooden cockle-basket from Poole) ready at the bottom of the stairs, he carried it up to ease Mrs. Bone. Mademoiselle Adèle, hearing steps outside, wanting something or another, and thinking that it was one of her two slaves, either Mathilde or Mrs. Bone, dashed out on to the landing in very extreme dishabille, and found herself face to face with William the Silent.

If she had had on her best dressing-gown, she would not so much have cared; but she had not—she had on nothing better than a very old duffle dressing-gown, and her hair was not done. When the doctor came to see her in her bedroom (there was never anything the matter with her, but she had the doctor sometimes to see if she could get some gossip out of him), she always had on quite another kind of dressing-gown, trimmed with blue; but William the Silent had seen her in the old duffle one, and she hated him from that moment. He, on the other hand, had had a rooted antipathy to that young lady; which, indeed, he carried to his grave. They were certainly not formed for one another, those two. He kept his dislike for her to himself; she never yet kept anything to herself, and most certainly not her extreme dislike for him. Their first battle-royal, which, ending in a disastrous defeat for her, increased her dislike for the "Nigaud," arose out of this business of the duffle dressing-gown. If she had had on the blue-trimmed one, the course of their history might have been altered. Does not Carlyle tell us that no one wanted the Seven Years' War except three women —Marie Thérèse, Catharine, and Pompadour?

She would have kept up a seven years', or a seventy years', war with him after this, had there been seven years to do it in, which there were not. However, she made herself as disagreeable as she could, which was not very disagreeable, for she was a loveable little soul, after all.

She complained to her father about the "Nigaud Anglais" being upstairs, and M. D'Isigny had a solemn inexorable bed of justice over the case of the duffle dressing-gown *versus* William. The result was that William left that bed with the highest honours, and that Adèle got an admonition about her habits of luxury and self-seeking which drove her half mad, and made it necessary for her sister Mathilde, who was ill of a cold, to sit up with her all night.

Monsieur D'Isigny never *scolded*, he only *admonished*. Mathilde could scold, and roundly too; but no one ever cared for her. Two minutes' admonition from M. D'Isigny was a far more terrible thing than twenty minutes scolding from Mathilde. See, for instance, the difference between a scolding from Lord Scamperdale in the hunting-field, and a *rating* from a judge, a bankruptcy commissioner, or an experienced police magistrate. No one is the worse for being called a " perpendicular Puseyite pig-jobber ; " but watch the effect of my Lord Judge's whip, or Mr. Commissioner's whip, in contrast to the whip of my Lord Scamperdale the scolder. It is the knotted cat, with half a minute between each stripe, giving just time enough to feel the pain of the first blow fully before the second comes, against the loose light stripe of the hunting-whip. Adèle had some three minutes of her father's admonition about this matter, and she disliked the innocent William to the last.

---

## CHAPTER IV.

### GOSSIP STILL, PRINCIPALLY ABOUT MADEMOISELLE ADÈLE.

ADÈLE was very like a little bird in some of her ways. You have seen on a winter day a robin come from you know not where to the crumbs which you have scattered : he comes perfectly silent, not making the sound of his little wings heard in any way, nor the motion of them seen. Can any Cambridge gentleman tell us at what angle a bird's wings (any bird, say a swan or a "Sabine snipe" for mere illustration's sake) hit the air, and how often they move their wings to go one yard? They can mete the bands of Orion for us, all thanks to them ; but the details of the great mystery of a bird's flight seem as far off as ever. Surely the greatest mysteries are the closest to us. One can dimly understand red, solid Mars, or blinking Venus ; but one cannot understand in any way the flight of a bird. There is an inimitable dexterity about *that* which puzzles one utterly. One can no more understand it than could Mrs. Bone understand how Mademoiselle Adèle was always at her shoulder before she heard her. "She came and went like a bird," said Mrs. Bone.

She was always felt before she was heard: her lovely little hand on your shoulder was generally the first notice you had of her approach. There is no irreverence meant, when I say that her approach was not ὡσεὶ περιστέρα. There was none of that gentle, beautiful fluttering of wings. She swept in like a robin or a swallow, and lit.

And if she lit on your shoulder, and "cheeped and twitted twenty million loves" in your ear, as she generally did, who were you to withstand her? Why, nobody. Do not even try it now that she is a very grey old woman: if you want your own way.

Yet her father and her sister distrusted her, and William the Silent could not bear her. But with this bird-like little way of pouncing down on people, without notice, with her beauty and her cleverness, not to mention her silliness, you would have guessed that in that age of conspiracies, she would have been a first-rate conspirator. If you chance to meet Mathilde hugging her breviary, I know not where, ask *her* about that. She will probably tell you that the qualities of a good conspirator consist in something more than a faculty of coming and going silently, and reading other folks' letters. Probably she will add, that the qualities of a *successful* conspirator involve the qualities of a first-class statesman, with illimitable courage superadded. She *ought* to know. She might possibly finish up by quoting the proverb, that "fools cast firebrands."

Adèle's nest above-stairs had got cooled from want of coals, so she wanted some, and M. D'Isigny allowing no bells, she had to descend and seek some. William and Mrs. Bone were engaged in something at the fire, and had their faces turned to it; when Mrs. Bone turning round, found that Adèle was standing perfectly still and silent beside her.

Mrs. Bone put her hand to her side, and gave a gasp.

"Law, miss, what a turn you give me! I thought you was upstairs."

"'Si vous avez d'alarme,
Prenez d'eau des Carmes,'"

sang Adèle, and then began laughing and talking in French.

"What does miss desire?" said Mrs. Bone, who called *her* "miss," and Mathilde "mam'selle," from some undefined idea that the latter title had precedence over the former. "Miss knows that I do not understand French; why does she speak it?"

"Because my father has strictly forbidden me to do so; and that is why," said Adèle, in English, nodding her beautiful head, until the gleams of light in her golden hair wavered like the reflection of sunset water upon a wall. "I talk French because I am disobedient and wicked of my own choice. That is why."

"Dear me, miss, what a pity that you should so vex your pa'."

"If you dare to tell him, I will—I will *pinch* you," said Adèle, with an almost gasping emphasis on the word "pinch."

Mrs. Bone laughed at the idea of Adèle's being able to pinch hard enough to hurt such a tough old subject as she was; and, indeed, it did not seem at all likely.

She was a very slender, middle-sized, but finely-formed girl, about eighteen, with the lightest golden hair, and blue eyes; perfect complexion and features; and a *tout ensemble* of such extraordinary and unapproachable beauty, that those who had once seen it never afterwards forgot it.

And she turned her beautiful face full upon Mrs. Bone, and watched the effect of it. When she saw the flush of admiration mantle over the honest woman's face, she gave a pretty little half laugh, half exclamation, and, sidling up to Mrs. Bone, gave her a little kiss.

"Am I not irresistible, my old dear?" she said. "Can any one in the world resist me? Hey, then?"

Mrs. Bone thought of her father and of a certain baronet. William had departed on Adèle's arrival, so she did not think of him, but reserved her thoughts, and evaded the question by saying:—

"*I* can't, my dear; that is very certain. Now what wickedness do you want me to do for you? for you never coax unless you want me to do something out of orders."

"I only want you to take me up some coals."

"And bring down a letter, I suppose, miss?"

Adèle turned the light of her beauty upon Mrs. Bone once more; but with an imperceptible effect this time. An artistic trick is seldom so successful the second time as the first, particularly when one has learnt the object of it. Turner's flat-headed pines, some say, are apt to pall on a man who has got the pestilent trick of looking at the quality of the sky beyond them. Adèle's little bit of acting did not tell now.

"Anything but that, miss," said Mrs. Bone. "I could not do it, really. Times are quite changed now. What I did before I can do no longer, now that Sir Lionel comes here habitually."

"But you don't know to whom the letter is written," said Adèle, in her most pleading tones, and kissing Mrs. Bone again.

"If there is nothing secret about it, send it to the post with the others, miss," said the practical Mrs. Bone.

Adèle had actually nothing whatever to say to this, so she began to cry.

"*I* know the direction," said the still apparently inexorable, but really half-melting Mrs. Bone. "'Capitaine Comte Carrillon De Valognes, Grenadiers du Dauphin, Tour Solidor, St. Servan, Bretagne,'" replied Mrs. Bone. "That's the only French I know, and I got that by heart from reading it so often. But I am going to forget it now in favour of 'Sir Lionel Somers, Ashurst Park, Stourminster Marshall, Dorsetshire.'"

"How did you guess the direction of my letter?" said Adèle, still crying. "It might be to some one else."

"I have daughters of my own, miss, to begin with, and I have brains enough to go on with; and when I am asked to carry ninety-nine secret letters all with the same direction on them, I am apt to conclude that the hundredth letter will have a similar one."

"But he will be so meezeraable," said Adèle.

"I dare say he'll get over it, miss. At all events, whether he does or he don't, he will get no help from me."

"But it is the very last one," pleaded Adèle. "I have told him in it that I shall nevare write to him no more."

Mrs. Bone found her principles going; she had to shake herself together. "This is one time too many, miss. Sir Lionel is come with your approbation, for you were not drove in the least manner, and any letters to M. de Valognes must go in the post-bag." So saying, she hoisted the coal-basket, and departed to toil up-stairs with it.

Adèle was very much vexed. Hers was a very innocent little

letter. She merely told De Valognes in effect that she was engaged to Sir Lionel Somers, that it was her father's wish, that she thought she should like it, that bye-gones were bye-gones, and that she would ever hold him as one of her dearest friends, or words to that effect. But she wanted him to have it, for she was really in her way very fond of him, and wished to prevent mistakes. Lady Somers of Ashurst would be a very fine lady indeed. And De Valognes was very poor; and his uncle, the Marquis, would never die; and Sir Lionel was very charming and young. And so she wished particularly that De Valognes should have the letter.

Her father would be absolutely furious at the idea of her writing to De Valognes. Still it must go, and go secretly. And Mrs. Bone was recalcitrant. What could she do? She sat at the table, pondering.

William the Silent came in. Would he do? Very doubtful indeed; but she was determined to try him.

I need not say that she was infinitely above trying any personal acts of persuasion with a man in his rank of life. She took the letter, laid it on the table, and put a guinea on it. Then she said,—

"When you take the other letters to the post, I wish you would take that one for me," was all she said.

William remained perfectly silent. Adèle tried to help crying, but she could not. At last, when William had finished what he was about, he took the guinea and put it on the table before her, and placed the letter in his pocket.

She pushed the guinea towards him again, and in pushing it back it rolled down and fell on the floor. At this moment the outside door was hastily opened, and some one, coming quickly round the corner of the screen, advanced towards them.

It was Sir Lionel. William was picking up the guinea, which he handed to Adèle, who was crying; but the letter was safe in his pocket.

## CHAPTER V.

LOUIS AND ANDRÉ TALK OVER THE STATE OF PUBLIC AFFAIRS;

HE tide at the mouth of the Rance, and amidst the beautiful archipelago of granite islands, which form the defences of the good old English-hating town of St. Malo, rises and falls, at least at the equinoxes, nearly fifty feet; a greater rise and fall, I believe, than even that of the Wye at Chepstow.

Unlike the water of the Wye, however, the ocean water which daily creeps up over, and drains away from, the granite rocks at St. Malo is exquisitely clear, and on a quiet day the Atlantic swell is so broken and deadened that there is little or no surf; and so you can lie on the rocks as the tide goes down, and look into the depths of the water which runs up between the coralline-covered crags, and see the bed of the sea bringing secret after secret to light, until the broad level of sand stands exposed, and you can descend and walk for miles on the floor of the great sea. A quiet day at spring-tide among the rocks and sands, to the westward of Dinard, is a thing not to be forgotten by a very old traveller.

But I scarcely think Dinard was in existence at the time I speak of. At least, very little of the present village looks as if it could have existed then. Certainly not the granite quay, for instance; that model of dexterous engineering at which a steamer can moor at any hour of the day, in spite of forty feet difference of tide. This pier is later-imperial, and has been imperially erected for the convenience of a village of some 800 inhabitants. Few seaport towns of 2000 or more inhabitants in England have such a wharf as this; and one only thinks of remembering it to call attention to the singular passion which every party in France has for fine public works. Arthur Young, with all the pre-revolutionary misery around him, is enthusiastic in praise of the *corvée*-built roads and bridges; and through the wild political changes of seventy-four years, since the abolishment of *corvée*, every successive government has, even in the wildest times, bidden for popularity by the continuation of great public works. Sometimes to gratify the national pride, sometimes as a sham-labour test: under the later empire to fulfil both these requirements.

In the spring of 1789, however, Dinard was but a very little place, and a very quiet one. Old St. Malo, a mile off across the bay, must have looked much the same as now, a close-packed town with mediæval walls, and alternately, as the tide rose or fell, a fringe of yellow sand or green sea-water; the cathedral, scarcely visible above the high-piled houses, for the present later-imperial spire was not built; Tour Solidor, in the suburb of St. Servan, probably the highest point, a very beautiful keep of the fourteenth century.

Then, as now, there were very few places more fit for a quiet walk between two young friends, of very high mental calibre and of great purpose, than the rocks to the westward of Dinard. Two such were there, sitting together on the rocks, watching the old town, the archipelago of dangerous islands, the airy white-winged gulls, which floated heedless over the salt-sea graves of the dead men — French and English — who had perished here for so many centuries in the attack and defence of this town; at times, leaning thoughtfully over the edge of the rock and watching the great, mighty Atlantic, as he gently withdrew his waters, and revealed cranny after cranny, secret after secret; and waiting until he should leave the sands bare and show to them the floors of the ocean for a time before he came back.

They were two young French officers who sat thus, their names André and Louis. They were both in uniform: André, the eldest, in a white uniform, with light-blue facings, and the cross of St. Louis, still popular, soon to be insulted. The second, Louis, also in white uniform, but with darker blue facings. A watcher, stealthily approaching them from the low down above, at first took them for two sea-gulls perched upon the rock, until getting nearer he saw that they were but flightless Christians, and that his quarry was safe. He might stalk on: those fowls would sit.

André, the elder of these two white-coated sea-gulls, is the most difficult to describe, for I have seen his portrait, and I distrust not the genius of the painter but the authenticity of the picture.*

---

\* It has been taken from the *picture* in the Tableaux Historiques, which flatly contradicts the *text*.

A high forehead, as large at the dome as at the eyebrows, but no larger; eyes steady and kind; nose large, straight, and thin, with immovable nostrils; a mouth absolutely immovable when in quiescence; chin long, but not very broad; physique magnificent in every way. This is all I can give about André.

Louis, the other young officer in the white uniform, had formed himself on his cousin so long that he hoped he was like him. Some people said he was in every way superior to his cousin André. One of these people "ventilated" this idea to Madame D'Isigny at one of her little suppers at Dinan. Royalist society at Dinan was in hopes that Madame D'Isigny had lost her temper so long that she couldn't find it again—that she had got into a mere state of chronic cynicism. Madame undeceived them; she laid her hand on her temper directly, and produced it for the inspection of an astonished and (as things went) seditious supper party.

"Compare Louis to André!" she said. "You might as well compare my daughter Adèle to my daughter Mathilde. Louis is a boy: his merit is that he tries, poor fool! to form himself on André. When the great crash comes, Louis will cry for his mother: André will *act*. Madame, you have said to others that I am *emportée:* allow me to say, in return, that you are no judge of men. That I dislike that young man André and distrust his principles is well known."

But Louis, cousin to André, as he was also to Mathilde, was a very noble young fellow. All anchors were dragging now, and all moorings were sunk as deep as the bodies of the English and French in the great bay of St. Malo. Louis's sheet-anchor was his cousin André; yet André was no *hero* to him. André was nearly of an age with himself, and they were familiar; but he had found in André qualities which he knew he lacked himself: counsel, forethought, and the power of *acting* on forethought. Besides, he loved him, and knew that André loved him in return, which may have had more to do with André's influence than mere intellectual respect.

His physique was a kind of feminine translation of his cousin André's. A very beautiful young man, with every good quality; for the rest, let Madame D'Isigny's judgment of him stand good for the present.

These two lay idly on the rocks, and watched the water. They had not met for some little time, and the mere satisfaction which each felt at being in the other's society was sufficiently great to render conversation almost unnecessary. There was plenty of time for conversation coming. The great fact at present was that they were together again, could touch one another and hear the sound of each other's voice. Earnest conversation was to come, and might wait. Meanwhile their habit of mind was that of idle complacency.

They had taken off their swords and laid them on the rock. During their idle, pleasant babble, tired of watching the rapid sinking of the tide from among the rocks, Louis, the youngest of the cousins, took up André's sword and unsheathed it, eyeing it over from hilt to point, at the level of his eye, as one sees a fencing master or other swordsman do.

"It is a good sword, André," said he. "It cost you money. See here: the point will almost come to the hilt."

"Pull it a little further, thou strong boy; break it in half, and cast it into the sea," replied André.

"I break thy sword, André," said Louis, letting the point of the blade fly back with a "ping." "There is one reason against my breaking it, my dear; I have not money enough to buy thee such another."

"It is a good sword enough," said André; "and it cost money. I had it from Liège."

"Can they make swords there, then?"

"They made that one," replied André. "Break it in half, and cast it into the sea."

"Why?"

"Because the age of swords is passed; and the age of gunpowder, which equalises the physical power of man—almost the physical courage of man—is arrived at last. What could I myself do with that splendid blade against one of those 'misérables——de la nation, dégradés par les vices honteux, regorgeant de l'eau-de-vie,' if he were ten yards from me, with a loaded gun in his hands? Break the sword, and throw it into the sea. It is only a mark of the Eques; and the Equites are being pitched out of the saddle very rapidly by their grooms."

"Are your men uneasy, then, André?" said Louis.

"My men are most of them uneasy, Louis; nay, some are almost mutinous. I have loved my men and cared for them most honestly and truly. They might know it, if they chose; but they do not choose. Am I not an aristocrat? My brother officers, in the main, distrust me because I am personally attached to Lafayette; and my men distrust me because I am an aristocrat. No man should leave his regiment now."

"And yet you have left yours," said Louis, laughing.

"Ingrate! only to see you. Break my sword: it is useless to me. See there! when I was at Malta once, I saw in the old armoury of the knights a weapon which was better than a sword; it was a short pistol with six breeches, every one of which came round true to the breech of the barrel. That is the weapon for an officer now. There is only one objection to it; it will not go off. If there were such a weapon now, I would give you the best sword ever forged in Damascus for it."

"You would give me anything I asked for, I know, my André. I have tried you once or twice, and so I can speak. But this wonderful pistol: would it be used against the democrats, or against the men of your regiment, or merely against the national enemy?"

"That would depend," said André. "I suspect that if I had such a pistol, the first use to which I should put it would be to shoot down a certain Sergeant Barbot. That fellow, my dearest Louis, is the most pestilent savage I have ever seen. He is destroying the regiment. I have been kind to him; I have had him in my confidence; I have offered to advance his views, if he would tell me what they are. But I have failed with that man, while he has succeeded with the regiment; and the regiment is mutinous."

"But you wish for the well-being of the private soldier as much as I do, André," said Louis. "You have spoken so boldly about their real grievances, the peculation of their pay, and other things. Surely, as soldiers and as Frenchmen, they would listen to a tried friend, who has faced class indignation for them more than once, sooner than a miserable man like this Barbot. Are they not Frenchmen?"

"They *are* Frenchmen," said André. "They can conceive a bitter hatred or love for an idea or a class. They have conceived a bitter hatred and distrust for one class, at which I do not wonder; and they are crying out for elected officers. They know me for a good friend, and yet, if election of officers were to become law to-morrow, they would elect Barbot over my head."

"The fools!" said Louis.

"Why, no," said André. "They are determined on change, and they have as much sense as this, that a change from me to such a man as Barbot, one of themselves, with whom they believe they could do as they like, would be at the least pleasant. The French army must be remodelled; and the remodelling, done at such a time of doubt and heat as this, when miserable hounds like Barbot are getting the ear of the people and being cast to the surface, will be but ill done, I fear, though God knows best. Democratic armies *have* fought and conquered," he added, with a smile.

"These are terrible times," said Louis.

"But there is hope in them," said André. "Stainville is furious at the fact that just at this very crisis almost every influential man should be called away from the provinces to attend States-General in Paris.\* But we must have States-General; and fifty Mirabeaus or Lafayettes will not prevent our having a republic. See, the tide has uncovered the sands: let us walk upon them, right down into the level base of the Atlantic, and see what strange creatures, of whose existence we have known nothing at high water, lie gasping in the sun."

So they walked out together, with intertwined arms, across the sands. There were many strange things lying about, only disclosed at the equinoctial tide. Such, for instance, as the *Adamsia palliata*, the parasitic anemone, strange sea-worms, and shells innumerable. But the strangest animal to be seen on that shore that spring day they left behind them, unseen and unnoticed and unheard.

A man who had been lying on the rock behind them for some time, listening to their conversation. A short, squat, hideous man, in a blue uniform. He was of vast personal strength, with very bowed legs, and an enormous chest and shoulders.

---

\* "Mille et mille gens propres à rendre des services essentiels, se trouveront tout-à-coup paralisés dans Paris." And Maréchal de Stainville goes on raging against the power of Paris and the causes of that power. "Paresse, orgueil, et curiosité." His protest seems to be the protest of an honest seigneur, disgusted at all the very worst vices of his order being openly exhibited in Paris.

All his features were too mean and bad for description, until you came to his mouth, an enormously long, lipless gash, extending right across his face ; firmly set enough, and yet curling into a hideous half-smile whenever he met your eye. The wolf-like, thirsty gasp of Marat was beautiful beside the smile of this man. It was Sergeant Barbot.

He stepped down from his side of the rock, and walked down the narrow alley of sand which led out on to the broader expanse, where the two brothers-in-arms were picking their way, and, with the vivacity of Frenchmen, laughing at the strange shells and creatures which lay about around them. Hearing the sounds of footsteps, they turned round as Barbot approached. Louis, thinking it was one of his regiment come with orders, advanced a few steps to meet him ; but Barbot passed him with a smile and a salute, and then went on to André, saying,—

"Pardon, monsieur ; this letter is not addressed to Captain Louis de Valognes, but to Captain André Desilles."*

## CHAPTER VI.

### —AND FINDING THEM UNSATISFACTORY, DISCUSS THE D'ISIGNYS :

ESILLES took his letter and walked away with his friend. Sergeant Barbot remained behind among the rocks on the sands, like an evil cormorant, watching the two white uniforms grow smaller in the distance, until they were only two white specks upon the vast expanse of sand which now stretched far and wide before him.

"Pistolling of patriots—hey?" he began saying to himself. "Pistolling of patriot Barbot, too. This is very well. Go thy way, Captain Desilles. I hate thee utterly. I hate thee for thine order's sake, and for thine own. I hate thy delicate white hand and thy delicately dressed hair. You are good, you are brave, and you are beautiful. Curse you ! I know you are all three of these things, and I hate you for them."

* Some authorities spell the name with the S, some without it. I began doing so with the S, and so I will continue it.

"What is your letter?" asked De Valognes.

"A recall to my regiment; that is all."

"So quickly!" said De Valognes. "Is anything wrong?"

"Is anything right, my well-beloved? My *congé* was granted under a misunderstanding by De Sartige, and has not been confirmed by Colonel Denoue; hence I am followed instantly by Barbot."

"Why by him?"

"Who knows. I never should have come, but that I wanted to see you; that I wanted to see if my well-beloved brother was yet firm in his faith and his principles; to have a clasp of the hand and a look into the honest eyes again. All these things have I done. Why should I not return then?"

"So short a time," pleaded De Valognes.

"Too long to be away from one's regiment: too long, my Louis."

De Valognes took his arm in a coaxing manner (these were Frenchmen, remember: our English manners are different), and remained silent, looking sideways at Desilles.

"What, now," said Desilles, gently, "are you going to ask for *congé*, then?"

"From you, from you only, André. If you refuse it, I will say nothing. I only ask for it under your approval."

"For how long, then?"

"A long time. Three months."

Desilles shook his head.

"I would not advise you, Louis; on my honour, I would not advise you, just now. The new principles are rapidly infecting every regiment; even here in Brittany some of your men looked sulky on parade, and talked in the ranks this morning; and there is no possible way of counteracting this, save by such officers as are possessed of brains and principle staying by their regiments, being familiar, confidential, and kind to their men, and counteracting the inconceivable folly and frivolity of your brother-officers."

"I acknowledge it," said De Valognes, sadly, but not leaving go of Desilles' arm.

"See," continued Captain Desilles, "how we are sometimes officered. Look at the majority, the great majority, of the men in your particular regiment. How many of them care for their profession? how many of them care for the well-being of their men? Insolent, quarrelsome, frivolous; dicing, drinking, intriguing; treating the lower orders *de haut en bas*, and yet demanding respect from them, on the only grounds, as it appears to me, of a superiority in vice; imitating, lastly, and clumsily caricaturing, all the inconceivably stupid and barbarous vices of the English, with the sole effect of making the very barbarians laugh at the ridiculous travestie of their own barbarism. In our garrison there are but four who do their duty, besides our colonel; they are Peltier, Enjolras, Cassaignac, and St. Meard of the Swiss."

"I acknowledge," said De Valognes.

"And yet you want furlough. You want me to advise you to remove for three months your influence from these disaffected men, with their real grievance of peculated pay, and whole hosts and swarms of dim and imaginary grievances forming themselves into practical shape in their heads day by day, and hour by hour. My dearest brother—for you are that and more to me—remember how short a man's time is in this world, considering the work he has to do; and remember that the effects of personal influence, except in extremely rare instances, vanish soon after the person has ceased to continue his influence either by spoken or written speech. The Second Epistle to the Corinthians might tell you something of that, if you knew it; and that refers to St. Paul. In the case of a noble little person like you, your influence would be gone the day you left. You squeeze my arm again. Are you going to persevere?"

"Yes."

"You have a strong reason, then," said Captain Desilles. "Louis, I have said enough; I should, like a tedious preacher, confuse you as to the main argument of my discourse by prolonging it. I only say, in conclusion, that it must be a very strong reason which should take you, almost the only hope of your regiment, away from that regiment just at this time. What is that reason?"

"I want," said De Valognes, slowly, "to go to England, and to see the D'Isignys."

The arm of Desilles, which De Valognes still held, moved uneasily, but for a very short time; and then Desilles' disengaged hand came over on to the arm which De Valognes still held, and pressed De Valognes' hand firmly and boldly.

"Is anything wrong, then?"

"So I greatly fear. There is a Sir Lionel Somers, a man of great wealth, of great personal beauty, of great talent, and of the noblest character, admitted there with the sanction of D'Isigny himself; and you know what that means with D'Isigny."

"I do. A close, just, perfect man like D'Isigny would never admit such a man habitually to his family circle, unless there was a deliberate understanding about his visits. D'Isigny is the most perfect man I have ever met. Would to God that the world was peopled by D'Isignys!"

"Do you love him, then?" said De Valognes.

"Love D'Isigny! Who could possibly love D'Isigny! No; my nature is far too inferior to his for me to love him. But he is the best of living men."

De Valognes looked up into his face to see if he was joking; but no, Desilles' face was sad, serious, and earnest. He added: "How did you learn this?"

"Mathilde wrote and told me of it, and advised me to come."

"Perhaps she was not quite correct, then; but you had better go. D'Isigny must have got the English fog into his brains to propose to marry Mathilde to an Englishman and a Protestant."

"Mathilde!" exclaimed De Valognes; "I am not talking of old Mathilde. I am talking of Adèle."

"Is he to marry Adèle, then?" said Desilles.

"Certainly," said De Valognes.

"A very good thing for her," said Desilles. "I cannot possibly see now why you can want to leave your regiment and your duty to go and interfere between that silly and petulant little chatterbox and a rich English *parti*. If he is fool enough to take her, in Heaven's name let him have her. I hope he will like his bargain; but don't lose my respect by leaving your regimental duties to go to England and put a spoke in such a wheel as that."

"André! André!"

"I abused the English just now; but some of them are among the noblest of God's creatures. I hoped, from your description, that this Sir Lionel was such an one; but the man must be a fool, though he be an angel."

"André! Be quiet."

"Why, then?"

"Because I love Adèle above all the world. That is all."

Desilles loosely dropped the arm which De Valognes held, and walked in silence. How could he possibly have offended him? thought De Valognes. "Surely, if there could be offence between us, it must have come from me." But Desilles had his silent ruminating fits, as De Valognes well knew; and this was one of them.

They had arrived, by their walk over the sands and by a short transit in a ferry-boat, to the Dinan gate of St. Malo. Old women then, as now, had stalls there, at this time of the year containing nothing but withered apples; old women who knitted, as they watched their two-pennyworth of wrinkled apples, as diligently and as sharply as ever did the *tricoteuses* of the Place de Grève. Unlike the rosy, cheery old dames who knit there now, these women were more withered and more worn than the most withered and unsaleable of last year's pippins. Seeing two white-coated young military "swells" (if you will forgive the word), one with the order of St. Louis, they bent their witch-like old heads and knitted the harder.

Among the people who were basking in the March sun, there was a vague, idle walking up and down which was remarkable. The year had been a hard one, and there were rumours of change even so far westward as this; want of change was visible on every face. There were not many declared patriots here as yet, but the few who were so were listened to with the deepest respect. As André and Louis walked up separately under the gate of Dinan, a fully declared patriot, a real "old man of the mountain," not to say "assassin," in a loose blue coat with a cape, an immense ill-tied cravat, and no visible linen, held a conversation with a neat, dapper, half-declared patriot, with immensities of clean linen, his coat-collar well up the back of his head, and his coat-tails down to his heels, short trowsers apparently cut by a Persian tailor of the old Greek times, foolish shoes, and his hat on the back of his head —a mild Girondist every inch of him.

Between these two men, and through the crowd which surrounded them, and which they represented, André and Louis passed, in their close-fitting, well-cut white uniform, like two felspar crystals in a heap of broken granite. There was no cry of "à bas les aristocrats," no "haine naissante" to the cross of St. Louis which André had on his breast; that only began in Paris on the night of the burning of the Fabrique of Sieur Reveillon, a month or so hence. The people were patient with them, and more than patient, for St. Malo is very far west. They admired and respected these two handsome, solemn, white-coated young men, who passed with bent heads among them.

"They have quarrelled, those two," said the Girondist, as we will call him—the man with his coat-tails down to his heels, clean linen, and foolish shoes—to the advanced patriot in the large cravat. "There will be a duel to-morrow."

"Curse them!" said the patriot. "I hope they will kill one another."

"I should be sorry for that," said the doctrinaire radical in the blue coat; "for that young De Valognes is a noble youth and a true friend of the people and will come in for a large property at his uncle's death. And Desilles also is a townsman, and a friend of all that is good."

"Curse them again!" said the patriot. "Do you not know that they are each of them to marry one of D'Isigny's daughters? You speak of their quarrelling; no such luck. Do you want D'Isigny back again?"

"D'Isigny is a just and good man. We do not agree; but you will go far before you find a better," said the Girondist. "He was the man the *bailliage* should have sent to States-General, in my opinion."

Then there followed a general clamorous babble, mostly facetious. Many jokes were made, all of them very bad; but the facetious proposition which was best appreciated by the mob was that Madame D'Isigny should be sent south by her party to terrify single-handed the Rennes boys, just now violent and rebellious, into submission.

Desilles and De Valognes, little heeding, passed through the arch of the gateway, and Desilles led the way to the left up a quiet street, and mounted the ramparts without speaking. De Valognes, puzzled and grieved at his silence, kept silent too, wondering whether he had given offence. Desilles leant over the rampart, gazing northward over the sands, across the archipelago of granite islands, across the blue sparkling sea towards England,—towards Dorsetshire. In a few minutes, without turning round, he put back his hand for De Valognes to take, and said,—

"I wish I had known this before. I wish to heaven I had known this before."

"You mean," said De Valognes, "that if you had known it, you would not have said what you said about Adèle. My good André, how could you dream that I could be offended with you? Your Quixotic, courteous heart takes such trifles as these too seriously. I shall scold you, or at least I should scold you were I not prepared for a scolding from you. I have practised a little deceit, not willingly on you, but on D'Isigny. He desired my alliance with dear, old, humpbacked Mathilde, at least so I believe; for poor as I am now, I shall be rich at my uncle's death, and one of the De Valognes' estates adjoins the D'Isigny estates. My uncle hates me, but he cannot disinherit me; and I let D'Isigny think that my visits were paid to her. You thought so yourself, did you not?"

"God knows I did," said Desilles.

"Then, why do you not scold me for my deceit, André? You are always used to do so."

"I have no heart to do so, my Louis. Hark! there is the first bugle for afternoon parade at Solidor; you must run, my Louis, or you will be late. Never keep your men waiting. If you are uncourteous to them, they will be uncourteous to you. Go!"

"Where shall I find you again?"

"I am going to church. I will look round to your quarters at St. Servan afterwards."

## CHAPTER VII.

### WHICH ENDS IN ANDRÉ GOING TO CHURCH;

DESILLES left the rampart as soon as De Valognes was out of sight, and went through the narrower of the narrow streets towards the church.

Calm, erect, and pale, but looking older than he had done in the morning, with his face slightly pinched, and a weary expression on it. The advanced patriot of the last chapter saw him go, and cursed him again. "The crimes of his ancestors are gnawing at his black, wicked heart," he said. Poor patriot! how little he knew of the truth. If it had been possible for him and Desilles to interchange confidences, it is quite possible that they might in a way have respected one another; but it was *not* possible. Distinct classes could never then personally interchange ideas; and look at the case now. Your Whig nobleman at his dinner-table is natural; your artisan at his fire-side is natural. Bring the best of them face to face, and in spite of their desire for conciliation they are in buckram directly. They must understand one another through print after all, and give and take. At St. Malo in 1789 there was but little print and no liberality, and the young men of Rennes had just defied the nobles and won; and so our poor patriot, with the piled-up memory of at least three centuries of misrule, merely cursed one of the best men living as a representative of his order.

It was a late day in Lent, and the priests were having a grand service. They had got a Cardinal in those parts, a Cardinal of the Rohan type, and he had come over from the château of that wicked and amiable old seigneur, Louis' uncle, among the forests to the South there, at Montauban, after a morning's boar-hunting and a heavy luncheon, to assist at the afternoon service. There was therefore a more than ordinary crowd in the cathedral that afternoon.

Desilles was a devout man, and this afternoon he longed very much for prayer, longed to try whether or no he could put himself in spiritual communion with that "*Bon Dieu*" whom he loved, and in whom he trusted so frankly. He thoroughly succeeded in his object, though not quite in the way he proposed.

When he passed out of the bright street, he found the great nave of the church filled with a mere mob. Patriots undeclared, declared,—nay, even now a few of them *"enragés,"*—walking up and down among the heavy, almost Doric, pillars, smoking; while from the other end, from behind the rood screen, there came fitfully a feeble droning of priests. Desilles, towering above the average of Breton heads, could see dimly, far away in the chancel, the fat Cardinal, in purple and scarlet, buried in his chair. He pushed through the crowd, and got into one of the side chapels near the altar, and knelt down, just as the Cardinal rose to take his part in the service.

Desilles knew this man, a man of abominable character, a glutton, a wine-bibber, a faithless friend, and a corrupt politician. The Church of England in her deadest days never produced such a man as this, or any imitation of him; but such as he were now swarming in the Church of France and ruining her. When Desilles saw this man going through what must have been to him a hideous mockery, he grew sick at heart, and felt less inclined for prayer than ever. He knew that this man, and such as he, although they swarmed in, and devoured (and alas! to many people represented) the Church, did not really represent what was alive of her, only what was dead. For had not the French clergy, in the famine of the cruel winter just past, risen to their work like true men, the glorious memory of Fénélon in the famine of *his* time bearing fruit one hundred fold? He knew this, and yet the presence of the Cardinal was a loathing and a scorn to him, and seemed to pollute the atmosphere.

At length the Cardinal had finished, and the congregation streamed forth, and the church was empty. Still he sat and watched the peaceful afternoon sun, caught only by the higher windows of the pent-in church, grow from yellow to crimson: leaning his arm wearily forward on the chair before him, and confusedly thinking of what might have been.

A quiet, steady step came along the flags of the church from behind, and stopped at the entrance to the chapel where he sat —the sacristan doubtless. He felt for some money to get rid of him and be alone a little longer, and turned towards him. It was not the sacristan at all.

It was a short and slightly built priest, with curly grizzled hair, fringing a large tonsure, very unlike the tonsure of his Eminence. His dress was, I think, the most beautiful of all the infinite Roman Catholic dresses; he wore the ordinary black gown or cassock, and over it a white loose jacket, the name of which I do not know, reaching to his waist or slightly below, so that the only break in this striking monotony of white above the waist and black below was his rosary and cross, which hung below the white garment before mentioned. You might have noticed that the one foot which was a little advanced from under the long gown, and which was covered with a silver-buckled shoe, was extremely small: you might have noticed that his hands were small and delicate also; and you might have had an eye for the grace, boldness, and vivacity of the man's carriage, if your eye had not, from sheer necessity, settled on the man's face.

Enormous grey eyes, and a rich brown complexion, describable no further. In age the face was about fifty, with scarcely a wrinkle, but so wonderfully beautiful and good, that it seemed as though it were growing into a new and more lasting youth; and Desilles, looking gladly and lovingly upon it, thought for an instant that the aureola of sainthood was already there.

Carrier! Carrier! what if there be a day of judgment, after all? And when you are judged before heaven as you are now in the memories of men, what if that face stands out as your chief accuser? Better any other than that.

There was no aureola of glory around that face as yet, save that which was made of intellect, goodness, and beauty. There was no extraneous light there, except the last beams of the spring sun. It was only Desilles' dear old tutor, Father Martin; he sprung towards him, calling him by name.

"My André!" said Father Martin. "Here, and all alone!"

"Father, Heaven has sent you."

"So, I suppose. Seeing that I am commissioned by Heaven, it would be strange if it were otherwise. And what are you doing here of all places, so far from your regiment, which is your wife? Will not madame scold her truant André on return?

You could not have come after me, for you did not know that I was here. I arrived from Nantes only two days ago on my route."

"No, but I wanted so earnestly to confide in you of all men," said André."

Father Martin said nothing; but taking André's eye, looked towards the confessional in the corner of the chapel.

"No," said André. "Not to-day."

"Good, then," said Father Martin; "we will walk and talk the while, son of my heart. To-morrow, the next day, or when God sends a wind, I am for Aurigny, in the most miserable of little Chasse-marées. At Aurigny I am handed over to the imperial and magnificent mercies of the Queen of the Seas. You have not forgotten the first piece of burlesque I ever taught you, when you were a quiet, silent little child of ten, somewhat difficult to please?

" 'Angleterre,
 Reine des mers.'

"And also,—

" 'L'Autriche
 Triche,' "

added André, refreshed already by the child*like*—or, as some might say, child*ish*—humour of Father Martin.

"And also," continued Father Martin,—

" 'La France,
 Danse,'

at the very time when she had better be doing anything else in this world. Now, my son, enough of babble. I see you have not forgotten even the very earliest of my instructions. Let me hear of yourself; and if anything is the matter, what it is."

"But first about you, father. Why this expedition to Alderney?" said Desilles.

"Did I not tell you? See, I will tell you again, then. I am to go in a lugger to Aurigny, at the risk of being *noyé*. At Aurigny I suddenly become the great gentleman, although I have but 200 livres, and a very small malle. His Britannic Majesty thinks that he has at his command a frigate, called the *Galatea*, which is under his orders. His Britannic Majesty, so lately recovered, must be again mad; at least, he is mistaken. That frigate is under my orders. That great ship, potentially containing five hundred thunderstorms, which could blow St. Malo as far as Dinan, and cause a temporary terror in the heart of Madame D'Isigny herself, awaits my coming to take me to England. The terrible Captain Somers, her commander, writes me, drolly enough, that he shall get into hot water about it: for that he has been ordered to Plymouth to pay out of commission, or some such expression; but that his brother Lionel wants him to be civil to me, and so that if I will make haste, he, as senior officer in harbour, will chance anything which Pitt or Sydney, or any other big wig, may do, for the sake of old Lionel. So,—do you see?—if I do not haste, M. Pitt will shoot his terrible Captain Somers, as they did their Byng; and his death will be at my door."

"But why are you going to England?" said André, confused at the recurrence of the name Somers twice on one day, and disregarding Father Martin's playful talk.

"I am going to stay with our old friends, the D'Isignys."

"And I wished to speak to you about them. How strange! But why are you going to them?"

"Merely because D'Isigny requires a resident priest; and because also Sir Lionel Somers, who is to marry Adèle, desires one also, Protestant as he is. Now tell me what you have to say. Hide nothing, any more than you would in the confessional, for I am anxious and uneasy at your looks."

André told him his story; and we will tell it for him, as shortly as is possible, but a little more fully than André told it to Father Martin: because Father Martin knew considerably more than three-quarters of it before.

# CHAPTER VIII.

## AND THE AUTHOR, HAVING TO TAKE UP THE THREAD OF THE STORY—

HE Desilles, the De Valognes, and the D'Isignys, all cousins, were all brought up as children together; and, as children will do, they had formed likes and dislikes among one another. In all coteries of children, there is one who, generally from an incapacity for play, is unpopular. Among some little people I was noticing the other day, there was one like this. The others first offered her twopence, and in the end sixpence, to go away and not play. She refused both the twopence and the sixpence with scorn, and retired to eat her own heart, possibly with such bitterness as we grown-up people are unable to know—*now*.

Real play is an art, and possibly the most singular of all arts, because the capacity for it is dead—at least in boys—after fifteen. Girls keep it longer. One has seen girls of eighteen actually *romping* with children, and enjoying it: but that was before the time of the fairy prince. Children despise the efforts of a grown-up person at real play, as much as a mediæval architect would despise our efforts at church building. Grown-up people when they romp are practising a lost art, while real professors of it are still alive and criticising.

But there are some children who never can play, and yet desire to do so, partly from a genial and sentimental wish to be well *répandus* with other children, and not to be thought singular; and partly from a desire for prestige, were it only in a game of romps. When grown up, the best of these children, in a free state, become the rulers of that state, or biography lies; the mediocres and the worst of them find themselves different places; yet all of them have a trick of making themselves heard in some way or another.

Mathilde D'Isigny was one of these quaint, sensitive children, who wished to play, and yet who was voted out of every game. Passionately fond of play theoretically, yet so undexterous that even André himself could coax her out of a game, and, giving up his own amusement, would sit by her talking to her, and pretending that he himself was tired. This was tolerable to her; but when André was not there, it was intolerable. Louis (De Valognes), Adèle (very tiny then), and the others, would laugh at her want of dexterity and her clumsy way of running, and tell her that they wished André was playing, because she played so badly that he would sooner give up his own play than see her make herself so ridiculous. And he had told them so, they said; which was one of those curious child's lies, which we dare not judge.

We at this time of our lives cannot remember or measure the bitter long grief of childhood. It is doubtful whether even Mathilde ever received a more cruel stroke to her heart than this.

The utter incompatibility of temper which existed between M. and Madame D'Isigny ultimately led to their separation. His extreme and inexorable precision was perfectly maddening to her; her coarseness and violence he considered to be a judgment and a discipline, sent to him by heaven in punishment for some secret sin. Madame, with her usual want of reticence, was accustomed habitually to tell her circle of friends at Dinan, that it was a wonder that they had got on together as long as they had, and used to add that it was only her own good temper which enabled them to do so. French politeness prevented any looks of wonder passing from one guest to another whenever this theory of Madame's was broached.

She lived at Dinan. When the separation was agreed on, he had politely left it to her to choose her residence. She chose his family house at Dinan; he, with a bow, selected her English house, Sheepsden, in the vale of the Stour, where he lived, as we have seen, with his daughters.

So there was a long separation between Mathilde and her much younger sister, Adèle, on the one side, from their old French friends, De Valognes, Desilles, and many others; and a little more than a year previous to the time we are speaking of now, M. D'Isigny, who had all the evening been writing diligently at his desk, under his lamp, next the fire, in the general room at Sheepsden, wiped his pen, turned to his two daughters who were sitting at the next table sewing, and said,—

"My dear children, you must give up all to-morrow to preparing and packing your clothes for a journey. We start the day after."

Mathilde, after a pause, spoke, knowing perfectly well that she would get into trouble, but so perfectly reckless that she did not care very much. "What clothes shall we want, sir?"

"Not being a haberdasher," replied M. D'Isigny, "I am afraid I must confess to a certain amount of ignorance on that point, at least in detail. I should say, gowns, shoes, stockings, under-linen, and things of that kind. I should have thought that you would have known. If I have made any mistake, I humbly beg you to forgive my ignorance."

"I ask pardon, sir, most truly," said Mathilde, knowing that the further she went the worse she would fare, but going on. "It was not the description of clothes which we should want, but the quantity, about which I wished for your directions."

"You *said*, 'What clothes!'" replied M. D'Isigny. "As usual, you are departing from your original proposition. Among men this is called tergiversation, and is visited with contempt. A *man* is *chassé* from the society of other men for shifting his position in this manner. We have an ugly name for it. I can only answer, that not being a ladies' maid, I can give you no idea of the quantity of clothes which you will require."

"What I wished to arrive at, sir, is this," said Mathilde: "how long are we to be away?"

Adèle, who had kept dexterously out of the engagement, by holding her tongue for once, stitched diligently, expecting a storm.

"Not having access to the councils of Providence," said M. D'Isigny, "I am unable to answer that question also. I may, however, say this: that this is the first honest and straightforward question that you have put to me this evening."

"If you were more honest and straightforward with us," said Mathilde, with desperate bluntness, "we might be more straightforward with you. We might have the courage to ask you a plain question, and receive a plain answer. You accuse me of fencing with words. You do the same yourself. I said, 'What clothes!' speaking in English, as you yourself desire that we should do on the majority of occasions; and then making a miserable *calembour* on the word 'what,' you accuse me of mendacity. Your mendacity, sir, is greater, morally, than mine, and without its excuse."

Adèle gathered up her work, and made for her bower. *She had feebly fought her father, but never like this.* She tried to make for her boudoir.

"Adèle," said M. D'Isigny, "come back and sit down." Adèle did so, trembling.

In a quarrel, if you will remark, the first person to speak, unless the case is very strong indeed, is the loser. It is like the English and French duel in the dark room, where both parties were afraid to fire for fear of showing the other where he was. So in this case. M. D'Isigny was disinclined to speak first. He had always managed these girls by calm indifferentism, and would now. As for Mathilde, she had said *her* say, and would take the consequence. *She* would keep silent till the day of judgment. So she sat and sewed.

She starved D'Isigny into speech, and consequently into temporary disaster. She would not speak, and as an eternity of silence is impossible, he spoke first.

"My daughter, you are in rebellion."

"I am," said Mathilde, "not so much in rebellion as in revolution. You pitch your standard of virtue so high and unattainable, that it is impossible for a person like me to be good ; and you make virtue appear so extremely disagreeable in practice that vice appears preferable. I strive continually to be good because I know it is my duty ; but I hate being good all the time."

M. D'Isigny answered not a word. He thought that would be the best course ; particularly as he did not exactly know what to say. Not only did he abstain from speaking to her that night, but kept an absolute silence towards her for exactly one month. On the thirty-first day, exactly at the same hour, he spoke to her again ; having succeeded in inflicting on her a month of absolute unnoticed liberty, and also of perpetual and ever-increasing torment. It was one of the most dexterous accidental "hits" he ever made.

He never even spoke of her all this time. She did all the drudgery of preparation, and only learnt their destination from Adèle. It was St. Malo first. "And then on to Dinan," suggested Adèle out of her own head. "Good heavens, can papa be going to live with mamma again?" At which terrible suggestion they stared at one another in silent dismay.

Had M. D'Isigny known that they were speculating on this point, he would have been the very last to enlighten them. It would have been what he would have called a "discipline" for them; and he loved "disciplines" both for himself and others. The two girls had for nearly a week to endure a discipline quite unknown to him—the terror of once more coming under the power of their "*emportée*" mamma.

Their fears were without any foundation. M. D'Isigny took them to Poole, and putting them on board a brig, carried them safely to St. Malo, where he took possession of one of his numerous houses there, at this time without a tenant. In a moment of unwonted confidence he told Adèle that his time would be much occupied with monetary business for a few months. His agent having declared strongly on the extreme democratic side in politics—he explained to her—was necessarily a rogue, a thief, and a scoundrel; and it was necessary to take his affairs out of his hands. They would go into society, but Adèle was to observe that his intentions as to her future being undecided, and God having been pleased to curse her with extraordinary beauty, she was to be very careful not to admit peculiar attentions from any man whatever.

So they began their few months' life at St. Malo. Old friends swarmed to them at once. Father Martin from Nantes flew to them directly, and took up his abode with them, in what he called the little prophet's chamber in the wall, and became one of the household instantly; having, bright good soul, his own good way in everything, save in the matter of the thirty-one days' silence towards Mathilde (and one or two others), which like a wise man he let be, seeing that he could not mend them. His Eminence the Cardinal of the Rohan type called on them, and fortunately, as Father Martin, Mathilde, and Adèle agreed, M. D'Isigny was not at home; for when he heard of the honour which his Eminence had done him, he continued for the space of half an hour to pace up and down through all the rooms of their suite of apartments, in a state of calm, bland fury, not to be interfered with even by Father Martin, saying, "The disreputable old villain! the perjured old traitor! the miserable, hypocritical, old atheist! daring to have the impudence to allow his lacquey to knock at the door of a French gentleman!" To an invitation to meet the Cardinal at Montauban, the Château of the Marquis de Valognes, to the South, he was induced by Father Martin's representations to reply *only*, "That he might possibly accept the hospitality of the Marquis at the first moment after the departure of Cardinal Leroy." The epithet, "pestilent scoundrel," as standing for the word "Cardinal" in the original document, was omitted after a sharp debate with Father Martin, who fought for and won this small concession; and congratulated himself, and gave thanks elsewhere for even *that* much. A hard, inexorable, fearless man, this D'Isigny, caring only, according to his light, for the right; but so indiscreetly bold, and with such a terrible biting tongue.

No one else who had the audacity to call on them met with such a reception as the man we have called Cardinal Leroy. Some got such a very dignified and profoundly polite reception, that they went home to ponder in the watches of the night over their political backslidings; and after tumbling and tossing for an hour or so, to ask their wives, if they (their wives) were awake; and if so, whether they could save them from madness by telling them what D'Isigny's political opinions *were*—a question which was never answered by either man or wife. These people had generally engagements or illnesses at the D'Isigny's later receptions. Then, other people were received with politeness and deference. Lastly, some were received with the profoundest tenderness and geniality; and among them De Valognes, not yet rich, but only a cadet, and Desilles, with his glorious and immortal elder sister, and his beautiful and brave younger one.*

St. Malo society was divided on one point. Would M. D'Isigny go and see his wife at Dinan, or would he not? The English habit of betting on an event, of risking cash on what you think to be an accumulation of probabilities, had not got so far west as St. Malo yet. If it had, the St. Malo people would have betted about the probability of M. D'Isigny going to see his wife at Dinan; would, after his first week there, have betted to a man against it—and lost. The favourite seldom or never

---

* Those who know the story, see at this point that I have altered it.

wins the Derby. For a man of fixed principles to bet about the actions of a man of unfixed principles, judging that man's principles by his own standard, is of course suicidal as regards his cash; but for a number of men without fixed principles to bet about the actions of such a man as D'Isigny, whom they know to have inexorably fixed principles of some kind, had they only known what, was still more ridiculous. The majority of St. Malo society—let us call them " the field "—ridiculed the idea of his seeing his wife at all, after his neglecting her for the first week. Nevertheless, the field lost.

For he got him a boat at the Dinan gate, and into it he got himself, his daughters, De Valognes, Desilles, and Father Martin, and went on the flood-tide to Dinan. They were back again the next ebb but one, and the wicked St. Malouins said that they all looked ten years older; which was certainly a fiction of theirs, because solemn André Desilles remarked to Adèle on landing, " Well, one feels ten years younger now that business is over;" and Mathilde got quietly rebuked by her father for laughing so loud with De Valognes on their way home. The laws against *tapage*, he remarked, were necessary, though strict.

So Desilles was walking with Adèle, and de Valognes with Mathilde. Now let Desilles himself finish this part of our story in his confession to Father Martin.

"D'Isigny received us both again like his own sons. Our intercourse with our mutual cousins was like that between brothers and sisters. I am not sure what D'Isigny designed then. I think that he had chosen both, or one of us, as eligible suitors for either of his daughters, and left Nature to take her course. What was the first result? I fell desperately in love with Mathilde, and I love her now, more deeply, more intensely than you, as a priest, can dream of."

"Very likely," said Father Martin. "And then?"

"And then? Why, I made love to her."

"So I should have conceived," said Father Martin. "And then?"

"Louis de Valognes made love to her also."

"That I should not have conceived. Are you sure?"

"I was," said Desilles. "He was always by her side. He gave all his little cares to her. He sent and brought her flowers and music and pamphlets. I was so assured of the earnestness of his attentions towards her, that I withdrew mine."

"That was very magnanimous," said Father Martin; "and you proved your fitness for entering, by marriage, that most remarkably inexorable family, by showing that you could feebly copy its very Spartan virtues. Still, on the whole, you were very foolish. Withdrawing your claims on Mathilde, because your friend Louis brought her flowers and pamphlets, is very fine and classical, no doubt, but the lady should have been consulted. I admire your friendship for Louis, and Louis' friendship for you: it is elevating. But what were the young lady's wishes? Your story is lame at present, André."

"It will march directly," said Desilles. "Mathilde disliked me. Some childish gibe, reported, as I believe, falsely to her, had set her against me; and, moreover, it was painfully evident to me, after a very short time, that Louis de Valognes' attentions to her had produced fruit; that she had believed in them, and that the whole of her great heart was given to him for ever."

"This is very serious," said Father Martin. "Louis has been terribly to blame. He loves Adèle."

"So I learnt for the first time to-day," said Desilles. "What is to be done?"

"Nothing," said Father Martin. "Of all the affairs which gave arisen in these most unhappy times, this is one of the most unhappy. Cannot you go back to your regimental duties, and forget all about it?"

"I can go back to my regimental duties. I go to-morrow morning; but I cannot forget her. She loves him, and he loves Adèle."

"And Adèle?" said Father Martin.

"Of that I can say nothing. She is courted by, and we almost think affianced to, an English lord. How far matters may have gone between her and Louis, I cannot guess. I was perfectly blinded."

"And I also," said Father Martin.

"He proposes to start for England immediately," said Desilles.

"That is of course ridiculous," said Father Martin. "He must be kept here. I shall see how the land lies."

"And I?" said André Desilles.

"Must bear your burden, and do your duty. I grieve over this business, because I know you, and know how deeply you feel it. But answer, son of my heart, is this a time for men of brains, of purpose, of energy, like you, one of the strongest hopes of a doomed cause, to be love-making? I wish that we two could tread the dark path which is before us together; but that, I well know, cannot be. Hold to the truth, as I have tried to teach it to you, and there will be a golden cord between us, which death itself cannot break. Now, you will come back with me to the church, will you not?"

They went back to the church together, and remained some time, parting at the side door which opens into the little square of the Hôtel de Ville. It was dark now. Father Martin leant against the stone ribs of the church, and watched André Desilles, tall, solemn, and clothed in white, pass slowly down the narrow lane under the few lamps which hung flickering there in those times, casting long swiftly-shifting shadows on pavement and wall. A darker shadow followed his; a solid shadow, which lurked in the gloom of the tall over-hanging houses. Sergeant Barbot crept after him, watching and listening like a black, unphosphorescent Scin Læca, or like one of Van Helmont's satyrs, born, it would seem, of woman, but having for father the incubus—the incubus of old misrule.

The stars were out over Father Martin's bare head, but he stood there yet, thinking of many things. There was a crowding of lights and tuning of fiddles in the town-hall opposite, and many groups had passed him, which he had not noticed. Then there came a blaze of torches, and a shuffling of footmen in liveries; then the Cardinal Leroy, walking delicately from his carriage, which had been left in the broader street below, and leaning on the arm of the most disreputable nobleman in those parts; a man with something like the reputation of Bluebeard de Retz. Father Martin realized that they were going to the ball in the town-hall, and that neither of them were exactly sober.

"You are the men who are guilty of our destruction," he said, "and of your own also. May God forgive you!"

## CHAPTER IX.

### LANDS THE READER ONCE MORE AT SHEEPSDEN.

IR LIONEL SOMERS had ridden over to bring Adèle the last number of "The Gentleman's Magazine,"—that for February, 1789. But he forgot all about this magazine in a moment. Here was Adèle crying, and the servant handing her a guinea. Now, what on earth was the meaning of this?

He was a young fellow, dressed in a caped riding-coat like that of M. D'Isigny, with top-boots, and wearing his hair in a very short *queue*. He had good health, good looks, good sense, good temper, and very great wealth; was a violent Whig, and the accepted suitor of Adèle, to whom these Dorsetshire estates were, by a recent arrangement, to go at M. D'Isigny's death, as those in Brittany were to Mathilde.

You may be a very extreme Whig, nay, a very extreme Radical, and yet not like to find your *fiancée* in tears, disputing with a servant about a guinea. Sir Lionel did not like it at all. He turned sharply to William at once, scowling and speaking as men did speak to servants then, and said,—

"Leave the place, fellow."

William the Silent went quietly out, and Adèle stood crying with the guinea on the table before her. She could have left off crying if she had liked, but she felt so very guilty about the letter to De Valognes, that she thought it wiser to cry on until she had time to make up a fib. Consequently she did so.

"Has that fellow been rude to you, my darling?" asked Sir Lionel.

The devil is popularly supposed to be always handy. He failed Adèle on this occasion, however, most conspicuously. If he was there he was maliciously enjoying her perplexity, for not a falsehood could she frame, and so went on crying, knowing that she would have to make up some sort of a fib very shortly, and getting more confused and frightened as the moments went on, and no fib would rise to her tongue.

"My dearest Adèle, speak to me, and give me leave to break every bone in the rascal's body," said Sir Lionel.

"I will tell you all about it in a minute," sobbed Adèle. "Don't hurry me." And so she waited, while he looked at her curiously and kindly; she unable to get to even any general plot of an explanation, and longing for some disturbing cause.

One came before she had necessity to speak. The weather was whirling and tearing more and more furiously every minute, and just as the very wildest gust of all was roaring in the chimneys, and lashing the windows with rain, the outside door opened, and the wind walked in and took possession—shaking the screen, irritating the fire, and banging and flapping all loose doors all over the house.

And in the roar of the wind was heard a voice, saying in somewhat shrill French, "I am not responsible for shutting the door. I have not the strength, and I will not be responsible for everything. If the house is destroyed and unroofed, I am not responsible for it."

William, as they guessed, dashed from some office and got the door shut. Then they heard a low, slightly petulant voice, arguing with him. Then came what Mrs. Bone called the clipperty-clopperty of a pair of sabots across the floor, at the sound of which they both said, "Mathilde," and recovered their good humour. The atmosphere of that woman was so much greater than her real diameter, that it made its influence felt as soon as the first sound of her voice fell on the ear. The tears, the guinea, and William the Silent, were all forgotten now. Sir Lionel and Adèle smiled on one another, and kissed. Surely none of our readers are so unfortunate as not to know some man or woman who carry this atmosphere of peace and goodwill about with them; as not to have known at some time some person, so consistently loving and loveable, as to make others amiable, if from nothing else, from sheer force of example. Mathilde, in her querulous way, was such a person.

She kissed her sister and said, "Is papa come back?" and being told "No," went on,—

"If I was to be visited with an illness for undutifulness, I must really say I am glad of it, for what I have suffered this afternoon no tongue can tell, and a good scolding at the end of it would have been altogether too much for me. I won't grumble any more than I can help; but the weather is so entirely wicked, and my sabots kept coming off in the mud, and he was dead before I got there, and so I might just as well have stayed at home as go out. However, my dears, we will have a fine little dinner all to ourselves, which Mrs. Bone and I will cook. A fish and a fricassée, and an omelette, and a bottle of Portuguese wine for Sir Lionel, and Grève for us; and also the man shall have an errand down the village, and have moreover a shilling that he may spend at the Leeds Arms, and a hint from me to take his own sweet time about his errand. And we will have a most charming evening altogether."

"You dear wicked little plotter and schemer against your father's desires," said Sir Lionel, "always trying to make other people happy, grumbler as you are. I could make your kind heart leap for joy if I chose."

"I wish you would, then," said Mathilde, pausing, and turning up her snow white cuffs from large, but beautifully-formed and white hands. "I have not much to give me pleasure; tell me this glad news."

"I am bound in honour to your father not to do so. He is very careful that you should not get too much pleasure out of any pleasant event, and he has forbidden me to speak to you about it."

Mathilde still looked at him fixedly. "Come," she said; "you may tell me, at all events, of what nature is this pleasure?"

"I do not think I ought to do even that," said Sir Lionel.

"Nor I either; but surely you will."

"Well, then, you have prevailed so far. Some one is coming, by your father's wish, whom you will be deeply glad to see."

A deep flush came over her face, and she turned away, while her heart beat wild and joyously. Little she thought that, by the suggestion of Sir Lionel, Father Martin was coming to live with them. Her thoughts were of one very different.

Sir Lionel and Adèle sat whispering together till late; but she sat apart, perfectly silent and perfectly happy. Sir Lionel went away, and Adèle went up-stairs; but she was still disinclined to move. De Valognes was coming. He was indeed coming, as it happened,——but not to her.

## CHAPTER X.

### MONSIEUR D'ISIGNY RETURNS.

SIR LIONEL had gone away, and Adèle had gone up-stairs; but still Mrs. Bone and Mathilde sat on either side of the fire, for William was not returned. Mrs. Bone sat with her arms folded: Mathilde sat with hers lying loosely, with the palms uppermost in her lap. Mrs. Bone did not speak, because she had nothing to say; and Mathilde was perfectly silent, because, in reality, she was unconscious.

Mrs. Bone was a good watcher; she had been well drilled to that in her former life, and was also well fitted for it by her natural temperament. Yet, after a time, she began to nod and yawn, and at the same time to entertain in her sleepy soul—she could hardly tell why—a wish that Mademoiselle would go to bed. This desire took possession of her more and more the sleepier she got; yet she was a woman who was a long time before she spoke her most settled convictions, still longer before she acted on them. She had slid half off her slippery wooden Windsor chair some three or four times, with her chin on her bosom and her knees nearly on the fire, before she went so far as to say, just saving a yawn,—

"He is very late, Mademoiselle."

Mathilde made her no answer. Mrs. Bone sat upright, and shook herself together once more, perfectly fresh and bright; but Mathilde sat there just in the same attitude, taking no notice of her whatever.

Four times more did Mrs. Bone slide half out of her chair and recover herself; the fifth time she slid too far, and the outraged laws of gravity, long trifled with, indignantly asserted themselves. She slid too near to the edge of her chair, whereupon the chair shot her dexterously forward into the fire-place, and there fell a-top of her.

Mathilde picked them both up, and restored them to their former relations. After which she said, either to the chair or to Mrs. Bone, "You had better go to bed."

"Had not Mademoiselle better go to bed?" suggested Mrs. Bone.

"No," said Mathilde. And Mrs. Bone discussed the matter no further; but set herself to the very difficult task of getting a comfortable snooze and preserving her consciousness and her equilibrium at the same time.

She succeeded in a measure. She kept from sliding, and soon was perfectly fast asleep, with the difference that she was triumphantly conscious of being broad awake. Mathilde's attention was first called to this comatose-clairvoyant state of Mrs. Bone's by that lady saying, with remarkable emphasis and distinctness,—

"Hi! ho! he! ho! hum! ha! All the whole family was soft in their heads; and her grandmother, the witch, as big a fool as any of 'em. She biled up some lords and ladies* in a brass pipkin with some dead man's fat, and a dash of rue, and said the Commandments backwards; but it never came to nothink, Lord bless you!"

Mathilde was aroused; she said very distinctly, "Mrs. Bone!"

Mrs. Bone giggled idiotically.

"Mrs. Bone!" said Mathilde, louder.

Mrs. Bone sneezed, coughed, choked herself, and said, "Fifteen ducks' eggs under a small game hen. The woman always was a fool, and so was her mother before her."

"Mrs. Bone!" shouted Mathilde.

Mrs. Bone returned to every-day consciousness with a start, smiling sweetly; and remarked that "it was a'most time to get up."

"You have been asleep, Mrs. Bone," said Mathilde, loudly.

Mrs. Bone denied this accusation with great vivacity, but dropped off again at once, with a cheerful stupid leer on her tired face. "She may as well sleep," said Mathilde, "so long as she don't fall into the fire. William is very late. Thank heaven, papa is not at home."

At first Mrs. Bone kept up the fiction of being wide awake, by opening her eyes every minute and winking foolishly at Mathilde. Then she went sound asleep, and had a nightmare,

* Arum Maculatum.

and exasperated Mathilde so by crying out, "Oh, Lord! oh, good gracious! I never!" and so on, that she got up, and shook her broad awake at all events.

"Oh, yes, my dear young lady," said Mrs. Bone, looking foolishly in her face, and yawning, "believe one that loves you well, that it will never come to no good at all."

"What then?" said Mathilde.

"Him and her, my dear young lady."

"You are not well awake, Mrs. Bone," said Mathilde.

"Haven't closed an eye, my dear mademoiselle," said Mrs. Bone. "But, Lord love you, it will never do!"

"What will not do?"

"Sir Lionel and Miss Adèle, to be sure," said Mrs. Bone. "She can't *abide* him at times even now; and she will like him less, if ever they have the ill-luck to marry. The Somerses are a near and hard family; and nearness and hardness will never suit *her*. And she is playing with him. Did you ever see his coach?"

"Yes," said Mathilde, looking shrewdly at her.

"What is painted on the door of it?"

"I have not noticed," said Mathilde.

"Why, a bloody hand," said Mrs. Bone, in a low voice. "And she is playing with him. She loves a Frenchman."

"Every English baronet carries a bloody hand on his coat of arms," said Mathilde; "there is nothing in that. And who is this Frenchman, then, with whom you connect my sister's name?"

"A captain from Brittany," said Mrs. Bone. "And keep that captain from Brittany away from Sir Lionel, if you love peace and hate murder. The Somerses are a *just* family, as just as your father, Monsieur; but they are hard and near, and they never forgive. They have been in the valley two hundred years. *We*, who have been their servants so long, should know them. Keep this Brittany captain out of Sir Lionel's path."

"I should recommend Sir Lionel Somers to keep out of the path of André Desilles," said Mathilde, the Frenchwoman all over in one instant. "I suppose André Desilles is the man to whom you allude."

Mrs. Bone, possibly confusing names, possibly wishing no further debate, nodded her head, and committed herself.

"What makes you think that Adèle has any communication with him?" asked Mathilde.

"Because I have smuggled letter after letter, and answer after answer, between him and her," replied Mrs. Bone.

"You have been a faithless and unworthy servant," said Mathilde.

"Not at all," said Mrs. Bone. "I have refused to take any more letters to Captain Thingaby——"

"Desilles?" suggested Mathilde.

"Ah! Desilles," said Mrs. Bone, not wishing to commit herself; "since Sir Lionel was received. And, besides, let like wed like, and kind, kind. French and English don't match, mademoiselle. Look at your pa and ma."

"Adèle is acting very badly," said Mathilde. "I shall certainly put the whole matter, from one end to the other, before my father the moment he comes home—— Hush! my dear Bone! hark!"

Mrs. Bone jumped up as pale as a ghost. "Good Lord! here he is," she said; "and William not come home."

"Now we are all ruined together," said Mathilde. "This is the most dreadful thing which has ever happened to me in all my life. If he serves us these tricks, I will go into a convent. I would sooner go and live with my mother at Dinan."

"Don't say such dreadful things, mademoiselle," said Mrs. Bone. "Whatever shall we do? Oh, whatever shall we do?"

"I shall fight," said Mathilde; "I can't stand this for ever."

## CHAPTER XI.

### "IPHIGENIA IN AULIS."

THE noise which had scared Mathilde and Mrs. Bone was the footfall of M. D'Isigny's great brown horse, approaching through the courtyard. The sound of the horse's feet ceased at the usual place, and the heavy stride of M. D'Isigny was soon after heard approaching the door.

The two women cowered together. "He has to put his own horse up," whispered Mrs. Bone. Mathilde nodded, calm with the calmness of desperation. D'Isigny opened the outside door with a clang, and pulling aside the curtain, came inside the screen and confronted them. One minute, while I tell you what he was like.

A very tall, splendidly-made man, as to body ; narrow flanks, deep chest, graceful carriage. As to features, regular ; as to complexion, perfect. From under his delicate prominently-hooked nose the long upper lip receded to a delicately cut close-set mouth, which the chin advancing, again left in a hollow. The whole form of the face was noble and grand, handsome and inexorably calm.

" Where have you sent William ? " he demanded.

" Sir Lionel came," said Mathilde, in French ; "and so I gave him a shilling to go to the ' Leeds Arms.' Sir Lionel objects to your plan of having the servants in the same room as ourselves at any time ; and, considering the relations which exist between Adèle and him, I thought that it would be wiser and more proper, at all events on this occasion, you being absent, to get rid of the man, and await your further instructions as to my future conduct on this point."

And having said this, she awaited the storm. D'Isigny said, quietly, " Come here." And she came to him.

"You have acted wisely and well, my good daughter," he said, taking her hand. " I am deeply sorry that you have forced me to praise you, because I know how bad praise is for the moral nature of any one ; but I am obliged, in common justice, to praise you on this occasion. Interests, which are of far higher importance than my own conclusions, render it necessary that I should yield to the idiotic class pride of Sir Lionel Somers. You have acted on your own responsibility in my absence, and you have done well and wisely. You are a woman of discretion ; you are a discreet sister, and a good and thoughtful daughter. May the good God bless you, Mathilde ! and make your life long and happy, if it so pleases Him,—if it may be possible. I pray God to send you the greatest blessing for which a father can pray ! May the husband of your choice be worthy of you ! and in your old age may you have daughters around you as worthy of your love and confidence as you are of mine ! "

She was utterly conquered in a moment. She asked so little love and kindness, poor soul, and here, suddenly and unexpectedly, she had got so much more than she ever dreamt of.

He might worry, tease, bully, call her Goneril or Regan, three hundred and sixty-four days in the year, if he would only melt to her like this on the three hundred and sixty-fifth. His will was hers for an infinite time now.

Did he know this? I cannot say. Did he calculate on it? I cannot say either.

She went quietly up to him, and laid her head on his bosom. "Love me a little more, father," was all she said; and then broke out into a wild fit of weeping.

"I do not think that I can love you more than I do, Mathilde," he said, calmly. "These are extremely foolish and causeless tears, and must be dried immediately. I knew, when I praised you, that you would in some way make a fool of yourself. I am rather glad that you have done so at once. This is not a time for a Frenchwoman to get wildly hysterical because her father tells her that she has done her duty, and gives her his blessing. If you begin now to indulge in this kind of sentimentalism, you will never be fit for the work which lies before you. In other times I might have been pleased by this exhibition of sentiment. At present it is offensive."

She recovered herself at once. "I will do the best I can for you, sir," she said.

"*That* is better spoken," he answered. "No tears, Mathilde, no tears *as yet*. My good girl, keep your tears until all is over, and lost. See what I have to say to you. I *trust* you. I trust you to obey me implicitly in all which is coming, without question."

"I will do so, sir, if you will only be kind to me sometimes."

"These are no times for sentimental kindnesses; you must obey me without that stipulation. I have been kind to you, in sheer justice I will allow, and you have rewarded me by tears. Girl! girl! in the times which are coming such an outbreak as that may ruin everything."

"I could die mute, sir, if needs were."

"I think you could," said M. D'Isigny; "and I think it very likely that you will have to do so. Tell me. Are you afraid of death?"

"I am your daughter, sir."

"And so is Adèle," said M. D'Isigny, quietly, "who certainly could not die mute. What I mean is this. Do you think that if everything went wrong, you could trust yourself to die without mentioning names?"

"I am sure I could, sir,"

"I am not so sure. You are not submissive; you break out at times, and objurgate me. And just now, when I complimented you about the management of a wretched domestic detail, concerning two fools, you burst into tears. I doubt I cannot trust you."

"You may trust me to the very death, sir, and I will die silent. I only ask this: Will you be kind to me?"

"No," said D'Isigny, shortly. "I was kind to you just now, and you made a fool of yourself. I shall be stern to you, and keep you up to the mark. In the business which is getting on hand we shall want a woman—a well-trained woman—without an opinion. I intend you to be that woman. And we may want a young man; and Louis de Valognes must be that young man. And you and he must act together. De Valognes and you are in love with one another, I believe, though I am not aware that I ever gave my permission to such an arrangement; you will work together in this business."

"I wish you could tell me in what business, sir," said Mathilde.

"I wish you could tell *me*," said M. D'Isigny. "We are waiting and watching, you know. We have not declared. Your mother, at Dinan, has added the last to her already innumerable catalogue of follies, and *has* declared. She has declared on the violent Royalist side. By-the-by, it is quite possible that I may send you to Dinan to listen to these asses, and report their conversation to me."

"Spare me that, sir."

"I shall spare you nothing. You are worthy of the work; and if the work requires you, you must go to the work. *I believe* that we shall none of us get out of it with our lives. Do you understand me?"

"Perfectly, sir."

"*My* head I consider as gone already," continued D'Isigny. "So is the head of De Valognes. The question is this: Will you join us?"

"But, sir, this is merely a political *bouleversement*. There is no question of life and death."

"Girl! girl!" said D'Isigny, "it is a question of life and death. Do you think that *I* do not know? We have ground the French people down until we have made them tigers; and we are only like the English officers in the jungle of Bengal."

"Well, sir, when I am wanted I will be ready. Your supper waits you."

"We will talk no more of these things to-night, then," said D'Isigny. "Come and sit by me. We now return to our rule of talking English, if you please."

"Is your horse cared for?" asked Mathilde.

"Yes. William, who has the instinct of a gentleman, has been sitting in the stable with a lanthorn, having looked in and seen that you were sitting silently wrapped in thought. Tell me one thing. Is that young man engaged to be married? has he a sweetheart, as they call it?"

"Yes, sir," said Mathilde, smiling pleasantly, for "Awdrey" was a little household joke among them. "He 'walks,' as they say, with Mary Hopkins."

M. D'Isigny prided himself on the "royal" habit of never forgetting any one he had once seen.

"That beef-faced, bare-armed fool, *avec les coudes écrasés*, which she is always scratching and keeping in a state of irritation; the girl with the uncombed hair, and some other girl's shoes and petticoats, who comes for the butter from Stourminster, and always tries to run away and hide when she sees me? I know her. But she is as ugly as a butcher's boy, and half-witted. He can't be in earnest about her."

"She is a very good girl, sir, and keeps her mother. He is very much in earnest about her."

"I am extremely sorry, and rather vexed to hear it."

"And why so, sir?"

"I am not generally accustomed to give reasons," said M. D'Isigny, looking sharply at her. "Certainly not to *you*. In this case I will gratify your curiosity. William's stupidity, his courage, his splendid honesty, his admiration for me, and his absolute ignorance of the French language, might make him extremely useful in France in the times which are coming."

"But 'Awdrey,' as we call her, would not interfere with that, sir; she is stupider than he, and quite as honest. As to fear, she ought not to be suspected on *that* account; for she faced

Hollinger's bull single-handed with a common hurdle-stake, and by dexterous and repeated blows over his nose, drove him triumphantly to the other end of the field."

"You utterly fail to follow my line of argument," said M. D'Isigny. "We shall want courageous, self-sacrificing simpletons in the business which is coming: as an instance, we shall want you; mind you act your part. I do not want to utilise this young woman at all. My regret at her connection with William arises from this. I have the strongest repugnance to enlist any man in the cause of French politics just now, who has any human tie on this earth. I therefore shall pause before I involve William."

"But, sir," said Mathilde, "let me talk to you now we are so pleasant together, for you will be disagreeable again to-morrow. William's marriage to this poor girl would only make him more devoted to our interests, more entirely dependent on us. You say you want a certain number of fools for the business on hand, and have done me the honour to count me off as the first, and I suppose the greatest. If you want such people for your business, I assure you, from personal observation, that you could not possibly find a greater simpleton than Awdrey. I assure you that she is a much greater fool than I am, little as you may think so."

"There is a *soupçon* of your dear mother's temper there, young lady," said D'Isigny; "a little dagger of spiteful badinage let in from under a cloak of affectionate confidence. I would not do that again if I were you."

"I was utterly innocent, sir," said Mathilde, aghast.

"So I believe; let it go. I return, then, to the argument about this William, which I will try to make you understand. If William's life had been but a single life, I should not have hesitated in sacrificing it. The mere fact of this red-armed girl's life hanging on his makes me pause."

"But, sir, in employing him in the work before you, you do not necessarily sacrifice his life."

"I tell you now, my daughter, that any man or woman who interferes in French politics now, risks his life. Therefore, although I could have got important service from this man, William, I shall spare him, because he is engaged."

He spared his groom. But with regard to his own daughter

and De Valognes, his cousin? Had the old Seigneur ideas got so deeply burnt into his heart, that he considered all his kith and kin, with all their individual ideas and opinions, as his own property as head of the house? It is possible.

## CHAPTER XII.

### NEWS FROM FRANCE FOR M. D'ISIGNY.

SIR LIONEL SOMERS, who had a will of his own, fought M. D'Isigny on the question of the servants living in the same room with them, and gained a trifling concession. He never for an instant moved M. D'Isigny as to his general principle (or was it his hastily adopted crotchet?). Sir Lionel (father of the present Earl of Stourminster) was a splendid match for Adèle, or for twenty Adèles. M. D'Isigny was perfectly well aware of the fact, and so, as a Frenchman, a host, a friend, and a prospective father-in-law, he gracefully waived his crotchet so far as ostentatiously to send Mrs. Bone and William to consider themselves in a cold and distant scullery whenever Sir Lionel came. This had the effect of making the good-humoured and considerate Sir Lionel very uncomfortable, and of costing him five shillings a visit—he finding it necessary to give half-a-crown a-piece to William and Mrs. Bone, as conscience money.

"No one never got their change out of master," remarked William, on the occasion of one of Sir Lionel's visits, just after this arrangement, as he smuggled the hot teakettle out of the sitting-room for Mrs. Bone to put her feet on, and so keep them off the cold stones; "and no one ever will. Yet he is a kind man, too; and a good man—a'most as kind as ma'mselle herself. When that awful-looking Mr. Marrer fell ill down town, he was with him night and day; and yet he hated him. I tell you, mother, I have seen Monsieur go into his bedroom to ask how he was, and shrink away all the time near the door, as if there was a mad dog in the room."

"My dear child," said Mrs. Bone, "don't talk about that man."

"What—master?"

"Bless his honest heart, no. That Marrer! As sure as ever

I eat any form of pig-meat, that man comes to me in my dreams, just as I see him lying on that bed, with his gasping mouth and his jagged teeth. Did I ever tell you the effect that that man's appearance had on my niece, Eliza? It was some time before she got over the sight of him coming along under the great yew-tree, just at dusk, on One Tree Down, hissing and gurring with his teeth. Did I ever tell you?"

William had heard the story a dozen or so of times; but he liked his stories as Sir Lionel liked his Madeira—old. He disliked new stories—they cost him a mental effort—just as Sir Lionel disliked a new kind of wine, with the flavour of which he was not familiar. William consequently intimated that he had never heard this story before; and Mrs. Bone, with her feet on the teakettle and her shawl over her head, set to work to tell it to him for about the twenty-fifth time.

It was a very long story, involving the pedigree of many people in Stourminster Marshall: involving questions, answers, and "interpellations" about nearly every one in that town and the neighbourhood around it. The story promised to be a sort of "Iliad," edited by Burke, and with as many episodes in it as in Carlyle's "Frederic the Great." The teakettle had got cold, and Mrs. Bone was warming to her work, when, in the middle of a long discussion about M. Marat—who he was, where he came from, why he had sold himself to the evil one and said the Lord's Prayer backwards, or something of that sort, they were interrupted by the arrival of the carrier's cart from Stourminster.

Sir Lionel and Adèle were sitting before the fire in the sitting-room, "engaged." M. D'Isigny was reading "The Gentleman's Magazine" under his lamp, and was bending so far as to approve of it in a patronising way. Mathilde was thoughtfully cutting out needlework, utterly absorbed in it; pleasedly thankful for present peace, let the morrow bring what it would — when William, after a cautiously noisy demonstration outside the screens, pulled the connecting curtains apart, and appeared with his arm full of parcels. M. D'Isigny took them from him and nodded to him.

William said: "Four-and-fivepence, monsieur!"

"Go with him and pay the man, Mathilde," said M. D'Isigny; and she went. "Don't disturb yourselves, you two," he said; "it is only my French budget. What you can find to say to one

F

another, I don't know ; but pray go on saying it. I did it myself once," he added to himself ; " and the result was, Madame ——I hope you will have better luck."

They went on, while he examined his mail. The first article in it was a packet of letters done up in a parcel, surreptitiously smuggled from Poole. He began to open them and read them.

" Here," he said to Adèle, after having read the first one, "put this in the fire. It is from Louis De Valognes, who proposes to come here on a visit. Let me catch him at it ; I will answer him to-morrow."

He threw the letter to Adèle, who was sitting between her father and Sir Lionel. She caught it, but turned ghastly white. With her English lover's kind and gentle eyes on her face, she dared not read a line of this letter. The sight of that handwriting opened her eyes to a fearful fact in one moment. She loved De Valognes more than ever. Until she had seen this letter she had believed that it was all over between them ; but now she saw the dearly-loved handwriting of De Valognes, as she threw it on the fire, and longing and desiring to read, and if necessary to kiss every letter of it, she turned from her English lover with dislike—almost disgust, making her beautiful face ugly ; and turned, as luck would have it, towards her father.

Horror of horrors ! He had opened, and had read another letter. She could see, under the blaze of his reading-lamp, that the letter was addressed to her, and was in the handwriting of De Valognes. She knew that it was the answer to the letter which William the Silent had smuggled for her, and she got desperate, for her father was calmly and inexorably staring at her over the top of it. His eyes were absolutely steady, his features absolutely immovable. He was merely looking at her ; that was all.

The loss of nerve, the want of courage, which caused sad mischief hereafter, came into play here. I cannot say whether it was physical or moral. But she lost nerve. When she caught her father's steady look from under his reading-lamp, she threw her little arms abroad, cried out piteously, " I am dying ! I am going to die ! " and then fainted away, as Mrs. Bone expressed it, " stone dead ; " her last conscious efforts in action being directed to tearing fiercely at the hands of Sir Lionel Somers, who put his arm round her waist to support her : her last conscious words running unfortunately, " Louis ! Louis ! my darling Louis ! Come and save me from this man."

Ladies do not faint now-a-days, at least but rarely. If one can trust a perfect mass of evidence, oral and written, syncope, at the end of the last century, and up to the thirty-fifth year of this, was a habit with ladies. A story without a swoon was impossible until lately. Let us thank heaven comfortably that our mothers, wives, and daughters, have given up the evil habit of becoming cataleptic at the occurrence of anything in the least degree surprising. Although society gains undoubtedly by ladies giving up the habit of swooning on every possible occasion, yet fiction loses. For a swoon, in an old novel, was merely a conventional and convenient aposiopesis.

Adèle, however, had managed to faint away fairly and honestly. Mathilde was beside her in a moment ; she had been in the room when Adèle committed the dreadful indiscretion of calling on De Valognes, but *she did not understand it.* " Who is this Louis on whom she calls ? " thought Mathilde ; " it is a mercy she did not call on André Desilles.—She must be thinking of our poor brother, Louis, who died years ago, Sir Lionel," she said aloud. "Give her to me, please. Pretty little bird, calling on her dead brother."

She might have added the particulars that this brother Louis was only four months old at the time of his decease, and had died four years before Adèle was born ; but she wisely suppressed all this. As for meeting the eye of her father, who sat immoveable, staring calmly from under his reading-lamp, she would have died sooner than do that.

" Let me get her away from you, Sir Lionel," she said, cheerfully. " She will be better soon. Poor Louis ! Ah, poor dear Louis ! Come away, Adèle, it is only your own Mathilde ; come away, darling. Poor Louis ! You did not know him, Sir Lionel. Ah, no !"

She knew perfectly well that Sir Lionel was about two years old when Louis died at the ripe age of four months. But she knew that Adèle had committed some sort of an indiscretion in calling for this unknown Louis ; and so, God forgive her, she made her fiction, and got herself to believe it, little dreaming how it touched herself. She got Adèle away to her bower, and was content.

There were left alone M. D'Isigny and Sir Lionel Somers,—

Sir Lionel, an honest young English gentleman, who would have scorned a lie, and would have very quietly bowed himself out of his engagement to Adèle on the appearance of a more favoured suitor, and have possibly shot at that suitor, and possibly have killed him, in the most polite manner, on the first occasion,—such, perhaps, as having some wine in his glass after drinking the king's health: and M. D'Isigny, who lived in a glass-house of ostentatious truthfulness, and was sitting and considering under his lamp this little matter.

D'Isigny himself had discovered Adèle's treachery, her relations with De Valognes. Sir Lionel must be an absolute simpleton if he did not understand, from her crying out for Louis, that he, Sir Lionel, was not the man of her affection. Now, M. D'Isigny, the man who would utterly scorn a lie, was wondering to himself whether or no Mathilde's outrageous lie about his dead baby Louis had succeeded. He hated a lie, and would die sooner than tell one himself; but he rather hoped that this one of Mathilde's would hold water, because——

Because the question resolved itself into this. Adèle's treachery was patent enough to him, yet if Sir Lionel called off his engagement, M. D'Isigny must have him out. That was absolutely necessary. D'Isigny knew about Adèle's treachery, and knew that his daughter was in the wrong. Sir Lionel, however, could know nothing of these things, and therefore, should Mathilde's falsehood not hold good with him, should the 17th-century baronet demand explanations from the 13th-century count, or demand explanations which could not possibly be given, it would become necessary to M. D'Isigny to go out with Sir Lionel and shoot him.

Sir Lionel had politely followed Mrs. Bone and Mathilde to the door as they transported Adèle, which gave M. D'Isigny perhaps two minutes to think. He spent that precious time in thinking how he would punish Adèle, and how he could make Mathilde smart for the falsehood she had told, and which had been so useful to him, without acknowledging its utility.

Sir Lionel came back; and he was obliged to decide in some way. He was a quick hand at a decision. He decided rapidly and wisely to let Sir Lionel speak first, and lose the advantage. Sir Lionel was not long in speaking; and his gentlemanly trustfulness was a stab at D'Isigny's noble pride.

"My pretty little love," said Sir Lionel, "I fear I was clumsy in offering my assistance to her. My mother has told me often that women hate men being near them when they are ill. Poor little thing: she shall get so used to me soon that she will not fear me. Has she ever had these faintnesses before? Do you think that this is serious? Shall I ride for a doctor, dear sir?"

D'Isigny longed to tell him the truth. He sympathised so with his noble confidence that he felt guilty in abusing it; but he thought, "I can whip this girl in and bring things right, which is the better plan;" and so he practically adopted Mathilde's falsehood.

"She has never fainted like this before," said M. D'Isigny. "She is doubtless unwell. Here is this big parcel of my mail from France. Guess what it contains. If you will wait a little longer, you will have a report of this silly child's health."

This challenge to change the subject was not responded to by Sir Lionel. He ignored the large parcel altogether, and would speak of nothing but Adèle; thereby involving D'Isigny in a labyrinth of prevarications, which exasperated that gentleman almost beyond bearing. Sir Lionel wondered why he was so short and almost snappish with him; but D'Isigny had let down the shade of his lamp so that Sir Lionel could not see his face. Could he have seen it he would have seen that it grew older and fiercer as the conversation went on. It was the face of a man who thought he lived only in perfect cruel truth, but who had committed himself to *one* lie, and therefore to a hundred.

"I will wait and hear of her health," said Sir Lionel. "I fear she has had some shock. She was perfectly comfortable with me just now. Don't you think that she has had some shock?"

"It is possible," said M. D'Isigny.

"I wonder what!" said Sir Lionel. "Do you know that I don't like that groom of yours?"

"I like him extremely."

"Well, then, I will say no more. Only in your absence a week ago, I found him disputing with Adèle about a guinea, and Adèle in tears. This is, of course, your business. It will be mine soon."

"I will inquire into it," said D'Isigny. "Until it becomes your business, leave it in my hands, if you will have the goodness."

"*You* are a tartar," *thought* Sir Lionel. "Lucky your daughters don't inherit *your* temper." And then said to M. D'Isigny, in perfect good faith, "Is it not curious that Adèle should have remembered her dead brother, and called on him to-night in her illness?"

"Most extraordinary!" said M. D'Isigny. "Have you any remarks to make on the subject?"

"Why, yes," said Sir Lionel, puzzling D'Isigny more and more in his perfect simplicity. "It shows one how curiously sensitive women are. Do you know that she has never mentioned the existence of this brother Louis to me before? I never heard of his existence until this evening. I suppose that there are some painful circumstances about his death?"

"There were," said D'Isigny.

"So I thought," said Sir Lionel. "How old was he; and when did he die?"

"Would you mind changing the subject?" said D'Isigny.

"I beg ten thousand pardons," said honest Sir Lionel. "I ought to have known that it was a painful subject. Pray forgive me. Mathilde will tell me all about it."

"I would sooner that you never mentioned the name of my late son Louis to any member of my family, Sir Lionel," said M. D'Isigny; adding mentally, "Catch me adopting a falsehood again."

And Sir Lionel said, "I will be most careful to follow your instructions, sir, and once more beg pardon." Adding also, mentally, "So we have had a fiasco in this saintlike family, hey! I wonder what this wonderful brother Louis was like, and what he did. He must have been older than Adèle, or she would not have called to him for protection. Gambled most likely; or went to America with Lafayette, or something of that sort. I'll bet myself a hundred pounds that he was in the American business. The old man is dead against the Americans, as he is against anything like motion, actionary or reactionary. I shall be pretty sure to have the history of my sainted brother-in-law from Mathilde before I am much older."

Diligence is a virtue. But we must credit the devil with it; because his diligence in the distribution and the development of lies is very great. With regard to the masterly way in which he works out the effects and consequences of those lies, I do not wish to speak, as I do not wish to compliment him.

M. D'Isigny, now regaining his good humour, resumed the conversation. "I have challenged you to look at this large parcel of mine from France, and to guess what was in it; you have evaded my challenge. You will bet, you English here, but only on what you think certainty. Will you bet on the contents of this parcel? Not you. If you *knew* what was in the parcel, or if you thought you knew, you would bet. You English invented betting (for which may——), but you are the veriest cowards about betting in Europe. You only bet on certainties; we French bet on speculation. I, for instance, in this case will speculate fifty guineas that you, with *your* intellect, don't guess what is in this parcel."

"You will pay up on the spot?" said Sir Lionel. "Will you say 'Done?'"

"I say 'Done,'" said M. D'Isigny.

"Then I will trouble you for fifty guineas. If you have notes in the house, I prefer them to a cheque; not that I distrust your balance at Childs', but there are three or four dear little dicky-birds likely to have a difference of opinion in Lascelles' park to-morrow, and notes come handy. Pay over."

"Why do you fight cocks? And you have not won your bet," said D'Isigny.

"I beg pardon. I had omitted the detail," said Sir Lionel. "That big packet from France contains the turnip-seed which Young in his letter urged you to send to Madame D'Isigny at Dinan. Now I'll tell you what I'll do. I'll let you off your bet if you will let me see the letter which accompanies the turnip-seed."

D'Isigny hummed and hawed and pished; but fifty guineas were fifty guineas. Then he confessed that, as a father of a family, with two daughters on whose actions he could never calculate, he had done wrong in betting fifty guineas on anything. Still he had fairly lost his bet, and fifty guineas were fifty guineas. Then he told Sir Lionel, in a feeble way, that he did not want to get out of his bet; on which Sir Lionel said, "Pay up, then." Then he asked him, "How did he know that any letter had come with the turnip-seed?" to which Sir Lionel answered, that if there was no letter the original bet stood, and that D'Isigny must pay, in notes or gold. Finally, D'Isigny showed Sir Lionel the note, and got off his fifty guineas. Sir Lionel read it, then put it down and looked at M. D'Isigny.

"You *would* see it, you know, at the expense of fifty guineas. Is your curiosity perfectly satisfied?" said D'Isigny.

"Not entirely," said Sir Lionel. "How many years did you stand this?"

"Close on fifteen."

"You must be a gentle-tempered man, then, in spite of your rigidity. Your daughters have but little of their mother in them. I may be allowed to ask, as I am about to marry into your family, and we are alone together—do you consider Madame mad?"

"Try a bargain with her. Come, you who can throw away fifty guineas, try a bargain with her. She is perfectly able to manage her own affairs, I assure you. No one ever got so much out of those Dinan estates as she does. You look at me still, and ask me a silent question with your eyes, and my answer is, No. Madame is the most sober woman in France."

"Are you right, then," said Sir Lionel, "in allowing her to grind these Breton peasants in the way she is doing? Why, from this letter it seems that she is exacting money for the Silence des Grenouilles, a thing which was never done but down in the Landes, has not been done for forty years, and never except the Seigneur's wife was lying-in. She never would dare to do it, were she not trafficking with *your* peasantry, on the value of *your* name, so deeply respected among them. Why don't you stop her?"

"You go and try."

"It is not my business, I think," said Sir Lionel. "I only warn you that she will get your château burnt about her head if she goes on like this. *Our* people could not stand one half of it."

"She is an Englishwoman," said D'Isigny. "You say that my daughters have nothing of their mother in them. I assure you that both of them have got her Teutonic mulishness to an immense degree, more particularly Mathilde. You ask me why I do not go to Dinan and interfere with my wife's proceedings, do you not?"

"Well, I *wonder* that you do not."

"Did you ever hear a story about me and a mad dog?" said M. D'Isigny.

"I know the story well."

"Do you consider me a coward?" said M. D'Isigny.

"One only requires to have seen your face once to answer that question, monsieur. You come of the bravest nation in the world, and you are the bravest specimen of that nation I have ever seen. You had no need to allude to the mad-dog story to make me acknowledge that in any difficulty involving danger I should value you beyond measure as a friend, and dread you greatly as an enemy. I know that you are afraid of nothing. As for the mad-dog story, I wonder at your alluding to it rather. I hope that I should have done the same thing myself, though with less dexterity."

"Your speech is logical and well rounded; you converse like an educated gentleman. For instance, a man less educated than yourself would have stopped his compliments to me without ending by the logical deduction from them, which was made on the words, 'you are afraid of nothing.' I beg to contradict you. I beg to inform you that, brave as I am, I am entirely afraid of Madame, my wife."

"But, dear sir," said Sir Lionel, "are you not doing wrong in yielding to her so much? She is out-heroding Herod. She will get *your* château burnt about *her* ears. Why on earth do you live here—acknowledged by all to be the best landlord in the vale of Stour—on *her* estates, and allow her to rackrent *your* estates in Brittany in this shameless manner?"

"You read the letter which accompanied the return of the turnip-seed," said M. D'Isigny. "Will you after that just go over to Dinan yourself, and argue with her?"

"No, I won't," said Sir Lionel, promptly.

"You had better not," said M. D'Isigny. "She has paid *you* a few compliments in ink; I wish you could hear her tongue. She is an Englishwoman, you know—a compatriot of yours—deeply religious, deeply loyal in her sentiments, with a morality which I could almost characterise as frantic. She is extremely clever, and her conversation is epigrammatic and lively; an admirable letter writer, as you have seen from your fifty-guinea turnip-seed letter. She is a nearly perfect person; there is nothing wrong about her but her tongue. Now do, before you marry into my family, go and try that for yourself."

" I think I won't," said Sir Lionel.

" She is enormously charitable," said M. D'Isigny, "as well as wonderfully shrewd. She spends fully one half of this 'Silence des Grenouilles' money (which was an original idea of hers, mind) in what you so coarsely call 'poor man's plaister.' I am sure you would like your countrywoman and future mother-in-law. She is a real Whig. Go and see how you would like her."

" I think that I will do nothing of the kind," said Sir Lionel.

" Then go home to bed, for it is late. Only again do not speak to me about my cowardice with regard to my wife. You flinch at merely reading one letter of Madame's, your countrywoman—I have stood nearly fifteen years of her. We French are braver than you English. You have a trick of firing your guns faster at sea, which we have not, from getting no practice, and you are the better sailors; but we are the braver nation. Bah! go home to bed. Our sailors always know they will be beaten by dexterity, yet they *fight* as well as yours. Ask your admirals."

M. D'Isigny, most truthful of men, had got things as he wanted them, but could not be content with his victory, which was only a victory over the trustful, honest gentleman, Sir Lionel. D'Isigny, extremely pleased to find that there was still time for deliberation about Sir Lionel and Adèle, went in for obscuration and confusion of counsel.

Sir Lionel, riding steadily home in the darkness, said to himself,—

" That wife of his at Dinan must be a devil of a woman. I never read such a letter in my life. He *says* that she isn't a lunatic; I believe that she is. I will find out some more about her from Mathilde."

## CHAPTER XIII.

### ADÈLE'S PENANCE.

MENTIONED that during the most anxious part of M. D'Isigny's late conversation with Sir Lionel Somers—at that point when, having discovered the correspondence between De Valognes and Adèle, he was entirely in doubt as to how much Sir Lionel might have guessed about her undoubted *fiasco* in calling aloud on Louis; when, in fact, he should have kept his wits about him to answer any questions which Sir Lionel might have put, and, if necessary, resent them; that he did nothing of the kind, but wasted his precious moments in devising a sufficient punishment for Adèle.

He could not think of one sufficiently agonising. His old trick of dead silence, which he had used towards Mathilde two years before, was stale. His genius for tormenting himself and others was far too original to enjoy thoroughly the same torture twice. Besides, Adèle, by prescription, had now got such a vested right in her "bower" upstairs, that it would have been revolutionary to interfere with it. He was not prepared for such a measure as *that*. And while the bower remained an institution and a refuge, his silence would lose half its terrors. Adèle was not always to the fore also, as Mathilde was, doing some kindly, busy piece of good work, and getting scolded for doing it more or less clumsily. The penance of his silence was terrible enough for *her*, but it might fall dead with Adèle. She might even like it, empty-headed little creature as she was, providing she was allowed to chatter on herself.

How, if he were to impose silence on *her?* he thought on his bed that night. How would *that* do? About as well, he was forced to answer himself, as imposing silence on her dear mother at Dinan. *That* would not do at all.

Towards the early hours of the morning an idea struck him, after which he went to sleep, and awoke early to act on it.

Mrs. Bone and William were "doing" the sitting-room; M. D'Isigny, ready dressed for his morning among the fields, in top-boots, buckskins, and redingote, appeared before them, and addressed Mrs. Bone.

"Will you be so good as to step upstairs, and take the compliments of M. the Comte D'Isigny to his daughter, Mademoiselle Adèle, and inquire respectfully how she finds herself after the fatigues of last evening?"

Mrs. Bone, looking steadily at M. D'Isigny, put her dust-pan and brush on the top of the papers and books on his writing-table, and then withdrew on her errand. She saw something was wrong, and in her way tried to mend it. She went to Adèle's bed-side, and delivered D'Isigny's message thus : "My dear Miss, your Pa's affectionate love, and wants to know how you find yourself this morning."

Adèle thought, "Oh, he is going to kill me with affection. One never knows what his next torture may be. Tell him," she added, "Mrs. Bone, that I send my affectionate duty, and that I wish I was dead."

"I can't take that message, Miss."

"You could take it, if you choose; but you don't choose, you wicked woman. You are in his pay; and that wicked William is in his pay also, and you three conspire to drive me mad."

"My dear Miss!"

"*Your* dear Miss," replied Adèle, little thinking how truly she was echoing her father's *real* message. "Take this message to him with my defiance. Hey, then! Tell M. the Comte D'Isigny that his daughter Mademoiselle Adèle is better than he wishes her to be."

Mrs. Bone, the peacemaker, delivered it in this manner. "Miss Adèle's affectionate love and duty, and finds herself better; though low, with a curious coldness of the nerves, which requires rest."

As soon as Mrs. Bone was gone Adèle got into one of her lamentable states of terror. "If the old fool should actually go, after all, and deliver my message to him! *Can* she be such a fool as to do it? I believe she is. What, on earth, did I say, last night? I wonder if I said too much. I might have said anything after his looking at me like that over the top of Louis' letter. I'll have that letter somehow, if I make Mrs. Bone steal it for me. I know that Louis has been horribly indiscreet; and that *he* has read the letter."

That "he!" Think of that, you parents who will not invite the confidence of your children ; not the friend, the father, but " he."

"He," she continued, "in one of his humours is as likely to tell Lionel the whole matter as not. I don't care if he does. If he allowed bells in this miserable house, I would ring for Mathilde. I think she might have come near me before this. She is at her prayers, I suppose. I think that she might have left them alone until she had come to her sister."

So Adèle : whom you must not judge, or at least, not condemn as yet, unless you can say that you were never petulant and unjust yourself. She was under the impression that the form of punishment which her father had prepared for her was that of affectionate solicitude. She never was more mistaken in her life. M. D'Isigny's carefully-studied torture, with which he contrived to punish her, and madden her almost beyond endurance, was profound and polite deference to all her wishes, however small.

I doubt whether my pen is sufficiently fine to give you all the little tortures which he inflicted on her by this new and brilliant invention of his, but I must try, even though I should stand as a mere Calcraft in comparison to the executioners of Damiens. They used to do these things better in France, and, indeed, can still do them better. Heaven help a weak English boy in a French school. Read that very charming and able book, " Les deux Nigauds," by the Comtesse de Segur, and say if the art of torture is lost in France.

Adèle, by way of deferring the beginning of her penance as long as possible, lay in bed until the midday dinner. She then thought it wise to descend, being carefully half-an-hour late. " I will come in towards the end of dinner quietly," she thought ; " that will make it easier for me. They will have nearly done, and I shall be not much noticed. He waits for no one."

Indeed. Pulling aside the curtain, and coming in, she perceived that the cloths on the two tables were laid, but that no dinner had been served. Her father was ostentatiously busy writing at his table ; and when she appeared, he called out, " Serve dinner, Mademoiselle has descended." This was quite enough to upset and frighten her to begin with : her father had waited dinner half an hour for her. If anything had been wanted to complete her discomposure, it was the fact of her father's coming forward, and politely and respectfully handing her to her seat. When she was seated, he inquired after her health with the greatest solicitude; was deeply anxious to know whether the room was too cold for her, in which case he would have the fire replenished. Was it too warm? in which case the man should empty half-a-dozen buckets of water on the fire, pull down the screen, and set all the doors and windows open. The house, he said, was entirely at Mademoiselle's orders. Did she object to the servants having their dinner at the opposite table? if she did, they should pack off to the scullery. She did not object, and was quite comfortable. Monsieur D'Isigny could not, in a sufficient manner, convey his thanks to Mademoiselle for her kind condescension. He begged her to believe that his house and his fortune were entirely at Mademoiselle's disposal.

He had forbidden Mathilde to go near her, or to communicate with her; and Mathilde, seeing that there was rather a larger storm in the wind than usual, never made the slightest effort so much as to acknowledge Adèle's presence, deeply as she sympathised with her. She bided her time for letting Adèle know that she felt for her.

M. D'Isigny's deep courtesy and respect to Adèle were fearful and maddening. He was Petruchio and Roger de Coverley all at once. The omelette was ill cooked; would she give him her kind permission to turn the cook out of the house? There was a draught where she sat, although her politeness would not allow her to acknowledge the fact; could not he persuade her to give her consent to having the house pulled down altogether, and rebuilt on a better plan? No. She was too kind; he would do it in a moment. He apologised for having asked her to live in such a miserable old barn, and said that he had only ventured to do so from knowing the thorough goodness of Mademoiselle's heart, her entire abnegation of self, and her studious consideration of others. And so he went on with her penance, until she was half mad.

Mathilde sympathised so deeply with her, that, after a time, she was determined to show it, and got into trouble as usual.

M. D'Isigny was putting the question of the separation of the orders in the approaching States-General before Adèle, and ostentatiously and respectfully asking her opinion, when Mathilde got behind him and caught Adèle's eye. Adèle was constrained to look over her father's shoulder at Mathilde, and felt, half-hysterical as she was, very much inclined to burst out laughing. She would have done so, if she had not known that she could not have stopped herself if she once began.

The first thing she saw was Mathilde's face, with a look of deep and solemn commiseration on it. Then Mathilde shook her head, and jerked her thumb towards her father; then she shook her head and waved her hands abroad, as if she would say: "It is a sad business, but no fault of mine:" and then she folded her arms, and wagged and nodded her head persistently.

Meanwhile M. D'Isigny went on, in his most ravishingly-agreeable manner. "Mademoiselle will therefore perceive, that while agreeing with De Stainville that it is to a certain extent impolitic to remove all the men of mark in France to Paris just at this time to attend States-General, yet, at the same time, I am obliged to agree with Alexander Lameth, that we must have States-General with the permanency of the English House of Commons. I perceive that Mademoiselle's attention is being distracted by the extreme imbecility of my eldest daughter, who is flourishing signals to her within six inches of the back of my head, under the impression that I am not aware of the fact. Mademoiselle's large sense and good heart will make allowance for the folly of a sister, however unworthy of her. I have to apologise to her for giving her so foolish a one."

Adèle had had as much as she could stand by this time, and broke out.

"I wish you would kill me."

M. D'Isigny turned round to Mathilde, who certainly looked very foolish, and said quietly,

"Imbecile! take Mademoiselle to bed. She is tired."

Mathilde did so, and came down again, taking up her work. M. D'Isigny calmly went on writing at his table, and said not a word. Mathilde spoke first.

"Why do you tease her like this? You will kill her."

M. D'Isigny looked up from his paper for one moment; and the look of pity which Mathilde had seen on his face the night before was there again. He said not one word.

"What has she done?" asked Mathilde, stoutly.

"Betrayed," said her father. And Mathilde said no more.

M. D'Isigny continued his treatment of Adèle until the day when he aroused Mathilde for a morning's walk, of which we will speak in the next chapter.

## CHAPTER XIV.

### MATHILDE WALKS OUT WITH HER FATHER.

A VERY early knock at Mathilde's door announced her father. She was already dressed; he entered and kissed her solemnly.

"Get ready to walk with me," he said; and very soon they were winding up the white road which led aloft over the down behind the house.

It was a very glorious, cloudless morning. The short sward which, dotted here and there with juniper, hung in abrupt sheets around and above them, was silvered with dew. Three hundred feet below them, the river wound like a silver riband through the beautiful poplar-fringed meadows, now wreathed with mist, which formed the floor of the valley. A little smoke was beginning to arise from the earliest chimneys of the distant town, and was curling in bluer wreaths amidst the cold white river-fog, which hung about and half obscured the red-brown roofs. The bell which hung in the square minster-tower told seven. There was a mingled noise of many sounds—broken, distant, but very delicious. The lowing of herds, the bleating of sheep, the whistling of herd-boys, the falling of water at mill-wheels, "the melodious armony of the fowles," as the "Boke of St. Albans" has it. I am but telling an old tale, better told by others before. It was a glorious English spring morning, and the agricultural world was awakening to its daily round of drudgery.

M. D'Isigny and Mathilde walked side by side in silence, winding up and up along the scarped terraces of the road which led over the down into the next eastward valley; now choosing some sheep-path which cut off one of the zig-zags, now walking on the short turf which bordered the road itself. Mathilde never dreamt of inquiring whither they were going, or why he had asked her to walk with him. He had only come into her room, and kissed her, and asked her to walk. But as he kissed her, she had seen deep love and deep pity in his face. She was perfectly content. She would follow him to the world's end if he would look like that at her sometimes. She asked so little, and he had given so much. She plodded on beside him, complacent in the mere animal feeling of contentment at being near him, and knowing that he was inclined to be kind to her. One has seen the same thing in dogs. The mere presence of one we love deeply gives one a kind of brute satisfaction which is very pleasant. William himself, by no means a refined young man, felt a very great pleasure in the mere company of Mrs. Bone. Mathilde, a very refined person, felt the same pleasure in the mere presence of her father. Whenever in her waddling walk she touched him, her face grew only more peaceful and more complacent.

He had looked on her with deep pity in his face that morning. She did not ask herself why he should pity her. She saw that he loved her also : and that was enough.

She walked clumsily, although she walked strongly and well. In spite of all the wonderful though half-concealed beauty of her face, she was nearly being a cripple. In spite of her enormous bust and her really great size, she was short in stature, and looked odd and queer in figure. As she walked beside her father on this morning, he was thinking to himself whether or no it would have been better if she had died in infancy.

"My child," he said, "do I walk too fast for you?"

"No," she said, with a laugh. "I *dandine* in walking ; but I walk strongly and well, and should never tire of walking with you as you are now."

"How am I now, then?"

"Your true self, without any of your nonsense," replied Mathilde.

M. D'Isigny left that matter alone. There was so much in hand, one half of which he was forced to confess to himself that he did not understand, that he let that little matter alone, as involving argument. And he had a great future in store for Mathilde; which she achieved, as the St. Malo folks can tell you ; and she must be led up to it gently. He changed the subject of conversation.

"Do you know where you are going?" he said.

"I would go anywhere with you in your present mood."

This was again dangerous.

"Have you any curiosity as to where you are going?" he put it once more.

"Not in the least," she said. "I am contented to be with you, and to touch you whenever I lurch in my clumsy walk. But I have no curiosity as to where I am going, if you will let me go with you. You are a just man, and will not lead me wrong. You have a just, cruel, and inexorable tongue, which would betray you if you were leading me wrong. I only desire to be near you, and to love you. That is not much to ask. I would go to my mother's at Dinan with *you*. You speak of *wanting* me. I will die for you, if you will be as you are now."

Once more he fought shy of the main question.

"It is a lonely road," he said. "How strange it would be to meet some one we knew on it."

"That is not likely," said Mathilde; "it is a cross-country road from Christ Church, and we are not likely to meet with anyone from there."

Madame D'Isigny always averred that Monsieur could not make himself agreeable if he tried. She never was more deeply mistaken in all her life. The veil over the earlier married life of those two was never withdrawn. Madame herself, the least reticent of women, mingled such evident self-justifying fictions with her account of it, that her story was incredible. From her account, they seem to have begun quarrelling at the church-door. There is no doubt that she, coming as she did of an old English Roman Catholic family, turned Protestant in two months, the wicked world said, to spite him. One fears that M. D'Isigny had certainly never made himself agreeable to *her*.

In which fact he certainly does not stand alone. A very great many men do not conceive it necessary to make themselves agreeable, particularly in small details, the neglect of which hurts love, to the women who have cast in their lot with them to their lives' end. I should think it probable that M. D'Isigny went further than this. I suspect that he was actively *dis*-agreeable to her. Yet when Madame D'Isigny, whatever her experiences, said that he could not be agreeable, she was deeply mistaken, as Mathilde could testify; for whether out of pity for her, or out of policy, he made himself profoundly agreeable to his daughter this day.

Nothing came amiss to him. The song of birds, the names

of flowers, the beauty of the land, the history of the country. Of France, of the painful troubles in their own Brittany, the Parliament trouble now gone by, and the still more dangerous trouble at Rennes in the winter just gone, he said nothing; to her wonder, for she expected, after what he had said, that he would have made political explanations to her. He was all peace and gentleness, and spoke only of the most agreeable subjects: the freedom and prosperity of England, the recovery of the King: admiring praise of Mr. Pitt,—nay, patronising admiration of Mr. Fox,—his favourite *bête noir*, the Prince of Wales, he never once mentioned during the whole walk, to Mathilde's intense relief.

They walked until half-past nine, and then he took her to an ale-house and gave her breakfast, carefully judging the reckoning. Then he told her that they would only saunter now; and they sauntered accordingly a little way through the pleasant spring lanes towards Christ Church, but not for long. D'Isigny's calculations of time and place were generally correct.

For as they were sitting on a pleasant bank together, tying bunches of primroses—(if his wife could only have seen him making such a fool of himself!)—there got over a style near them, but a little further down, and came into this Protestant Wiltshire lane, a Roman Catholic priest, clothed in the usual long black garments of a French secular, who chanted a psalm of David in the Latin tongue as he walked along swiftly, and raised his beautiful face towards the lark, who also sang overhead in the sky, as he did so.

They heard him singing as he came, and M. D'Isigny watched Mathilde :—

"' Salva me ex ore leonis : et a cornibus unicornium humilitatem meam.' " \*

Those words, chanted loud and melodious, fell abroad into the fresh spring morning. Then he paused before he took up his jubilant strain, and rolled out,—

"' Qui timetis Dominum, laudate eum : universum semen Jacob, glorificate eum : timeat eum omne semen Israel.' " †

---

\* "Save me from the lion's mouth : for thou hast heard me from the horns of the unicorns."—Psalm xxii. 21.

† "Ye that fear the Lord, praise him; all ye the seed of Jacob, glorify him; and fear him, all ye the seed of Israel."—*Ibid.* 23.

Mathilde was listening now, with starting eyes and parted lips. The priest took up his glorious melody once more :—

"'Quoniam non sprevit, neque despexit deprecationem pauperis : nec avertit faciem suam a me ; et cum clamarem ad eum, exaudiit me.'" *

Mathilde knew him now. She ran towards him with outstretched arms, and without one word. She should have knelt for his benediction by right, but her love got the better of her decorum, and she merely cast herself into his arms and kissed his noble old face twenty times over.

"I am a good calculator," said M. D'Isigny, beaming down on them, as soon as Mathilde had got over her first outburst. "I gave you the route pretty correctly, I think?"

"You did nothing of the kind," said Father Martin ; "I have kept *time*, but I have not followed your route at all. I have kept *time* with you ; but do you think that I was coming into a foreign land without seeking adventures? I have come across country like a fox-hunter. Found at Ring Wood, went away at a slapping pace over Woolbridge Common for Charlbury, where there was a slight check (for breakfast) ; then away again with a good scent to More Critchill ; and so by Tarrant Monkton to Pimperne—where, as you see, we have killed. A fast thing, fifteen miles in less than six hours !"

He parodied all this in French, to D'Isigny's great amusement.

"Thou Anglo-maniac, thou Orléanist, whence hast thou gotten this insular '*Argot*' so soon?"

"So soon !" said Father Martin. "Did you not tell me once that you had sat up all the night before and learnt Spanish? I am not such a quick learner as that, yet I know all about fox-hunting, and have, what is more, brushed up my Aristotle and my Plato ; learnt a great deal about the system of education at Oxford ; of the antiquities of the neighbourhood ; of the state of politics in *France*—mind that—and all in one afternoon and evening. Knowledge—or, at the very lowest, *news*—is better diffused here than in France. At St. Malo, when I sailed, no one discussed much about the separation of the orders in the

---

\* " For he hath not despised nor abhorred the affliction of the afflicted ; neither hath he hid his face from him ; but when he cried unto him, he heard."—Psalm xxii. 24.

States-General. My friend of last night pointed shrewdly out to me that the whole thing hinged on it."

" But who was your friend ? "

" Hear my adventure. Having read the travels of Moritz\* in this benighted land, I became aware that a pedestrian is an object of suspicion and distrust. Captain Somers tried to dissuade me from my plan of walking here: not only, he said, because I was a pedestrian, but because I was a priest; and reminded me that only nine years ago London was sacked, and priests were hunted when there was an attempt to remove our disabilities. But I said to him plainly, as we walked the quarterdeck together as we came through the Needles—(have you seen these Needles ? No ! You should.)—I said to him, ' Dear Somers, the French Church is going to reap what she has sown. I will get in train for it. I will learn to face scorn ; therefore, I will walk. But martyrdom as yet ! No ! Therefore, with the map you have given me, I will go across the country, and will stay only at the houses of the Protestant priests.'

" He turned on me suddenly and sharply, and he said : ' My dearest Padre, of all things I wouldn't do that.'

" I said : ' Why not ? '

" He said in answer : ' Because you had better do anything else.'

" I asked again : ' Why ? ' And he answered again, English-like, by repetition : ' Because, my dear Padre, you will find it a mistake.'

" Well, I was right, and he was wrong. He kept possession of my portmanteau, to be sent to his brother, Sir Lionel ; and his sailors landed me at a place they call Key Haven. Have you seen those English sailors ? No ! You should. They are kings among men, gently ferocious and ferociously gentle. The tide was low, and there were deep holes among the mud banks. I thought I should have to wade to shore ; but they fell to

---

\* Moritz travelled in England in 1782, chiefly on foot. His book will be found very interesting to such readers as care for little scenes and incidents in the country inns and farm-houses of the England of our immediate fathers, seen by foreign eyes, from the pen of an intelligent though poor German parson. Gonzalez, also, the Portuguese Arthur Young (commercial, however, not agricultural), is also interesting. He travelled in 1730.

quarrelling which was to carry me, until their noise was stilled by the voice of a little boy-officer in a gold-laced hat, who steered the boat. Then the biggest giant carried me on shore across the mud; after which he refused my money, declined my benediction, and would not even let me kiss him; at the same time, in very coarse language, giving me to understand that I was as fine a man as he had ever met; which is hardly likely. This sailor—captain of the foretop was his rank, as he informed me—volunteered to put me on my road, as he claimed to belong to those parts. I wish that he had not done so, for, meeting a custom-house officer in the road, he suddenly studied the weather in an abstracted manner, walked accidentally against that custom-house officer, knocked him down, fell heavily on the top of him, and then used opprobrious epithets to the officer because he declined to box, but proposed an appeal to the law. I, as a man of peace, tried to make peace between them; but, speaking bad English, was unsuccessful. From my limited knowledge of English, I gathered that my tall sailor-friend was possessed with a burning desire to knock off all the heads of all the *douaniers* in the British islands; and also that the custom-house officer was prepared to 'pull' any sailor who attempted to do so. The threat of the custom-house officer evidently refers to the penalties for high treason. He meant, doubtless, that he would 'pull him on a hurdle to the gallows.'

"Finding that my sailor-friend was but a dangerous companion, I was glad to leave him, in spite of his kindness; and to start across country towards you. Somers was wrong about my reception among the English clergy; and I was right. With the map he had given me, and walking fast, chanting my offices as I walked, I made Ringford Magna that night. The peasantry objected to me strongly. They would have objected to anything else they did not understand, just as strongly. They hooted me, they set their dogs at me; but I understand dogs. In one little village where they set many dogs at me, I sat down upon the stocks and called the dogs to me one by one. The dogs all came one after another, but the villagers stood in a circle, and would have none of me at all. The *jockei* of the seigneur of those parts, a young man of great personal beauty and large stature, came with his hat in his hand to me as I sat on the stocks, and begged me to notice that none of his lord's dogs had joined in the attack on me, advising me respectfully to come to the seigneur's house, where I should be well received. 'Our people, sir,' he said, 'are not used to the sight of a priest.' That must have been a good young man, you know.

"Well, I determined to adhere to my determination of using the Protestant priests just as the Protestant priests would use us. So when I got to Ringford Magna, I asked the way to the Rector's house, who was also Rural Dean; and they told me the way, and laughed at me the while. I went through his park, through his flower garden, up to his front door. I rang the bell, and there came out a footman in velvet breeches and a butler in black; and there stood I—a poor dusty little secular Catholic priest, in full array. And I said, 'Somers is right. He knows his people. I had better have gone and called on Cardinal Leroy, Cardinal de Rohan, or the Archbishop of Sens, than done this.'

"'Was the Rural Dean at home?' I asked.

"No; but the Rural Deaconess was. Mrs. Tomkins was at home.

"My dear D'Isigny, I had never realised a married priest before. As there is nobody listening, I am not at all sure that I object to it so strongly as I am bound to do. I was utterly abroad for a moment, but soon recovered myself. 'I would do myself the honour to see Madame, if she would allow me.'

"Madame would do me that honour. She took me in: she put at my disposal everything which the house contained. Her mother followed suit. There was nothing which they would not do for me. When the Rural Dean came home, he seized on me as a great prize. We talked politics until dinner, divinity till coffee, classics until the ladies went to bed, and then—a neighbouring lord coming in—sporting, principally fox-hunting, until three in the morning. I saw that my host and his friend, the lord, wanted to talk about hounds; and yet, being gentlemen, did not like to do so, lest they should be uninteresting to me. So, hating the very name of all kinds of field-sports, I professed an ignorant interest about this wonderful fox-hunting, and gave them their will. I deserved anything for my shameless hypocrisy, but the devil was permitted to pay me in *his* coin, for I was very much interested at first, but rose with a bad headache and an ill temper this morning. Ha! this is your valley! How beautiful and peaceful! And I am actually to rest here a little! Not for long."

## CHAPTER XV.

### FATHER MARTIN'S ADVICE.

ATHILDE went quickly up into Adèle's room, and said, "Here is news, then, good news."

And Adèle said, "What news? Has my father determined to send me into a nunnery? I wish he would. He has puzzled Lionel, and made him distrustful by his treatment of me. I wish he would let me go into a nunnery, and have done with it all."

"Adèle, hear," said Mathilde. "One has come who will set it all right. Father Martin has come."

"I am sure I do not know what he wants here, prying and peering, and asking questions. I would much sooner that he was anywhere else," Adèle replied, petulantly. Still, she was glad. He was, at all events, a pleasing distraction for her father; and she had had too much of her father's attentions lately. Only from that point of view his arrival was an advantage; and, moreover, his was a fresh face, which was something; and a Frenchman, which was something more; and a very agreeable man, which was something more still. And so, after having dismissed Mathilde in a state of deep disappointment at not having pleased her, she gradually worked herself up until she persuaded herself that Father Martin's arrival was a great godsend, and that he was a very charming and delightful old man. Knowing, also, that he had more influence with her father than any one else, she argued, entirely from instinct, that his arrival was somewhat the same as a cessation of hostilities, or, at least, of a truce. That there must be a battle-royal with her father some day, she very little doubted; but she felt that, in consequence of Father Martin's arrival, the day was postponed for the present.

M. D'Isigny had found an early moment to consult Father Martin about this matter between De Valognes and Adèle. He showed him the dreadful letter, and awaited his advice.

"Serious, my dear friend," said Father Martin. "It is undoubtedly serious. I knew most of this just before I sailed."

"I always thought that De Valognes was in love with Mathilde," said M. D'Isigny.

"So did others," said Father Martin. "I knew how matters stood even before André Desilles told me."

"André Desilles!" said M. D'Isigny. "How did that very self-contained young gentleman ever lower his intellect so far as to take cognizance of a love affair?"

"I do not think that you understand André Desilles, my friend," said Father Martin.

"Possibly not," said M. D'Isigny. "I am not sure that I should ever take the trouble. An old martinet is sufficiently intolerable, but a young one more so. How came he to take an interest in this business?"

"Louis De Valognes is his most intimate friend."

"True; he *has* a friend. I had forgotten. Well; and so Tiberius Gracchus Desilles put a spoke in the wheel of his bosom friend on this matter, and betrayed him to you."

"You will know him better one day," said Father Martin.

"I doubt it, if my wishes are consulted," said M. D'Isigny, coldly. "That young gentleman does not seem to have behaved well in this matter."

Father Martin longed to tell the whole truth. That André Desilles loved Mathilde, while Mathilde loved De Valognes. He kept that part of the matter to himself: he did not quite see how to act about it.

"He seems to have offended you in something else also," said Father Martin.

"*N'importe.*"

"You ask my advice, and I strongly advise you to do one thing."

"And that is——" said M. D'Isigny.

"To do nothing at all. Let it go. It will be pretty sure to right itself. Have you been unkind to the girl over this matter?"

"I have been giving her a certain form of discipline."

"Leave it off. You will drive her to something rash and underhand. Your hand is too heavy for that kind of thing. And reflect again. This letter of Louis De Valognes is only one in answer to a letter of hers, in which she cast him off—I think regretfully, but certainly cast him off. Dear me, she may be exceedingly fond of this Sir Lionel Somers, for aught we know. It will all go right, if you will only be kind to the girl, and if Louis De Valognes will keep away. *She* will forget him soon enough, if she could write the letter to him she evidently has written."

"Louis De Valognes wrote to me proposing a visit," said D'Isigny.

"He spoke of the same thing to me. I dissuaded him."

"Is there any fear of his coming?"

"Fear? yes. Chance, no. At least, I do not think he will come. He was a little rebellious about it. *Laissez aller!* See! here is Adèle herself. What a wonderfully beautiful little woman!"

## CHAPTER XVI.

### THE FRENCH REVOLUTION IN THE STOUR VALLEY.

A WIND-BEATEN, solitary grange, like Sheepsden, perched up high in a hollow of the bare chalk down, facing the wild south-west, is pretty sure to be dull at all seasons of the year. Sheepsden certainly was—nay, it was more than dull—it was profoundly melancholy.

Even in summer, when the valley below was still, peaceful, and calm, some wandering wind always found its way into the hollow where this old house stood, and in some way raised mournful music; either sighing through the dry grass of the wold; or whispering to the scattered junipers; or raising fitfully a lonely sound like distant falling water among the elms which surrounded the house. The furious south-west from Brittany, from the wild quicksands of Mont St. Michel, from the tossing woods of Dinan, from the desolate Druid rocks of Morbihan, was the most refreshing wind they got; and that howled and piped and raved among their caves and chimneys, as if each cairn and menhir had yielded up the spirits of the dead priests, and they were riding on the blast, full shriek with their immeasurable woes.

The east wind—the worst of English winds—should, from the

position of the house, have passed silently over it.  Yet some former proprietor of Sheepsden, some ancestor of the dreadful Lady of Dinan, would not have it go by, at least unheard, and had planted Scotch firs on the summit of the down to catch it and make it musical; so when the rest of the valley was almost unaware of the sad, steady, blighting wind of spring, the inhabitants of the Grange were kept fully in mind of it by wild tossing, wailing boughs close overhead.  Summer or winter still, the winds of heaven made Sheepsden one of the most mournful houses in the world.

The internal economy of the house was not likely to make it very lively either, as my readers have doubtless perceived.  The charmed circle of comfort was bounded by the light of the great fire upon the screen which shut them in.  They were comfortable enough inside that space, and the wandering winds which rumbled about among the rafters overhead only made them feel more so; but even after prayers Adèle would sit and yawn herself blind sooner than she would go in the darkness up to bed without Mathilde (or as a *pis-aller* Mrs. Bone).  William and Mrs. Bone a hundred times over confided to one another that the house was very "unked"* indeed.  Mathilde, who *said* nothing, considered on the whole that it was preferable to her mother's at Dinan, and she could not well have said less.  As for M. D'Isigny, it suited him and his temper to perfection.

Father Martin went over the whole establishment in perfect silence, with his clever, handsome Celt-Norse head on one side, and at the end he said,—

"You keep your women in too tightly, D'Isigny.  Believe an experienced man, it does not do."

"You ought to know, as a priest," replied D'Isigny.  "The women are your stock in trade."

"They *are* my stock in trade, and I *do* know," said Father Martin; "and I tell you that they will not stand this kind of thing a moment longer than they can help it.  You have been using your power to the utmost, and have very little capital in hand.  You have brought your women to the edge of rebellion."

"Women like being bullied," said M. D'Isigny.

"*Do* they?" said Father Martin.  "I was not aware of the

---

\* "Unked;" probably only "unkind," after all.  A very common word in Hants, Berks, and Dorset.

fact myself. *We* never do it, except in extreme cases, even with *our* claims to their obedience. You have gone too far with these women. You can keep them in hand here, in this desolate, isolated old house ; but they would be too much for you in the world. If you want to have any influence over them at all, you must show more tenderness. You speak vaguely of using Adèle's beauty and Mathilde's shrewdness in politics ; we will speak at large of that afterwards ; but I tell you plainly that you will lose your hold of them by this extreme severity. Why, one of *our* people could not do it ; and what hold have *you* over a religious woman like Mathilde compared to mine ? I could take her from you to-morrow. She has spiritual necessities which you are unable to supply, and she would follow me away from you at any time. You must not grind these women as you do."

"I am an old witness of the way in which priests abuse superstitious women for their own ends," said D'Isigny ; "and I respectfully bow to the great influence of human folly. I cannot fight it single-handed. Have your way with me and with the women. I shall require both priests and women for my work, and so I will keep terms with you. Have your way."

"What *is* your work ?" asked Father Martin.

"To check the Revolution," said M. D'Isigny, quietly—"to keep it in hand, and prevent it going too far. You cannot understand. Well, then, to prevent them, as one item, from hanging all you priests up in a row. You can understand that."

"Quite," said Father Martin ; "but we shall be hung in a row notwithstanding. Hah ! so you are going to keep the Revolution in hand, are you ? You have the best intentions."

This conversation between Martin and D'Isigny had the effect of making the old home much more agreeable to Mathilde and Adèle. Uncertain in politics as he was, M D'Isigny was a devoted religionist. La Fayette's rose-water republicanism he loved ; but La Fayette's expedition to America was in his eyes disgraceful piracy. He was bent on making the new monarchical republicanism fit with the old monarchical division of Europe, and also with *Roman* Catholicism—a hopeless task, which none but a Feuillan pedant would have undertaken. We have only to do with this, however—that he gave up the spiritual management of his house to Father Martin, *ex officio*, and that the house was much better managed by the clever and amiable priest than by the crotchety doctrinaire.

No allusion was ever made to Adèle by her father to the dreadful De Valognes' letter. What was in it, and what became of it, she could not find out, and of course did not dare to ask. Sir Lionel continued his visits as usual ; M. D'Isigny was quiet, kind, and agreeable, and all went smoothly : all angles were rounded off by the influence of this one man.

The house placed up so high above the distant town, above the noises of the valley, which only came faint and indistinct on the ear, was solitary still, but no longer melancholy. Father Martin explained ostentatiously that his mind required relaxation and amusement ; that after the cheerfulness of St. Malo, and the excitement of the Rennes riots, the sadness of their house was disagreeable to him. He demanded to be taken out on expeditions in the neighbourhood ; he wished to make the acquaintance of a few of the neighbours ; he liked sometimes a game of cards, and sometimes asked for some reading aloud in the evening : making it appear that it was all done for him.

The Rector, a gentlemanly, well-read man, called on him at once, and they became great friends. They organised parties to visit the local antiquities together ; the Rector and Sir Lionel generally casting up at the rendezvous on horseback, but the French party invariably walking. M. D'Isigny himself unbent at these gatherings, though like an Englishman he took his pleasure sadly.

Then every one was made busy for some time in making a chapel out of a room which had evidently been used for the purpose before. It was astonishing to see what good taste and good will did in a very short time. A very handsome little chapel was shaped out, and one by one the various ornaments were got together, Sir Lionel assisting nobly. Indeed, they could hardly have done without him, for he fetched and carried like a dog for them, sturdy Protestant as he was. In fact it was he, and no other, who drove over to Lulworth when everything was finished, borrowed and brought home in his curricle the very vestments in which Father Martin first said Mass, before the new ones ordered from France, and presented by him, had arrived. From Stourminster Newton to Christ Church the whole valley groaned at this awful backsliding. Every one believed that Sir Lionel (with his 19,000 acres) was already in the bosom of Rome. As he flippantly remarked to a venerable nobleman who remonstrated with him : " It is lucky that the election is just over. They will have forgotten all about it by the next one, or I will do something else to put it out of their heads."

When entering that house, Father Martin had, after the beautiful old custom, paused at the doorway and said, " Peace be to this house." He verily had fulfilled his own benediction, and brought peace.

Not, however, by quietly letting every one have his or her own way, but by a quiet though courageous activity. Probably that slightly-built man had as much determination as all the rest of the family put together, though he was utterly without obstinacy. Convince his reason, and he would yield instantly; leave that unconvinced, and you could do nothing with him at all. This man had determined that there should be peace in the house, and, lo ! there was peace.

He had the most violent objection to arguing on religious subjects. The Rector would have very much liked a quiet and gentlemanly passage of arms, foils carefully blunted, with him; and, indeed, brushed himself up for the battle, but Father Martin declined.

" We are not likely to convert one another," he said, " so why should we argue ? We each believe the other wrong, yet can respect one another ; so why argue ? If you desire an intellectual contest with me, I am charmed to join battle with you, but it must be on another subject than religion. See what we have come to in France with all this arguing."

" You are a sensible man, Father Martin," said the good-humoured Rector. " But you are attracting a congregation up there at Sheepsden, you know. I doubt I shall have to borrow a sermon from my neighbour, the Hon. and Rev. Cosmo Knox, and preach it at you. I know of an elegant, spicy piece of his, which he preached the week before the Gordon riots. It is so calm, so logical, and so charitable, that it would quite finish your business, if you were rash enough to tempt me to use it against you. Be warned in time, for I shall certainly use it, if you continue to erect the abomination under my Protestant nose, and seduce my sheep."

"I have seduced no sheep of yours," said Father Martin, earnestly and eagerly; "not one. Believe me, ten thousand times, dear Rector, not one. Do you think that I, in the face of the horrible state of things in my beloved France, would be the man to set Christians quarrelling on dogmas? Do not, as a fellow-minister of the Gospel, believe such a thing of me."

"My dear sir," said the Rector, seriously, "I was only joking."

"I am glad of that. I am sure of it. See here, then, dear Rector. What is my congregation? At most, thirty. Who are they? Hidden Catholics of whom you did not know; and there are many such in all England. These few who come to Sheepsden are only a faithful few, who in past times, and at the great festivals, crept wearily across the down to Lulworth. There are no others. You have, I think, complained of Mademoiselle D'Isigny for leaving Catholic books of devotion with the sick whom she visited, but I have pointed out to her that, without direction, they are as bad as useless."

"Say no more, my dear sir," said the Rector. "I have collected Mademoiselle D'Isigny's books which she left with the sick and poor, and have them tied up with tape in my study, all except one, 'Thomas à Kempis,' a book which I use myself. Say no more."

"I would have wished, I would have prayed," said Father Martin, standing before him, with his hands stretched towards him, and his beautiful face flushed with emotion, "that England might become Catholic. I wish for it still, but now I only pray that she may keep with Christ. The religious future of England is in the hands of such men as you. I would strengthen those hands instead of weakening them. This is no time for arguing on details, when the basis of all religion is in danger. Your flock has nothing to fear from me."

"The religious future of England is in the hands of such men as you." A subject for contemplation. The day was mild and warm, with a S.W. wind blowing gently up the river, and raising a fine ripple. It struck the rector that this was a good day for contemplation, with the assistance of the "contemplative man's recreation." He accordingly stepped across home, and told Mrs. Rector confidentially that he was going to see what Sir Lionel's jack were like.

She mildly suggested that it was Saturday; and was his sermon ready?

"I shall preach an old sermon, my dear. My very best. They have not heard it for two years, and ought to hear it once a month. No. 67. Text, you remember, 'Paul planteth, and Apollos watereth, but God giveth the increase.'"

"I am glad of that," she said. "I will get it out, and put it ready. I like that sermon. Do you want one of the men with you?"

"Certainly not. I shall carry my own net. I wish to be alone."

"I am glad of that. I am going to have them all in the flower-garden. Are you going to dine at home?"

"Yes."

"I am glad of that, because I have eels, which you like. Do you think you shall catch any fish?"

"Certain. A splendid day."

"I am glad of that. I wish, if you fish as low as the village, that you would leave a fish with Eliza Rigden, who has just got a boy."

"Are you glad of *that?*" asked the Rector, taking his rod and net from one of his men.

"I don't know, I am sure. I think I am glad that she is well through with it, though she is deeply to blame. I wish you would leave her a fish."

"*Pour encourager les autres,*" growled the Rector, as he passed towards the river. "She would have got precious few fish from that little French priest. Here is the wife of my bosom urging me on to the encouragement of immorality, and pleading Christian pity for her conduct."

Those who care about the noble science of angling, who are adepts at it, and who like to pursue the solitary vice without interruption, would do well to take to heart the words which I am about to write down, and to act on them. Always go fishing on the very worst days. You then have the river to yourself, and can do as you please, which I take it is one of the great charms of fishing. In the May-fly season, when men are almost in rows on the bank, when one man catches a large trout close to the legs of another man's servant, who has been sent into the water to regain his master's flies, fish are not very precious. One good fish caught on a foul and sulking day is worth a dozen caught on such a day as this. The Rector was a fair-weather man, and always knew when the fish would run, as well as a poacher. This was an undoubtedly fine day for jack fishing, and so he went out, as did every one else.

Sir Lionel Somers preserved his part of the Stour in the most careful manner, but as he gave every one who asked him leave to fish, partly to keep up his interest in the borough, and partly from sheer good nature, it all came to the same thing in the end. The first person the Rector met, with his rod over his shoulder, was his own clerk, who simpered and bowed; the next was the horse-doctor, who was profoundly civil, but obviously raced him to get the first turn on the long shallow; and when they arrived there, the master chimney-sweep from Stourminster Newton was there before both of them, but half-washed, and more than half drunk, looking as if he had been acting Othello the night before, and had since tumbled into a horse-pond. Then there was a disreputable young blacksmith, with a live bait and a float, watching every other comer out of the corners of his evil young eyes. There was the father of the present Dick Martin, who was a great poacher, looking very innocent, but keeping a sharp look out lest any of the numerous fishers should get hold of any of his cleverly set night-lines. Nay, infancy itself was not unrepresented, for the village tailor had come and brought his numerous family, part of which were watching their father fish, while the rest were running about the meadow, stark naked, howling.

There was neither fishing, peace, nor contemplation to be got here. There were, however, three or four fine reaches of the river which ran through Sir Lionel's park, which were more carefully kept, and to which the Rector and a select few had the *entrée*. He pushed on down the meadows towards the park.

The Rector was a handsome man, about forty, but looking much younger; and was not clerically dressed. He was extremely cross at finding his favourite piece of water being fished to death by tag-rag and bob-tail; moreover he wished to be alone: and so, when he had hoisted himself over the sacred park-palings, and was wading deep in Sir Lionel's grass, he saw a young gentleman leaning over the side of the river, and calmly picking out a night-line with a jack at the end of it; he got fractious, and began to think about his friend's interests.

The young gentleman beckoned to him, and said in French,—

"Look here, then, fisher. You shall have fish in your pannier, and no one shall know anything at all. I have been sitting here on this log, and have watched the grass grow under the rain; and then I have looked upward for a sight of heaven, but always the sad grey clouds. And then I heard cloc! cloc! in the river, and I saw this string, and here is the fish."

A scandalous transaction. The sporting instincts which had flowed in the Rector's blood for centuries rebelled against it; he said, in French also,—

" Has Monsieur the *entrée* here?"

" The *entrée?* No. Why?"

" This is Sir Lionel Somers' park, and, although he is absurdly lenient with regard to trespass in other parts of his property, he draws a line with regard to his park."

The young gentleman arose. "Are *you* Sir Lionel Somers?" he asked, quietly. "Yes, I am sure you are, and I can understand all about it."

"I am not Sir Lionel Somers, sir," said the puzzled Rector. "I am but the priest of the parish. I hope I have given you no offence; but Sir Lionel is very particular, and it is impossible to see whether a man is a gentleman or not, if he chooses to lean over in the long grass, and pick up poachers' night-lines."

The Rector was not in the least degree a man likely to be troubled with any form of physical fear; but when De Valognes rose up from the wet grass and confronted him, he was strongly possessed with a moral fear. He was afraid that he had been rude to a gentleman, a Frenchman, and a stranger.

For he was by no means prepared for the extraordinary beauty and elegance of the young gentleman who stood before him. He wore the usual caped great coat, long riding boots, and a three-cornered hat; but it was such a beautiful little hat, so extremely neat and sober, and yet so very confident. And the boots were such beautifully cut boots, and the man himself was so splendidly set altogether, that the Rector saw he had made a great mistake; and, moreover, the perfection of his features and complexion, and the manly grace of his carriage fixed the Rector for a moment in dumb astonishment, and he could do nothing to put himself right.

Meanwhile De Valognes smiled pleasantly on the Rector, and said, "Trespassing has become such a habit in France in these later months, that you see it has even infected the most loyal of us. I ask Monsieur's pardon, and retire."

The Rector once more apologised, and they parted bowing and scraping, and kootooing against one another, as if for a large wager.

"Now who may *you* be, my fine sir?" soliloquised the Rector. "And why have you got on your best clothes on a week-day, and why have you got a rose in your button-hole, and why are your eyes so bright, and why does your breath come and go lightly between your parted lips? I doubt you are come a courting, my young sir. And, upon my word, with a pretty good chance of success, *I* should say."

A very little further on he met Sir Lionel fishing, the day was so good for fishing that even he had come out. M. D'Isigny was at his elbow. Now, Sir Lionel was a splendid fisherman, and M. D'Isigny knew nothing whatever about it, yet he was instructing Sir Lionel. Superadded to an exhaustive acquaintance with all the traditional lore of angling, Sir Lionel had a shrewd, observant brain, a quick hand, and a steady eye; yet M. D'Isigny proved him to be philosophically wrong in a dozen ways, and condescendingly showed him how the thing should be done. He had, at an odd time, made out a theory of fishing, in which every thing was considered except the will and habits of the fish; and he was somewhat contemptuously giving Sir Lionel the benefit of it now. The Rector said to himself: "Bother that Frenchman. I wanted to speak to Lionel alone."

It was a dim instinct more than anything else which made him begin comparing and contrasting Sir Lionel Somers with the young Frenchman, whom he had just seen. Sir Lionel was the taller of the two, and was in a different way quite as handsome; and there was a calm, deliberate majesty about the English Norman, which the French Norman, with all his grace and dignity of carriage, wanted. Even in dress the contrast between the Gallicised and the Anglicised Norman was apparent. Each had, of course, after the manner of his race, adapted himself to the land of his adoption. The Frenchman had gained clegance from the Celt, and had idealised that elegance until it was almost perfect. The Englishman had gained rude, homely, coarse strength: and had equally idealised that. Against the perfectly-made clothes of De Valognes, Sir Lionel showed the dress of an English gamekeeper, in expensive material, and of the most perfect fit. His shooting-coat and waistcoat were of velvet; his finely-shaped leg was clothed in grey breeches and leather gaiters; his feet were in well made lace-up boots; all fit to resist weather and brambles. His continual devotion to athletic sports had given him a carriage more rude and less refined than his French rival, yet quite as dignified, and almost equally graceful.

"I'll go to pillory if I know which is the finest fellow of the two," thought the Rector. "It would be a pity if two such fine fellows were to fall out on any subject."

Alas! good Rector, for five-and-twenty years—the first of which was near at hand—Sir Lionel and De Valognes were, by proxy, to be at one another's throats; and the Frenchman to this day—in spite of Aboukir, Trafalgar, the Peninsula, and Waterloo—declares that he never was in the least degree beaten; and least of all people by the Englishman. The stars in their courses fought against Sisera, that was all. Surely war is the most unsatisfactory amusement in the world.

M. D'Isigny began on the Rector:

"Your rules of fishing are a mere collection of ill-digested legends. They should be tabulated and sifted: those which are obviously puerile rejected, and the others subjected to the light of philosophy. Somers here has come out fishing because the wind was south-west. Can any man be foolish enough to believe that a fish which lives under the water, can care which way the wind blows?"

"Long tradition and long personal experience show us that they do," replied the Rector.

"You argue from an insufficient number of facts," said D'Isigny. "You have got the idea into your heads that the fish only bite in a south-west wind, and so you never come to fish but when the wind is in that quarter. The wind was east yesterday before the thunder-storm, yet neither of you fished. Believe me the fish would have bitten just as well."

At this obvious piece of nonsensical ignorance they both laughed.

"Long tradition and long personal experience," continued M. D'Isigny, "proved to us that the French peasantry would not rise against their villainous misgovernment, yet they have risen, and who shall lay them?"

After saying which he departed, and left them to their folly.

"There he goes with his half truth," said the Rector. "A man sharp and keen in action when once roused; but, I doubt, totally muddled in his convictions. If he knew what he wanted, he'd have it, though Satan was in the way; but he don't know what he does want. His school will play more mischief with the French monarchy than either Royalists or Democrats, before they have done. I say, what do you think of that French priest they have got up at Sheepsden?"

"A very noble man," said Sir Lionel.

"A suggestive little person," said the Rector. "He has set me thinking. A most pestilent and dangerous Papist, I fear."

"I should say so," said Sir Lionel, dryly.

"Will you spin across this pool, or shall I?" said the Rector. "Shall I? Good. What is the news from France?"

"Dead lock. The *tiers état* refuse to vote."

"They will make a mess of it," said the Rector.

"For France," said Sir Lionel. "You have got a fish, and a fine one, Rector. Keep the point of your rod up, or he will be down into the weeds. Lost, by Jove! You should keep your fish better in hand."

"He was too strong for me."

"So I saw; a Mirabeau of a fish. You have not fallen out with that priest, have you?"

"Not I," said the Rector; "I am scandalously fond of him. Tell me, Lionel, is it true that you fetched vestments over from Lulworth to enable him to commit the abomination of desolation?"

"It is perfectly true."

"We shall get into the most awful trouble about him," said the Rector, almost petulantly.

"Very like," said Sir Lionel. "I don't see why *you* should, however."

But the Rector did. However, instead of preaching the sermon which he had told his wife to set out, he sat up all night and wrote another, the text of which was, "Other sheep I have, not of this fold;" and in it he made such scandalous allusions as to the possible salvation of Papists, that the parish churchwarden waited on him, *proprio motu*, immediately after church, and remonstrated. Now the valley was not contented with believing that Sir Lionel had gone over to Rome to please his Papist bride elect; but also insisted on believing, in face of all facts, that the Rector of Stourminster Osborne had gone too—nay, had been there for years; nay, had never been anywhere else. No protestations, either from themselves or their friends, availed them anything. They were always at Sheepsden, where there was mass performed: of course they attended it. They were marked men.

The Rector had a hard time of it, for the Gordon Riots, it must be remembered, were but nine years past. A considerable number of his congregation seceded under a pretence of dissent, though many of them were never seen in the dissenting chapels. His church-rate was violently opposed and scarcely carried. The parish churchwarden insulted him in the vestry, and Sir Lionel, *his* churchwarden, unhappily mislaid his temper in that same vestry, and rated the parish churchwarden soundly. The numerous dissenters in the valley preached against him and denounced him; all except the quiet, good old Wesleyan minister at Stourminster Newton, who stoutly stood out for him as a gentleman, a Christian, and a scholar; the result of which was that his chapel was emptied, and his life shortened by worry.

And after the general election in the next year, Sir Lionel remarked to the Rector:—

"Do you know that a Papist priest in this valley is a most expensive luxury? I had that borough of Stourminster Osborne under my feet, until I persuaded D'Isigny to send for poor Father Martin. Such is the sound Protestant feeling of our English electors, that I have had to pay away 1,446*l.* in sheer hard bribery to regain my rightful influence. This, mind you, is in addition to the old regulars; the amount of which you know as well as I. Why, man, I had that borough in the hollow of my hand before I sent for that little priest."

"And drove over for the vestments to Lulworth," suggested the Rector.

"Exactly," said Sir Lionel. "Who could have thought that

such a very quiet little man would have made such a noise in the valley?"

These were the old times, we must remember; the Gordon Riots but nine years old, when Protestant feeling ran high. And bribery at elections was carried on to a fearful extent at the end of last century. We live in happier times.

## CHAPTER XVII.

### THE FIRST SACRIFICE.

OWN in the valley the meadows were deep in grass, across which the tall and thickly-crowded hedgerow elms, now in full leaf, threw dark shadows, which grew ever darker as day waned. The air was faint and rich with the scent of woodbine and meadowsweet, and the gentle air merely moved the flower-spangled grass for one moment, whispered to the leaves, and died into stillness.

The long glorious day succeeding the last of which we have spoken, had blazed itself almost into twilight, and the valley was getting more peaceful every minute, when Adèle, quite alone, crossed a cornfield, and passed into a long, dark, and beautiful lane, which led towards an unfrequented ford in the river.

She glided along in her silent, bird-like way, but looked round stealthily many times. She, as her sister Mathilde had remarked to herself when she saw her furtive start, was after no good whatever.

"She will get into the most fearful trouble," thought poor Mathilde. "She has had a letter in a French hand by the English post. I got close enough to it to see that. It is my firm belief and persuasion that André Desilles has come over, and that she is going to give him an interview. Adèle is really, of all people I ever saw, the least capable of guiding herself. There is an utter want of discretion, an extreme reckless *abandon* about her conduct, which is actually terrible. We shall be well out of this without a fatal duel."

She followed her instantly.

"I can at all events screen her somewhat by walking home

with her. I doubt I shall have to lie a deal over it. It is shameful of André to behave so. Yet it is so singularly unlike him. Poor dear André and I never were friends—at least, I never got on so well with him as I might have—but he was always the most discreet and honourable of mortals. It seems to me an inconceivable thing that he has left his regiment and come here after Adèle, after knowing of her engagement with Sir Lionel Somers. Besides, it never seemed to me that he cared anything for her. I should have thought that he liked me by far the best. Yet, according to Mrs. Bone, he has been in constant communication with her. I cannot make the matter out completely; only it is evident that Adèle is bent on making a fool of herself, and ruining herself, and must be saved."

So she followed the unconscious Adèle two fields off. She was quite sure that her walk would end in a painful scene; that there was trouble before her that evening, the greatest part of which was sure to fall, somehow or another, on her unlucky head. Yet she was one of those who, as far as they are personally concerned, live in the present mainly. She had a happy habit of making the most of the present, and of leaving the future and the past. Many exceedingly sensitive and conscientious natures have exactly the same habit. Consequently, with illimitable and unknown trouble before her, she improved the present, and, poor soul! to a certain extent, enjoyed herself.

For the early English summer glories had voices, sounds, and scents for her, as much as, nay more than, for the lighter, thinner nature of Adèle. Mathilde could love with a deeper love than Adèle, and she loved De Valognes as Adèle was incapable of loving him. There was not a whisper of the summer wind across the flowered grass, not a scent of rose or woodbine, not a rustle of air among the trees, but what spoke of him, and of her love for him. Her whole great soul was filled with a tender love for him; and as she walked under the gathering shadows and thought of him, and of the honour he had done her among all women, her noble face developed a radiant and glorious beauty, to which that of Adèle was small and commonplace. Sir Joshua Reynolds was right. She was a wonderfully beautiful woman.

Voices in the lane which led to the ford. She hesitated what to do.

"I had better listen," she thought. "I need not tell. I *will* listen, and I will scold them afterwards. I will break suddenly in on them, and denounce them. I can look through the hedge here and see them. I consider myself justified in so doing."

She looked through the hedge, and then sat quietly down among the wild parsley, and the arums, and the budding clematis, and the fading primroses and violets, and put her hand to her head.

They tell one the story of Ginevra, lost to human ken on her marriage-day. They tell us in our own times of a beautiful bride, lightning-stricken and dead under a sheltering crag. Dead these two, leaving sorrow to the living. Mathilde lived on.

She had seen Adèle in the arms of De Valognes; she had heard them interchanging that foolish lovers' babble—indescribable, not to be translated—of which all of us have had, or shall have, experience. She saw in an instant that she had been shamefully deceived, and she sat down, in the lush growth of the English hedgerow, with her hand upon her forehead.

If it had come to her by degrees; if she had been able to get a suspicion of the state of affairs, it would have been easier for her to bear it. But in the full flush of her gentle, honest love for him, she had found him false, and herself a dreaming fool. Coarse hinds have a horrible habit of knocking down their wives and kicking them on the head. In all England or in all Ireland no woman was worse served that day than was Mathilde by the gentle and thoroughly noble De Valognes.

The two lovers walked away towards the ford; but Mathilde sat still behind the hedge with her hand on her forehead. "It is so hard to die like this, ma'mselle," said William the Silent to her once. "Bless you, I have died before this," she replied; "it is nothing when you are accustomed to it. The details may be made more or less agonizing, but it is only a matter of time, and the result is the same."

Mathilde had died one of her deaths, and when she arose from her seat in the hedgerow she felt giddy and ill. Her *self* had hitherto been her self in relation to De Valognes, and that self was dead; so her own self, being now worthless, dead, and a thing of nought, she began to think more particularly about others.

What would be the first effect of Adèle's indiscretion? To Mathilde, with her ideas of propriety, the indiscretion was something absolutely monstrous and unheard-of; it was immeasurable. She had deceived her—that was nothing; but she had deceived her father, and had most shamefully deceived Sir Lionel Somers. What on earth was to be done? Discovery was almost certain, and then——

She determined most positively at once that she would lend herself no longer to the systematic deceit which was being practised on Sir Lionel. "I never heard anything so monstrous in my life," she said; "Adèle's conduct transcends human belief. I will not lend myself to this deceit any longer; it must end. Yet I must save her somehow."

Adèle rarely or never walked out by herself. Others beside Mathilde must have seen the way she went, and it was growing from twilight to dark. She would be missed and followed. Suppose her father should follow her. Which came first—the idea in her brain, or the sight of M. D'Isigny approaching in a leisurely manner three fields off? They came so quick one on the other, that she never could decide. Others besides herself had watched Adèle, and had given M. D'Isigny the route. He was not far off now, straight on the track.

Suppose she were to lie perfectly still now. Would it not serve them right? How would it end? De Valognes would be reprimanded furiously, and would most likely rebel, and Adèle would be sent to a nunnery. She could well revenge herself on them now by merely remaining quiet; but she had no spirit. She wanted spirit sadly in one way; and there were her father's broad shoulders advancing steadily and inexorably through the standing corn.

So she went through a gap in the hedge and confronted them. They were not in the least degree surprised or taken aback. No one cared for old Mathilde: she was nobody. De Valognes held out both his hands towards her, and when she was near enough took her in his arms and kissed her. She submitted quite quietly. Was he not her cousin?

"You must fly, Louis," she said, quietly and earnestly. "My father is at the end of that field, and is coming straight towards us."

"Now we are all undone together;" cried Adèle, pulling her

beautiful hair in sheer desperation. "Now, I *do* wish I was dead. Now, I wish I had never been born. Now, I wish that I was with my mother at Dinan. Now we are all undone together. My father will kill Louis, and I shall be sent to a nunnery and be *ennuyée* to death ; and it is all thy fault, thou false and cruel sister. Thou hast followed me, and by doing so hast given our father the route."

Mathilde took no notice of her. She turned to Louis De Valognes. "Time is very short," she said ; "my father approaches. You must fly and hide. What do your eyes say, then—that you scorn it? You can add nothing to your deep dishonour, not if you were to hide under the manger in a stable. Your honour is gone, yet I believe that you love *her*. Think of the consequences to her if you remain here one instant longer."

Louis de Valognes went at once. He was taken by surprise at her appearance, at her words, and at the voice of his own conscience. Three minutes afterwards M. D'Isigny entered the lane, and approaching the ford, saw his two daughters.

Adèle was sitting on the bank, weaving a garland of clematis round her hat. Mathilde had got off her shoes and stockings, and was washing her feet in the river. His steady persistent bullying had made them as false as this.

M. D'Isigny found it necessary to account for his situation. He had no right to follow and watch his daughters, and he felt it now. His daughters, I regret to say, did not help him out of his difficulty. Adèle invoked the archangel St. Michael, in her surprise, quite vaguely, as the first saint, and, of course, the most entirely unappropriate one, who happened to come into her giddy head. Mathilde, with a vague impression of being near a ford, somewhat more logically invoked St. Christopher, and began putting on her stockings. Between them both M. D'Isigny was thoroughly puzzled.

And he deceived them on his part. He affected a pleasant surprise at meeting them, and asked for their company home, which was most willingly accorded. So those three walked home together through the gloaming, each of them feeling very guilty towards the other, and all extremely afraid of one another. Under these circumstances, I need hardly say, that they were most ostentatiously agreeable and affectionate. Adèle was in a state of fairy-like, airy gaiety, and innocence; Mathilde with her aching heart, walked beside her father, and talked with her usual calm sensible logic about the new-born revolution, about politics generally, about religion. As for M. D'Isigny, he surpassed himself. He was dignified and conciliatory; he was mildly dictatorial, yet tolerant. He opened up the store-house of his mind, and displayed its treasures to Mathilde. There was not much to see there, but he showed it off well. He discoursed beautifully about the beauties of nature, which were spread about their path in every direction; pointing them out with his walking-stick. He pointed out to Mathilde that nature was now in her creative mood, but in a few months more would pass into her destructive mood; from which he deduced the beautiful moral, that life was short, and that you should cull the blossoms while they grew; with a great deal more nonsense, equally original and important. Mathilde pretended to listen to this balderdash with rapt attention, while Adèle danced on before them, and strewed their path with wild flowers, plucked in the innocent gaiety of her heart. It would have been uncommonly nice if either of the three had believed in it.

As it was, three self-convicted and self-conscious humbugs arrived at the door of Sheepsden together, and parted. Adèle to her bower, with a worn, old, ay, cruel and vindictive look in her beautiful face; wondering what Mathilde would do, or what she would say. M. D'Isigny to his reading-lamp, to ponder over what could possibly have taken his daughters to the ford, and what trick they were serving him; Mathilde to Father Martin's room, to lay the whole truth before him, in sheer desperation.

She entered abruptly and stood before him, and he said to himself: "You are wonderfully handsome. All the men are fools, with the exception of André Desilles. *Can* he be right about De Valognes!" And then he added aloud, "What is the matter, Mathilde?"

"De Valognes has come; and we are all undone together," said Mathilde. "That is what is the matter."

"Will you explain further?" said Father Martin, quietly.

"What will one gain by explanations?" replied Mathilde. "Louis de Valognes has come, and has come for Adèle, which surprised me, for one moment. And Adèle has committed herself. And there will be bloodshed. She has scandalously deceived Sir Lionel Somers."

"And Louis has deceived you," said Father Martin.

"No, not particularly. I am silly and vain, and he is very agreeable. I do not speak of that. But we are in sad trouble. Adèle's indiscretion is immeasurable."

"Are you angry with Louis de Valognes?"

"No. Who am I that I should be angry? I thought that affairs were different; but who am I that I should think? He was kinder to me than any one else ever was, and encouraged by his kindness a certain kind of folly; but that is all dead and buried. Help Adèle out of the consequences of this awful indiscretion, that is all I ask. Do not mind me."

"I will see her through it somehow," said Father Martin. "Is that all you have to say?"

Mathilde was turning to the door, but when he said this, she turned again and spoke.

"That is not all I have to say. I loved and still love that man with all my soul. He made me believe that he loved me. I love still the ground he walks on; but that is no matter. If I ever had a share in him, I give it to Adèle; for who am I? Regard this, and remember it. I loved him beyond all men, and he has deceived me. Yet my love has not turned to hate, for I love him still. Stay, silent; and hear me, father. I have always loved Adèle, as you know. She has deceived me and supplanted me; yet I love her better than ever, because I now see that she is capable of loving that man. I love her the more strongly because I see that she is capable of loving Louis to the extent of indiscretion, to the extent of ruin. Do you understand?"

"I think I do," said Father Martin, seriously.

"You will then," said Mathilde, "be pleased to use your influence in order to protect her from the consequences of her madness."

"I am not sure," began Father Martin.

"But *I* am," said Mathilde. "*I* am the person to be considered. You have little or nothing to do with the matter, save to do the usual priest's duty of making matters fit. Do that."

"You are in rather a heathenish frame of mind to-night, Mathilde," said Father Martin.

"Possibly," said Mathilde. "I have been lying all the evening, and I am sick of lying. You can set these matters straight for us. Do it."

And with a humorous smile in his face he did it. When he appeared before D'Isigny the next morning, D'Isigny thought that Father Martin was going to tell some good story about the Rector, or the dissenting minister. It was not at all a humourous story which Father Martin told M. D'Isigny, for he told him the whole truth. And when he had finished, M. D'Isigny sat before him quite quiet and calm, but white with indignation and fury.

## CHAPTER XVIII.

### ASHURST AND SHEEPSDEN.

HE general opinion throughout Stour Valley had been that Sir Lionel Somers had "married his mother." That is to say, they all thought that old Lady Somers would be sole mistress of Ashurst until she folded up her gold spectacles for the last time, and got into her coffin, with much the same air of dignified and graceful humility with which she was accustomed to get into her coach.

"I hate men marrying their mothers," said our friend the Rector once on old times. "It never does. There is certain to be a left-handed family to begin with, which produces all kinds of complications. After his mother's death, the man is certain to marry a *lady* later on in life, when he has gone beyond falling in love; and she is certain to marry him with her eyes blindfolded by her mother, and to hear all about the previous business through her maid. Then the man, if he be a man and not an animal, is certain to have a sneaking *tendresse* for his left-handed children, and very likely—though I as a clergyman ought not to acknowledge such a thing—some remains of a *tendresse* towards the woman he has ruined; and that is the very mischief, sir. Consequently, I am extremely glad that Lionel has engaged himself to this little French creature now, while her character is so pure and unspotted. Believe me, sir, a man had better marry his mother's dairy-maid than his mother."

Sir Lionel had come home to his mother one day and calmly told her what he had done. She had said,—

"I would sooner it had been an English woman, and I had much sooner that it had been Mathilde than Adèle; but this is no earthly business of mine. I have never recommended you a wife, because I believe that a man who would choose his wife on his mother's recommendation is entirely unworthy of a wife, at least, a wife worth having. My dear Lionel, I am profoundly pleased. I cannot tell you how profoundly pleased I am at your choice."

"I was afraid you would be angry, mother," said Sir Lionel. "You said once that you thought her silly and vain."

"I am a very silly old woman, my Lionel," said Lady Somers, "and say many things which I do not mean. Forget what I said then, and hear what I say now. She is the most beautiful person I have ever seen (except her sister Mathilde). She is clever; she is good-humoured; she is good-natured; she is amiable. What would you have more? She is, again, splendidly born. Of her mother, my old schoolfellow and neighbour, I wish to say little. Mary Price and I did not suit one another. It was probably my fault. Yet Mary Price, now the terrible Madame D'Isigny of Dinan, had remarkable elements. Most wonderful elements. In her style of objurgation for instance, she as a mere girl showed the highest genius. I conclude all by saying that we did not suit one another. About your choice, again, what is there against her? She is French; my dear boy, we cannot all be English. She is a Roman Catholic; my dear boy, we cannot all be Protestants. Your eyes are open concerning the confessional, and you can keep your domestic priest in order. I really think you have not done at all badly on the whole. Nay, I think you have done very well indeed."

It was one of the most serious parts of the practical creed of such old ladies as Lady Somers, never to say a single thing to wife with regard to husband, or to husband with regard to wife, which should make the one in the least degree vilipend the other. She despised and disliked Adèle, but this was all she *said*.

As to what she *did*. She received Adèle with open arms. She petted and caressed her beyond measure. She praised her beauty gently and kindly to her face. Adèle never appeared at Ashurst without some delicate little refreshment being brought in for her—nay, more, Adèle never went to Ashurst without the old lady going away and rummaging out of her very precious old stores some exceedingly handsome present for her beloved Lionel's young French bride elect.

Presents of very great beauty indeed ; all kinds of things. A pair of old Dresden shepherds in blue tights, and their lady-loves in green petticoats and gold stars ; a (well, I cannot use another word for it—a spade is a spade) *grattoir pour le dos*, with a beautifully carved ivory hand, a two-foot shaft of twisted whalebone, and an ebony handle, with which Adèle was supposed, after the manner of her grandmother, to allay any temporary irritation on her spine. A set of amethysts, then rare and expensive, now no longer so. A Prayer Book with the Service used "At the Touching" (for the king's evil) in it, date 1710, one of the very last. There was also a set of Indian chessmen ; a lock-up liqueur case in oak, with iron bindings ; and a missal bound in real cedar of Lebanon, overlaid by delicate silver filigree work, with a piece of the true cross set in emerald in the centre. And this last present was a thing after which Mathilde's great soul lusted.

This was the last thing which Lady Somers gave her. She and Mathilde were going home together in Lady Somers' carriage, and this priceless treasure, perfectly unique (the binding being Levantine, put on to a Spanish illuminated missal of the time of Ferdinand and Isabella), lay unnoticed in Adèle's lap. Mathilde had never seen a piece of the true cross before, and desired very much to kiss it ; but Adèle had been more than usually *difficile* that day, and wanting to get the bauble into her hands, she felt it necessary to lead up to the proposition gently.

"May I look at your book, dearest ? " she said.

Adèle, who was lolling back, splendid in her beauty, and perfectly silent, roused herself at once.

"Take the wretched thing and throw it out of the window, if you like. Or better, then—yes, indeed, and once more yes, indeed,—I am not always to be stared into silence by your great stupid eyes,—I say still, better throw it at the head of the wicked old woman who gave it to me."

"My sweetest little bird," said Mathilde, gently. "Why do you call the dear old Lady Somers wicked?"

"The *dear* old Lady Somers. But why do I speak? You are on her side. She is a nasty, wicked, venomous, odious old snake."

"She is not well," thought Mathilde. "These English cooks ruin French digestions as they do their own." "My dear love," she added, aloud, "why do you speak so of Lady Somers?"

"Because she treats me like a baby, because she treats me like a child. Because you, and she, and Lionel, discuss about me apart. Because you all three think of me as a fool, as a *cr-r-rétin;* and because that wicked old woman wants to make Lionel break off from me, and for him to marry you. And I believe you want to marry him yourself."

"I marry Lionel!" said Mathilde. "You are *emportée*, my love. You little know the truth, Adèle, when you make these wild accusations."

A few days afterwards Mathilde herself knew the truth—but only when De Valognes came. But she got her wish just now. Adèle let her handle the missal, and Mathilde took it off to bed with her.

Adèle published her Memoires lately, and very interesting they are, if one could believe them, which one cannot altogether. The *ex post facto* wisdom is too strong in them, as indeed in most Memoires. Sir Lionel Somers, on the other hand, never published his Memoires; and so we have only Adèle's statement of the case.

"My engagement to Sir Lionel Somers," she frankly writes, "was a mistake from beginning to end. It was the work of my father, and was based on fiscal considerations entirely. I was strenuously opposed to the arrangement from the beginning" (oh, Adèle), "not only because I saw that it was impossible that Sir Lionel Somers and myself should ever get on well together as man and wife; but because I perceived very early that his heart was given to my unfortunate sister. Of old Lady Somers I wish to say as little as possible. The subject is not a pleasant one. She was kind, I will allow; but there is a certain sort of contemptuous kindness which is very hard to bear."

So stood matters between Sheepsden and Ashurst at the time of De Valognes' indiscreet visit. If D'Isigny had known everything, he need not have taken William the Silent into his bedroom, and told him to clean his pistols. William's father had been a game-keeper; he himself had not only learnt how to clean guns, but also on occasion, in the dark, to hurl a poacher over bodily, and hold him until he had recognised him, which does not matter as yet. He need not have told William that the gig-horse was to be ready at any time; and that in case of anything happening, Martin the dealer was to have the pigs at five-and-sixpence the score. He thought that there would be a quarrel. There was none.

## CHAPTER XIX.

### M. D'ISIGNY'S EXPLOSION.

S was remarked very cleverly by a daily paper only the other day, in alluding to the threatened war between France and Prussia, "When an offended Frenchman gets pale, calm, and polite, he is not far from striking." Monsieur D'Isigny was very pale, very calm, and profoundly and carefully polite; but nevertheless his wrath, or, to speak more correctly, his fury, was so great, that from time to time he gasped, and moistened his thin, dry lips with his tongue.

He sat and played a little tune on the table with the fingers of his right hand; he was very careful to play his little tune in perfectly correct time, lest Father Martin, who was perfectly aware of his state of mind, and had calculated on it, should think that he was in any way put out. Father Martin, on his part, had said his say, and remained, like a wise man, on the defensive, waiting until D'Isigny should make a fool of himself, as Father Martin calculated pretty surely he would do, and also until D'Isigny's underlying good sense should show him that he *had* made a fool of himself, and until D'Isigny's sense of honour should make him confess that he had done so. "After which things have happened," said Father Martin to himself, "we will begin to talk."

M. D'Isigny had to speak first.

"I should feel deeply obliged to you, as a very good old friend, if you would be kind enough to give me the benefit of your opinion on this miserable and dishonourable business. You, I perceive, smile at it. That is natural, from the elevation you keep above social faults and follies. To me it means utter dishonour, and most likely death; for Sir Lionel will certainly fight me, and I most assuredly will shoot Louis de Valognes before twenty-four hours are gone over my head. If you could possibly be grave over such a very trifling matter, I should be glad to hear your opinion; not that I shall take it, but it might be as well to hear it."

"You shall have it, dear friend, in the most business-like manner," said Father Martin. "In the face of two duels, with two quiet, cool young shots like Sir Lionel and Louis, we cannot be too business-like. These Dorsetshire estates are settled on Madame for her life?"

"Certainly," said D'Isigny.

"And your living on them is merely a verbal arrangement?"

"That is true also," said D'Isigny; "though I hardly see where you are going. The separation between Madame and myself is merely, as you say, a verbal arrangement. She preferred my estates in Brittany; I, to get as far from her as possible, preferred hers in England. What then? I have given her *procès* to draw my rents in Brittany, and she has given me power of attorney to do so here. It is a family arrangement, to avoid squabbling on money matters."

"And the tenor of your will?"

"Well, I of course, not having an heir, have left everything in Brittany to Madame for her lifetime. It is the rule in our part of France. After both our deaths, the Dorsetshire estates, under present arrangements, which must now be altered, will go to Adèle, and those in Brittany to Mathilde."

"Then after possibly the first, certainly the second, of these two duels, Mathilde and Adèle will be left at the mercy of the terrible Madame of Dinan, who is left with full power of altering her will. You have managed cleverly."

"I will make another will this night," said D'Isigny, still white hot.

"Make a new will in England, which, under the present law, will not hold good for one instant in France? Again, I say, you have managed cleverly."

"S——!" cried D'Isigny, rising and thumping the table with

his fist. "I ask you for your advice, and you confine yourself to proving to me that I have made an utter fool of myself."

"Exactly so," said Father Martin. "Such was my deliberate intention when I began."

To say that D'Isigny "raged" now, is to say short of the truth. The first part of Father Martin's plan was that he should make a fool of himself, and so he assisted nature. D'Isigny was really furious.

"I consented to your coming into this house, sir, because I saw, and because it was pointed out to me, that I could not rule my two idiots of daughters without the intervention of a priest. I am a religionist, sir, and I have respected priests *ex officio;* what is my reward? The first priest I have had into my house after many years begins, has begun, by attempting to bully Me, and to force his opinions down My throat. That priest will end by setting my daughters against me, and by bringing discord into a house over which he has given the blessing of peace. Don't deny it, sir. Be honest, if you can, and don't deny it. You are on my daughters' side, sir. I see it in your eyes."

"I am rather on the side of your daughters, certainly, knowing their strength and weakness," said Father Martin, who was now winning his race in a canter. "We will come to that directly. Let us see what you, in your anger, have said of me. You say that I am trying to bully you, and to force my opinions down your throat. As how, then? I have only as yet pointed out to you that your business arrangements are exceedingly faulty. You then go on to say that I shall end by bringing discord between you and your daughters. Now, my whole aim and object is to make you and your daughters one."

"You have begun pretty well, sir."

"So I say, myself. You have bullied them until you have made them deceitful, and so one of them has deceived you."

"Both, sir."

"Well, both, if you will; though Mathilde's falsehood is more noble than some people's truth. You would never have known one word of all this until the catastrophe, whatever that might have been, if I had not greatly violated her confidence, and put you in possession of facts. And because I do this, you furiously accuse me of siding with your daughters. Any person in full possession of his faculties would say that I had done my best to forfeit their confidence, and had moved boldly to your side. I never did such a thing in my life before, and see how I am rewarded."

It was undoubtedly true. Father Martin saw that he had hit D'Isigny hard; but he also saw that D'Isigny's temper had not cooled, and that he must wait a short time for his apology. He therefore went into generalities, while D'Isigny remained silent.

"Mathilde is a very noble person," he said; "if you will allow me to praise a member of your family without giving offence. She has been very badly treated, and seems to have behaved very well. As a very dear old friend, D'Isigny, I must ask you, as a personal favour, that she is entirely spared in this."

M. D'Isigny rose and walked up and down the room.

"I wish, dear old friend," continued Father Martin, "to point out to you the extreme self-sacrificing nobility of Mathilde's behaviour. Our beloved Louis——"

"*Our* beloved Louis, sir!" snapped out D'Isigny. "Speak for yourself."

"So I will, if you will not interrupt me. I say that our beloved Louis has certainly behaved very badly to Mathilde."

"You say nothing of *me*," said D'Isigny.

"He did not pretend to make love to you, and then throw you aside. No, I say nothing at all of you. I speak of Mathilde. Mathilde believed that his attentions were for her, and suddenly discovered that she had been only used as a stalking-horse to get at Adèle; discovered his treason suddenly, when her whole great soul had gone forth to meet him. Do you know Mathilde's wonderful power of love? Do you appreciate how great a blow it was for her?"

"I do," said D'Isigny, softening.

"How would you have had your daughter act, then? What should she have done to prove herself a D'Isigny?"

"She should have stabbed him to his false heart," said D'Isigny. "She should have sent the dagger home."

"Right," said Father Martin; "and so she did. She knew where his heart lay, and she stabbed him there. See! She followed and watched, and you followed and watched; but she was first. She learnt his falseness, and then she stabbed him.

She saw you coming, and warned him in time to fly. She had but to stay quiet, and she would have been avenged in a way; but she knew that she had a great and noble heart to deal with, and she drove her knife into it—home to the hilt."

"Did I not tell you, Father Martin," said D'Isigny, laying his hand good humouredly on the priest's shoulder, "that you were siding with my daughters against me?"

"It is true," replied Father Martin. "May I ask, as a matter of detail, if you have recovered your temper?"

"I have perfectly recovered my temper."

"That is good."

"Will you forgive the words I used to you in my anger?" said D'Isigny.

"On condition that you do not allude to the subject again. Now, with regard to the future, what do you propose to do?"

"I must fight Louis de Valognes. That is imperatively necessary, or I could never put myself right with Sir Lionel."

"True. That is of course absolutely necessary to begin with. But then a voyage to France just now would look very much like eluding the natural wrath of Sir Lionel, if you are determined, as of course you are, to tell him everything."

"Has that coward fled to France, then?"

"I know of no cowards, and of no flight," said Father Martin; "Louis does not come of a family which produces cowards, or which flies. He has gone back to his regiment at St. Malo, by my advice, having gained the sole object of his journey to England; that is to say, having ascertained the exact state of Adèle's affections."

"And leaving her to my vengeance," said D'Isigny, calmly.

"But under my protection," said Father Martin, steadily.

"Truly, sir!" said D'Isigny.

"And truly, sir!" said Father Martin. "Come, D'Isigny, don't let us quarrel. You would have known nothing of this if it had not been for me."

"That is perfectly true, as far as it goes," said D'Isigny.

"It is absolutely true, without any reservation," said Father Martin. "Now, what do you propose next?"

"I must, in honour, put Sir Lionel in possession of all the facts, and await his challenge."

"Precisely so. Await his challenge. Nothing can be wiser. Now, about the two girls?"

"As for Mathilde, in spite of her gross deceit towards myself, I consider her worthy of my esteem, almost of my respect."

"You never thought so before, then," said Father Martin.

"Your are sarcastic, and will not serve her by that."

"I do not care to serve her. She can serve herself by her noble and blameless life. Those who cannot appreciate her are unworthy of her. *Dixi!* About Adèle?"

"She must of course, after this, go into a nunnery," said D'Isigny, coolly.

"I beg your pardon."

"I said that, of course, she must go into a nunnery," said D'Isigny. "It is the usual thing after a *fiasco* of this sort. It is always done."

"Ho!" said Father Martin. "Yes; by the bye, so it is. Shall you keep her there altogether?"

"That is more in your way of business than mine. She had better take the first vows, *I* should say. It is the correct form in these matters."

"Have you any particular establishment in your eye?" asked Father Martin, *fishing* for a reply which would lead up to his own proposition quite naturally, and catching a better fish than he expected.

"I don't know," said D'Isigny, carelessly. "Dinort, on the Rance, is a well-conducted establishment. My sister is superior. A most respectable woman."

"A most respectable lady," said Father Martin. "A most profoundly respectable lady. With none of the temper of her good brother, yourself; but profoundly respectable. 'Difficile' yet. A woman with a great object in life: that of squabbling with the De Valognes family."

"By the bye," said D'Isigny, "it is so."

"Yes," said Father Martin; "it is so, indeed, as the Parlement at Rennes well knows. If you remember the dispute, it was between the Lady Superior of the Convent of St. Catherine, at Dinort, and the Marquis Carillon de Valognes, uncle of our poor Louis, as to who shall furnish the *corvée* on the road between Vasansdire and Vaurien. You remember it all? The

Convent holds the land at what the Rector here would call a pepper-corn rent from the Marquis. Your dear sister excuses herself from the *corvée*, putting it on the shoulders of the Seigneur. Now, on the other hand, the Marquis——"

"For Heaven's sake!" said D'Isigny, "don't go into this farrago of nonsense."

"Why not?" said Father Martin. "It is very interesting. I sat myself for whole hours in the Parlement at Rennes listening to the arguments; and I give you my word that my interest was as high at the end as at the beginning; they were as far off the crisis of their argument as ever. I will not go on, however, if you do not like it. Let us change the subject. What is the value of these De Valognes' estates?"

"Very great," said the unsuspecting D'Isigny. "I should say 600,000 livres a-year. Worked with tobacco and turnips, more. Arthur Young and I were talking the other day about those lands, and he confessed that he had not done them justice. I pointed out to him that they were the finest lands in France, and he promised to go and look at them; in fact, he is there now.* They are very fine estates, indeed. Montauban is one of the finest places in France."

"It is. The estates come to Louis at his uncle's death, I believe."

"Louis will be Marquis —— certainly," said M. D'Isigny, uneasily.

"Not a bad provision for Adèle, hey?" said Father Martin.

"You come to the point too quickly," said D'Isigny, testily. "You are too blunt. You are too short. You should not, if you had any tact, have said that for the next quarter of an hour at the very least. You should have led up to that carefully and slowly. You always speak as if you were dictating to women, while you are consulting with men. I wish you would not be priest with me."

Although Father Martin was shaking with laughter, his well-trained face showed no sign of it. "You are right," he said. "I am too blunt. I should have been bishop, but for my bluntness. We will therefore consider my last remark as expunged from the minutes of the conference."

* Arthur Young never seems to have gone, however. He had a great contempt for this part of the country, with all its works and ways.

"But we can't," said D'Isigny. "No one but a priest, with all his tortuous insincerity, could have proposed such a line of action. You have said the words, and they stand on record."

"What between rash bluntness one moment and tortuous insincerity the next," said Father Martin, laughing, "I seem likely to get into trouble. However, as my remark is to stand on record, I will make it again. It would be rather a fine thing for your daughter Mademoiselle Adèle to be the marchioness of that fugitive young scoundrel, my beloved Louis, with his estates of 600,000 livres a-year." *

"That is just the whole trouble," said D'Isigny, sitting down again and drumming the table. "Any one but a priest would have seen that long ago. That is the very matter under consideration. I would have given Adèle to Louis de Valognes with the greatest pleasure, but it seemed to me that he liked Mathilde best; and I let things go. Lionel Somers, in the meantime, had paid Adèle the most marked attentions, and on his renewal of them after our return from St. Malo, I was delighted to find them renewed. I accepted them formally, thinking that Adèle was safer with a great park in this safe island than in our unhappy and disturbed France, she being an utter fool, and safer here than there. Again, I believed that De Valognes was in love with Mathilde, which would have suited me very well——"

"Very well indeed."

"But they deceived me."

"Of course they deceived you," said Father Martin, testy for the first time during the discussion. "You bully all the people who choose to believe in you until they habitually deceive you. You have actually been trying to bully *me* this very night. With what success I leave you to judge."

"What do you advise me to do?" asked D'Isigny, in perfect good humour.

"Send Adèle away for a time. Send her to her mother."

"I could not send her there. She has behaved very badly; but I could not do *that*."

"Very well, then, send her to her aunt at the Convent at

---

\* Say £25,000 roughly. Duc D'Orleans was worth about £500,000 a-year.

Dinort. Mind, my *distinct* advice is to send her to her mother; but if you are too great a coward for that, send her to her aunt. One thing is certain: she can't stop here. She has made a perfect little fool of herself, and has, according to her own account, involved you in at least two terrific duels."

"But why do you propose that she should go to her mother?" asked D'Isigny.

"Because her mother will knock some of the nonsense out of her, whereas Madame the Superior of St. Catherine's will knock a good deal of fresh nonsense in. Madame of Catherine's is a fool; Madame of Dinan is a dragon, but no fool. *I* should send her to Madame of Dinan. But wherever you send her, mind that Louis de Valognes has the *entrée* to her. They might marry soon; the sooner the better."

"But what am I to do with Sir Lionel Somers?" asked D'Isigny.

"Tell him all about it, of course—that is very easy," said Father Martin.

"Easy enough for a priest, protected by his cloth," retorted D'Isigny; "but not so easy for one *gentleman* to another."

"That is true enough. That is as true a thing as ever you said. You are very right there. See, my dear friend,—shall I, protected by my cloth, tell him?"

"That would prove me a coward," said D'Isigny.

"You are right again. Then, tell him yourself."

"But, how?"

"How? Are there two ways? Go quietly and categorically through the whole story yourself, without the slightest omission. Point out to him that you have both been deceived. He is not the first man who has got his *congé*. Dear me! it is not such a very terrible affair."

"We shall have to fight over it," said M. D'Isigny.

"Then there will be two more silly people in the world than I thought there were. You, however, put yourself in the right, and lay the whole truth before him."

"By letter or speech?"

"I should say by speech, if I could trust your temper; but I cannot. Write a frank and cautious letter to him to-morrow morning. Suppose we talk about something else."

"I shall be delighted," said M. D'Isigny. "For my part, I

have had as much lecturing as I am inclined to stand. I do not dislike having my daughters lectured by a priest, but too much lecturing on my own person unnerves me. Let us talk of more agreeable matters."

## CHAPTER XX.

### NEWS FROM FRANCE.

"OF the Revolution, for instance," said Father Martin; "for it has come to that now."

"No; of people, of persons. Let me recover my temper in a quiet talk with you about those we have known. You have had a large budget of letters from France to-day; let me hear something of the old friends who wrote them."

"Goneraile and Regan are gone to bed; Mrs. Bone and William do not understand French. Come, then, I will recover my temper and tell you about our old friends. I believe that André Desilles is in love with Mathilde!"

"I dislike that young gentleman. Pass him."

"Why?"

"Because he does not suit me," replied D'Isigny.

"Humph! then I will pass him. Here is a letter from Barbaroux at Marseilles."

"Barbaroux is going too far, will go further than he intends; I am not bound by Barbaroux. I wished to speak of personal friends in France, and you begin on politics."

"Unintentionally," said Father Martin. "The part of Barbaroux' letter to which I wish to call your attention is purely personal, and to me, I confess, pleasant. Shall I read it?"

"Anything from my beloved old France," said D'Isigny. "Read me Barbaroux' letter."

And so Father Martin read it.

"'I hear,' wrote Barbaroux, 'that you are gone to England, to stay with that man, D'Isigny—a man too just not to be undecided; and, at the same time, too undecided to be perfectly just. Your object is, if I understand you, to float Christianity in his house; and if any one could make the bar of iron float, I think it would be yourself. We have nothing left now of which we can speak in common, except this—my intense and devoted love for you. If Christianity had been represented by such men as yourself, there need have been no revolution. What are we doing, after all? We are aiming at the morality of Christianity, without its formulas. We are not fighting against such men as you; we are fighting against the Leroys and De Rohans.

"'D'Isigny is a man who should declare. He is a purist; but we want purists. What line will he take? He and his daughters seem wonderfully amiable. I was last night with the nightmare. You only have the nightmare when asleep—I see it while awake. I was last night, while broad awake and sober, sitting face to face with the nightmare. The nightmare has tawny curly hair, a large mouth, and moistens its large lips while talking. It has a wolfish face, this nightmare, and snaps and snarls in its speech. It is hideous, awful, and portentous; yet not all ill, for it spoke kindly of these D'Isignys. It said that D'Isigny was a good and just man, and that his daughter, Mathilde, was the most perfect and best of all women who ever lived. The name of my nightmare among men is Jean Paul Marat.'"

"Marat!" cried D'Isigny. "Why, that is the man who was lecturing here two years ago. Nightmare! I should think he was a nightmare. He was taken ill here, and was desperately poor. I used to go and see him."

"You mean that you kept him comfortably while he was ill, and gave him a handsome sum of money to take him back to France as soon as he was well," said Father Martin.

"Well, we need not talk of those things," said D'Isigny. "Mathilde nursed him."

"So I understand. Barbaroux was a pupil of his at one time."

"Heaven help Barbaroux, then, if he learnt anything from him except horse-doctoring and optics."

"What did you think of this M. Marat, then?" asked Father Martin.

"Think!" said D'Isigny. "Well, I can scarcely tell you. To begin with, I shall never forget either the face or the man as long as I live."

"Why?"

"He seemed a man removed from the ordinary pale of humanity. That is a platitude, you will say; but I know what I mean. If he had told me that he had come from the moon, I believe I should have told him that I suspected so from the first. I can see him lying there in his bed, with his rough curled hair on the pillow, and his mouth open, gasping, now. He had a way of moistening his lips with his tongue, and swallowing before he spoke too——. Heaven preserve us from him!"

"Did he behave well?"

"Very well and very gratefully. Mathilde and he grew very much attached to one another, I believe. I myself had a very strange fascination for him before he went. I am afraid that I should have got to like him."

"The man is *hors de la loi*. He wants 280,000 executions. He is worse than Nero."

"It may be. I can only say that from the most profound and utter loathing for the man I got to a curiosity about him, and at last got into a hideous state of semi-fascination about him. I can say no more."

"He ought to be shot like a mad dog," said Father Martin.

"Yet a dog may have been to some extent loveable before he went mad," said D'Isigny.

"That is possible. It is very late; and you have a hard day's work before you. You will have to ride over and tell Sir Lionel all about it to-morrow morning."

"To-morrow! oh, that's sudden. Spare him—spare him!" said D'Isigny, who appreciated the melodramatic and Frenchy points in Shakspeare like any Frenchman, and yet who considered Falstaff, the greatest wit of all ages, the dexterous and shifty man whose first order, when he heard of the change of kings, was "Carry Master Silence to bed," as a mere English beer barrel. "To-morrow!" said D'Isigny. "Surely the day after will do?"

"I should have it out with him at once," said Father Martin. "You will put yourself completely in the wrong by concealing it from him an hour longer than is necessary. Just think if he were to see Adèle by accident, and she were to accept his endearments after what has occurred!"

"That is true," said D'Isigny. "We must have it out."

## CHAPTER XXI.

### SIR LIONEL FINDS HIMSELF AGAIN IN THE MARKET.

A VERY busy and pushing young Whig, like Sir Lionel Somers, devoted to all kinds of new ideas, particularly in agriculture, which was his *spécialité*, was not one likely to lie in bed of a morning. An intimate friend of Mr. Coke and Arthur Young, he had gone fiercely into the turnip and improved sheep experiment, and was hot on it.

Not that it was an experiment with him. Mr. Bakewell and Arthur Young had proved that it *could* succeed, and he had at once determined that it *should*. There were to be no doubts about it in his case. This was the first year of both his new Leicester lambs, and also of his turnips, and he was up at five o'clock every morning to see how they were getting on.

His mother told him that "a watched pot never boiled;" but he watched his pot nevertheless, waiting eagerly until the time should come when his lambs should be lambs no longer. The lambs, however, were still lambs in July, and his sole satisfaction was leaning over the hurdles and watching them.

"These are the finest lambs I have ever seen," he said to his shepherd, one of the innumerable Martins, this morning.

"I have seen bigger," replied the shepherd.

"That is wholly impossible," said Sir Lionel; "these are the biggest sheep in the world."

"Them I speaks on," said the old man, with that cool familiarity which existed then between lord and hind, but which exists no longer, "are out of the world. I've seen bigger ship than they, of the same age."

"These sheep will go six-ty-pound-a-quarter, Bob," said Sir Lionel, calmly and sententiously.

"Sixty which, Sir Lionel?" said the shepherd.

"Six-ty-pound-a-quarter."

"Oh, indeed," said the shepherd. "Ah, yes! A fine sermon of the Rector's last Sunday, Sir Lionel."

"Indeed!" said Sir Lionel. "I was not at Church."

"Better at church than at chapel," growled the peasant.

"There was a fine to-do when I went to chapel, I think. And a Methodist is as good as a Papist any day. I am sorry you missed the sermon, Sir Lionel."

"What was it about?" asked Sir Lionel, good-naturedly.

"Faith," said the shepherd, "the virtue of believing everything that is told you; just the same as you believe that these French ship are freer from footrot than Southdowns, and will go sixty pound a quarter."

"Some *have* done so," said Sir Lionel.

"Well, I never disputes with gentlefolks," replied the shepherd. "They know better than we what is good for us, and for themselves too. As for me, as far as a man, who has took ten shillings a week, with cottage, garden, and wheatpatch, from your family for fifty years, may speak: I am again all French notions."

"These are not French sheep," said Sir Lionel.

"Baint 'em! they're forrin anyway. What's forrin is French, and what's French is bad."

"But these sheep are from Dishley."

"That's as bad as forrin parts; and if they as sold 'em to you says they'll ever go sixty pound a quarter, or forty, wuss. That is French all over, that is. Here is one on 'em acoming across the fields now. I wonder what kite he is agoing to fly. Drat 'em, they're all tarred with the same stick; and you are agoing to marry one of the wust on 'em."

The last sentence was merely growled out after Sir Lionel had made out M. D'Isigny approaching him rapidly across the field, and had turned to meet him. With all the traditional humorous impudence of the Martins, the shepherd would never have dared to say this within Sir Lionel's hearing; but if the reader will have the kindness to contrast the relations between Sir Lionel Somers and the old shepherd with those between the majority of French seigneurs and their hinds, he will see one of the very many causes which saved us from a revolution. D'Isigny's narrow, just mind saw this when he issued the order for his servants to eat and live in the same room with him. A true French manner of cutting the Gordian knot; as if the effects of the habits of ages, among twenty million souls, could be altered by the personal habits of one single family!

Sir Lionel advanced to meet his future father-in-law through the growing-corn, and held out his hand to him. To his astonishment his proffered hand was gracefully and politely waved aside. "Not at present, Sir Lionel," said M. D'Isigny, in very bad English, which we will not reproduce, "not as yet. Before I take your hand in mine again it is necessary that there should be some personal explanations of the most delicate nature between us."

Sir Lionel was in buckram at once. He was conscious that he had behaved with the most blind and chivalrous honour; he had been more than half bullied, while in a sentimental mood, once before, and he was half inclined to be tired of it. He had never been in a similar position before. Yet he knew what to do. *Tradition* told him how to behave. Before his father prosed himself into his grave he had told his son a baker's dozen of stories, a baker's dozen of times, all about the most undeniable gentlemen, under circumstances such as the present or similar. Consequently, Sir Lionel knew how the traditional English gentleman ought to behave under the circumstances, and he behaved accordingly. There are few finer *ideals* than the old English gentleman possibly, and indeed there were more good points about him, on the whole, than bad, even in practice; Sir Lionel had got his part from tradition, and acted it well.

"I am rather at a loss to understand," he said, "what explanation we have to make to one another. I can only begin by declaring that my conduct towards you, and towards your family, has been most trusting and most loyal. I have refused to ask for explanations when most men would have demanded them. I see that something has gone wrong, and, before we go any further, I must request, my dear D'Isigny, that you allow this. Otherwise——"

"Otherwise?" repeated M. D'Isigny. "Otherwise, what?"

"Well, you push me rather hard. I wish I had not said 'otherwise;' but my 'otherwise' meant this. In case you did not admit that I had behaved with the most entire loyalty towards your family, I should feel it my duty to tell you to your face that you were doing me a very great injustice. I fear I should be obliged to tell you that."

D'Isigny knew that he was treading on the edge of a volcano.

He knew that it was he, D'Isigny, who had to make his case good, and not Sir Lionel. Yet his inveterate habit of bullying was too strong for him even now. He could not help it; and that is the only lame excuse which I can give for him. The better Sir Lionel behaved, the more he bullied him.

"This is very well, sir," he said. "But suppose that I choose to deny your propositions *in toto?* How then?"

"In that case," said Sir Lionel, "I should be forced to the conclusion that you had been affected with temporary access of stupidity."

"And your remedy, sir?"

"My remedy would be, sir, to get your daughter Mathilde to pray for your restoration to serenity."

A man who *won't* be bullied is the man who wins the game. The man who kicks and fights, at the very best compromises the matter so far that no one can say who had the best of it. The man who *turns the other cheek* until the other man puts himself in the wrong, is the winner.

"It is about my daughter Adèle I wish to speak now, Sir Lionel."

"Well, sir?"

"You take this matter rather coolly," said M. D'Isigny, who felt the awkwardness of his position more and more, and was beginning to be profoundly anxious to get himself into a rage, and Sir Lionel into another, and so finish the business with an explosion of fireworks, during which Sir Lionel would have a chance of putting himself slightly in the wrong, and make the subsequent explanation somewhat easier and more mutual. Sir Lionel would give him no such advantage. He only said,—

"I am very cool over this matter for two reasons. In the first place, I don't know what the matter is, and in the second, whatever it may be, I don't see the use of losing my temper. Proceed."

It was getting very bad for M. D'Isigny.

"May I ask, Sir Lionel, whether the relations between you and my daughter Adèle have been the same as usual lately?"

"Exactly," said Sir Lionel. "There has been no change whatever. I have continued to treat her with the most deferential affection, which she, on her part, has responded to in a way of which the most jealous lover could not complain. There has not been a shadow of a cloud between us of any sort or kind."

Things were getting worse and worse for M. D'Isigny. What on earth he was to say next he could not conceive; and so, like a wise man, he just said nothing at all.

That was all very well and very wise; but the unlucky part of the business was that Sir Lionel Somers said nothing either. An old lady said to me once that two men had far better quarrel than sulk; that it was in the end less exasperating. I should conceive that few things in life could be more exasperating than for a man, who was entirely in the right, and to whom you owed an explanation, possibly an apology, to have spoken last, and to refuse to speak again, leaving you to begin your explanation without one single word to say for yourself. Such was the position of the unlucky M. D'Isigny.

His temper entirely broke down under the trial. He broke out, made a fool of himself, burring his r's like a corn crake.

"*Sacr-r-re mille tonnerres! Sacr-r-re vent gris!*" he cried. "*Ces insulaires!*"

"Something seems to have disturbed your equanimity, my dear D'Isigny," said Sir Lionel, very quietly. "I wish you would tell me the cause of it. I like and respect you very much, and might possibly do something to remove the cause of your extreme disquietude."

There was no doing anything with this man—a man who would put every one who disagreed with him in the wrong by acting as a perfect gentleman. D'Isigny, who was as noble a man as Sir Lionel in his way, felt it; he turned away from him and said,—

"You have beaten me. Let us walk side by side for a few minutes in silence."

"I will walk side by side with you for any time, under any circumstances," replied Sir Lionel. "I like being in the company of gentlemen and men of high honour, like yourself. Allow me to say one thing. At the beginning of this interview I was a little short with you, because you refused me your hand. Now that I see you are really disturbed, accept my apologies for that behaviour. Will you allow me to lay my hand on your shoulder? Good. My dear D'Isigny, there is something amiss between us. Be frank and honest with me, and tell me what it is."

"I cannot *now*," said D'Isigny. "I wanted to make you quarrel with me, and put you in the wrong; but you have been too noble for me. I cannot speak now; I *cannot* humiliate myself so far."

"Yet you will do it. Come, I will put you on your mettle. If it is anything about Adèle, it is your duty, as a French gentleman, to tell me."

"You will not strike me suddenly," said D'Isigny; "you will meet me in fair duel."

"I will do neither the one nor the other," said Sir Lionel. "Now, do let me have the truth."

"Adèle is false to you. You have the truth. Take it."

"Good heavens! What do you mean?"

"What I say. Her heart has never been yours. She, and a false young panther, whom I reserve for my own especial vengeance—mind, I will have no interference here—has deceived us all. He has followed her here; she has, in the presence of Mathilde, given him proof of her *tendresse* for him, for which I could kill her."

"She has not behaved well to me," said Sir Lionel, calmly.

"Then what do you think of her conduct to *me?*" replied M. D'Isigny.

"Doubtless, most undutiful," said Sir Lionel. "I, for my part, never thrust my attentions upon her."

"Nor did I," replied D'Isigny, "ever force your attentions on her, beyond what a French father is accustomed to do. I have been shamefully used by her."

"So it seems. It is all over, then?"

"She is yours still, if you choose to take her," said D'Isigny.

"Oh, no! that would never do at all, now; that would be mere life-long misery to both of us. And you must allow, my dear D'Isigny, that *you* have given me my acquit."

"I acknowledge it frankly. You have been badly used. Do you acquit me of blame?"

"Most fully," said Sir Lionel. "I know how bitter this must have been to you, with your rigid rules of honour, and I sympathise with you profoundly. I have not been well-used in this matter, and I *demand* a compensation."

"Name it, sir."

"I demand," said Sir Lionel, "that there should be not the slightest cessation of friendship between you and myself. That I demand as my right."

"Lionel, Lionel, you are very noble. I wish to God she had been worthy of you. You are very noble."

"Pah! my dear sir. We have, in our family, traditions as to how we should act under circumstances, and we merely follow them. Now, I wish to speak further with you. Who is this French lover of Adèle's, whom she has so sensibly preferred to myself?"

"He is reserved for my vengeance," said M. D'Isigny.

"For heaven's sake don't talk such nonsense! There has been a mistake, and it must be corrected; but don't add to the complication by shooting the man. Poor little Adèle's reputation would not be worth a franc if there was any further *esclandre*. We can keep everything quiet at present. No one knows anything but ourselves. You will excuse the liberty I take in saying so, but she ought to marry this man at once."

"You take things uncommonly cool, Sir Lionel," said D'Isigny.

"I do," said Sir Lionel. "I have been taking things very coolly for a very long time. I can see my way to a great many things now. My dear friend, it is quite as well as it is. I have seen more than you have. Anything is better than continual suspicion. What is the name of Adèle's new-old *fiancé*, again?"

"She has no *fiancé*; she goes to a nunnery."

"The poor, tender little bird," said Sir Lionel, eagerly. "You must not do that. I will not stand that, before Heaven, sir! Poor gentle little thing. No, I will not stand such a thing as that. I have been deceived and ill-used; I have been made ridiculous, and people of my name, sir, are not accustomed to be made ridiculous, still less to sit down under it with perfect good temper, as I have done. The poor little thing has used me badly; but allow me to tell you, sir, that with all her silliness and frivolity, she is a very loveable and gentle little thing, sir; and that if it had not been for your way of bullying your daughters, this business, which has ended by making you only more ridiculous than myself, would never have happened.

*I* am to be consulted, sir, in some measure, I believe ; and I can tell you, sir, that if you make any attempt to immure Adèle in a nunnery, I will—I will do something dangerous. A seventeenth-century baronet can, in spite of taunts, be quite as dangerous as a lapsed thirteenth-century marquis."

When one door steeks, another opens, says the Scotch. It was now Sir Lionel's turn to lose his temper, and he lost it accordingly; but D'Isigny had recovered his, which is fortunate for the progress of this story.

"You need not enrage yourself, dear Sir Lionel," he said ; " I am perfectly open to reason. I have no particular wish to murder De Valognes."

"De Valognes ! Why, that is Mathilde's lover."

"He has deceived us all. He is Adèle's. The rascal, he is safe back in France, if you can call France safe. Well, my dear Lionel, after I have sent Adèle off to her mother at Dinan, Sheepsden will be open to you as usual ; until then we must meet at the Rector's."

" That will be worse for her than a nunnery," said Sir Lionel.

" It is not done yet," said D'Isigny. " Good-bye. You have behaved like a gentleman !"

It was this very evening,—a day which Mathilde called the vigil of the holy St. Swithin,—that is to say, the day in the middle of July when the weather almost invariably breaks up, when Father Martin, having other things to think of, had forgotten all about the matter, and was quietly reading Van Helmont before the fire, and quietly wondering whether or no Van Helmont was the greatest ass who ever lived, or whether, by more diligent study, he could find out a greater,—it was on this very evening when Mathilde entered to him with a basket of flowers, hollyhocks, stocks, sweet Williams, and bee larkspurs, —pelargoniums and verbenas were not as yet,—and proposed that they should decorate the altar in the chapel for the next day's festival, little dreaming what had happened in Paris.

Father Martin consented at once. "We all talk sad nonsense at times," he said, "but seldom worse than Van Helmont. Yes, my dear Mathilde, I will willingly go with you and lay these flowers on the altar of the purest morality which the world has ever seen;" with which platitude the puzzled Father Martin went with her into the dark chapel, directing her as a practised man in those *details* of ornamentation, which seem to me and to others so singularly unnecessary.

They were a long time before they said anything worth recording. At last Mathilde blurted out,—

"It is all over between Lionel and Adèle."

"I am glad to hear it," said Father Martin. "You would make him a much better wife than she would."

"I never thought of such a thing," said Mathilde.

"I don't think you ever did," said Father Martin. "But why do you think it is all over?"

"Martin, the shepherd, told me. Lionel and Father scolded all across the big turnip field, and he heard every word."

"Well, Mathilde," said Father Martin, "I desire to hear no more. There is one thing certain, that whatever may have happened, you have a good conscience."

"I hate having a good conscience," said Mathilde.

"It is the best thing the world can give," said Father Martin.

"It is the very worst," said Mathilde. "It makes you so conceited. I am twenty times more of a Christian with a bad conscience than with a good one. I hope and pray that I may always have a bad conscience. Come, then. The Pharisee had a good conscience, whereas the publican had an exceedingly bad one. How do you get over that?"

Father Martin, being more of a man's priest than a woman's, did not get over it at all; he only said, "Those white lilies should be laid crosswise before the pyx. You must not touch the pyx with them."

"Stretching the old formula to meet the new fact." I know that it is an unpopular thing to quote Mr. Carlyle in any way. Yet just think, in common honesty, how he has expressed this matter for us. Think how such men as Martin were trying, in 1789, and are trying now, to stretch the old formula to meet the new fact.

## CHAPTER XXII.

### THE FOUNTAINS OF THE GREAT DEEP ARE BROKEN UP.

M. D'ISIGNY, having left Sir Lionel Somers, after the grand explanation, came quietly home, got William the Silent to get him his valise packed secretly, while he waited in the stable,—took his horse, and rode off across the downs to Lulworth: as he said, "to get his ideas together without any more discussion;" in reality, because he wanted to avoid any more scenes, and because the Welds had a very pleasant accidental French party there, and had asked him to join them, if it was in any way possible.

His hosts were so very charming that he was really in no hurry to return. He had to tell them of the breaking off of the engagement between Sir Lionel Somers and his daughter. They were so gently regretful over the matter, and showed such perfect, kindly tact, that he was at home at once, and enjoyed himself so much among the three or four compatriots of his who were staying at the Castle; that Sheepsden, with a weeping Adèle, a downright father confessor, and a wondering and possibly scandalised, certainly inquisitive, neighbourhood, seemed to him by no means a change for the better. He had never allowed any human soul to raise the least question about his times or his places. He was comfortably assured that his family had not the least idea where he was. He knew perfectly well that Father Martin and Mathilde would think that he had followed Louis De Valognes to France, after the interview with Sir Lionel Somers, with the view of shooting that unfortunate Louis; and would be in a state of miserable, feverish anxiety. Consequently, M. D'Isigny enjoyed himself thoroughly and entirely, and made himself so wondrously agreeable, that his compatriots, some old French Catholic aristocrats, agreed that there was nothing like a real French gentleman after all, and what a pity it was that D'Isigny was ever so slightly tainted with the new opinions. D'Isigny, between one thing and another, enjoyed himself thoroughly, and stayed on.

On the fifth day of his stay, the weather, wild, dark, and dim ever since his arrival at Lulworth, was darker and wilder than ever, rushing into the cove from the westward with sheets of wind-driven rain, and making the yacht, lying snug, with topmasts sent down, surge at her anchors. M. D'Isigny said he must ride homewards. A bright boy of nine, looking out into the weather, told him that he was much better where he was; for that there was plenty more weather coming, and that he was going on board the yacht, as soon as the sailing-master was ready, to see to her moorings.

"Joseph is right," said the charming old Madame Mautalent, close to him. "It is impossible to start in such weather. The English St. Swithin, who guides the English weather, is against you. Since his day, the weather has broken up as usual."

"He was impatient this year, madame," said a bowing and smirking abbé, joining them, snuff-box in hand. "The saint had evidently heard of madame's intention of departure on the fifteenth, and antedated the weather in order that madame might wait for a pleasant passage. The weather changed on his vigil. On the night of the fourteenth the fountains of the great deep were broken up."

True, oh, Abbé! in a way you little dreamed. But what between madame's charming nonsense and the abbé's charming nonsense, D'Isigny felt less and less inclined to go back to his dull house, and his weeping daughters. Nevertheless, the weather having mended on the eighth day, he condescended to ride quietly into his own court-yard and dismount.

"You have not been out of England, then?" was Father Martin's greeting.

"No, I have been at Lulworth. Where are my daughters?"

"Adèle is very ill, and Mathilde is, of course, watching her. That matters nothing. Had they heard the news at Lulworth?"

"What news?"

"Lionel Somers got it first from his friend Mr. Jenkinson, who saw it happen. It has come by Havre and Southampton. The mob have risen, and have taken and sacked the Bastille, and murdered the garrison."

"In-deed!" said D'Isigny. "So the game has actually begun. I suppose, then, that I had better go to Paris at once?"

"Why not to Dinan?"

"I would rather be at head-quarters, and study things. I think I will go to Paris at once. There is another thing: you tell me that Adèle is ill. As soon as she is well enough to be removed, will you take her to Dinort for me?"

"Certainly; and Mathilde?"

"Will do very well here. Things will manage themselves here. It is impossible, after what has happened, that Adèle can stay here. No, my dear friend, take her to Dinort for me. I will start for Southampton to-night."

"That is short notice," said Father Martin.

"One cannot be on the spot too soon," said M. D'Isigny.

"Doubtless," said Father Martin. "I want a word before you go."

"I will write."

"I *said* a word before you went, and that would be a letter after you had gone. Quite a different matter. Here it is. Is Louis de Valognes forgiven?"

"No," said M. D'Isigny.

"I think yes."

"I think no."

"Again I think yes. Come, I must have this done. You will do it, will you not?"

"He has behaved dishonourably to me, and has insulted me."

"Granting that, you might yet forgive him. I am not curious; but I *should* like to know how you got over your business with Sir Lionel."

M. D'Isigny gave him an account of the whole interview; and Father Martin patted him on the shoulder. "I knew," he said, "that no harm could come of two perfect gentlemen and good Christians meeting and explaining matters. I am sorry I advised you to write to him; I was silly there. You did right in going so nobly, and explaining matters to him face to face. Your wisdom was far higher then than mine."

"And then?" said D'Isigny.

"And then," pursued Father Martin, "you, as a Frenchman, would never allow yourself to be outdone in generosity by an Englishman. Sir Lionel has forgiven Louis; and his injury is greater than yours."

"Well," said D'Isigny, laughing, "you have stroked the cat the right way, and I will agree. You priests have just the same trick as women. You flatter us; and while we see through and often despise your insincerity, we yield to you for the sake of peace. Louis may go to the devil his own way, and I will do nothing to send him there. I concede so much."

He departed that night, without bidding good-bye to his daughters. His heavy luggage was to follow him to Southampton, and he rode away with only his valise, to be in time to get his papers—a thing, I believe, not as yet difficult. Father Martin watched him as he topped the downs against the gray, rainy sky, and said,—

"Why he is going to Paris, and what on earth he means to do when he gets there, I know as little as he does himself. There is one thing most certain: he will begin by laying his life and his purse at the service of the King, and will then bully and dictate to every one else who has done the same, until they will, like Adèle, 'wish they were dead.' He will probably point out to the King himself the course which he wishes him to pursue. Yes; and the King will say, 'You seem to me to be a very sensible man, monsieur.' And then ask after his wife. Well, I congratulate Paris on the accession of the most impracticable firebrand I have ever met in my life."

He passed into the hall-kitchen, and went behind the screen, pondering deeply. Mathilde happened to be there, and he, in an absent way, and to her great astonishment, took up the thread of his thoughts aloud, and addressed them to her.

"He will insult Lafayette about the American business. He has sworn to me that nothing shall ever induce him to speak to Mirabeau; he has vowed to me that he will insult him whenever he meets him. For the rest, why give details: he will insult and denounce them, every one. If heads are lost in what is coming, his is the first head which will go. He denounces the aristocracy, and denounces Mirabeau as a disgrace to his order at one and the same time. In short, he belongs to the party 'D'Isigny,' which consists of himself; and every other party are a congerie of rogues and vagabonds. He will lose his head, whichever party wins."

But he kept it on his shoulders nevertheless, while heads not half so deeply implicated as his fell like wheat-ears in harvest.

Mathilde looked quietly up at him. "You were talking to yourself," she said. "Is anything wrong which I can mend? Who is going to lose his head?"

"Your father, Mathilde. He will lose his head among these politics as surely as I have lost mine in thinking of them."

"He has lost his head among them already," said Mathilde, smiling. "I am to help him at something some day, as he says, at peril of my life. But I do not understand what he means, and I do not think that he does either. All this trouble will blow over, will it not?"

"Yes, it will blow over," said Father Martin, as they looked out of the window over the rich corn-fields in the valley. "It will all blow over, as this storm has blown over. See, there is a red arch of light in the west, which rises and gets more glorious each moment."

"The west wind and rain have 'laid' the wheat," said matter-of-fact Mathilde. "It will not get up again before harvest. The storm has gone over, but the wheat is destroyed."

"Yet the wheat will grow as well as ever next year," said Father Martin.

"But not in those fields," said Mathilde, simply. "There will be barley there next year, and then clover, and then turnips, and wheat again only in four years."

"But there will be wheat again at last. Let us change the subject. You are speaking in all simplicity; yet, by accident, your words are painful to me. One is so blind, and one has to look forward so very, very far."

"To what?" asked Mathilde.

"To harvest, child. Your father has gone to Paris, by the bye, and commissioned me to bid you adieu."

This changed the subject with a vengeance. It took away Mathilde's breath, and enabled Father Martin to continue his explanations without any "interpellations."

"It is absolutely necessary, you see," said Father Martin, "that Adèle should leave this part of the country; and it is quite impossible that she should travel alone. Consequently, your father and I have arranged that I should take her to her grand-aunt at Dinort, as soon as she is well enough to move. The sooner the better."

"She can go well enough now, if you like," said Mathilde.

"I think she would be better there than here. But *you* will come back again, and not leave me entirely alone?"

"Oh, yes; I will come back again. Do you really think she *can* be moved?"

"It will do her all the good in the world," said Mathilde. "But I could take her there as well as you. Why should not I take her?"

"Because your father has ordered otherwise; and because," he added, speaking very slowly, "Louis' regiment is still quartered at St. Malo, which is very close."

"Are they to marry, then?" asked Mathilde, in a whisper.

"I think so," said Father Martin, also in a whisper.

For one of the few times in this story she burst out into wild weeping. He let her weep. He had nothing to say to comfort her, and he held his tongue. "God knows best," he thought; "I shall not interfere with her. Let her cry till she is quiet."

It was not long before she was quiet. He waited until her sobs grew less and less frequent, and at last became mere sighs. Then he spoke to her.

"Are you quite ready to speak to me about arrangements?" he asked.

"Yes."

"Good; will you then arouse yourself? Tell Adèle of her destination. Prepare her mind for immediate departure. Get her to submit decently to the plan. Pack her things for her; for, I fear, she will never pack them for herself. And if you have any difficulty in gaining her acquiescence, tell her that Louis is at St. Malo, and that she will see him very often. She will go fast enough then. Will you obey?"

"I will obey," said Mathilde. "I always do. But *you* surely might hold out the attraction of Louis de Valognes before her. That is rather a bitter pill for me to swallow, advertising him to her after what has passed."

"It will do you good," said Father Martin. "Louis has grossly deceived you. Show him that you despise him, and hate him."

"But I don't," said Mathilde.

"Make believe that you do. Show your spirit. Say 'You want her, hey? Then take her!' Show your courage."

"I have none," said Mathilde. "I am the greatest coward in the world. But I will do as you say. And what is to become of me? Am I to be left here all alone?"

"Certainly you are. You will have to manage matters here. You are, allow me to tell you, more lucky than the rest of the family. You do not know what has happened. While you and I were decorating the chapel on St. Swithin's eve, the people of Paris having succeeded—how I cannot conceive—in capturing the Bastille, were amusing themselves by massacring De Launay and the garrison."

"Have they destroyed the Bastille?" said Mathilde, with sudden animation. "Why did you not tell me of that before? Thank God! there is life in old France yet. And so there *is* a God which judges the world. I thought He was dead, or asleep like Baal. So the wicked old place is down. I wish I had been there: this is very glorious news, indeed."

"My daughter, do you not think of De Launay and the garrison?"

"What of them?"

"Murdered!"

"I am sorry for that—that was a mistake. I think I could have saved them, had I been there with a strange friend of mine. I am very sorry for that. But, then, they were maddened, you know. Naturally, no people in the world are so kind as the French—they will regret this. I wish that my friend Marat had been there; he would have prevented this."

"Mathilde," said Father Martin, "you should never name that man. It is inconceivably horrible to me to hear you call that man your friend. I am seldom angry, but I am angry now. This Marat is the most inconceivable scoundrel in all France. Since the days of the Old Man of the Mountain no such villain has appeared on this earth. I thank God that he is not a Frenchman, but a Swiss! And you call him friend!"

"If you are angry I will say no more, of course. I liked him because he loved the poor. He was odd, and I am also very odd. I am sorry that he is proved to be wicked. I think that in future some one should tell me whom I am to like, and whom I am to dislike. I want guidance sadly."

"I think you do."

"Well, I will be amenable to it. I am to stay here, all alone, and manage matters?"

"That is what we wish you to do."

"Then, of course, I will do it."

## CHAPTER XXIII.

### SIR LIONEL COMES TO SHEEPSDEN.

HERE was but little summer that year. Nothing but wild, sweeping, westerly rains, folding Sheepsden in the mist of the low carrying cloud, and rushing among the elms about the house, and moaning in the fir-trees aloft on the summit of the down. A wild and melancholy season, only made more melancholy and more tragical by the news from France, which got more and more lamentable as time went on. Mathilde had to pass this time alone at Sheepsden, with no other domestic company than Mrs. Bone and William the Silent; for Father Martin and Adèle were away to Dinort.

She heard of them now and then. Madame D'Isigny of St. Catherine's, with whom Adèle was staying, was lady visitor of La Garaye, and used to go once a month to see how the blind and the imbecile were getting on there. Adèle wrote to her that these monthly inspections of the hospital of La Garaye were the pleasantest days she had; and adding that her aunt, the Abbess of St. Catherine's, was wonderfully well qualified for her office of inspector of the "aveugles" and "imbéciles," seeing that she was more than half blind and utterly imbecile herself. Adèle did not add the fact that Louis de Valognes alway met them at these gatherings, but Father Martin did; and Mathilde fully understood that the match between De Valognes and Adèle was merely a thing of time. So when she actually heard that it had taken place, she was not so very much put out; for—well, she had got some good advice, other than Father Martin's, before the marriage took place.

Things seemed to be going on pretty comfortably at St. Malo, Dinort, and La Garaye; things, however, were not quite so comfortable at Dinan. We will get through our friend Mathilde's correspondence in these few months before we begin with her life during that time. She got one letter, spotted with tears, from Adèle, in which that young lady began, as usual, by wishing she had never been born, and ended by wishing that she was dead. These were the only two coherent propositions in the whole letter. The middle and incoherent part of it was taken up with vague denunciations of her mother, Madame of Dinan, and of Mathilde herself. Mathilde was very much puzzled, and wondered what she *could* have done, but was somewhat enlightened by the letter of Father Martin which came by the same post. It appeared that Madame the Lady Abbess of St. Catherine's had been holding her monthly inspection in the garden of La Garaye (a fête, I suspect, very similar to our present school fêtes, though without croquet), when Madame D'Isigny, the terrible Lady of Dinan, had appeared, and had, as Father Martin put it, "conducted herself as usual." She had, it appeared, used those great powers of objurgation alluded to by old Lady Somers, with such remarkable force and dexterity, that she had left every woman on the ground in tears, except Adèle, the principal victim, who was in hysterics. Madame D'Isigny, it seemed, had used such dreadful language to her daughter Adèle, about her desertion of a real man like Sir Lionel Somers, for a miserable creature like De Valognes (who was present); had scolded also so fearfully about her husband's political tergiversation; about the Lady Abbess of St. Catherine's trying to make up her quarrel about the *corvée* with the future Marquis de Valognes; about the shameful way in which Mathilde had been treated by that future Marquis, bosom-friend of the double-dyed Lafayettist, André Desilles; that Adèle had been carried into the hospital of La Garaye in a swoon. After which Madame of Dinan had gone back to Dinan triumphant.

After this plain proof that her dear mother's temper was by no means improving, Mathilde came to the conclusion that she was just as well where she was. Still it was dull for many reasons. Her relations with William, the servant, and Mrs. Bone, the housekeeper, were as pleasant as ever. She was very fond of them, and they loved her. All that was well. These three had to consult every morning about the farm, about the household expenses, about the horses, about the fowls, and after the consultation she gave her orders, which they obeyed with goodwill and diligence. As being a thing of the past, as being a thing which will never be seen again, this diligent, trustful, affectionate obedience after consultation is worthy of notice, just in passing. However, she got things *done*, which is more than we can do now; and so found that she, with two common, honest souls to help her, could make the microcosm of Sheepsden spin on better than ever.

But it was dull. William and Mrs. Bone were not "company." She found that out in the first fortnight. Their talk was, first, about the scandals among the gentry, which she always stopped at once; second, about the scandals among the farmers and lower classes, which she stopped also; and thirdly, about agricultural prospects and the health of horses, which she let go on, but which bored her. It was very dull for her, and it rained so persistently, that her precious red umbrella seemed to be a part of herself; and having borrowed Mrs. Bone's English Bible, she read the account of Noah's flood with dismay.

She knew that she was doing wrong in reading this Bible of Mrs. Bone's. She was perfectly aware that Father Martin would be angry with her for doing so. But she was bored, and she read it. She could confess and have absolution for having done so hereafter. She may be excused for such a sin, considering how dull it was for her, and that she had no spiritual director.

She read it with a hungry soul, and put her old book aside; for here, in this forbidden Bible she found every phase of her soul satisfied. "Why have they kept it from me?" she said; and there was no answer.

Dull, very dull, at Sheepsden; long days spent on the farm and among the poor; long evenings with Mrs. Bone and William. Mathilde was a thorough *radical*. She had absolutely no class prejudices whatever. She would as soon sit with a rheumatic old woman as she would with a duchess. She began to sit with the old women and gossip with them. And her Catholic language was half forgotten, and some of the poor whom she habitually relieved and attended to were Wesleyans and Independents; and after a very short time it seemed to her that their formulas were nearly as attractive, nearly as spiritual as her own, and moreover that they were wonderfully similar.

The necessity for public worship which had lain dormant so long, but had been aroused again by the ministrations of Father Martin, was very strongly felt by her. Still she had a dislike to appear at the church where she would be seen by people in her own rank of life, and set down as a renegade. She spent her first Sunday or two of freedom among the fields.

It was on a very wet Sunday when she wandered solitary among the lonely lanes, in one of the remotest of them—one which was deeply shadowed by over-arching elms, deeply rutted with the winter's rains, and which ended in the sudden, abrupt down. She had just made up her mind to climb the down, and enjoy herself three hundred feet aloft, alone among the driving mist, when she paused and listened with eager curiosity.

It was the sound of many voices singing a hymn to a simple and easy, yet bold and majestic tune. They sang the first verse, as she listened, and there was silence; then they took up the harmony again with still more strength, precision, and simplicity. Not only was the effect of the music itself inexpressibly fine, with the adjuncts of wild weather and solitude; but the words of the hymn, touched, with a hand quite uncultivated, on the highest and deepest spiritual questions—the immortality of the soul and the ultimate mercy of the Deity. Rude as the words were, they were purely religious; that is to say, they involved humble inquiry of God for something more than He has revealed, which is the basis of all the higher forms of religion. I should say that even a really thoughtful Roman Catholic\* would not deny this position.

> Thou wilt not leave my soul
>   To perish in the dust;
> It lives in thy control,
>   Thou canst not be unjust.
>
> The more my spirit sees
>   Of Thee and of Thy ways,
> The more my soul agrees
>   To sing Thee songs of praise.
>
> Do with me as Thou wilt,
>   I trust alone in Thee;
> Thou knowest all my guilt,
>   Yet Thou wilt pardon me.

She was aroused, interested, nay, almost excited. She had read and loved legends of travelling knights in their adventures coming on secret romantic little chapels, where a few monks, in

---

\* I should hope not the author of "Lead, kindly light."

the midst of the lonely woods and the wintry weather, were singing God's praises amidst the surrounding desolation; and she had read of, and, radical as she was, had loved and admired the Scottish Cameronians, singing their wild hymns in unison, beneath the solemn crags of Wardlaw and Cairntable, until the melody was extinguished amidst the shattering fire of Claverhouse's carbines. Somehow she seemed to have found in her lonely summer ramble some adventure of this kind; for she was of that romantic nature from which come our martyrs, and she went on with her adventure.

Just round the end of the lane she found a little chapel, from which the singing came. Without thinking for one instant of her duty as a Catholic, or of what Father Martin would say, she quietly passed inside the doorway, just as the singing ended, and sat down.

No one seemed to notice her, though there were many there whom she knew. As she passed in, with the instinct of many years, she looked to the right for the stoup, but seeing nothing but an alms box, only crossed herself, and bowed her knee slightly. The moment afterwards she remembered that she was among extreme Protestants, and had given offence; but she sat down, and no one seemed to see her.

The minister of this little tabernacle among the English hills was a very young man, dark, atrabilarious, fanatic in appearance, but of extraordinary beauty, and evidently not long for this world. The large bold eyes, the sunken face, the prominent nose, the thin lips, and the melancholy expression of his whole face, told of consumption. She saw before her, in that young man, the highest type of the saints of her own Church; and while she looked on him, pitied him, he began to pray extempore.

And his prayer took this form: it was an address to his congregation about the infinite mercy and goodness of God. There was very little direct petition whatever. It seemed as though he merely wished to put the great goodness of God before his congregation. The only direct petition came at the end of the prayer, and Mathilde knew that it alluded to her. Here this young man made a direct personal appeal to the Deity, "Other sheep you have not of this fold, whose good works and whose labours of love we have known. In Thy hands we leave them.

Grant, then, that we may sit with them in Thy kingdom." And all the simple folks said, "Amen," for she was well known among them.

Then he preached, but not at Mathilde the Papist. She was utterly beneath him now. His text was the casting down of the golden crowns; and believing in his inmost soul that his own glory was near at hand, he soared away into an atmosphere almost as high as St. John's. Under the spell of his rude eloquence, these starved and storm-beaten Dorsetshire hinds became kings and princes, with an inheritance, after death, grander, infinitely grander and more glorious than Hapsburgh, Hohenzollern, or Hanover dared dream of. And you wonder at the power of these men! Mathilde by degrees raised her head, and watched his face; but she was nothing to him. She believed, as all Catholics do, every word that he said; and she was forced to confess that she had never heard a grander sermon. Every word of it suited her. She seemed as he went on to be rising into a clearer atmosphere every moment; every sentence roused her to the contemplation of some noble deed. But at his peroration she bowed down her head and wept.

"My time is short with you. I am going, in a very short time, to this unutterable glory of which I have been speaking. And you will weep and lament for me. Why for *me!* I can understand your weeping for yourselves; but I am at a loss to conceive why you should weep for me in glory. Yet I could weep myself even in glory, for my faith is not perfect. Tears will be wiped away from all eyes I *know*, yet see what an imperfect worm I am. I will lay my poor soul bare before you. I find no assurance in the Book that those who have loved on this earth will meet again. And without the wife of my bosom, what will glory be to me? Yet I trust. Yet I trust."

Mathilde being next the door, was forced of course to go out first, which she did with her head bent modestly. Some one's hand, the hand of some one who stood before her and opposed her passage, was laid on her shoulder, and she looked up into the frank, genial face of Sir Lionel Somers.

"Oh, dear!" she said, eagerly and quickly in French, "I am so very glad to see you. I am so very lonely. However did you come here?"

"I followed you. I came to see you at Sheepsden, and got your general route; asking such few as were about, I followed you, never dreaming that you could be in the Dissenting Chapel."

"I suppose that I have done very wrong," said Mathilde, "but I must complete my crime. There stands the minister, and I must go and thank him."

"I will introduce you," said Sir Lionel. "He is an old friend of mine."

The young man was standing on one side with his young bride, for, like most other pure and enthusiastic young men, he had married young. The wife was a gentle, pretty-looking, delicate creature, and was looking anxiously up into her husband's face, which, now the excitement of preaching was over, was ghastly and wan, but very handsome. Sir Lionel took Mathilde up to them, and said,—

"Evans, let me introduce a young French lady of the high nobility, who wishes to thank you for your sermon."

"I know mademoiselle very well," he said very respectfully. "I, though coming from a little distance, have known of Mademoiselle's good works, and her labours in the Lord."

"You made me weep profoundly, monsieur," said Mathilde in a downright manner. "And I am grateful to you. I am hard-hearted, and not easily moved to tears. Will you allow me to shake hands with you?"

But to her surprise and Sir Lionel's, Mr. Evans hung back and hesitated. They thought that it was because she was a Roman Catholic, until he stammered out,—

"I beg your pardon, Sir Lionel; but I think I should wish you to explain to mademoiselle that I—I am only a common village shoemaker, and that I return to my bench to-morrow. I doubt," he added, again hesitating, and in perfect humble simplicity, "that her ladyship does not understand that."

"Why, then, this," said Mathilde, brightening up, "is more beautiful than all. This brings us back to the time when there were no trained priests at all, and they were all carpenters, fishermen, and tentmakers. I am backsliding more and more," she said, smiling on Sir Lionel. "All this will go to Father Martin, and my penances will be terrible. *Now*, sir, will you shake hands?"

When they had all four done so, and were at ease among one another, Sir Lionel asked Evans which way he was going.

"I preach at Pimperne to-night, Sir Lionel; and walk back over the Down afterwards. I have a very important order to execute to-morrow, which must be done. I am heeling and soling Sir Arthur Martin's shooting-boots. Disappoint him, and I lose his servants' custom; lose that, and I lose half my trade. I and my wife must walk home to-night."

"Il ne faut pas," said Mathilde, emphatically. "Trente mille fois, il ne faut pas," and so on to the amount of the half of one of these pages in French, partly to herself and partly to Sir Lionel. Then she got hold of Mrs. Evans and walked on before.

Sir Lionel said, when she had done:

"Mademoiselle D'Isigny says, Evans, that she will not hear for one moment of such an arrangement as yours. She declares that it is perfectly monstrous of you to pull your wife over the Down after dark in such naughty weather, and insists that you and Mrs. Evans shall sup and sleep at Sheepsden, and be driven over in the morning. Just look at your wife, man, and be reasonable."

Indeed, she was but a delicate little thing, and there was another life beside hers. Sir Lionel had touched him.

"But it is a Papist house, Sir Lionel; and I am not without my enemies."

"Do an honest thing like an honest man, and let your enemies be——" not scattered—something worse. For it was a coarser age than ours; and yet there were gentlemen on the earth in those days, too.

Evans still hesitated.

"See here, then," said Sir Lionel; "I will sup there myself to countenance you."

"Your character for Protestantism does not stand very high in the Valley just now, Sir Lionel," said Evans, somewhat slyly. "However, I will come, for the wife's sake. We turn off here."

Mrs. Evans joined him, and Sir Lionel and Mathilde were left standing in the road together.

"You have done a fine thing," he said, "asking a red-hot

Primitive Methodist home to Sheepsden! You are a nice young lady to be left in care of your father's house!"

Mathilde began nodding her head rapidly: she nodded it till she was tired, but she never said anything; yet these nods were made by a Frenchwoman, and so were as good as words.

"Your father will be furious."

A nod, which somehow—(who is able to analyse French gesticulation?)—expressed, with raised eyebrows, a scared acquiescence.

"Father Martin will be very angry."

Another nod, perhaps with a slight turning of the head on one side, and a trifle of a shrug of the shoulders, as if she would say, "That is no such terrible matter."

"Adèle will laugh at you for ever about it. She has the whip-hand of you now. You, so particular! You, so religious! You, so Catholically correct!"

A nod, a shrug, a raising of the eyebrows, and, superadded, a slight shaking of the sides, as though of a laughter which never got reflected on the face.

"You have committed a terrible indiscretion. I will tell you what I think will be best. Let me come home with you to Sheepsden, and help you to entertain these people. It will save a great deal of scandal," continued this consummate hypocrite.

"*Allons!*" said Mathilde, taking his arm, and "right-abouting" him up the lane towards Sheepsden "This is a fine way to save scandal, and you are a fine man to save it. You are in trouble now with the orthodox, on account of us Catholics; now you will be in trouble once more with the orthodox, for receiving Dissenters. It is all trouble together, Lionel, is it not? But let us walk fast, for I will have a good supper for my shoemaker. See here, now! I complain of Adèle for her indiscretions. She is more often indiscreet than I. But when I *am* indiscreet, I show a greater genius for it than she. She never equalled this."

Sir Lionel said, "I believe you are the best little soul in the world," and bent down and kissed her, just as the Rector came swiftly round the corner of the lane, on the way to reading prayers to some old people in an outlying dame's school, in red-hot argument with the radical master-sweep from Stourminster

Marshall, on the subject of the last church-rate.  These two, being in haste, passed on with only a salutation; and Sir Lionel, reflecting about his public recognition of Evans, the dissenting minister, set down, in the account-book of his mind, 800*l.* extra towards his next election expenses.

When they got comfortably inside the screen at Sheepsden, Mathilde left him for a time with a book, while she assisted, or rather directed, Mrs. Bone to get supper.  He had not read long, by M. D'Isigny's lamp, when a very quiet, *good* voice said to him, " I ask your pardon, Sir Lionel ; but will you allow me to take off your boots, and give you shoes ? "

It was William who spoke.  He had a sort of unreasonable dislike of this young man ; but he said " Yes," and William knelt down.

When his head was under the lamp, Sir Lionel saw what a really noble head it was.  The down-going light from the lamp threw but few shadows on the face, because the face was so strong that in the lower part it caught more light than shade.  It was a nice, honest face to look at; and Sir Lionel thought, or imagined, that he should like to stand well with every one in this establishment, and so he spoke to this objectionable William.

" You have a good place here ? "

" Yes, your honour."

" You come of a good stock.  I hope you will be faithful to Mademoiselle.  Here is a guinea for you."

" I will be faithful to M. D'Isigny and his daughter without a guinea, your honour."

" Will you not take this one ? "

" Thank your honour, no.  There was trouble about a guinea before between you and me, and I nearly lost my place through it."

" Well, but take this one and make friends again."

There was no resisting this, and William was won.  We can say no more about him just now.  We only record the fact, that Sir Lionel could not have bought him for fifty guineas, but won him with one, which he at once expended—buying Mrs. Bone a grey silk gown for fifteen shillings, and his sweetheart, Awdrey, a cotton print for six.

Then Evans came, and they had a pleasant evening, with conversation, noticeable among which was this :

"I wish I had learnt the French language," said Evans. "If I had known what was going to happen, nothing should have prevented me."

Mathilde, thinking he meant some compliment to her, asked—"Why?"

"Because, my lady, I would have gone as a missionary to France, and have done vast good among the people. Two dozen such as I could have stopped this revolution. Primitive Methodism is the religion of the poor, and they have not got it in France."

"Our parish clergy—at least, in my Brittany," said Mathilde, "are just as simple, as good, as devoted as yourself, sir. I can pay them no higher compliment, sir. The people in Brittany will follow their priests to the death. You say they have not got Methodism. That is true; but they have priests who understand every thought and wish of theirs, as well as you do those of your own sect; and, sir, they will die for them."

"I do not doubt it, my lady; you should know. This good Father Martin of whom I have heard is one of them. The Abbé de Firmont, lately at Lulworth, is another."

"Edgeworth is a good fellow," interposed Sir Lionel—"Irish, but good." *

---

* The French call him "de Firmont," the English Abbé Edgeworth. He was the man who was on the scaffold with Louis XVI. I have heard it surmised that he was actually *uncle* to the great Miss Edgeworth, of Edgeworth's-town. But if so, how did he get his territorial title of "De Firmont"? Surely some correspondent of SYLVANUS URBAN can set us right here.—H.K.

This challenge in the GENTLEMAN'S MAGAZINE was answered by a lady well known for her knowledge of French literature, in the following most interesting note:—

"MR. URBAN,—Having observed in your September number, p. 286, that Mr. Henry Kingsley, alluding in the course of his novel, 'Mademoiselle Mathilde,' to the Abbé Edgeworth, makes a foot-note inquiry as to how that ecclesiastic obtained his territorial title, 'De Firmont,' I think it possible that an answer to that question contained in the following brief statement, may not be unwelcome to some of your readers, more especially as it involves one or two other points referred to by Mr. Henry Kingsley with regard to 'the man who was on the scaffold with Louis XVI.'

"Henry Allen Edgeworth, son of Essex Edgeworth, and said by French biographers to have been *cousin* to 'the great Miss Edgeworth,' was born at Edgeworth-town in 1745. His father, a beneficed clergyman of the

"But is it the same in Paris?" asked Mr. Evans, after the interruption.

"Je ne suis pas une Parisienne, frivole, moqueuse, vaine, et inconstante," said Mathilde emphatically. "Je suis habitante de l'excellente Bretagne. I ask your pardon for speaking French. Go on, sir."

"I would not speak of religious Brittany," said Evans. "I would not disturb their faith *there;* but I think that my pure Methodism, preached with unction among the priest-ridden population in Paris, would have done great things."

"Protestantism has not flourished in Paris, sir," said Mathilde.

Church of England, having inherited a certain estate in Ireland, was called 'Edgeworth of Fairy Mount;' but when Essex Edgeworth became a convert to the Roman Catholic faith, and consequently made his permanent residence at Toulouse, his Irish territorial title lapsed into 'De Firmont.' Henry, Essex Edgeworth's son, was educated in France, first at Toulouse, and afterwards at the Sorbonne. When ordained priest, he entered the fraternity of 'Les Missions Étrangères' in Paris, and became Confessor to Madame Elisabeth, who introduced him to her brother Louis XVI. That monarch's earnest appreciation of this ecclesiastic's character was best evinced on the scaffold; but after the king's execution, so imminent was the danger to which the loyal Abbé Edgeworth de Firmont was exposed, that he dwelt in seclusion at Choisy, under the name of 'Essex,' until enabled to escape in disguise to England. There, as afterwards at Mittau and elsewhere, the Abbé Edgeworth de Firmont was entitled to all honour; but when the second William Pitt generously desired him to accept a pension, he refused it. By special request of Louis XVIII. at Blankenbourg, he conveyed the order of the 'Saint Esprit' to Paul, Emperor of Russia, but although the best friend of the exiled royal family of France, he declined every personal mark of distinction which princes more prosperous at that time than those of France would fain have conferred on him, and devoted himself to the service of the friendless sick and poor. In the summer of 1807, the Abbé Edgeworth de Firmont died of a fever caught in the discharge of his spiritual duties at the Military Hospital of Mittau. Louis XVIII. composed a Latin epitaph in honour of that name, concerning which I have thus presumed to address you.*—I am, &c.,

"A. E. C."

---

* "Letters of the Abbé Edgeworth, with a sketch of his life prefixed, were printed, one vol., 8vo, in Paris, 1818. The compilation was originally made by the Abbé himself at the urgent request of Louis XVIII. Brief notices of his life are also to be found in the 'Nouvelle Biographie Générale,' and the 'Biographie des Contemporains,' and in other works more inaccessible to the public, but of equal value to French students.—A. E. C."

"You dream, you dream, my good Evans. The history of the whole thing is that they want an equalization of property," said Sir Lionel.

"Quite naturally," said Evans. "*We* are Socialist, you know."

"The deuce you are!" said Sir Lionel. "Here is pretty company in exchange for my good nature."

"*Theoretically*," replied Evans.

"Not practically, you are quite sure," replied Sir Lionel. "Ashurst is, of course, at your service."

"Theoretically, sir, only," said Evans, "as in the primitive Church. It is only a principle of ours, carried into practice against the law only among a select few of ourselves. We are subservient to all rulers and magistrates. For the time of the prince of the power of the air is not passed, and will not pass, sir, for seventy weeks of years."

"Bedlam! Bedlam! and once more Bedlam! There never was a better fellow than that, and yet, give him his head, he will talk himself into as great a state of nonsense as D'Isigny," said Sir Lionel, as he walked home to Ashurst over the Down. "Everybody is mad, and, upon my honour, I am as mad as ten hatters myself—madder. It would be very nice, but it would be so ridiculous. Nevertheless, she is extremely charming."

Then he walked above a mile in deep thought, after which he took up once more the theme that every one was mad, and spoke it out aloud among the dripping junipers,—

"We are all going mad together. Every man is saying, with an air of calm conviction, the first thing which comes into his head, and quarrelling with every one else who don't agree with him. This, I take it, is the ultimate outcome of Whiggery. I can understand the Tory position, and I can understand the Democratic, but, upon my word and honour, I cannot understand ours. We began removing the landmarks, after all. Nothing it seems is, by our creed, to be ultimately *sacred* except 'property.' I'll be hanged if I see why. Why, any brute might get property. It seems to me the first thing to go instead of the last. The advanced people in our party are pitching every formula to the winds except this 'property.' The prestige of birth is gone; the religion of the land is going, —both bad things, but not so bad as this last one, which is, after all, the great evil of the land.  I am getting somewhat sick of this rosewater Whiggery ; D'Isigny has cured me, I suppose. He is a born Whig—a man who will calmly pull to pieces the old state of things, quietly advance every argument which logically leads to pure democracy, and then expect that everything is to go on exactly as it was before.  I'll be hanged if I don't turn Tory—they *do* know what they are about ; or Democrat—they also know what they are about.  I will wait and think."

The Stour Valley people were right in saying that Sir Lionel had got very unsettled in his opinions since he had been so much at Sheepsden, and that he never would be the man his father was.  Both propositions were undeniably true.  That he might be a better and nobler man than his father, the old fox-hunting baronet, they never thought.  They meant that he was going the wrong way altogether.  He had first slid away from the path of righteous Philistines by engaging himself to a French woman.  Then he had encouraged Papists, and brought over the abomination of desolation in the shape of Popish vestments in his curricle from Lulworth.  Lastly, he had been known, in a public manner, to go to a dissenting place of worship in company with a Popish young lady, to walk home scandalously alone with her, and to assist at the entertaining at supper of a dangerously democratic nonconformist cobbler. His sins were so great, so innumerable, and withal so complicated, that no one could exactly lay hold of them.  All parties, however, agreed that he had broken loose from every tie, and was going to the devil.  I am not wise enough to say whether toleration is a good thing or a bad thing.  I have only to say that there was none of it in the Stour Valley in 1789.

The Rector, best of men, turned against him.  He did not mind Sir Lionel's *faux pas* about the vestments from Lulworth ; that was in a way respectable.  There were Howards, Talbots, Petres, Welds—people of the most undeniable respectability— who still, unhappily, clung to the more ancient form of faith. This indiscretion of Sir Lionel's was tolerable ; the last one was, however, intolerable and *un*gentlemanly, after all the Rector's long-continued efforts to "uproot dissent" in the parish ; after he had so frequently undergone the fatigue of preaching for nearly an hour at a time against it (after having previously murdered our noble Liturgy by reading that extraordinary congeries of prayers, lasting an hour and a half, and which they are pleased to call Morning Service); after all these sacrifices, his beloved Lionel, his Absalom, had taken up, in a scandalously open manner, with a dangerous dissenting cobbler, and had "sat at meat with him," as the Rector put it, who got the more Scriptural as he got the more angry.

"Angry!" I beg pardon—I should have said "hurt." The Rector was friendly with him still, met him as of old, and called him "My dear Lionel;" deferred to him in every way; was more polite than ever; begged him, by note, to undertake once more the responsibility of being his churchwarden for another year; but he declined his invitations to dinner, and, what showed his displeasure more strongly, refused formerly, through the gamekeeper, to fish in his water.

As for the squires and baronets in the Valley, they were deeply angry with him. He had allowed his bride to be taken away from him by a Frenchman, and no one had been shot (not that any one of them dared give a Somers the white feather), and "Whig and Tory all agreed" as the song goes, that he had no principles whatever. He was a hunted man, almost without a backer and without a refuge except his own house.

But not quite. He *had* a backer—a backer that few of them dared face, old and quiet as she was—his own mother, Lady Somers. This strenuous old lady suddenly grew twenty years younger, and offered battle-royal to the combined forces of the Valley. When the Rector committed the overt act of treason, of refusing to fish in Sir Lionel's water, she wrote him a note regretting that she should be unable to receive him in future, and requesting that her prayer-books and hymn-books should be delivered out of the family pew to the bearer. Old Lady Morton, who came cackling over to her with the tale of Sir Lionel's misdoings, she *did* receive. What passed we don't know; but it would almost seem as though gentle Lady Somers had taken a leaf out of the book of her old schoolfellow, Madame D'Isigny of Dinan, for Lady Morton was observed to be in tears when she went away.

What had passed between son and mother? what made her fight his battle so furiously, defying scandal, the Valley, and the Rector? Who knows?

He had one backer, and he also had one refuge, Sheepsden; he was always there now. Reader, if you chance to be a man, young, handsome, clever, gentle, and agreeable,—just for mere experiment sake,—get into the habit of sitting alone, before the fire, with one of the most beautiful, charming, and original women you ever met in your life, keeping your head close to hers, talking in a low voice of all things in heaven and earth; and then see what will happen to you. Much the same, I doubt, as happened to Sir Lionel Somers.

Again, my dear reader, if you happen to be a woman, just let us reverse the former position. Suppose that you are one of the most beautiful, charming, and original women ever met with (as of course you are),—just for mere experiment's sake,—get into the habit of sitting alone, before the fire, with a young, handsome, clever, gentle, and agreeable man, keeping your head close to his, and talking of all things in heaven and earth; and then see what will happen to *you*. Much the same, I doubt, as happened to Mathilde.

And if you are both of you all alone, and have both just been irritated and insulted by a scandalous deception, why then *tant mieux* or *tant pis*, as the matter ultimately turns out.

There was a ghost at Ashurst, which always appeared, said the old women, to the Somers of the time, when loss or misfortune threatened him. The traditions of the ghost were, however, very dim, because, probably, the Somers had been a lucky family ever since they had paid " Non-such James," their thousand pounds for their baronetcy; and so the ghost's services had not been required. Sir Lionel, sitting over the fire late one night this autumn, after returning from Sheepsden, actually thought that he had seen this ghost for a moment; but it was only his grey-headed old mother, in her chamber costume, who came towards him along the dark hall, with the light of her solitary candle flickering on her withered old face, and who said,—

"I believe it is as I wished it to be from the first. What on earth you could ever have seen in that girl Adèle, I am at a loss to conceive."

And Sir Lionel was silent. For Adèle, with all her petulance and frivolity, was a most irresistible little creature; and the memory of her was strong on him that night.

## CHAPTER XXIV.

### LA GARAYE.

HE deep green of the boscage of the Brittany woods was deeper in the year 1789 than it is now. In the pre-revolutionary times, before the woods were cut down, the oak and the elm grew and flourished; now, one sees little except poplar and other quick-growing colourless trees, planted to hide the effect of revolutionary violence. France in the evil old times was green; now, in the better times, she is grey: like the head of one who has passed through a great affliction.

It was a late and wet season, and the green leaves still hung bravely to the trees. In the old oak and elm time there was the old autumnal silence in the woods; now, in the poplar age, each tree rustles and whispers suspiciously to every breath of wind. In the old time the thickly-pleached elms and oaks kept the sound of the coming storm from the shepherd, until the roar and crash came on him together; in the new, the tossing, up-turning leaves of the poplars give him better warning. In the old time news travelled slowly; it flies fast enough now.

It was a dripping, dull day in November, when André Desilles turned out of the quiet country road, and entered the long-drawn chestnut avenue which led, and leads still, to La Garaye. Nature was wrapped in steaming, rotting silence; no sound was to be heard beyond the drip of the mist from the trees, the downward fluttering of a leaf, or the rattle of a ripe chestnut, as it fell upon the sodden turf beneath among the rapidly springing autumnal fungi. Hopeless decay was all around him, and one dared not in that year think too much of what spring would bring; and yet there was a look about the whole man which savoured far more of April than of November.

He was dressed carefully and beautifully, as he always was, but now in civilian's clothes, of as perfect cut as those of his friend Louis de Valognes, but rather less dandified. His three-cornered hat, though small and jauntily worn, was untrimmed, and he wore no powder, his hair being done in a carefully tied club. The cape of his riding-coat added breadth to his otherwise powerful figure, and the whole of that very becoming garment showed off his noble carriage to perfection.

His top-boots were faultless in make, yet thick and strong, and although on foot, he carried the universal riding-whip of those times in his hand. A practised eye could see that he was perfectly dressed, but that he was dressed for travelling. A practised eye might also see that there was expectation, if not hope, in every movement of his carriage.

So he entered the long avenue of La Garaye, the whole vista of which was empty, save that far before him, among the dull autumnal lights and shadows, a priest walked swiftly with fluttering cassock—a hard, black figure among the decaying greens.

"A priest everywhere," said Desilles, laughing a low and gentle laugh, which might tell a tale to a lover. "Well, I will give you a good start, my worthy father, whoever you are. Priests are not exactly good company just now. They have mainly brought this business about, and now they seem inclined to drive one mad by jeremiads over their own handy-work."

So he let the priest flutter on round the corner, out of sight, before he quickened his pace. If he had known that it was Father Martin, the man of all others he wished to meet, he would have run after him as hard as he could; but he did not, and so missed the opportunity of getting Father Martin alone. Which was a great pity.

His thoughts, as he walked down the avenue among the dropping chestnuts and the springing fungi? They began here and ended here. "It is impossible that I have miscalculated—it is totally and entirely impossible." The reader will not be puzzled for many minutes.

So he came out into the quaint square flower-garden in front of the Château of La Garaye. It was then, as far as I can make out, from examination of the ruins, a largish mansion house, dating probably from the early part of the 16th century, superadded to some heavy older Norman work. The few windows which remain are what are loosely called "Tudor," but with wonderfully light and thin mullions. What André Desilles saw, as he debouched among the flower-beds, was a fine enough *façade* of yellowish white stone, not very much unlike a small piece of Bramshill House (if you happen to know it), in point of architecture, but lighter and finer. I turn to Oxford and Cambridge for an illustration, and can find none, either in colour or form. There are pieces at Audley End more like it than anything I have seen.

In the centre of this *façade* was an entrance porch, and in front of it lay a square flower-garden, with turf walks among the beautifully-kept flower-beds. In these flower-beds, there grew at that time of the year the old Michaelmas daisy, and a brother flower, the Aster Novæ Angliæ; the chrysanthemum also, introduced in 1764 in its earlier and more uncultivated form, was here. It may interest some of my readers to know this; and I think they will not find me wrong.

I calculate on my readers knowing that La Garaye was a great hospital for the imbecile and blind; and, also, that they have read Mrs. Norton's noble poem about it. With all this I have nothing to do; it has been done better by another hand. I have only to do with what André Desilles saw.

The rain poured steadily and heavily down; so steadily that André himself thought of shelter. He knew perfectly well that this was the monthly *fête*-day at La Garaye, and supposed that they would all be enjoying themselves in-doors. He was right so far. There was not a soul in the garden but three, and they stood there, in front of the porch, without umbrellas.

Louis de Valognes and his bride Adèle, likewise a religious woman of mark in a wimple. Adèle had got in under the cape of her husband's redingote, and was pretty well off, considering. Louis had on his very best clothes, but did not look impressive. The rain was weeping off the swan's down in his hat, and making maps on his white buckskin breeches. As for the eminent religious woman, she was in a worse case than either. The rain had taken all the starch out of her wimple, and her wimple had fallen over her nose; and from the tip of her nose the rain dropped steadily on to the ground. Yet there they stood.

"My dearly beloved souls," said André Desilles, coming up to them, "I thought I should never see you any more."

Louis de Valognes stretched out his hand. Adèle put her lovely little face out from under the cape of her husband's redingote, with her beautiful hair all rumpled, tumbled, and wet, and said, "And indeed we thought that we should never see *you* any more; and that you had given up those who love you best in this world." After which she retired under the cape of the redingote again.

"I am so glad to see you," said Louis de Valognes. "You know the Lady Abbess of St. Catherine's." And he bowed towards the religious lady with the rain running off her nose.

"I beg a hundred thousand pardons," said André Desilles; "but to tell you the truth, I did not recognise Madame D'Isigny —I ought to say the Lady Abbess of St. Catherine's. My dear madame—I mean, my Lady Mother—are you not very wet? Let us go in-doors."

"Tell him," said the Lady Abbess, solemnly.

"The fact is, my dear André," said Louis de Valognes, "that Father Martin is in-doors, giving the galette and cider to the patients."

"Father Martin!" said Desilles,—"the very man I want to see."

"Yes; but he is being assisted by Madame D'Isigny of Dinan, which accounts for our standing out in the rain."

"The devil!" said André Desilles. "But look here! Madame of St. Catherine's must not be kept out here in the wet. You are without resource, you. Go into the *conciergerie* there, and dry the wimple of Madame. You are without resource."

"She will come there," said the Lady Abbess, extending her arms before her with her fingers stretched out. "She will come there. And what matters a little more or less rheumatism to a poor old woman who has given her life to religion? Let us stay in the rain. She will not find me here."

However, André's suggestion of taking the Lady Abbess to the *conciergerie* was acted on, and André Desilles went into the refectory and confronted Madame of Dinan.

What passed is not on record. André came to them in the *conciergerie* after a time, looking old and thoughtful. "I don't think she will come here," he said. "She *may*, but I don't think she will. If she does, we can get out by that door into the corridor, and lock it after us."

Louis and Adèle had got off the Lady Abbess' wimple, and were drying it: she sat before the fire, drying her bald scanty old hair. Louis said, "Have you had a quarrel?" and André said, "It takes two people to make a quarrel; and I, for my part, said nothing. I know more about the faults of my character than I did a quarter of an hour ago. That is all. Consider that a frank friend is a great possession."

"Lock the door!" cried out Madame the Abbess, starting up in extreme perturbation, with the steam coming from her grey old hair. "Lock the door, and put something against it. I hear her voice. She is coming here. Stand between me and her, and I will give you each a *novena*. Think of that, dear young friends. *Apage, Satanas!* where is my rosemary—I mean rosary?* Plenary indulgence, three *novenas*, and in case of death, masses. Think of it, and lock the door!"

They were indeed scarcely less alarmed than the poor old Abbess. The dextrous André Desilles just had time to lock the door before it was beaten violently on the outside, and a terrible hoarse voice said:—

"Come out, you half-hearted revolutionist, and face an Englishwoman! Come out, you poor miserable drenched old Abbess, and let me scold you! Come out, you Americanized Lafayettist, André Desilles, and hear your doom from a witch! Come out, thou wretched dandy-bridegroom, De Valognes, and bring thy silly bride, married on the vigil of the destruction of Sodom! Hah! you sit cowering there silent, and dare not face Old Cassandra. Help me to beat this door down, Father Martin. You inside there! What have you done with Mathilde?" (here she beat at the door again). "What have you done with the only individual of the family worthy of more than the name of animal. Let us beat the door down, father."

The sharp, clear, decisive voice of Father Martin was heard next.

"Madame will gain little by that. The instincts of Madame are, in the main, right. I on the whole agree with Madame; yet it would be better for the Church and for the Throne, if Madame were dead. Madame's fury alienates all the honest souls who are wavering."

"My fury!" said the terrible hoarse voice again. "I tell you, Martin, that the Revolution *is* fury. The Revolution lies in Marat's hands and in mine. I can match his fury; but he is

---

* Romorin : Rosaire. The slip of the tongue is more absurd in English than in French.

backed, and I am not.  Well, I will leave these few frightened sheep, if you desire it."

The few frightened sheep looked out of window, and saw the awful Madame D'Isigny of Dinan get into her carriage.

She turned towards their window once or twice before she went, and they saw her clearly.  Desilles had not seen her lately until just now, and confessed his astonishment to the others.  The voice which he had heard outside the door, was like a voice from a mad-house.  The lady he saw getting into her carriage, was a well-dressed and noble-looking woman of singular beauty.  She scowled, and held her arms tightly folded across her breast, but she was to all appearance a perfect lady. He was utterly unable to connect the hoarse, rude, terrible voice and words, with the elegant lady who stept into her carriage, and with a smile made room for Father Martin beside her.

You will have to remember more than once, if you read this tale, that we are speaking of 1789, when people were wilder, fiercer, and more exasperated than now.

Let us return to our half-hearted sheep locked into the *conciergerie*.  André Desilles was the first to speak, and he said, "Well, she is gone ; and, what is more unlucky, has taken Father Martin with her.  I wished very much to speak to him. I wanted to ask him about Mathilde."

"Well," said Adèle, somewhat pertly, "we can tell you as much about her as he can."

Indeed, Adèle, you could not.  She never made a confidant of *you*.

"Is she all alone at Sheepsden?" asked André Desilles.

"All alone," they answered.  Father Martin could have answered differently, but they only spoke as they knew.

"Then look here, dear people, and Madame the Lady Abbess, also.  I wish bygones to be bygones entirely.  I do not wish to bring the past into the present.  In fact, I refuse to do so. Dear Louis, you, now so happily married to a wife in every way worthy of you, will confess that there was at one time a little confusion."

"Louis is not to be called to account for poor dear Mathilde's vanity," said Adèle, promptly and pertly.

"By no means," said André Desilles, bowing to Adèle, and thinking her on the whole the most contemptible little person he had ever seen. "But all I wish to learn is this. Is it an actual fact that Mathilde is in perfect solitude, without one single friend?"

"Such is undoubtedly the case," replied Adèle. "Louis, my dear, poke my aunt with your cane, for she is nodding off, and will have her head in the fire directly. Mathilde is, undoubtedly, all alone. She made her bed, and is lying on it."

"Adèle, be quiet," said Louis de Valognes.

"I beg your pardon, Louis," said Adèle. "I did not catch what you said."

"I said *be quiet!*" said Louis, with great emphasis.

"Certainly," said Adèle, "I will be perfectly quiet."

Louis was so very decisive in the way he said "be quiet," that she, like a thorough little coward as she was, never fought him again. However, André Desilles was not her husband, and so she revenged herself on him. If she had only had the weapons—if she had only known about Sir Lionel Somers, as Father Martin did, she might have made herself exasperatingly disagreeable to André Desilles, and moreover have saved a deal of useless trouble.

"Yes," she said, "Mathilde is absolutely alone at Sheepsden,—alone, I mean, with the groom and the housekeeper. Unless indeed, my father has gone back there."

"You know that he has not, Adèle," said Louis de Valognes, somewhat sternly.

"He had not a week ago," replied Adèle; "but he might be there by now, nevertheless."

"You have heard from M. D'Isigny, then?" said André Desilles.

"Yes, we heard yesterday," replied Adèle. "I would show you his letter; but there are allusions to you in it, and truth, for truth is in me a perfect fault, compels me to say that they were by no means complimentary."

"I am aware of M. D'Isigny's objections to me; I know them to be trivial, and I know that they might be removed by ten minutes' explanation. I do not doubt, knowing and respecting your father as I do, that they are strongly expressed. I know also, Adèle, that your father would face Satan and his companion angels single handed; but if he was driven to call for assistance, he would call on André Desilles."

"This is strange talk; you *ennuyez* me with your fallen angels!" said Adèle.

"You cannot understand it, my pretty bride. Let it go. Can I do anything for you at Sheepsden?"

"Why!" cried Adèle, laughing a shallow little laugh. "You are never going *there?*"

"Adèle, be silent," said Louis de Valognes, more emphatically than ever. "I say, be silent. André, may God go with you! You may do one thing at Sheepsden: take this kiss to Mathilde. Now let us have cheerful badinage. How about thy regiment, thou turncoat? Did you not lecture me once for going to England and leaving my regiment? Now, faithless and false, thou goest thyself."

"With regard to the Regiment du Roi," said André Desilles, with a calm, humorous smile, "it could not be much worse, and might be somewhat better. My presence has done but little— my absence may induce regret; and regret, penitence. It is at least worth a trial."

"And a journey to Sheepsden?" said Adèle, demurely.

"Precisely," said André Desilles, laughing. "Well, the Athenians regretted their Aristides. Let us hope, and laugh a little before the night comes. What a strong smell of burning! Thousand thunders! the old woman is on fire!"

In fact, the Lady Abbess had done more than dry herself, and fall asleep during the process. She had put her undergarment so near the fire that it had caught and was smouldering, sending up a handsome and hopeful little column of smoke. André and Louis had hold of her directly, and put it out. The old lady woke up, thanked them, lamented about her petticoat to them, told them what it cost, and fell to telling her beads; but Adèle, meanwhile, had started up and darted along the corridor, crying *Au feu! au feu!* until she had fallen almost fainting into the arms of a vigorous old *Sœur de Charité*. The alarm spread. The idiots began to screech and giggle; and the blind began praying, and feeling about for an exit to what had long been their home, but what they now began to believe was to be their grave.

Everything was in confusion in one moment, as would of course be the case in an establishment composed of the blind and the idiotic. I said everything—not quite everything; for there were seven well-trained Sisters of Charity, oldish women, tried for nerve and for gentleness, trained scientifically under the best doctors: religiously, with such light as they had. There were seven of these; and the Lady Superior, clearest-headed of them all, glided—a tall, dark figure—out of her room, and made order out of disorder in one instant.

"Sister Margaret and Sister Lucy, you will go to the source of the alarm, and immediately report to me. There are gentlemen in the house who will assist you. Sisters Cecilia and Anna, you will go to the blind, and keep them quiet. Sisters Veronica and Martha, you will amuse the imbeciles. Sister Elizabeth"—to the sister who was assisting Adèle—"you will continue your present avocation, and try to calm the excessive terrors of Madame de Valognes. I will go and rouse the men."

Everything was in order in five minutes. By the time that the Lady Superior had roused the hinds outside, and had followed the alarm of fire into the *conciergerie*, Madame of St. Catherine's had ceased to lament the damage to her petticoat, and was going on with her prayers. The Lady Superior pointed out respectfully to the Lady Visitor, the Abbess D'Isigny, that Madame de Valognes had raised an alarm of fire, and the Lady Abbess had piteously pulled up her serge dress, and pointed out her burnt petticoat beneath it. Meanwhile, Desilles was saying to De Valognes,—

"I don't think much of your wife's nerves, Louis. My cousin is everything to be desired; but I don't think much of her nervous system."

"She *is* nervous," said Louis.

"Most confoundedly so," said Desilles. "She will get some of us into trouble with her nerves. She would be much better in England. Nerves won't do in France just now. Tell me, what is D'Isigny doing?"

"He is hard at work at politics. You know, of course, that he is elected for States-General?"

"No. How?"

"Sieur Gaspard, of Avranches, getting sick of things generally, has been so wise as to commit suicide. D'Isigny came down at once, and—as the English say—'stood' for the place, and the baillage has elected him. He has pledged himself not to commit suicide, but what other pledges he has given I cannot say."

"Did he come here and see you, while he was so near?"

"Not he," said Louis de Valognes. "We wrote to him to ask his consent to our union, and he replied that he was not going to interfere with any arrangements we might have made for going to the devil together. That was all we could possibly have wished, you know."

"Exactly," said André Desilles. "Marries his daughter to a Marquisate and a great property, and gets the credit of having submitted to the affair unwillingly. You get, however, the Dorsetshire estates with her?"

"Yes; and you the Brittany."

"I have got neither wife nor estate yet," said André. "Tell me, then, what line of politics is D'Isigny taking? To what party does he belong?"

"To the party D'Isigny," said Louis, laughing. "He belongs to the club of the Feuillants, and they listen to him when he is not in a state of distraction, which is seldom. He has quarrelled with everyone except Mirabeau, the man he vowed to insult. They, somehow or another, have come together; but this has led to worse things."

"How, then?" asked André Desilles.

"Well, thus. Mirabeau, the younger, has an itching palm—loves money. Now, her Majesty, seeing D'Isigny and Mirabeau often together, made the mistake of offering him money. Not only made this mistake, but sent, as her ambassador, Cardinal Leroy to offer it to him."

"The devil!" said André Desilles, for the second time that day.

"I quite agree with you," said Louis de Valognes. "If genius combined with indiscretion could ruin any one, they will ruin her Majesty. The effects of this negotiation I leave to your imagination."

"You do wisely. It is inconceivable. The Queen is so clever and so politic."

"This is not a time for clever people," said Louis. "Some of the clever people will find their heads off their shoulders before long."

"I am sorry that D'Isigny is so quarrelsome. He is honest."

"It is not a time for honest people either," said Louis. "So look to *your* head."

"He is wise also," said André Desilles.

"It is scarcely a time for wise people either," said De Valognes. "I am smaller and cleverer than thou. I can see things which thou canst not. I am nearer to the earth than thou, and can see the things on the earth better. Trees like thyself will be cut down, and shrubs like me will remain and grow in a regenerated France. We will talk of other matters. Are you justified in leaving Sergeant Barbot to corrupt your regiment in your absence?"

"Barbot goes with me as my servant," said André Desilles.

"That is wise," said Louis. "I hope that he does not murder you. By the way, that William, D'Isigny's servant—who seems from Adèle's account to be another person of the same stamp—may fall out with him and box him to death."

"It is possible," said André. And he departed for Sheepsden.

## CHAPTER XXV.

### A GROUP OF OUR GRANDFATHERS.

IN those days, there used to be held at Stourminster Osborne a foolish old fair; nay, such is the persistency of human folly, that it is held there still. It was not a cattle fair, because Welsh, Hereford, and Devonshire beasts were by this time half fat on the latter math; it was not a hiring fair, for old quarter-day had passed and gone this two months. If you asked for the reason of this foolish fair, the only answer you were likely to get, was—"that it was a pleasure fair." And then, looking from the sloppy mud below to the leafless trees above, you begun to wonder.

It was held on the 4th of December, and was utterly and entirely aimless, causeless, and purposeless. In one of the most purely witty books which has been written lately—"Alice's Adventures in Wonderland"—Alice asks why they only drew things which begun with an M. The March hare puzzles her by asking, "Why not?" So I suppose that the only reason why this Stourminster Osborne fair was held, was that there was no overwhelming reason for its suppression.

There were booths in the main street, where they sold gingerbread toys and twopenny articles of jewellery. There were a few poor shows, a fat woman, a lean boy, a tall young man, and something in spirits too horrible for description; the *dramatis personæ* of Mrs. Gamp in one of her most celebrated passages.

It was enough to attract a crowd. The agricultural labourer of those times could take a holiday. He was not the overworked slave that he is now, any more than he was the long-suffering, overburdened man, who remains gentle, quiet, honest, and obedient, under his almost unbearable wrongs. In those days they would not have dared to do what they habitually do to my neighbours and friends now. The times were hotter. Let this question pass—for a time.

There was a great crowd, however,—a foolish, wondering crowd; the young men with ribands in their hats, staring and gaping almost idiotically, while their brother agriculturists in Dauphiny, more especially, were combining. These young men were the brothers of the men of Aboukir and Trafalgar; nay, there were some of the Aboukir and Trafalgar men actually present. Grand-looking boys of about eighteen, with bold, keen, dangerous-looking eyes, who swaggered about, on leave from Portsmouth, clothed only in their blue shirt and trousers, with their white chests bare in spite of the cold; boys who developed a somewhat remarkable creed, perhaps one of the lowest, perhaps one of the highest ever developed—that of keeping on firing their guns rapidly, and with perfect precision, until the French had stopped.

At this silly twopenny fair, there were also the men of Albuera, Vimieira, nay, even of Waterloo. The Waterloo man was represented by a little child of three; a Martin of course, who laid in the gutter in a passion, scandalously exposing himself, and kicking at his mother. He was ready for the French twenty-five years afterwards in the heights of Mont S. Jean,—nay, he is there still.

One would have liked to see this crowd, for it was one of the last groups of an older form of English life which was passing away, we hope and believe ultimately for the better; though these hinds were undoubtedly better off than are their grandsons. The position of every class in the community has improved since then, with the solitary exception of the agricultural labourer. He was a serf then, and remains a serf now; but he was better treated in the last old days of a dying feudalism, than he is now under the new laws of supply and demand. Never mind, he will be better off than ever soon. I wish to draw no moral, only I confess that I should have liked, from mere honest curiosity, to see the brothers of the men of the Nile and Trafalgar amusing themselves.

Their amusements, I should think, were coarse and rude, including a great deal of horse-play. Marryat and Michael Scott describe them for us, after they had grown refined and ennobled with much fighting, and say a trifle or so of beating; and have shown us their violence and their tenderness; their strength and their weakness; their babyish superstitions, which were inconceivably great; and their practical wisdom, dexterity, and shiftiness, which were inconceivably greater. The breed is not extinct, though in the extreme south somewhat debauched by good living. Among the northern collieries the breed seem to flourish, and their natural leaders seem to be alive also; for instance, Mr. Mammat. Who was Mr. Mammat? I can find no deed of valour like his.

There were two figures among the crowd which were made way for, and looked up to with universal respect; those of Sir Lionel Somers, and the Rector. They were both dearly beloved by the common people, who had been given to understand that they had quarrelled: they were pleased to see them reconciled; and could none of them avoid remarking that they looked a pair of gentlemen, every inch of them. The old *women* said that they were the best grown couple for miles, and were not far wrong.

The head and leader of the Martin family might well compare with either of them, however. A man of a very high-bred family (there is very good breeding, and there are some very good names among the agricultural labourers). He came of a somewhat ne'er-do-well, but restless and high-spirited family; the principal *specialités* of which were, that the men were fond of fighting and poaching, and the women, though all beautiful, never had a taint upon their names. This Martin, the representative of the family, was now sixty-five, a magnificent old man, over six feet high, who might have been in a farm if he had not been a poacher; but was only a labouring hind after all, and who, even above the rest of his family, was known for a kind of reckless impudent humour, not quite unrepresented in the present day among the same class. This man walked straight up to Sir Lionel and the Rector, and confronted them. And the crowd, knowing all the circumstances, gathered round, seeing that there would be fun, and grinning in ready anticipation,

"Martin," said Sir Lionel, "I wonder you can look me in the face."

Martin immediately put on a look of foolish wonder, and scratched his head, which brought down the laughter of the crowd at once; but he said nothing.

"Where did you get those trout, sir, which you sold at the 'Leeds Arms' on Tuesday?" asked Sir Lionel. And the Rector echoed, "Ay, come now. Let us hear something of *that*."

The crowd listened with their laugh ready. "I won't deny, Sir Lionel, that I am a short-tempered man."

"The trout, sir?" said Sir Lionel.

"I'm a coming to 'em," said Martin, solemnly. "I've as fine a plant of cabbages, Sir Lionel, in my little garden as goes down to the water as ever you see. And they went, and they went. One time I thought it was the papists, another time I thought it was the gipsies, another time I thought it was the excisemen. But last Saturday midnight, I ran out on a sudden, and I'm blessed if I didn't catch five brace and a half of your trout, hard at work in among my cabbages, like rabbits. I won't deny that I lost my temper, and knocked about a couple of brace of them about the head, so hard that they couldn't get back to the river. If you don't keep they trout of yours out of poor men's gardens, I'll summons you."

This suited the crowd very well, but they did not laugh very much; they were many of them looking the other way.

"This is sheer folly, sir," said Sir Lionel.

"Others may be foolish too," said Martin. "Do you mind, Sir Lionel, the time I was teaching you to swim in the mill-head, and you on a sudden, half-wiped and naked, catched hold of the rod, hooks a three-pound trout, and cuts away after him, just as you was, through the miller's bees, oversetting six skeps?* You bears the marks yet, no doubt."

* "Hives." This is no great specimen of a style of "chaff" of which you may yet hear a great deal among the older agricultural hinds in a few parts. The best forms of it are always too coarse for this age. It generally

This would certainly have turned the tables against Sir Lionel, but there was a dead silence. Martin, finding his wit falling dead, turned to see the cause, and Sir Lionel Somers and the Rector looked up also.

The crowd had parted, and had made a circle elsewhere, and in the centre of it stood a man quite as noble, and more remarkable than either Sir Lionel, the Rector, or Martin.

André Desilles, dressed in a long grey redingote, top boots, and a three-cornered hat; a man with a name for all time; tall, calm, majestic, gentle; looking patiently over the heads of the hinds who surrounded him, until he should catch the eye of the two gentlemen he saw beyond.

Martin with his nonsense made way at once, and the crowd divided, while Sir Lionel and the Rector advanced towards the stranger. Three hats were lifted, and three bows were made, while the rustics looked on, admiring the manners of the gentry.

There was no doubt about his nation. The perfect elegance of the whole man, though not so much ornamented as that of Louis de Valognes, bespoke the Frenchman. Sir Lionel Somers, whose colloquial French had lately been improved in a way which André Desilles would have little liked had he known all, anticipated the Rector and spoke in French, with such an imitation of the *haute noblesse* as he had learned at Lulworth.

"I wait to receive the commands of monsieur, and I hope that monsieur will conceive himself welcome to our rude little English village."

Monsieur considered himself welcome, with a smile, which might be more natural by means of his welcomer's pedantic French. He felt, he could not say why, accurate certainty that his welcomer was Sir Lionel Somers. "Nature," he said, "seldom or never produced repetitions of her highest and noblest models in a limited area. He was in the domain of Sir Lionel Somers, and nothing except the given word of Sir Lionel, should ever persuade him that he did not, at that moment, stand face to face with Sir Lionel himself."

Sir Lionel was forced to admit his identity after this wonder-

depends for its point on subjects which have been more than sufficiently handled by Smollett. It may be urged that this example is silly, but it is authentic and characteristic, and so not utterly worthless.

ful piece of Frenchism. As for the Rector, he opened his mouth, and never shut it again until the interview was over; after which he said, " What a fool he was to take that line with a Frenchman. Why didn't he leave him to *me* ?"

But André Desilles had taken the wind out of their sails in the complimentary line, and left them staring. So he was forced to speak again.

" I scarcely come into this valley as a stranger," he said. " My name is André Desilles, and I come to visit my cousin, Mademoiselle Mathilde D'Isigny, at Sheepsden. I only am beginning the route to that place; and behold! I meet two very old friends by report. Sir Lionel, and surely the Rector."

The Rector now, in his turn, had to reply to the politeness of this splendid Frenchman. His attitudes were, comparatively speaking, those of a bear which has danced too often on the same day. I resist a dangerous temptation when I refuse to reproduce his colloquial French. They gave him the route across the fields, and saw him go. Then Sir Lionel said,—
" That is *her* cousin, you know."

" So I understood," said the Rector.

---

## CHAPTER XXVI.

### THE FOOLISH REASONS FOR MATHILDE AND SIR LIONEL GETTING IN LOVE.

ATHILDE was a woman with a very hungry heart. Yet, like many hungry-hearted women, she was easily satisfied. She wanted so very little love to satisfy her, but she had never had even that little.

Out of the abundance of her own great heart, she could love. God only, who made that great heart, can say how much. Could love, I say,—*did* love ! Everything she met she took to her great capacious bosom and loved them. High and low, rich and poor, dogs, cats, and dormice. There was an enormous capacity of loving in her which expressed itself in her face. It was this which made Sir Joshua Reynolds pause opposite her; but he passed on, and left the riddle unread. And again, she loved Marat, because Marat loved the poor. Ay, and Marat loved her too, for Marat could love; though he was a better hand at hating than loving.

Mathilde had never been loved but by one man, André Desilles, and he had never told her of it. Desilles, unless I am mistaken, was a man of the Havelock-Willoughby type; the sort of man whom we only develope in the solitudes of India. This man had always loved her. But with his purist reticence he had never told her of his love; nay, he had done worse than this: by a clumsy remark, clumsily and falsely reported, he had insulted her in regard to her physical gait and appearance. No one takes more to heart a fancied insult of this kind, than a very sensitive woman, who has her heart bare and open before the world. And then, once more, Mathilde had been told as a child that she was beautiful; and the first person who had ever dared, as she thought, to say that she was unbeautiful and clumsy was the ill-reported André Desilles—the man who loved her best in all the world.

Louis de Valognes had deceived her, and insulted her; yet she loved him whilst she forgave him. Why? How well I know why. The reason should be told by a lighter hand than mine, yet I think that even I can make you understand that reason.

Adèle. Their house had been what the Scotch call a "dour" house. All rules and regulations: a weary house, a dull house. The only bright beam of sunshine in the house, the only radical thing which had rebelled against dull formulas, had been Adèle; and her naughtiness and rebellion had been infinitely loveable.

Mathilde, again, had only one person to love, and that person was Adèle. I fancy, although I do not know, that Mathilde was a woman who ought to have had children to take care of, for she loved those best who teased her most. This is the reason why she loved Adèle so dearly. To her Adèle, the plague, ay, and more than the plague of her life, she gave up Louis de Valognes with scarcely a murmur.

She was left alone, as you have seen. Sir Lionel Somers was also left alone. And these two people, meeting at the dissenting chapel, at which they had no business to be, to the unutterable confusion of all counsel, fell in love with one another. You urge that they could not help it, and I quite agree with you. But they did.

She was a woman with a great longing heart, which had never been satisfied.  She had asked so little, but now she had got so much.  She got the heart of Sir Lionel Somers, which was worth having.  She had also got the heart of André Desilles, which was worth more : the heart of a man who will fold his arms, and stand calmly before a cannon, face to face with levelled muskets, handled by infuriated hands, is worth something, young ladies, if you will only believe me.  Mathilde had such a heart at her feet always, but she never cared for it.  She wished for a demonstrative man, and men of the type of André Desilles, calm, thoughtful, religious men—men who carefully calculate the time when their morality will allow them to commit suicide for their country—these men are not demonstrative towards those they love : even Sir Lionel Somers was more so.

How many times did he meet her alone before he laid his life at her feet?  Three times : the old number.  Once at the door of the Methodist chapel; once at the bedside of one of his gamekeepers—a delicate young man, who, like most other beautiful young men, died of consumption; and yet once again.

It was in the crystal October morning.  He was out shooting, with a brace of spaniels and a foolish old flint-locked gun.  Pointers were hardly known then, and "shooting flying" was in its infancy.  The system of walking to your birds, which has done so much for the richer classes, by teaching them to use their legs, was only beginning.  Sir Lionel Somers was one of the first men who took up with it.  And on this particular October morning, with the autumnal scents floating round him, making him somehow think of death, of peace, and of quiet churchyards, his spaniels, or his legs, or his inclinations, carried him to Sheepsden.

D'Isigny had given him right of shooting there.  He was not unwilling to exercise it.  Before he got there he banged off his gun at birds which were clearly not in shot; so often, that his attendant keeper (a Martin, of course) went about with him on the subject.  Sir Lionel told him to "go about for a fool."  When they got close to Sheepsden the man "went about for a fool," and held his tongue, which is more than servants will do now-a-days.

For from under the golden-boughed elms came Mathilde herself, with the light of the morning sun blazing on her face.

The Martins represent the genius of that Stour valley. When the Martin who was attending Sir Lionel saw Mathilde approaching, his genius was so good to him as to advise him to retire. I should fancy that when the lion and lioness walk side by side, the leopard retires. Martin had the sense to retire, while Mathilde, coming from under the golden elms, with the morning sun strong on her quaintly beautiful face, approached Sir Lionel.

Martin the hind, the gamekeeper, knew that the business was all over, done, and finished from that moment. *He* went home with the birds, leaving Mathilde and Sir Lionel together.

## CHAPTER XXVII.

#### ONE OF THE SADDEST CHAPTERS IN THE WHOLE STORY.

POOR Mathilde's life at Sheepsden was, after all, very sad and miserable.

She loved Mrs. Bone and the silent William; she talked to them both habitually. But then they knew no French, and she had to talk to them in English. The effort of forming her ideas into English was quite enough to counterbalance the pleasure she felt in talking to them. After all, while speaking to them, she was practically alone.

She got a lover, Sir Lionel Somers. But then, again, her English was better than his French; so she never had a chance of speaking her great thoughts to him. Moreover, did she ever love Sir Lionel Somers as a man wishes to be loved? I cannot say; she fell in love with him as he did with her. But did she *love* him? This part of the story should be written by a woman.

Her position offered to her father remarkable opportunities of disciplining her, which he was not the man to neglect. His letters to her were extremely short and formal; he gave her no information either about politics or about himself. When he alluded to any personal matters at all, it was only to point out to her the inestimable advantages she was enjoying at Sheepsden, and what a splendid opportunity it was for her, in her contemplative seclusion, to think over and correct the numerous faults which he had, with the deepest regret, noticed in her character. *His* letters were always folded and put by as soon as read, with a sigh.

She had letters from Adèle, which she loved better, though not well. Adèle was, under some influence or another, developing the habit of smartness and sharpness in speaking of other people, which is so very charming in her Mémoires, but which people of larger natures, like Mathilde, think silly and ill-conditioned. Every new person whom Adèle met was sent over to Mathilde, dressed with Adèle's sauce piquante.

This habit of mind was so utterly unakin to that of Mathilde, that it distressed her. She was utterly unable to sneer at people. Adèle never did anything else now.

Mathilde had, moreover, letters from Father Martin, which she loved. They were more like the letters of a kindly man of the world than of a priest. They were not intended to instruct her; they were intended to interest and amuse her. She saw the intention, and was grateful.

News she had. The handsome and intelligent young Mr. Jenkinson, who lived to be the gentle and well-beloved Lord Liverpool—a man who got men to work together by the personal respect which they all bore to his mild wishes, who could never have been got to pull together by intrigue; this gentle Mr. Jenkinson sent his old friend and schoolfellow, Sir Lionel Somers, plenty of news, and, of course, Sir Lionel brought it to her. Things in her beloved France were getting darker, wilder, and fiercer as month after month went on. The châteaux were catching fire now. Sir Lionel read out to her the account of these burnings, and worse, from the letters of Mr. Jenkinson in English, and from the *Moniteur* in *his* French.* The people which Mathilde loved so dearly and so well were getting maddened under these wrongs. And everywhere, appearing, disappearing, and re-appearing, was her maniac old friend, Marat, whom she had liked because he cared for the people: the man who licked his dry lips when he spoke: the man who looked steadily, though fiercely, at you from under his lowered eyebrows; the man who, when he had spoken, held his wild, curly,

* If this is a blunder, it is a very slight one. I do not know the date of the first appearance of the *Moniteur*. In the *next* year we have plenty of it.

hideous, head on one side, waiting for your answer,—an answer which in those times you could not give.

Everywhere, in the dim dribble of news which came to her, this man's name turned up: more and more frequently as time went on. Dog, scoundrel, maniac, swindler, were the sort of names which were given to him. She had liked this man; and she was not the only person, by a few millions, who liked him. She had a happy or unhappy trick of believing everything which was told her. She grew puzzled about her old friend; and she had no one to consult except Sir Lionel Somers, and so she consulted him.

A hopeless, barren business. Conceive a sentimental woman consulting a well-formed and decorous Whig on the subject of Marat. The most frantic Tory would have understood him better, and would have hung him up on a forty-foot gallows. Sir Lionel's Whiggery became volcanic on the subject of Marat. Any one of his Tory neighbours would quietly have put Marat out of the way, as one would shoot a mad dog, or kill a savage horse. Sir Lionel, with his Whiggism, would have had him die a thousand deaths first; he had betrayed the cause of orderly freedom; he had utilised the Whig or Gironde formulas too logically; and so Satan was a gentleman to him.

Mathilde got no comfort from her English lover. Her heart hungered to talk to an intelligent Frenchman, in his own language, on the wild whirling storm which was beginning in France. She had that queer love for the poor—that queer, overwhelming desire to assist them at all hazards, which a great many people retain to the present day. Marat was with her in this, as was also Father Martin. But the decorous Whiggery of Sir Lionel Somers would fit in nowhere.

At last she got a talk with a Frenchman in her own beloved language. One afternoon Sir Lionel Somers — after having pointed out to her that a two-pennyworth of democracy, mixed with ten-pennyworth of Whiggery, would exactly make a shilling; and that no other current coin could be accepted—departed to the air to meet the Rector, Mathilde going about her domestic duties.

Adèle, in her Mémoires, sometimes hints that Mathilde, who suffered so much for her, was little better than a very dear fool. It is possible that Adèle is right; but on this particular afternoon she hardly behaved well. It was her cousin, doubtless—

that is an excuse. It was a man whom she had often declared had insulted her: that goes against her. On the whole, she behaved with the grossest indiscretion. But she was all alone; and the sound of her native tongue was dear to her.

This afternoon of the fair she was inside the old screen, bustling about with her pots and pans, employing herself with that domestic economy in which very high-class women take an interest, which is puzzling to me: when, turning round, she saw her cousin, André Desilles, in his manly beauty, standing and looking at her. And then, like Genevieve in Coleridge's almost unequalled ballad,

"Fled to him, and wept."

She put her noble head on her cousin's bosom, and looked up into his quiet face. "André! André!" she said; "you have come after me, you well-beloved! André, dear, they have all gone away from me, and left me all alone among these English."

He thought that it was love; it was only sisterly affection. It was a time of mistakes; she wanted a Frenchman to talk to, and he was the first who came to hand. Although she had disliked André Desilles and his precisionism all her life, she loved him for the moment because he was a Frenchman. She did not suffer for deceiving him; she purged her fault on other grounds. As for him, *Nanci!*

## CHAPTER XXVIII.

### ANDRÉ, LIONEL, AND MATHILDE.

ENGLAND was quiet that autumn. Here and there were a few wild democrats casting about what seemed to be wild whirling words—words which sounded strange enough then, though now grown familiar; nay, even—let us hope for good—reduced to practice. In the autumn of 1789, the words of those few early democrats sounded in the ears of the people like idle tales. They were like the scattered patches of nimbus, which the sailors call "prophet-clouds," which come sweeping up from the south-west, and herald the storm which follows. Lands-

men, when they see these prophet-clouds sweeping swiftly and steadily across the western sky at evening, say, "They are clouds, and we shall have rain." Sailors, more experienced, say, "We shall have wind with it, and wild wind, too ;" and send down the top-gallant masts, and bend the best hemp cable on to the best bower anchor.

But this autumn the landsmen who said only cloud, and the real sailors who said wind, storm, ruin, and destruction, were agreed on one point. They both said "wait." "Let us see," said both parties, "if this frightful thunder rattle, to the south there in France, is coming our way." In the next year the French Revolution stood before the eyes of men as almost the greatest fact of all time; and Englishmen, in a somewhat puzzled way, began to range themselves on different sides. But in the autumn and winter of 1789 the attitude of the English people was that of wonder and expectation. Both the inexperienced landsmen and the experienced sailors agreed that it would be better to wait, and see how the thing would go.

Sir Lionel Somers, André Desilles, and the Rector talked one day,—a strange trio,—much as men were talking in those days, I think. André Desilles said, "The seeds of democracy are very easily sown, and they grow also very easily, for they fall in fruitful soil. Democracy promises so much, and with such good hope of a harvest. I can forgive a man for being a thoroughgoing democrat, so long as he is honest."

"If one might speak and live, one could ask," said Sir Lionel, "Where is there such thorough-going radicalism as real Christianity? But as one cannot speak and live in these days, I do not ask that question, but put it aside, and decline to ask it."

"Martin and D'Isigny, however," said André Desilles, calmly, "refused to put this question by. They both—the one violently and furiously, the other mildly and with tact—declare that Christianity and democracy are one and the same thing. Here one gets into a perfect maze of differences, which the most patient listener could scarcely take the trouble to puzzle out. Martin declared himself a Christian and a democrat, on the ground that democracy meant Christianity and nothing else, and *vice versâ.*"

"D'Isigny," said Sir Lionel, "took other grounds. He wasf elaborate in his arguments. You will spare me the pain of going into the lamentably illogical arguments of our friend. They amount to this: Christianity could be proved to be untrue; but it was the best system of morality which had been ever seen, and was necessary for the government of the masses. Now, who are the fanatics? I should say D'Isigny. They, too, are toiling and labouring in their various ways," continued Sir Lionel. "I, as a headlong Protestant, love and admire Father Martin, the Papist, beyond most men. It is impossible to avoid loving men who give up their whole lives to doing good. Helping to burn down his chapel is one thing; loving and respecting him is quite another."

The above-mentioned opinions are not, as will be seen, my own. They are merely the fag ends of many discussions held between the Rector, Sir Lionel Somers, and André Desilles; for these three were much together now, for one thing had been clear to the Rector—it was absolutely impossible for André Desilles to stay with his cousin at Sheepsden. Again, another thing had become evident to the Rector—that it would be utterly inhospitable for him to allow the cousin of his old friend M. D'Isigny to stay at the Leeds Arms. Consequently, the Rector had insisted on André Desilles taking up his quarters at the Rectory. Mrs. Rector had made a feeble little moan about having a Papist in the house, but not to her husband; she carried her little wail to old Lady Somers, and pointed out to her how terribly it would undermine her husband's influence to have a Papist, and he a Frenchman, in the house. Lady Somers advised her to make no objection.

"I," said the old lady, "am glad that my son should marry Mathilde, who is a Papist. It is not much, my dear, that you should yield in the matter of having her cousin into your house. I think that your husband is both weak and ungrateful. My husband gave him this living at my solicitation; and last month he turned against Lionel because he, as a Whig, should encourage a Nonconformist. Your husband refused to fish in my son's water; and I, of course, at once sent for my prayer-books. I have now received your husband again into favour, and have sent back my prayer-books, and shall leave them there until your husband repeats his offence of ingratitude. With regard to having a Papist in the family, I should advise you to yield: firstly, because it is your husband's wish; and, secondly, my dear, because you know that you would give one of the eyes out of your head to have a Petre or a Weld to stay in your house."

Mrs. Rector gained but little from her conversation with this very strenuous old Whig lady; and went elsewhere for advice afterwards.

So André Desilles, the Lafayettist, found himself the denizen of a respectable Philistine English rectory; a very strange arrangement, if you will think about it. The rectory way of making things go was a different one to any André had ever seen before. It puzzled him while it amused him; it must have seemed strange, even to a man who had been familiar with the extraordinary number of offices filled by the French clergy. In addition to his having the sole cure of souls of the parish of Stourminster Osborne, the Rector was a magistrate; nay, even chairman of the bench. Again, he was a scholar, and kept his scholarship alive. He was the busiest and most correct antiquarian in the west of England. Then again, since Sir George Somers had given him the living, he, by the death of his elder brother, had come into a good estate, of about two thousand a year. He was likewise a very fair sportsman. But André Desilles noticed, and mentioned to Barbaroux, that the man seemed to fail in none of his positions. He was a good parson, a good antiquarian, a good magistrate, a good landlord, and, moreover, a good husband.

"You do not know these English," said Desilles.

Barbaroux said: "Nor would I. A nation which, under Cromwell, was once free, now trodden under the heels of the worthless Norman aristocracy. I do not desire to know them."

"But they will beat us," said Desilles.

"It is possible," said Barbaroux, "but they will not beat democracy. Sleep well assured of that matter, my soldier."

It was perfectly necessary, considering the utter solitude of Mathilde's position, that Sir Lionel Somers should not be the acknowledged suitor of Mathilde. She was so perfectly defenceless and alone, that it was totally impossible that the matter could be talked about in any way. At least, this was Lady Somers' decision, and there was no appeal from it.

Sir Lionel's argument was that it would be fairer on her to give her the recognised position of his *fiancée*, and there was a great deal in what he said. Still, however, Lady Somers carried the day.

"Before you spoke to her," she said, "I had no right to connect your name with hers. Now that you have spoken the irrevocable words, which I would not have unsaid, she has become, as it were, one of the family; and I, as mother of the family, can offer advice which I could not have given before. Before you spoke to her, I had no authority over your movements; now I claim some. In the very peculiar situation of the poor girl, deserted by both her natural guardians, I think that you should be exceedingly delicate, and should, in short, go to Sheepsden as little as possible."

"While Desilles goes as much as he chooses," murmured Sir Lionel.

"I never thought to have heard an unworthy word from my son," said the old lady, drawing herself up rigidly; "and *that* word was unworthy of him. Mathilde has done you the highest honour which woman can do to man; and when you hint even indirectly that you are not sure of her faith, you show yourself unworthy of your name, and unworthy also of her."

"That is all very well, mother," still grumbled Sir Lionel; "but when a man is engaged to a French woman, he does not exactly like to have an exceedingly handsome Frenchman admitted to her society when he himself is banished. You would not like it yourself."

"He is her cousin," said Lady Somers.

"Confound him—yes! and he talks French like a nightingale. My French after his is like the gobbling of a turkeycock. I wish he would go back to his regiment. I wish he was hung."

"If you distrust Mathilde, tell her so," said Lady Somers, getting still more on her dignity.

"Oh, hang it all, mother, I dare say you are right in the matter."

"I should suppose that I was. I have usually been considered an authority on these subjects."

"I do not pretend to doubt it. I have been a dutiful son to you, and will continue to be so. I will do as you desire. You know better than I what the cackling male idiots and foolish female busybodies who compose the population of this valley are likely to say. There, now, don't be angry; you have behaved most kindly in this matter, and I thank you for it. The poor child, God help her, has no one but you. I will be guided by you, and be grateful. Can I say more?"

And so what threatened to be a slight disagreement went off in an embrace, and a few tears from Lady Somers. And the old lady was perfectly right: she knew what she was talking about. She had seen the splendid Frenchman with his cousin several times, and she saw that there was no danger. She nodded her old lace cap, and she said to herself, "If that had been going to happen, it would have happened long ago. She has got too used to him and his elegances. He is no more to her than her brother. There is no danger."

So the secret between Mathilde and Sir Lionel was supposed to be only known to them and to his mother. As for Mathilde, she kept it from André Desilles, because she was afraid of him, and still more afraid of his rigid, soldierly Catholicism: was afraid that he would quarrel with her for proposing to marry a Protestant. And she was so happy with him; for did he not sit and talk to her about France, and what was almost as good, in French: quote little jingles of French verse to her, so delicious after the long, heavy, swinging Teutonic rhymes which her father had made her learn for penances. And he could see how she was dressed, which Lionel never could. He had been unkind to her once, but that was long ago. He was a Frenchman, and her own dear brother. She liked him, though she was afraid of him; but she loved Lionel best. André's was an old familiar face. She would as soon have thought of falling in love with old André as she would with Mrs. Bone. It was only old André, and who was he? Why, old disagreeable André. *Voila tout!* Lady Somers was perfectly right.

Somebody has said that a woman always knows when a man is in love with her. It may be true in England, but I doubt if it is true in France. An Englishman certainly takes care that there should be no mistake about the matter. A Frenchman is, or was, so fearfully polite to every woman he meets, that the woman herself must get puzzled sometimes. Moreover, poor André's courtship was of such an extremely dignified nature, that Mathilde never saw anything of it at all. Once or twice she was a little puzzled about what made him so consistently kind to her, but she said, "He has come to me with his kind heart, because I am all alone, when every one had left me;" and very nearly determined to tell him the words which Sir Lionel Somers had said to her—but was afraid, because Lionel was a Protestant.

His company was a great delight to her. But alas for poor André! He was left terribly in the dark.

One thing was evidently necessary for Sir Lionel to do. He must inform her father of his position towards his daughter. What, then, was M. D'Isigny's address? He asked Mathilde. She had not the least idea, and so he simply wrote to him as deputy to the *National Assembly*.

"Do you never correspond, then?" asked Sir Lionel.

"Oh, never now. They have all left me alone, except my dear old André, who has come in his kindness to talk French to me. Lionel, will you do me a favour? It is the first I have ever asked you."

"I will do it."

"Try to like André. I assure you that he is worthy of you; he is so very good and noble, and I have been unfair and unjust to him all my life. He offended me once, and I never forgave him until lately. I was utterly in the wrong, as he has proved by being the only one who came to me when I was alone. That, Lionel, is what makes me so tender and affectionate with him now, and I do love him so very dearly, Lionel, and I have used him so badly all his life. Do try, for my sake, to like him."

"I do like him very much. If he will give me his friendship, God knows he shall have mine. But, Mathilde, are you never afraid that he loves you?"

"How?"

"Are you not afraid that he loves you?"

"Loves me?—He loves me entirely. Would he have come here to see me if he had not loved me? He loves me very dearly, and I am proud of his love. *His* love is worth having."

"I mean this," said Sir Lionel, very slowly, "are you not afraid of his loving you too much for his—peace of mind?"

Mathilde stared at him. "Do you mean loves me sentimentally? That he loves me in the same way as you do?" pointing her finger at him.

"I meant that, certainly."

"Why, then, see what it is not to understand the other's language. My dear Lionel, you talk ridiculous, I assure you. Old André, then—listen—André and I have had a long quarrel, and it was all because he said, years ago, that I was so ugly that it gave him pain to see me play."

Mathilde rose at this point, and spread the fingers of one hand before Sir Lionel's face, she paused also for one instant, and then went on—

"He said that—or those two others, he and she, Louis and Adèle, you know—*said* that he had said it. Perhaps he did not, for they can be very false those two, Lionel. I would die for them, but they can be very false. They told me that he said that, and I enraged myself against him, for I am not ugly; have you not yourself told me that I am beautiful?—your word is as good as his."

There was no mistake about her beauty now, even to her, for she saw the reflection of it in the face of Sir Lionel, as in a glass.

"That is right; you confirm your words by your eyes. But he never thought as you think. He always thought me half *crétin*, an object of pity. Besides, again, he is my brother. Besides, once more again, Lionel, you do not know him. His heart is not for woman, oh, you blind! He is priest. He is, if necessary, martyr! Do you not see it in his face?—and for him to love me sentimentally, my old, cross brother André; bah! For me, I love sentimentally only you. I now really think that you were the first, and you shall be the last."

So Mathilde, to the entire satisfaction of Sir Lionel. But Mrs. Bone and William had other opinions. While Sir Lionel was waiting for his answer from D'Isigny, he decorously followed his mother's advice, and went very little to Sheepsden. But André Desilles went, and Mrs. Bone and William used to hear them, and see them talking over the fire, in French. And Mrs. Bone remarked to William that their voices were like the chiming of silver bells.

## CHAPTER XXIX.

### BARBOT'S FIRST REVENGE.

T seems to me, in any good story which I have ever read, that there is a kind of pause, or breaking line, about the middle of it. The author, in spite of himself, puts his causes before you in the first half of his story, and gives you the effect of them in the second. I do not know a readable story which does not fulfil this rule. I fancy it is the great rule of story-telling. It is certainly so well recognised, that some experienced novel readers omit the ceremony of reading the second volume of a three-volume novel, as old playgoers are in the habit of having a quiet game at billiards during the second act of a new three-act play.

I would have provided for my audience a quiet time of this kind, when they might, to use the theatrical simile, have had in their ices, and talked to their friends; but I fear I cannot. I have cast the time of my story in the times of the French Revolution: and there can be no pause, no peace, with a story which begins in 1789.

In solitary Sheepsden, folded among the calm Dorsetshire hills, one might have thought that there was peace, if there could be peace anywhere. Winter came down, and shrouded the Down with its winter's snow—yet there was little peace there. André Desilles and Mathilde were at cross purposes; Sir Lionel and Desilles did not understand their relations towards one another; and Desilles' time was getting short.

He had every reason for encouragement; he thought that he had nothing to do but to speak. He knew what had been the relations between Sir Lionel and Adèle. He never dreamt that there were any similar relations between Mathilde and Sir Lionel. His idea was, that he had only to speak the word to Mathilde, and that she would fly to his arms, or do something of that sort;—that he could have her when he chose. He did not want to hurry her; he knew that she had at one time some sort of prejudice against him. Yet she was so affectionate, and so gentle and loving towards him; and Sir Lionel and his mother kept their secret, like English people, so uncommonly well, that he never guessed it.

If he had known English, he would have heard of the relations between Mathilde and Sir Lionel very quickly; but English was a mere barbarous jargon to him, which he could not learn. He was as much isolated from his species as a deaf and dumb man. The people who spoke French to him, were—Mathilde, who did not wish him to know about her relations to Sir Lionel; Sir Lionel, who was still jealous of him; Lady Somers, who twittered out her little Frenchisms with a perfect accent, like an aged piping bullfinch who has nearly forgotten his art; and the Rector, who spoke French like a bulldog. He begged the Rector to teach him English colloquially, so that he might escape the Rector's French—it was so fearfully painful; but the Rector only retorted on him by asking him to talk in English while he spoke in French, as that was the best way of mutual improvement. So poor André had really no chance of hearing the truth. The only man, beside these four, who ever spoke to him in French, was his servant, Barbot. So André, until just before his departure, had no doubt whatever that he had only to speak a few words to Mathilde, to be accepted. He did not want to hurry her in any way, and so put off the speaking of them until they were never spoken. The man who prevented those words from being spoken was Sergeant Barbot, the man whom he had brought with him as a servant, because he was the most dangerous man in the Régiment du Roi.*

Mathilde was very particular about this man. She asked William, as a particular favour, to be very attentive to him; and William, of course, was so. When he was left alone together with Barbot, William instantly came to the conclusion that there were two kinds of Frenchmen; the one like D'Isigny, Desilles, and De Valognes, the other like Barbot and Marat. The one the most elegant person in the world, to whom Sir Lionel was a cart-horse, the other hideous, wild, and strange beyond understanding. There was a wild, lurid light in the red eyes of Marat and of Barbot, which William could not understand.

When Barbot was first left in William's care, they soon found

* I have chosen my name unluckily. This dreadful Sergeant was no relation whatever of the charming and kind Madame Barbot, of Dol.

out that neither understood the other's language. William was puzzled at first to know what to do, but he, after a moment's consideration, went through the pantomime of drinking. Barbot understood *that*, and they went to the public-house together.

William was no glass-breaker, merely taking his modest pint of beer; Barbot, like most of the inferior agents of the French Revolution, vacillated between alternate doses of strong tobacco and raw brandy. William thought that French gentlemen kept curious servants, and consoled himself by thinking that probably they could not get better. He told his beloved confidant, Mrs. Bone, that he was surprised to see such a real gentleman as Mr. Desilles, with such an exceedingly "ornery" * servant as Barbot. There was a curious light in Barbot's eyes, which William was unable to understand, but which he did not like. Still Barbot had been committed to his care by Mathilde, and he was civil to him.

They used thus to drink together at the Leeds Arms. André Desilles, who hated the very sight of the man, and had only taken him as his servant, in order to get him away from the regiment, had quartered him in the village. William used periodically to pay for his drink, and Barbot used to drink it, while William sat and looked on.

William was sitting and looking on at Barbot drinking one night, when he felt some one tug the hair at the top of his head. Looking up to see who had taken this very strange liberty, he looked up into the handsome face of Martin, the old poacher.

William laughed, and Martin facetiously boxed his ears; after which he sat down beside William, and then setting his keen, hawklike hazel eye on Barbot, to William's unutterable astonishment, began talking French to him.

William knew that Martin, the poacher, had been a soldier at one time; had been a prisoner at one time; but he had never had the very dimmest idea that old Martin could talk French. He was stricken with astonishment, and sat with open mouth, while those two very strange beings,—Barbot, the French democrat, and Martin, the English poaching loafer, the man

* "Ornery,"—with which word the English public are now mainly familiar from Artemus Ward—is an expression as old as the hills in Hampshire. It is merely a corruption for "ordinary."

who had nothing to lose and little to gain—interchanged ideas. I must translate for them.

Martin said: "You have a good service, and seem to thrive on it. I was prisoner in France once, and in those times service was bad, unless—" I will pause here; Martin went into details which are unnecessary.

Barbot said: "You do not seem to thrive on your service. Your master is a hard one." For indeed old Martin's "turn out" in the way of clothes was very far from impressive.

"I have no master," said Martin. "If I had submitted to a master, I could have been in a good farm. But I could not."

Barbot came round to his side of the table at once. "Then, I suppose," he said, "that you are one of those who are going to do as we are going to do."

To which Martin answered, rather provokingly, "*Quoi donc !*"

"What!" said Barbot, in a fury at once. "What! Why rise against them,—against these masters? Who, then, should have a master at all? What do they with the land? The land is ours. They are mere robbers and thieves, debauched by every vice. Take from them this land, then! Wrest it from them!"

"But what would they have to live on," asked Martin the poacher, "if you took the land from them?"

"Live?" said Barbot. "Why should they live? Let them die! Do as we are going to do: cut them off and take possession."

"There seems some sense in that," said Martin. "What would you propose, for instance, in the case of Sir Lionel Somers?"

"Assassination. Our French aristocracy are intolerable, but your English aristocracy are more brutally insolent. Sir Lionel Somers walks often, and alone. You know the use of a gun; and you seem *répandu* among the wretched peasantry. He has prosecuted you for killing his game. Your chance at him is continual. Do you not see your advantage? If there were a thousand such as you in England, the cause would be secure."

"But there aint," said Martin to himself. To Barbot he said—"You think, then, that the best way to begin would be for me to shoot Sir Lionel Somers?"

"It would be a good beginning," said Barbot; "a great example."

"Yet we should miss him in hard winters," said Martin, "not to mention his mother; and winters are devilish hard in these parts, comrade; and they come in very convenient, do these lords and ladies. They are very kind."

"Curse them! I know it," said Barbot.

"I have no doubt you do," said Martin. "You seem to hate them so very strongly that I very much suspect you have had a favour or two from them. Well, *bon soir!* I will think over this proposition of yours about killing Sir Lionel. If I find my prejudices go against it, perhaps *you* will take it in hand? Let me know when you are going to do it, because I should like to see the job done."

Barbot said, "Who am I, in a foreign country, to undertake such a thing? Who is he to me? Are there not two hundred and fifty thousand aristocrats at home?"—So Martin said, "Then you had better leave the job to me;" and Barbot said, "Certainly," and so separated.

"You have got into nice company, young man," remarked Martin to William, when Barbot had gone; "uncommon nice company, upon my word. For a respectable young man, hailing from these parts, I don't see you could have got into worse."

"I doubt he is no good," said William.

"You need not doubt," said Martin.

"What has he been talking about to you in French?" asked William.

"Murder," said old Martin.

William sat aghast; and repeated, "Murder! Who does he want to murder?"

To which old Martin replied, very vaguely, "All the whole lot."

"Then there is no particular young woman in the business, then?" asked William, whose ideas of murder as an art were derived from the only cases which had come under his knowledge: that of a young man who had murdered his sweetheart, and idiotically hidden her body in a saw-pit; and of a young woman who had murdered her baby out of spite.

"Young woman!" said old Martin, almost contemptuously. "What does such as he want with young women? I mean murder wholesale. Murder of the whole lot of the gentle-folks."

"What the deuce would be the good of that?" asked William.

"The poor folks would get the land," answered Martin, with his shrewd old eye on William.

"And what the deuce would they do with it when they got it?" answered William. "They've got no money to farm it with, and it would pretty soon fall back into the hands of them as had. This lot of landowners are well enough; let 'em bide. You might get a worse lot in their place."

"We will talk about that again, old boy," said Martin, the old poacher. "I knew you were all right, but I want to speak to you about this Frenchman. We have no call to grumble against the French, for there is M. D'Isigny and Mademoiselle his daughter; but I tell you some of the French are devils alive, and this Barbot is one. Why, what is wrote in his face?"

William, though interested in the conversation and anxious to prolong it, was unable to say what was written on Barbot's face.

"Why, murderer!" said old Martin. "Bill, listen to me. You asked me what he had been saying to me in French, and I will tell you. He was asking me to murder Sir Lionel Somers."

William moved quickly; the thing was so incredible to him. He little dreamt to what place his fate would ultimately lead him; little thought that he should take a human life himself; still less thought *whose* life, but he was extremely agitated (if such an expression can be made with regard to a young and stolid English horse-minder) at the idea of the assassination of Sir Lionel Somers. Sir Lionel was the man of whom they were all so proud, the favourite of the valley, in spite of all his fallings away in the direction of Romanism and dissent; these poor peasants were foolish enough to love the man. And now here had come a Frenchman who had proposed to old Martin that he should be murdered. To ask a Martin to murder a Somers! William turned his eyes on the old poacher inquiringly.

Martin went on, and William's face was quite close to his.

"That Frenchman, Bill, proposed to me, you sitting there and not getting up and breaking his back, that I should shoot down Sir Lionel!"

"How could I have broke his back—he is a stronger man than me—and me not knowing French?" asked William.

"There is a deal in that," said old Martin. "That is true, that is. But what odds? that Frenchman wanted to egg me on to murder him."

"But there's no odds between you and Sir Lionel," said the very much puzzled William.

"Odds betwixt me and he!" said the old poacher; "no, except on my side. I ain't been fair to him, Bill; I've poached out his trout; I groped out they trout that he kicked up a row about last month. My dear young man, don't you get looking too much at they dratted trout, or you won't be able to keep your hands off them. I can't; I would risk my life after them; I can't help it."

William said, in some form or another, that Martin should try if he felt himself in any way able, to get over this temptation.

Martin said in reply, "That is all very well for you; you have never been tempted in this way. You have been brought up among they horses, and your temptations lies among they; they are the curse of England, they horses. I don't say that you would go as far as to steal a horse, as I could steal a trout; but if you found a sound piece of turf you would *gallop* a horse when you was sent out with orders to walk him; much as I would go stark naked, old as I am, into a stream in December, after one of they trout."

The old man was getting discursive, and to a certain extent personal; William recalled him.

"About this Barbot, this Frenchman?" asked William.

"Well, Bill, he has proposed that I should shoot Sir Lionel. You are a young man, and a simple man, and don't understand Revolution."

"What is that?" asked William.

"Blessed if I exactly know myself," said Martin. "But the Revolutionists don't seem sharp to me. For him to ask me to shoot Lionel!"

"But you wouldn't do it, you know," said William.

"I taught him to swim, I taught him to shoot flying, I taught him the main of all the learning he has got, and then this Frenchman comes and wants me to shoot him. Poor Lionel! He and my Bob were born the same weck——"

O

William said nothing now, with the instinct of a gentleman, and indeed Martin paused. They were on very delicate ground. Robert Martin had been the only blot on the family escutcheon. To say that he had *got* into bad company would be incorrect, as none of the Martins were ever in good. But the Martins had always kept on the sunny side of the hedge with regard to the law, except on the question of poaching. Now this unhappy lad, Robert Martin, had nearly broken his father's heart by marrying a gipsy woman. This was bad enough, but worse came of it. One of his brothers-in-law stole a sheep, and Robert, as a matter of civility to his wife's brother more than for any other reason, received the carcass. They were convicted together, and under the cruel old laws were both *hung* at Dorchester. I am not "fighting extinct Satans," as Mr. Carlyle says, when I mention this fact. I am merely trying to give an idea of the state of society then ; to give some idea of the extraordinary way in which the doctrine of obedience had worked itself into the English mind at that time. We should not utterly despise this instinct of obedience, for it gave us Trafalgar. At the Nore there was an attempt at rebellion, but habit, mere habit, quelled the mutiny, when the mutineers had won.

Old Martin, a hater of all laws, had lived under these cruel laws, and had lost a son under them. Let us see, for curiosity's sake, how he spoke of the class who made them and enforced them.

"My Bob," said the old man, "was always a favourite with Sir Lionel. When he got into his trouble, Sir Lionel was up and down, night and day, to see him through it. But Lord bless you, forty Sir Lionels weren't no good at all. The sheep's life was took, and the farmers would have my boy's life for the sheep's : and the farmers got my boy's blood for their sheep's blood. And Lionel, he come to my place, and read the funeral service, him and me, the time my boy Bob was hanging at Dorchester ; and now this French devil comes and wants me to murder he. Why, I would have as lief murdered you."

I hope certain people will not pronounce the above to be what they please to call vulgar. It is pretty *true*, which is something. What saved a general Jacquerie here the last ten years of the last century was the simple fact that our upper classes had contracted habits of friendship and familiarity with the peasants.

D'Isigny pointed that out before. That is all past and gone. I am merely writing for the past, and expressing no opinions, only speaking of what venerable gentlemen have told me were facts. Will you hear Martin again? I honestly think that I am not misleading you in bringing his voice out of the past.

"There's Lionel. He has not used me as well as he might. He had no call to kick up a row about they darned trout a month ago," continued the old man, unable to forget Sir Lionel's last cause of offence. "I can't keep my hands off they darned trout, and he knows it. I suppose it's a instinct which Providence has put in me. Bill, I tell you, as a respectable young man without that instinct, that I can't keep my hands from them. He knowed it well enough; but for he and the Rector to go along at me about they trout was not fair."

"They were *his* trout, you know," said William, quietly.

"So I believe," said Martin. "I will say no more about them. But, look here. Lionel came to me, when my boy was hanging at Dorchester, and he read the service; and we cried together, we two. And now that —— Frenchman could have me murder him. That Frenchman wants watching, and you are the one to watch him."

"You would be the best; you are always round with Sir Lionel."

"*He* won't touch *him*. *He* has no grudge against him. *It's his own master*, I tell-ee—that young Frenchman, Desilles. Can't you warn him of what I have told you?"

William nodded his head. "Will you drink with me, Master Martin?" he said.

"Ah! I dearly love my drop of drink," said the old man. "You was always a civil and dutiful young man. I am getting to feel the rheumatics, and a drop of drink puts life into me now, though I cared little about it when I was young. I am a poor old vagabond, and I ain't done much good; but I can care for them as are kind to me as well as a better one."

Desilles was walking calmly up and down in the Rector's garden, when William approached him and entered into conversation. He pointed out to him that he had better take some precautions, had better use the law, for that Barbot was a declared assassin.

Desilles put his two hands on William's two shoulders, and

looked, with sad and tender eyes, gently into his face. "Dear young man," he said, "I thank you very much for this, though I have known it a very, very long time. But I am safe from him; he knows no mercy, and so he will let me live. You do not understand? No. Good-bye, and thank you. Good-bye!"

And so he departed, leaving William wondering; and William never saw him again, for that morning Barbot had had his revenge for the words he had overheard on the rocks of St. Malo. He had taken André Desilles down a thick pleached alley in the rectory garden, and had shown him Sir Lionel and Mathilde. Her head was on her lover's bosom, and he was playing with her hair. With one deep sob, and only one, André Desilles turned away; and Barbot saw that his dagger had gone home to the noble heart, hilt deep.

## CHAPTER XXX.

### SILENCE THAT DREADFUL BELL.

"HERE," said André Desilles, to the Skipper, "there is at least peace." And the Skipper said in reply, "Hm? Is there peace on that rock, think you?" and pointed to Mont St. Michel.

The little brig in which André Desilles had taken passage from Poole to St. Malo had been driven too far east in a smart gale of wind, and was now making up her westing. The sea had not gone down; but they were very lazily and comfortably toiling on, reeling, rolling, and diving before the gentle easterly wind. To their left, with the hills of the *bocage* behind it, lay Avranches, a line of white houses, topped by the grandest of all cathedrals * in the land of cathedrals—Normandy. Nearer, the dim smoke rising from little Pontorson, but close by, rising from green sea and yellow sand, four hundred and fifty feet in air, with the free sea birds skimming around it, rose the glorious and mighty stone flower which they call Mont St. Michel.

"Not much peace even here, monsieur," said the Skipper,

---

* Since utterly destroyed to the very last stone; not, however, by the Revolutionists. It fell, I believe, by decay.

resuming. "You won't find much peace in France anywheres for a year or two, in prison or out of prison; I doubt. It's the king's prisoners as are biting at them bars just now. There'll be other prisoners soon."

So said the honest English sailor, and André said nothing. No, indeed; there was but little chance of peace for him. He had had his last peace in the two months at Sheepsden. During that time he had scarcely realised what was going on in France. Mathilde had been his siren, and he had slept. This rude and noble old Hatchway Cuttle had roused him.

Do you know the infinite value of a sailor's bluffness? Do you appreciate the extraordinary value of the outspoken truthfulness of a really fine sailor? A soldier will never lie, but he tells the truth, by the tradition of his profession, so very gently and so politely, that you miss the point (unless you are of his mess—the truth is told boldly enough at the mess-table). Now, my sailor tells the blunt, plain truth in a most disagreeable manner very often, whenever he sees occasion, in a way which I can only liken to a green sea walking in over your bulwarks. Nobody likes it; but it is not bad for them.

He had taken a fancy to this rude old English sailor when he had first got on board, and had told him much—more than an Englishman would have been likely to tell—quite enough, indeed, to make the shrewd, gentle old man understand matters. When he had told him all, the Skipper (a Dorsetshire man, who knew the parties) had said somewhat bluffly, "Well, sir, my opinion is, that you had better have stuck to the ship, and not gone ashore after the young lady. If you undertake to do a thing, sir, do it. You undertook your company in the Régiment du Roi, and you went philandering after that saint of a woman (I know her), and left your men to take care of themselves. You will live to regret it."

That was the first thing which this quaint old English Skipper said to arouse André. André had been getting but little intelligence from France, while this old fellow had been going to and fro. André had been asleep. The old man had told him about burning châteaux, and other matters of which we cannot speak; and André, when they were sailing past Mont St. Michel, had said, "There is peace here, at all events." And the old sea-dog had answered as above.

"Peace, sir?" continued the Skipper; "Who are you that you should either desire or deserve peace? Look at that Mont St. Michel, there. The French priest whom I have carried over lately, Mr. Martin, told me how to admire it: he says there is not such a thing in Europe. Very like; I am glad to hear it. It is beautiful enough; but it would look prettier, in my mind, without the white fingers of the captives clawing at the bars. And you talk of peace! Talk about furious resistance to the death;—talk about blood, and fire, and fury; but don't let me hear any French gentleman talk about peace. That time has gone by, sir. I have sailed from Poole to Cherbourg and St. Malo too long, sir, not to know. I hear the wharfmen and stevedores talking as they unload my cargo; and their talk is about you, and such as you, sir; and they hate you with a deep and desperate hatred. Your order is doomed."

The conversation then turned again on the progress of the Revolution; and André once more saw that he had been asleep; that the conflagration had come without his knowing it. Still, all day they sailed quietly on until Mont St. Michel was only a pearl-gray cloud and a recollection, and the low Rochers de Cancale lay eastward from them, jagged as the Bernese Oberland, black as Fogo, and they sighted the innumerable granite islands in the bay of St. Malo, on the largest of which Chateaubriand now lies buried.

"And there," said André Desilles, "is my dear old home. You would like St. Malo, Captain."

"Should I?" said the Skipper. "Oh! I don't much think I should at the present moment. Can you make out the colour of that flag at the battery?"

"How curious. They have got a red flag up," said André.

"Ah! they've got a red flag up," said the Skipper. "You never said a truer word than that in your life. Now, Bob," he continued to the man at the wheel, "don't go a-writing your name with the ship.* There is eight knots of stream and a strong northerly suck of wind. Mind your —— ship."

"I was a-looking at that there flag," growled Bob; "and a-waiting for they to run up the bunting for a pilot."

"Mind your ship," retorted the Skipper. "If you don't know

---

* Sailor's chaff for bad steering.

the channel yet, I can show it to you. Close the Tour Solidor with the round hill inland, and run her straight up the Rance on the tide. That is all the pilotage *you'll* get."

Bob was an old man-of-war's man, and said, "You are putting her right under that old battery at Dinard."

"We will chance that," said the Skipper.

"What's the good?" said Bob. "I'd get her round now."

"Knowing what we have aboard?" asked the Skipper.

Bob swore, and put her at it.

"What does all this mean?" asked André.

"Revolution!" said the Skipper. "Put her at it, Bob."

The brig raced in on the tide, and André could see the rocks on which he had once sat with De Valognes quite plainly. The sea, raging and foaming, had nearly submerged them, and was rising every minute. He was thinking of how much had come and gone in so very few months, when he heard some one laughing behind him. It was Barbot, whose eyes were fixed on the same place. He moved away to the Skipper.

"Do you dread violence to your ship, then, my friend?" he said. "Our governments are not at war."

"But there is mischief in St. Malo," said the Skipper. "Listen."

He listened as the ship drove on, so close to shore that they could see that there were only three persons on the wharf under the walls: a feeble old blind woman, bowed by age, who felt her way with a stick; a drunken man, who danced wildly round by himself, fell against the wall, and then danced again; and a quiet man, who angled with a rod and line in the rising tide for mullet. These were the only three to be seen upon the wharf. But over the heads of these, cling clang, cling clang, went ringing the sound of the cathedral bell, which only half deadened a dull sound of confusion which arose from the close streets, and which seemed to take the place of a dull, ill-sung bass to the maddening sharp treble of the bell.

"What is the meaning of this? What is that awful bell?" said André.

"Le tocsin, Monsieur le Capitaine," said Barbot, who was at his elbow. "The people have declared. Voilà tout. Enfin!"

## CHAPTER XXXI.

### M. D'ISIGNY MEETS STRANGE COMPANY.

I SHOULD be inclined to think that in the history of the whole French Revolution there was scarcely a man who did less, or influenced other people less, than M. D'Isigny. He was a precisionist and a bully; and, if I may be allowed to remark about anything which I have seen, I should say that precisionists and bullies have infinitely less power than any other class of people going.

Is the moral of Aristides quite forgotten? D'Isigny was as good as Aristides; and when his little world grew old enough to think for themselves, they rose in rebellion against his goodness. They might possibly have stood his goodness, if he had not been such a bully. He would let them see that he was good on every occasion: and they, not being absolutely perfect, disliked it;—indeed, Adèle rebelled. Mathilde took him as a matter of course, and went to bed every night lamenting and accusing herself, because she was not as good as her father. The Girondists were, some of them, dreadfully good, but

"Roland the Just, with ribands in his shoes,"

was not so dreadfully good as D'Isigny. I want you to understand that D'Isigny was a perfectly faultless and perfectly determined man; and also one who never made anyone do what he wanted them to do, with the exception of old Mathilde.

Now his wife; you shall see her, but I am not going to explain her. She said truly, when she said that Marat represented the fury of the Revolution; yet old Lady Somers, whose schoolfellow she was, never *hated* her. I am not Madame D'Isigny's apologist. Lady Somers used to say that she was a wild, violent high-spirited woman, who had been driven into her almost maniac state of fury by her husband's precisionism. She is a ghastly character, and I will deal with her as little as I can until——. The spectacle of a furious old woman—still calling herself Protestant, cut off from the ties of religion, home, country, family, husband—is not a pleasant one. I love to write about pleasant things, and the contemplation of a coarse, half-maddened Tory Englishwoman, in the scenes of the French Revolution, is not pleasant. *Her* intense *apparent* dislike of her husband, and *Mathilde's* intense devotion to her father—one and the same person—is, to a certain extent, worthy of notice.

D'Isigny went stalking about Paris, in his new *rôle* of a deputy, admired by every one for his extremely noble appearance, and well put-on dress. Admired by every one, but by none so much as himself. There was never a pie but his fingers were in it. There was never a plot but what he heard of twenty-four hours before it ever entered in the mind of another man to conceive anything so foolish. We shall have more to do with him afterwards. He went about button-holing and boring every one; a fussy politician, who believed that he was pulling the bell-rope, while he was only trying to make the bell itself shake. So good, kind M. D'Isigny went up and down Paris, saying to himself: "Mirabeau can't last. He was *ébloui* at dinner yesterday, and he was extremely short in his answers, even to me. His temper is going with his health. I shall not have to wait long."

"Dickens, George Eliot, and me:" I heard, said on one occasion. D'Isigny had fully persuaded himself that Mirabeau out of the way, he was the man who would be summoned to save France.

He was as brave as a lion; nay, he was as brave as a tiger, which is more. Yet one morning in this dark winter he got a letter which tested all his courage. It was dated ominously from the Rue Jacquerie (now swept away by Boulevard de Décembre, down which your rifled cannon can go, blasting away revolution); but in the winter of 1789, it was not a quarter of the town into which a decently-dressed man cared to go. The letter dated from such a dangerous place, was very emphatic. That was nothing to D'Isigny, *he* could be as emphatic as any one; but it was an appeal *ad misericordiam* from a sick man, for assistance. That was an appeal which he never could resist; good works among the poor had been a habit of his family for generations. So he started on this,—to a man of his very aristocratic appearance,—very dangerous errand of mercy.

He did not know who had sent to him. The letter was merely signed, "One who loves your daughter." I think that he would have gone without this personal appeal.

So he started on foot, with nothing to defend him but a riding-whip. That he could not have gone into St. Antoine one knows; but this was a quarter a little more respectable than St. Antoine; yet one which would turn out to the tocsin scarcely a quarter of an hour later than St. Antoine itself. It was a dangerous journey. Bailly, to whom he spoke of it, told him that he should disguise himself, and go *en polisson*, if he *would* go; but D'Isigny never condescended to *that*.

He stalked on through the rapidly-narrowing streets until the people began to observe him. At first they were silent, and merely stood out of his way. But the fatal word "aristocrat" was passed on quicker than he could walk, and the squalid wild crowd, in the hideous filthy street, divided before him, and ranged itself on what should have been the *trottoir*, in a way that D'Isigny did not, as a practical man, like.

D'Isigny had heard—nay, D'Isigny knew—that drunkenness prevailed to a very great extent in St. Antoine; but looking at the awful wall of quiet faces which fenced his way, saw that there was no drunkenness among them. These people were of an order above St. Antoine. They were sober enough, dangerously sober, but they were, if such an utter confusion of metaphor may be allowed, calmly infuriated.

Not a single drunken man for a thousand in St. Antoine. Only one, whom D'Isigny may thank. There was a drunken giant, fearfully *ivre*, who carried a child of three years old in his arms. This fellow, reeling from his sober companions to insult D'Isigny, tripped on the rough pavement, and cast the child heavily on the ground.

D'Isigny had it in his arms in a moment. "Mon pauvre petit! Mon cher petit! Regardez donc, et ne pleurnichez pas.

"Madame About viendra,
Avec ses gâteaux et noix,
Et sous son tablier tiendra
Les objets de choix."

So he sang aloud to the quiet little face which lay on his arm, too quiet to please him.

"Mon dieu! I am afraid it is dead. C'est impossible! Madame, I beg you to approach," he went on with a gentle appealing face to a tall, gaunt woman who was nearest to him.

"The child is seriously hurt or else dead. I pray you assist me."

There were a dozen women round him at once: the quarrel between the two orders was so heavy now that they had hesitated to approach him for one instant; the women carried off the child, and the word was passed that it was dead.

D'Isigny was now surrounded by a wild, gaunt crowd of men, and gave himself up for lost. He was very much mistaken, indeed. The eldest among them spoke first.

"Patriots, this man is no aristocrat. This man is not of the breed of De Rétz, or De Sade. He is no monster. He is a good citizen, this man, and is tender and humane."

"I am an extremely good citizen, my dear friends," said D'Isigny, who though brave as a tiger, thought, that under the circumstances, there could be no harm in being on his best behaviour. There was a murmur of acclamation.

"And where is the patriot going, then?" said a very advanced patriot indeed, shoving his way to the front: a gentleman who appeared to have stolen a ragged blue blouse, a ragged pair of black trousers, and an odd pair of sabots, and with no other garments than these: a man who looked like a lunatic who had escaped, and had stolen his two only articles of dress from a broken-down butcher. This man repeated, "Where is the patriot with the fine clothes, and the silver-handled whip, going then? He has been in great danger, this citizen. Where is he going?"

"I am going, my dear friends," said D'Isigny, "to Numero Seize, Rue Jacquerie."

If one of that very advanced patriot Orsini's bombs had fallen among these patriots, it could scarcely have caused a greater effect. They started and stared, and quick words of intelligence, inaudible to D'Isigny, passed among them. "I am going to have an adventure," he thought.

"I am no De Sade or De Retz," he said; "I am, as you saw, deeply grieved by this unhappy accident. I have once lost a child myself, and I deeply feel, also, for all your sufferings. I am bound on an errand of mercy now. Will any kind citizen guide me to Numero Seize, Rue Jacquerie?"

It was singular to see how the greatest blackguard among them all instantly assumed the command. The patriot who seemed to have strayed out of St. Antoine, and who looked like a lunatic butcher, instantly gave the word, "Follow then, citizen," and was submitted to by the others, and by D'Isigny himself. They were, he noticed, comparatively respectable people round; but this horrible man was evidently their master, and his. He followed him.

The crowd stared strangely as they passed along to see such a figure as that of D'Isigny following such an one as that of the man who led him. Yet they did not molest him in any way. The story of the child had passed on among them, and with that frightful figure as his escort, he was safer than with a squadron of dragoons.

Clop, clop, went the sabots over the heavy stones, and the man seldom looked back. They soon left the larger street and got into a labyrinth of narrower and narrower streets, from which D'Isigny doubted if he could ever extricate himself. At last the man stopped, and rang a bell at a low, mean, and very dangerous-looking door.

It was opened by a wild-looking woman of some thirty years. Before the man had time to say anything, one of the strangest-looking women ever seen came out, and said, hurriedly, "Is that M. D'Isigny?"

The strangest woman! Dressed like a Swiss of some canton or another, D'Isigny could not tell of which; with short petticoats, banded hair, and a strange provincial head-dress, white stockings and low shoes, neat and clean as she could be; a strange contrast to the dowdy woman who had opened the door. Such a strange little face, restless, wild, yet tender and piquant, with eyes which attracted his own, and made him set his handsome thin lips as a man does in the effort of memory.

D'Isigny bowed to her in acknowledgment. She said, "Come in, Monsieur. Jean Bon," to the patriot, "I thank you. Go." And the patriot went. D'Isigny went in, and the door was shut behind him.

The dowdy woman disappeared into a room from which there came a smell of cooking—he fancied, principally of onions. The young Swiss woman led him up a rotten old staircase, and pausing at the top, before a door, said, "Go in; he knows that you are come. Don't irritate him, he is really ill."

He was determined not to flinch in his adventure now. He

turned the handle of the door and went in, seeing in an instant that he was among the patriots with a vengeance.

It was a large room, but very squalid; and in the corner was a bed with a sick man in it. Besides the sick man there was only one other person in the room, a young man, about thirty, who confronted him; D'Isigny, saying to himself, "Now I wonder who *you* may be." A middle-sized young man, with a high narrow forehead, a long, thin, hooked nose, and a loose restless mouth. His long hair fell down over the high collar of his swallow-tailed coat. He was not badly dressed, and looked like a gentleman, holding himself very upright, and though slight of figure, seemed almost athletic. One of the first things which D'Isigny noticed about him was his extreme restlessness; his body was never at ease, but was always in an attitude.

He was by way of passing D'Isigny to go out, and D'Isigny calmly drew on one side, raising his hat, to make room for him. The bow was not returned, and the young man was passing on, when a voice from the bed, which made D'Isigny start, said,—

"Do not go, Camille Desmoulins; I have nothing to say to him but what you may hear."

D'Isigny advanced at once to the bed, and looked down on the sick man. It was Marat.

The pillow was white and clean, for the Swiss woman, his sister, the sister who lived so long, had ordered things well for him, as much as Madame the Dowdy would allow her. And on that pillow lay that terrible head soon to be the most deeply loved and the most deeply detested in France. "Hideous?" D'Isigny thought: "Yes. Powerful?—Yes. Beautiful?—No. Well," thought D'Isigny, "it is certainly *bizarre*, and that is one form of beauty."

The head was quiet on its pillow, and it was laughing, which some said was a more terrible time at which to see it than when it scowled. D'Isigny, on this occasion, did not think so. Although the complexion was deadly, the lips were gasping, and the terrible fell of hair was half covering its forehead; he did not feel the deadly shrinking from the head that he had felt before, in England; the laugh was almost pleasant. He was puzzled beyond measure, and, considering to whom he was speaking, what he said was almost comic.

"M. Marat, I deeply regret to see you indisposed."

Marat laughed again.

"I knew I could fetch you here. A mystery or an errand of mercy would fetch you anywhere. Now I hate you, and I hate errands of mercy—or, at least, what *you* call errands of mercy. You, with your handsome clothes and your handsome face, are an abomination to me. I have brought you here to revile you, and to tell you ill news. News which will make you eat your heart."

D'Isigny was the gentleman and the Christian in an instant. He was on his mettle.

"M. Marat, you are disturbed by your sickness. I have never offended you."

"Bah!" said Marat. "Look at this fellow, then. He acts gentleman to me—to *me!*—by heavens, to *me!* Me, who hate a gentleman as I hate a toad or a serpent. If I could get up, I would kill you."

He ended his address in a tone of voice which it would not be unfair to call a scream.

Camille Desmoulins came quickly over from the window in which he had been standing, and laid his hand quietly on Marat's forehead.

The fit of shrieking fury was soon succeeded by a reaction. "Camille," he said, "kiss me. This man has irritated me beyond bearing. I received favours at the hand of this man when I was in England; and they were thrown to me like a bone to a dog. I brought him here to-night for amusement partly, because I know he thinks that he can save his soul by charity, and I had ill news to tell him. And he has behaved like a gentleman, and he has never said one single word of the favours he did me. And I hate you, and will have your head," he added to M. D'Isigny, quite quietly now, for Camille Desmoulins' hand was in his hair.

"M. Marat is excited and feverish, I fear," said D'Isigny. "I am not aware of any cause of quarrel between myself and M. Marat."

"Coals of fire on my head!" cried Marat. "That is the old Christian trick," he cried. "See here, D'Isigny; let me see if I can exasperate you. Our people in Brittany have burnt down your château and pillaged your estate. I had you here to give you the good news."

"Jean, I hope it was not by your orders," said Camille Desmoulins.

"Not by my order, Camille. No," said Marat. "I would have spared him. But when it had happened, I thought that I should like to see his cursed cold proud face flinch for an instant, and so I sent for him. And, curse him, it won't flinch."

"He is behaving like a true gentleman and a good man," said Camille. "You are *enragé*."

"Not quite," said Marat. "See, then. If I hate him I love his daughter. You, *man*, D'Isigny, mark me in this. I know more than you all. Mathilde loved me for my own sake—loved me, because I loved the people. It is not for your sake that I say this, it is for hers. You are all going to the devil together. I know the temper of the people; but I would save her, for I love her, Christian as she is. Now, mark me. If you allow her to set foot in France, she may perish with the rest of you. Mind that you are not her murderer."

## CHAPTER XXXII.

### LA GARAYE AGAIN.

MARAT'S news about the burning of the château was perfectly true. Madame of Dinan had got herself burnt out of her husband's château. The act was an unpopular one in that part of Brittany, as those who did it found to their cost afterwards; for this very furious lady was famed far and wide for deeds of charity, and the country was only gazing at the revolution. Yet it was done, and Madame the Furious was in an old house belonging to her husband, in an alley which takes off to the right, above the gateway, halfway up the Rue Jesouil at Dinan, threatening, in the most indiscreet manner, fire, sword, and fury to the perpetrators.

D'Isigny started at once, and in eight days was looking at the scene of the disaster—looking at the pretty château, where he had been born and bred, now a noble mass of smoke-grimed ruin. They had trampled and torn about the garden, but he found a rose tree which his mother had planted, with one frost-bitten bud upon it. That was all he found of his property which he could carry away, and so he took that.

He rode across at once to his sister's at Dinort. The Convent of St. Catherine's, which was perched on high, looking down upon the swift tideway of the Rance, was strangely quiet under the winter sun, which was paling in the west. It is all gone now, with much else; but in those times it was a high-roofed château-like building, which had been added at a later time to the *ogival* chapel, which had formed part of the original building. The chapel was at the other side of the building to that which he approached, and all was perfectly silent, barred, dead. He knocked, and there was no response.

There had been no violence here as yet. At this time of year there were of course no flowers, yet the parterres were all in order, and a few Christmas roses were beginning to push up through the mould.

He shouted once, twice, and at the third time he thought he heard an echo, and a very singular one. He thought he was dazed.

For it was an echo of music, very feeble and very faint; almost wiry in tone, yet perfect in tune—a chant.

"Bah!" he said. "It is the nuns in the chapel at vespers. Poor souls, are they undefended?"

He went round under the chapel windows, and heard the thin chant go on. It was feeble, yet singularly plaintive and beautiful. But it was not its plaintive beauty which touched him, so much as its unutterable helplessness. He had seen his own house in wreck and ruin, and he began to appreciate the awful tornado which was upon them; and here he found eight or nine lonely, unprotected old women, retreated to their chapel, trying feebly, yet with good faith, to whistle away the wind. So he put it at first.

Yet it was more solemn and more awful amidst the surrounding silence, than the most furious thunder-rattle. D'Isigny's horse, which he was leading, shook himself and rattled his bridle.

"*Cochon!*" hissed D'Isigny; and shading his eyes with his hand, stood there listening to the shrill well-sung chant, until it was ended.

There was a side door into the chapel opposite where he

stood; and when all was silent he beat upon it, somewhat loud, to attract the attention of the nuns. It was answered in a singular way. The nuns inside, at once, with emphasis, struck up—if I dare use such a vulgarism about such a glorious piece of music,—

"Stabat Mater Dolorosa,"

with an emphasis and precision which sent the blood tingling into D'Isigny's ears, and made his eyes hot with emotion. He tried the handle of the door before him, and, lo! it opened, and he passed suddenly into the dim chapel, leaving his horse outside.

He never thought of crossing himself, the sight was too strange and wonderful, yet I fear too common in those days. Nine nuns, too feeble, too friendless, or too brave to fly, had ensconced themselves in the dim, little Gothic chapel, to wait for death. They had determined that they would die singing, like the Scotch Covenanters, and the hymn they had chosen was the Stabat Mater; so when D'Isigny had beaten the door they had begun it. They were all kneeling together when he passed in and reverently advanced towards them; and, seeing only him, they ceased.

"My sisters," he said, "forgive me. I am D'Isigny, the brother of your Superior. Is my sister here?"

A withered old nun rose from her knees, and came towards him calmly.

"Your sister is gone, monsieur," she said, very quietly.

"Do not tell me that my sister has deserted her post, madame—I mean mother. Do not tell me that," said D'Isigny, passionately.

"She has only left this post to take one of greater danger," replied the sister.

"Thank God!" said D'Isigny. "Thank God for that."

For men's hearts and heads were hot in those times, and he had just been looking on the beginning of the great ruin, on the blackened ruin of his own house.

"Yes," said the nun, "our sister has gone to her real post, and I am left to teach these few sheep how to die, as brides of Christ should die."

"And where is my sister?" said D'Isigny.

"By now," said the nun, "she is preparing herself, by a short probation, for the vision of God. The blessed Saint Catherine, whose servant she was, pleads for her, and her time in purgatory will be short; not to be shortened by our masses, for our turn comes to-morrow."

"Explain, madame. Is she dead?"

"The attack of the Revolutionists—for whose forgiveness we pray fasting—on La Garaye," said the nun, "was to take place this afternoon at vesper time. It is over by now. She put it to us, as lady visitor of that hospital, whether her post was not there, as we are not to be attacked till to-morrow. We, weeping, bade her go."

"She was a D'Isigny!" shouted he, waving his hand wildly over his head; and then recovering himself, "Ladies, let me urge you, save yourselves; I have no hospitality to offer you, for my château is in ruins, or by heaven," he added ferociously, "it should have been ill for those who violated it. Disperse yourselves among your friends."

"We have no friends," said the nun. "The young ladies our pupils, and those who had friends, we ordered away under their vows of obedience. We are quite friendless and quite contented."

D'Isigny ran out of the chapel, uttering a furious oath, and leaping on his horse dashed straight away through the *bocage* towards La Garaye.

"Why, this is madder work," he said, as he rode, "than Marat and Desmoulins. Is France gone mad? Where will it end?"

We can answer him now, after the fact. France had gone mad. Where will it end? That question is still unanswered.

The country is very thick between St. Catherine's and La Garaye. The peasants had attacked the smaller game, but as yet had not got either the dexterity or the arms with which to attack the larger. Many a buck went stotting off before him in his wild ride; many a wild boar rushed snorting away; he broke into the chestnut avenue very near the hospital, and paused to listen. Everything was perfectly quiet, save that he could hear an idiot, who laughed at certain intervals a long loud laugh, which ended in a whine.

"It is all quiet as yet," he said; "they will make a night attack." Still he rode cautiously round the end of the avenue into the garden. The usual sounds were going on in the house, but only one man was to be seen. André Desilles, tall, calm, and erect, standing outside the porch.

"Great heavens!" said D'Isigny, as he rode up; "what are you doing here?"

"Keeping guard," said André. "Your sister is inside, keeping the *crétins* quiet. We expect them every moment. Do you know that your château is burnt?"

"Yes, Marat told me, when I went to see him in bed last week."

"Marat! Are *you* gone to the left?"

"Not I. I shall be extreme right soon. This will not do."

"It will certainly not do," said André Desilles.

"It will not do in the least degree," said D'Isigny; and here the conversation came to an end.

But not for long; André Desilles spoke next.

"M. D'Isigny, we are both, I very much fear, near death. I have had very good reason to fear that I have in some way offended you. Father Martin has more than hinted as much to me. Would you tell me what I have done? for at this moment one can say that I love and respect you deeply, and that my offence must have been utterly an unconscious one."

"Bah, what matters it now, then?" said D'Isigny. "Well, I thought that you truckled too much to the new ideas; and I thought, moreover" (for D'Isigny always put the truth last, although he always did put it), "that you had not made up your mind between my two daughters. I know better now. I found you where you should be, at your post. If you have done wrong you are forgiven; if you have done right I apologise; let there be an end of it. What measures have you taken here?"

"None whatever. There are none to take. We shall probably die like rats in a hole."

"H'm," said D'Isigny. "This is very pleasant. How is my sister behaving?"

"Splendidly. Let us go in and see her. Have you quite forgiven me?"

"I have forgotten what I had to forgive; I always loved you in my heart. Let us come in."

"And see the last of it," he might have added, for the end

was very near. They went into the hospital, and *saw* the last of it.

In a large mullion-windowed room, looking on the flower-garden, were the *imbéciles* and the *aveugles*, standing, sitting, walking about, some spinning cats' cradles, or knitting, some playing with toys, some merely moping; the blind sitting mostly silent, in dumb expectation; for although the situation had been very carefully kept from them, they knew that something was going wrong. Among them all moved the five brave sisters whom we have seen before, and in the centre of all sat calmly poor Mademoiselle D'Isigny of Dinort, a woman not considered wise even among her friends, but now calm, brave, dignified, and grand. D'Isigny, with a proud flash in his eyes, went up to her and kissed her, saying,—

"My brave sister! after so long do we meet like this!"

She held her arms lovingly round his neck, while her delicate fingers played with his hair. "My loved one, my brother——"

André Desilles walked once more to the door. D'Isigny soon joined him in a very softened and saddened mood. "André, I *cannot* urge her to fly; I cannot. Would you have me do so?"

"I cannot say. I am really not capable of giving a decision; but I think you would only disturb her mind, for I am sure she would not go. I have something to say to you."

"Say on, for the time is short."

"Do you know that Mathilde is to be married, subject to your consent, to Sir Lionel Somers?"

"I have just gained the intelligence. I thank God that in these times the noblest and best of my children should have a shelter. Though I dread, I very much dread, that there is something of pique in it. They have mutually changed their minds so very suddenly, I cannot altogether understand it. Still a marriage between two such entirely amiable people *must* be happy."

"They kept their secret well," said André; "I was two months at Sheepsden without discovering it."

"You at Sheepsden!"

"Yes, I. I went over to see if I could gain her, and thought that I had done so until I was undeceived, rudely and suddenly."

"Did Mathilde deceive you, my poor André?—surely not."

"No! no! I only deceived myself."

"I am deeply sorry for this," said D'Isigny.

"I am sure you are; but it is not a time to speak of such things. Do you know the news from St. Malo?"

"No, I avoided the town."

"The Revolutionists hold it, but the 18th Bretagne regiment, perfectly loyal, hold St. Servan."

"Can we not communicate with them?"

"I have sent messenger after messenger, but I fear they have no means of crossing the Rance, with the Revolutionary band which destroyed your château between them and us. At all events it is too late now, for here are the Revolutionists."

Here they were, evidently a very dangerous and earnest set of men. They had approached in perfect silence, but with the swift jerky tread of the French peasant when barefooted or lightly shod, which is now idealised into the march of the Zouaves. With one figure in advance they poured rapidly round the corner of the avenue, in a confused, yet compact mass, and the foremost man was face to face with D'Isigny before the latter had fully appreciated André Desilles' last words. Then they halted.

Who can *describe* a mob? Dickens himself has to be very general when he does so. D'Isigny saw before and below him (for he stood on a step) a quiet crowd of silent men, which he calculated to be between three and four hundred strong. The colouring of the crowd was a dull olive brown, with here and there a patch of brighter red and blue. He did not notice what arms they carried, for every face in the crowd was turned on him where he stood.

And ah, such faces; most of them finely shaped—for the French have a large *average* of beauty—but ruined, hungry, quietly exasperated, yet deeply determined. If they had howled and yelled it would have been better; if they had borne him down furiously it would have been better; but there they stood, calm, desperate, in perfect order, with their wild wolfish eyes fixed on him alone, waiting while their chief parleyed with D'Isigny. Verily the wolf had come to the door. He was known to most of them, and known as a just and honest man. They waited for him to speak. A young man in one of the front ranks burst out into a hollow barking cough, which he could not restrain: those round him *sacréd* him, and silenced him.

"My friends," said D'Isigny, with great dignity and calmness, "listen to me."

They were listening to him. The laugh of the idiot inside was painfully audible in the silence.

"I need not ask you what you are going to do. God help me, and forgive you! I stood just now before the blackened ruins of my own home—of the home where my mother nursed me, and my sister, given to God and God's works all her life, played with me and prayed with me fifty years ago. I utter no curse, I invoke no vengeance. Our order may have sinned against yours; but these poor sheep here, what have they done? They are your own flesh and blood; the idiots and the blind of your order. Surely you may spare *them*. Let me plead with you, if you be human."

"I am not," said the spokesman, a very handsome soldierly looking young man. "You have made us devils."

"Let me plead with you one moment. There are none here but two unarmed, a few charitable women, and some unfortunates whom Judas himself would spare. I pray you, by the God who made us, turn from this most wicked expedition, and send your wrongs and your rage elsewhere."

"D'Isigny and Desilles are friends of the people," cried a voice in the crowd, with a strong Breton accent, and there was a distinct murmur.

"Hog! be silent!" shouted the spokesman. "D'Isigny," he continued, "we are not provincials, with the exception of certain grovelling pigs, whom may the devil confound! We are one of the general bands, and we know nothing of you. You said you were unarmed. You lie! you have your sword. Give it up, and stand aside! This house was built by an aristocrat, and must burn!* Stand aside!"

D'Isigny quietly and quickly joined André Desilles in the doorway. "Give me room, André, and good-bye," said he, and André, like a good soldier, obeyed orders; D'Isigny stood alone in the doorway.

The infatuated young man, without giving any order to his

---

\* I can conceive no other possible reason for the most wicked and wanton destruction of La Garaye. Yet there stand the ruins.

followers, dashed up at him, armed with a heavy cutlass.  There was a sudden graceful, rapid movement on the part of D'Isigny, as he drew his sword, and something flickered before his hand like a brilliant spark of lightning.  There were just one or two clicks heard, as D'Isigny parried in *carte*, and then went under his adversary's guard in *tierce;* the next instant the young leader's head fell heavily on the pavement at D'Isigny's feet, and the leaderless Revolutionists saw D'Isigny wiping his sword in a cambric handkerchief, with the dead body of their champion before them.

His triumph was only momentary.  They swarmed on him like wolves.  How long it was before he was beaten down, disarmed, and bound, who can say?—not long.  He was never insensible in the frightful ruin and havoc which followed, but he was stunned and dazed.  He saw a hundred things which it took a great effort of memory to remember: André Desilles, fighting furiously, until crowded and disarmed ; his sister, standing among the other sisters, with some of the blind round them, singing, as it seemed to him, odd verses of all kinds of incongruous hymns, as was very likely to be the case with that poor lady ; again, his sister, with her wimple torn off, and her poor, close-cropped head nearly bald, being pushed along, bound, out of the door, and of a furious fight around her among the Revolutionists themselves ; a tall, quiet sister, with whom no one meddled ; a fierce, bare-headed little sister, who fought bare-headed, and scolded and was laughed at, exhibiting the Old Adam most unmistakeably ; idiots who laughed and cheered wildly ; idiots who shrank into corners and under benches ; idiots who did nothing, and who thought nothing, but were swayed about among the crowd, with a sickened feeling of submission, like logs on a storm-tossed sea.  Blind people who, after each rude push, felt about with trembling fingers in their external darkness ; blind people who shrank terrified into themselves, and with bowed heads, and arms crossed on their breasts, waited for the end ; blind people who, in their darkness, feebly wailed out the name of this sister or that, to come and help them.

Three or four men had stayed by D'Isigny all the time, guarding him ; and what is more, taking care of him.  Once or twice there had been furious demonstrations against him from knots of three or four, but these men who stayed by him always said, "He is a friend of the people, and must be tried." On which they had been cursed for provincials. These men now told him it was time to move.

"Where are we going, then?" said D'Isigny.

"Out of the way of the fire," said one of them.

So he followed them out of the door, and lo! it was dark, and quiet moonlight; and when they had taken him a little way, he was told to sit down, and he found that he was beside his sister and André Desilles, and that two of the sisters were tending on his sister, and two on André Desilles. The fifth, and more furious little sister, was still *emportée*, scolding and raving, but they never heeded her. La Garaye, in the moonlight, was before them.

But as La Garaye never was before. Blotting the moon, rose three great columns of smoke, already red at their lower edges.

"The rat-hole burns," said one of the Revolutionists who guarded them. D'Isigny, with his usual tact and discretion, turned on him at once.

"Of all the foul and dog-like deeds done since France was France, this is the most foul and abominable, aimless, stupid, foolish, cruel, wicked beyond all telling. You have ruined your cause to-day. And do you think that God will not plague France for this? Ask in fifty years hence," here he raised his hand, and the Revolutionist who was nearest to him knelt down suddenly, saying aloud: "He will break his cords, this furious aristocrat;" but adding, in a whisper, in D'Isigny's ear: "For God's sake, monsieur, keep silent. You are among friends, who have risked their lives for you and yours more than once to-day."

La Garaye blazed aloft, fell, and smouldered into the ruin we see it now. The idiots and the blind, in their mental and physical blindness, went wandering off, in a night for both of them more hideous than is the darkest for us—whither? God knows. To waysides, to beg; to alleys in the forest, and to lonely rocks on the shore, to die.

If this happened in kindly, gentle Brittany, what must it have been in Auvergne and Dauphiny?

So our party sat in the winter's moonlight, until La Garaye was burnt, and the scolding sister had scolded herself into quiescence. Then they began to compare notes. André was not badly hurt, only bruised; and Madame D'Isigny, the lady-visitor, passed from loudly desiring martyrdom (which she had been very nearly getting) through a general statement of her woes, until she came to her rheumatism. She had behaved nobly and splendidly the last two days; had made an effort such as very few women, or men either, are capable of. But the danger seemed over, and her rheumatism had been very dear to her for many years, and so she solaced her honest soul with it. And as the few Revolutionists who were guarding them kept them sitting there, on the ground, in a smartish frost, the Lady Superior's rheumatism did really promise to be one of the finest rheumatisms ever seen, likely to cover her with honour and glory for the rest of her life.

D'Isigny once or twice asked why they were kept there. The answer was now—"*Taisez, monsieur!*" Madame of St. Catherine's gathered from this that the Revolutionists had gone towards Dinort; and mingled regrets and anticipations about her rheumatism, with regrets that she had not been permitted to die among her own nuns. Hark! What was that? Musketry.

## CHAPTER XXXIII.

### EXPLANATIONS.

THREE or four well-delivered volleys followed by silence. Their guards left them and departed into the forest.

"It does not matter much," said D'Isigny, "how we are murdered; but I feel a kind of growing curiosity about this new disturbance. What, my dear André, has been the effect of the day's proceedings on *you*, as a matter of curiosity, for instance? How has this burning of La Garaye affected *your* opinions?"

"I have broken with the Revolution, and when I am free I shall instantly rejoin my regiment at Nancy, and do my duty there."

"The sack of La Garaye has done so much for you, hey?" said D'Isigny. "Well, it has done much the same for me. It matters little—our time is short. What do you make of that last fusillade, then?"

"There is no doubt that the loyal regiment from St. Servan has crossed the river, and has met with the insurgents. Which have won I do not know, but here comes our party. It is the regiment, by heaven! I congratulate you sincerely."

Directly afterwards Louis de Valognes was beside them.

"Here they are," he shouted, "safe and sound. Bring torches, that we may see them; bring knives, that we may cut their cords. Great heaven! what happiness. Come quickly, wooden feet."

"Do not haste," said a loud, fierce, strident voice, which they all knew, and at which Madame the Lady Superior betook herself to her prayers. "Pray, do not haste, messieurs. Let me see these fools, tied head and heels like rabbits: think that had it not been for me you would not have been here at all, and let me look at them."

"My dear madame, consider," said Louis de Valognes. "Pray think, my dear madame——"

"Out of the way, sparrow!" said Madame D'Isigny; "let me look. Ah, *ciel!* there sits on the cold grass the great and dignified D'Isigny himself, bound like a sheep. But he looks grand, this husband of mine! but he looks noble!—oh, yes! So you have been tampering with the Revolution, my dear? Ah! and how do you like it now? Not very well? And how is your Mirabeau, my dear? Bah! untie the man; he is too pitiable a sight—untie him. And my sweet sister of Dinort, and her singing nuns,"—here the Lady Superior turned her face and trembled,—"are they all murdered? No; the wicked old woman of Dinan has saved them by showing manhood and generalship. You may sing again until next fortnight—until the *revanche* comes for what I have done to-night: then your nuns must go. The men who could have stamped out the fire —D'Isigny, De Valognes, and Desilles—have let it spread, and it will burn you, my dear, in time. I, a poor, weak woman, have stayed it for a time, but not for long."

The Lady Superior began, "My prayers, sister, are at your service——"

"*Your* prayers!" said Madame D'Isigny, with a snort of the most unutterable contempt, and a theological opinion which I cannot reproduce. "*Your* prayers ! Here, messieurs, untie this other one : this man of oil. *Man,* did I say ? This creature of every Christian virtue, this André Desilles, who has just allowed that English booby, Sir Lionel Somers, to carry off my daughter from under his nose, and has neither shot him nor run him through. Unbind the man who has given up my daughter Mathilde without one blow, and let us see if he can stand upright, or if he crawls on all fours."

"Madame ! madame ! for the sake of the forgiveness of heaven !" interposed Louis de Valognes.

"You mean that I require the forgiveness of heaven for coupling the name of André with hers ?—You are right ; but I doubt if I shall have it. Mathilde !" continued Madame D'Isigny, now white with fury, "Mathilde and he ! Ah, heavens, go. She who is worth us all put together ten times over ; she to think of *him !* Ah ! well, that also is ridiculous once more. I do not wonder. Sir Lionel is the best, after all."

She had scolded herself into—not quiesence—but simply exhaustion, and André Desilles' voice came in very calmly and quietly.

"Madame has been talking extreme nonsense, and most mischievous nonsense. Is it possible to make madame understand that she is making of herself a spectacle extremely humiliating?"

Madame immediately gathered herself together for departure.

"My dears," she said, quietly, "if I stayed longer I might get *emportée* and angry. At present I have been perfectly calm, and have said things which will rankle in your hearts, and come to you when you wake on your beds for some time. At present I have the best of it ; and as I do not intend to have the worst of it, I will make my *congé.*" And so she departed, firing a parting shot at her husband, who had had nothing to produce against her but a very dignified attitude. "*You* tampering with the Revolution ! It would take a man to do that !"

So she was gone, and they looked after her as she sped away, gaunt under the moonlight, through the soldiers, away towards the forest. When she was out of sight they began to talk again. D'Isigny, feeling a certain loss of dignity, drew himself up and began to bully at once.

"Well, my good son-in-law," he said to De Valognes, "and so I find that we have to thank you, of all men, for this disgraceful business. The country is well served, *par Dieu!* Here is my son-in-law, in command of his regiment, who I may say looks on and allows his father-in-law's château to be burnt, and as if that was not enough, stays in garrison while one of the most beautiful and useful charitable institutions in the country is utterly ruined and sacked by a horde of miscreants of whose existence he must have been perfectly aware."

"Monsieur, mon père——" began Louis.

"What matters it. You have a fine story to tell, no doubt. For me, I look only to results; and what do I see? My château burnt, and the hospital sacked and destroyed. *N'importe.*"

"Mais, mon père——" said Louis.

"Mais, mon fils," said D'Isigny, "this is scarcely the time for telling a lame story. Some other time when we meet again; when France is once more tranquil, for instance, we will hear this little story of yours, and laugh over it. For the present, I must see to my sister and her rheumatism. My sister, come with me to your convent. I will protect you, and we will tell those poor nuns of yours that even if their throats are cut, they will be avenged three or four hours after by M. Louis de Valognes."

So he departed, leading his sister, and having succeeded, by mere groundless assertion, in putting every one else apparently in the wrong. He had practised this trick so often that it was no wonder he was perfectly *au fait* with it. He went off towards Dinort, affectionately leading the Lady Superior through the forest by rough and rude bye-paths, well known to him from boyhood. The poor old lady had a sad time of it; for although he was most gentle and affectionate, he was so ostentatiously careful of her, that she would almost as soon have been alone. Her shoes kept coming off in the clay, and D'Isigny put them on again: her wimple was torn by briers, he rearranged it. Nothing could be more tender; yet she was afraid of him, as she always had been; she loved him, as she always had done; she revered him beyond most men. But he had neglected her for very long, and his ostentatious kindness on this occasion over-powered her. She was glad when she got safely to her dear old convent, was welcomed by her nuns, and found herself in her old simple parlour. She was somebody *here*, at all events, though she might only have a week's lease of the place.

The nuns welcomed her "with effusion." I wonder if the habit of self-assertive bullying is catching, and goes by example? This gentle old lady, if she had found her way home entirely alone, would have thrown herself into the arms of these nuns, and they would all have bewept and behowled themselves together. But arriving under the escort of D'Isigny, Madame stood on her dignity, and put them aside.

"My daughters," she said, "save your tears until there is occasion. Unless your hearts were stubborn, you would be singing hymns of joy for the deliverance which my brother has wrought for us." (A pure fiction, but one in which she believed the moment she had spoken the words.) "Be humble, my daughters, and make our deliverer welcome. He and I have borne the burden and heat of the day: see to him. As for me, I will go to my room and pray. Has Father Martin been?"

Father Martin had not been.

"I suppose they have murdered him. Sister Priscilla, come with me to my room. Good-night, brother; the sisters will see to you. I am utterly spent. Good-night."

Sister Priscilla, who followed the Lady Superior to her room, was surprised and alarmed at a very singular fact, one she had never seen before. Madame the Superior was cross, nay, almost fractious. Sister Priscilla, good soul, generally the most *difficile* sister of the lot, was in a condition of loving sentimentalism at welcoming back the dearly beloved mother; but the dearly beloved mother was decidedly cross, for the first time in her history. Even when sister Priscilla had got the mother's legs on the fender before a good fire, and had given her some hot wine-and-water, the mother was not quite herself. The patient and good sister Priscilla looked on her so tenderly and persistently, that the good mother gave way at last, and called herself a wicked old fool; on which sister Priscilla dissolved herself into tears, and the two foolish women fell into one another's arms without explanation.

It has been noticed often by those who knew M. D'Isigny best that, although he was possessed of every Christian virtue, the effect of his society upon the temper was always unfortunate.

Meanwhile there were left on the lawn before the still smoking ruin of La Garaye, Louis de Valognes and André Desilles. When the brother and sister had departed, they looked at one another, and fairly burst out laughing.

"How cleverly he turned the tables on us, and went off with flying colours," said Louis.

"He couldn't turn the tables on his own wife, though," said André Desilles. "But then who could? What is the history of *this*? How did *she* come here?"

"The regiment of Morbihan was beaten out of St. Malo yesterday by the Revolutionists, fairly beaten from street to street, and were forced to retreat to us at the Tour Solidor. We knew of the revolutionary bands over here, but we had no means of crossing the Rance, and were utterly puzzled. This mad old woman, this mother-in-law of mine, was not at fault though. She got a sufficient number of loyal fishermen to drop down their boats on the tide and take us across; and what is more, came herself, and saw that all things were done in order. We left the Morbihan regiment in garrison, and came on. That is all."

"Where is Adèle?"

"In the Tour Solidor, quite safe."

"How does she stand all this?"

"Very badly. She is in a delicate situation, and has utterly lost nerve. What is this between you and Mathilde?"

"Nothing."

## CHAPTER XXXIV.

### THE SHEEPSDEN LETTER-BAG.

T was night, and Mathilde was alone, when Mrs. Bone came in to her by the fire, holding three letters in a corner of her apron, between her finger and thumb. "Letters, miss," she said, "from France." Whereupon Mathilde fell upon her, and kissed her, after the manner of her nation. The three letters flew far and wide in the struggle, and the first one which Mathilde got hold of was from her father.

### M. D'Isigny to his Daughter Mathilde.

"My Child,—

"A fortnight ago I received a letter from Sir Lionel Somers—much delayed in the transmission—which I am bound to say gave me the deepest grief and pain.

"I thought that there was one single soul left in this false and hollow world in which I could trust. I actually, at my time of life, believed that there was one being whom I loved, who was not entirely false and treacherous to me. How I have been deceived, Sir Lionel's letter has shown me.

"I am myself utterly at a loss to conceive in what manner I have so entirely forfeited your confidence and your duty. I am unaware in what way I have failed in my duty to you as a parent. That I am an imperfect character I am aware, and I may not have done my duty to you; I may have erred in my affection for you, by hesitating to point out with sufficient emphasis and persistency the faults which I saw in you. Let all that be granted. But how much better would it have been had you calmly pointed out these shortcomings of mine, instead of treating me with what I am forced to call treachery and deceit.

"I had designed you for nobler things. I believed, as I told you last year, that you could be trusted as few women could. I then asked you, were you prepared to act with me in any complication which might occur? Your answer was 'Yes; that you could die mute.' Your conduct says 'No;' and I have done with you.

"Done with you; that is to say as a trusted friend and an obedient daughter, I can trust no longer now. I can only command; and when the time comes I *shall* command, and you will obey. For you, with the traditions of our family, to have taken up with the discarded and deceived lover, and, without consultation with me, to have engaged yourself to him, is a dereliction of duty and propriety so utterly monstrous that I confess my inability to deal with it in anything like a reasonable temper. I can go no further with the subject at present.

"At the same time I call your attention to one fact. In case you are required here, to look after your sister, I shall demand and command your attendance. I have no more to say.

"D'Isigny."

Three days before he had quietly told André Desilles that the marriage was a good and convenable one; but there are men who will bully their women as long as their women will let them; and so D'Isigny revenged the fearful bullying he had got from his own wife on poor Mathilde.

It maddened her. She believed every word of his foolish ill-temper, and abased herself utterly. Her horror at his silly, cruel letter was so great that she could not weep,—only walk to and fro, moaning, believing herself to be the most worthless, false, and ungrateful being under the sun. Mrs. Bone and William heard her walking up and down, talking to herself, and forbore to go in as usual. "Mademoiselle has heard bad news," they said. Indeed, she had.

"He cannot trust me? Ah, heavens! he might, if he knew all. Would I not give up Lionel and life for him or for Adèle. Ah, so cruel, papa, yet so just and so true. Ah! he cannot love as I can; yet, what matters? The angels in Heaven do not love—only contemplate. And I was the last in whom he could trust, and I have deceived him. That is very true; and I am so wicked. I was the very last in whom he trusted, and I have deceived and betrayed him. Why did he leave me alone, without his guidance, here? Because he trusted me. And I am never to have his confidence again? Is there no way? Yes; he speaks now—as he spoke before—of a trust he had for me to fulfil. Let him put me to the test, and I will fulfil it. He asked me, 'Could I die mute?' Yes, by the holy crucifix! Yes, by the holy presence——"

She paused, as if shot. Her great Protestant lover stood before her, looking down on her, and on her raving with a disturbed and puzzled face. For one instant, and for one instant only, she felt ashamed that he should have seen her in her passion and her despair. Another moment she had wound herself around him, and was crying, "Lionel! Lionel! I have no one left me in the world but you. Kill me before you cast me off, dear. I will die mute, as my father asks. But kill me before you leave me; for I have none left but you."

English gentlemen, in those days, had, if all stories be true, a remarkable faculty of making themselves agreeable to women,—a sort of love-making instinct, in fact, more or less dangerous, which they seem to have lost in the march of civilisation. Sir

Lionel, though not a man of the world, seems to have had some dim idea as to what was the best thing to do under the circumstances; for he quietly drew her to a chair, and said only, "Come, and tell me all about it, dearest." It was not much; but the little was well done. There was a quiet, cool strength about this young man, which had a wonderful effect in quieting Mathilde. He took the letter from her, and read it, keeping his arm round her waist. When he had done he said—

"Have you pledged yourself to go to France, if he demands it?"

"Yes, Lionel. You will not leave me all alone?"

"I will never leave you, my beloved."

"Thank God! for I have no one left but you now."

"There you are mistaken, my little one," said Sir Lionel; "you do not understand your father as I do. This letter is mere temper. He evidently approves of our engagement. Be quiet now: if you are forced to go to France by any bargain with him, I will go with you, and will never leave your side. I tell you, point blank, that there is great danger in going to France just now. Your mother is behaving with the greatest indiscretion on the Royalist side; and Jenkinson believes that there will be a Jacquerie which will throw the old Jacquerie into the shade. Yet, if you have to fulfil your bargain with your father and go, I will go with you. Now, to pleasanter matters: is this the only letter you have got?"

"Nay," said Mathilde, cheerfully; "there were two others. Mrs. Bone brought them in on the corner of her apron; and I, in kissing her, dispersed them somewhere. There they are."

Sir Lionel picked them up and brought them to her. The first she read was more pleasant than her father's letter; it made her smile and laugh with honest happiness.

"DEAREST DAUGHTER,—

"The blessing of our Lord, of the Virgin, and of all saints be upon you! until we both, after our necessary trial and purification, meet face to face in Heaven.

"I thank the Lord always for you. In your rising up and in your sitting down; in your going and your coming, I praise God for you. I praise God because he has let me, in these later times, behold a Christian. Christianity, my daughter, means an utter abnegation of self; and I have seen that in you. I, therefore, praise God for you always.

"They say that you are to marry this Sir Lionel Somers. I am content; for he is noble, good, and Christian. I could have wished him a Catholic; but one cannot have everything. He will hold your faith sacred; be careful to hold his equally sacred. I am no believer in proselytes, now-a-days. He has had time to form his opinions. I think them erroneous; but if they are disturbed, you will have dangerously to disturb much else with them. My daughter, always remember that the duty of a Christian is edification—the *building up* of faith of any kind, not the *destruction* of it. Our own Voltaire, of whom, as a Frenchman, I should be proud, has pulled the edifice about our ears. *Enfin.* But he puts nothing in its place. My dear, the destruction of the Christian religion was as well done eighteen hundred years ago, by the Scribes and Pharisees, as it has ever been done since, even by Voltaire. The petty and miserable formulas which these destructives give you in the place of our grand Christian morality, developed through so many centuries, are as vague as the wandering waves of the Dead Sea, and are as bitter and as dusty as the apples of Sodom in the mouth. Have I not tried them myself then? Was I not nearly prosecuted for heresy by Cardinal Leroy?

"I say this to you because you are about to marry a Protestant, and because your father, in whom you trust among all men, is blown about with every wind of doctrine; going in here, going in there, until he has lost the respect of his best friends. *I would sooner see you a Protestant than see you such as your father is.*

"Keep, my daughter, to the Catholic faith, in which you were born. Let no man delude you into the idea that you can 'change your faith.' Such a thing is utterly impossible. A change of faith presupposes an examination of arguments. *No* faith will stand such an examination. Stay by our old Catholic formulas; they may not be absolutely perfect, but they are well enough.

"One word more. I speak these words in the face of *death.* Do not come here. We French are beginning a total *bouleversement* of all things. I cannot say where it will end. Your old friend Marat is in retirement; but his demand for three hundred thousand heads will be answered, unless I am mistaken. We secular priests will have to pay, in our lives, for the wickedness of such regular priests as De Rohan and Leroy. *Do not come here.*

"God bless you! As I said before, I thank the Lord always for you. I shall have no grave, or I would ask you to come and weep over it. Still, we shall meet again before the night. The night is very dark, and grows darker hour by hour; but Christ is risen, and has become the first-fruits of those that slept.

"MARTIN P."

"So they do not all hate me and despise me, you see, Lionel," she said. "There are some who think me worthy and good."

"Do not I? Does not every one?"

"Well, my father does not; and that just now is a very bitter thing. I wish you had not seen that letter of his."

"If I had not seen it, I could not have comforted you."

"I could have eaten my heart out in quiet," said Mathilde. "I want to gain your respect, and how can I ever gain it if he writes me such letters as that, and if I let you read them?"

"Do you think they would make any difference to me, knowing your worth as I do?"

"*You* think not; but I do not know. Your respect for me may survive this attack on my sincerity, made by my own father; but it would not survive many such attacks. You are in love with me just now, and all that I do is beautiful in your eyes. The time will come when the mere sentimental love which you have for me now, must develope into something nobler and higher—into respect, confidence, and perfect trust: so that we two may go hand in hand towards the grave together, without one single cloud between us. How then will it be, Lionel, when our honeymoon is over, when my beauty is gone, when I am grey and cross, and old and unattractive; and you and I are left all alone together in this weary world, waiting for death? Will you not say then, 'I cannot trust this old woman; her own father, a just man, accused her of treachery and of deceit?' The bitter words which you have read to-day will come rankling up in your heart then, and we shall go to our graves side by side, but not hand in hand. Ah! but it is cruel of him."

Sir Lionel was very quiet with her. It was some time before

he spoke, for the simple reason that he thought over what he was about to say before he said it; and when he spoke it was to the purpose.

"Mathilde, I do not wish to speak hardly of a father to his daughter, unless it were absolutely necessary. But it *is* necessary that I should tell you that I have a growing contempt for your father, and that selfish attacks, from him on you, like this one, only bind me to your side more closely."

"So you think now, Lionel; but if he attacks me thus, you will get in time to believe in his accusations, and they will undermine your respect for me. You think not; but a woman knows, when a man thinks. Instinct! Ah! yes, then, instinct. Your dog knows to which bush the wounded bird has crept, and leads you to it, when you yourself would tread upon it without seeing it."

Sir Lionel's reply to this was that of a lover, silly and foolish beyond measure. A kiss, and a few affectionate sentimental platitudes; earnest enough and sincere enough, but utterly out of place with *her*. The woman was in earnest, the woman's heart was on fire; she had been bitterly wronged by her father, the man in whom she trusted beyond all other men. She had tried—clumsily enough, perhaps—to state her case to Sir Lionel and make him understand it, and he ended by answering her by a mere common-place, sentimental love passage: put his arm round her waist, and by doing so showed her, once for all, that he was incapable of understanding her.

She acquiesced in his embrace with a sigh, which he did not understand either. Yet she felt that there was some one left who loved her; and in weariness laid her head upon his shoulder, and looked up into his face.

The next letter was from Adèle:—

"*St. Servan.*

"I suppose that you thought I was dead. I am, however, not dead; though nearly *ennuyée* to death. I think you might have written to me. I do not ask either for commiseration or for sympathy; I only ask for a sister's love. I do not doubt that I have it, only I wish it would express itself more often. However, I utter no complaints, further than remarking that the total desertion of me by my own family seems to be utterly heartless and cruel. I say no more. I can bear my own burden.

"I suppose that you will reply, that you did not know where to write to me, and also that I had never written to you. I should conceive such a line of conduct on your part to be highly probable. I am not at all clever, and am but a poor judge of motives and actions, but I should not be at all surprised if you took that line.

"Sheepsden was triste enough, but this country is utterly unbearable. We are besieged and threatened always by an atrocious Jacquerie. Louis is but very little with me. He is as kind and good as ever; there never was anyone kinder or better. It may interest you to know that the Marquis was very ill last night, and that I shall soon be the Marquise de Valognes. It may interest you to know that. That I as Marquise de Valognes will ever be as great a lady as you will be as plain Lady Somers, I very much doubt. My dear," (this expression was erased), "they are burning the châteaux, the wretches! They have burnt our father's, and have burnt mamma out. They have destroyed La Garaye, and, therefore, what will they do with *my* châteaux?

"My dear" (not erased this time, she was getting over her petulance), "I must speak to some one, and I have no one to speak to but you. I am leading the life of a corporal's wife, in an atmosphere of drums, and, for the last few days, musketry. The day before yesterday, part of the regiment in which my husband holds commission as Captain, was beaten from St. Malo. Here I am in the Tour Solidor, without a soul in life to speak to. Lady S—— is here, and Lord C——: with their stupid insular coarseness they seem to enjoy the escapade. But, as Marquise de Valognes, I am forced to show them the difference in our ranks; and they laugh much, these English: what is more, again, they laugh at me. *I* heard them. Aha! my Lady S——, you laugh then. This is well enough in times of *émeute*, when one herds with anyone. Wait, my Baroness, till I meet you in Parisian society, with all the prestige of my great rank,—I will say nothing of my beauty. No, my dear lady, I am not so tall or so fat as you; but I have my attractions. Wait then, my lady, until we meet in the old Parisian society. She is Orleanist, this woman! She is Palais Royal, this woman! Let us wait until we meet at Versailles; when the King has stamped the Jacquerie out under his feet."

Wait, indeed, my poor Adèle; and if you will forgive a vulgarism, wait a very long while.

"I have enraged myself about this woman, and have wandered. It matters not, my dearest old Mathilde; I tell you that she is unbearable, and that Lord C—— is a pig. I will say not one other word about either of them. Lady S—— is Catholic, and Lord C—— is Protestant; yet they both court favour with the people by fussing about among the wounded. They were welcome. But when Lady S——, after laughing at me, finds that I am in the way to become the mother of a Marquis; then that she should suddenly change her tone, and become pitifully affectionate to *me;* then——but I will speak of these people no more, not one word.

"I heard Lord C—— say, 'She is a terrible little fool;' and Lady S—— said, 'She seems so. Lionel Somers will do better with the elder sister.' For my part, my dear Mathilde, I am sure I hope he *may*. You have qualities which I am sure will grace the fireside of Ashurst, when dear Lady Somers is in Heaven; but I have a growing conviction that it would never have done for me."

Mathilde had a precisely similar conviction. And it is remarkable that the Rector, the Rector's wife, Mrs. Bone, William the Silent, Lady Somers, the Dissenting Preacher, and even Martin the Poacher, all held this same fact, put above by Adèle herself, as an article of faith. They said, in different ways: "Mathilde is the one for him. When she is Lady Somers there will be good times in the Valley."

"And Father Martin sides with these people—that is so exceedingly bitter. If there was one person more than another whom I thought I could have trusted, I thought it was Father Martin. He sides with these English. I must seal up here, Louis tells me, for the mail is going."

She had stopped here; but had gone on again a few days later:—

"*Montauban.*

"My very sweet, old, dear Sister,—

"I have not heart to read over the first part of my letter, for I am sure that I was cross and *difficile*. I am at times, as you well know, dearest; though now I have not you and Mrs. Bone to vent my poor little temper on—(Ah! Mathilde, it is a very little one)—and I was shut up in that horrid Tour Solidor, and I was very cross and very frightened. Here! Ah me! I must sit down and tell you everything.

"Of course I was late for the mail: I always *am* late, you know; so I can add to my letter. And the most astonishing and beautiful things have happened which one has ever heard of.

"My lord and master, Louis, came in to me, that night when I was so cross, and when I wrote I do not know what of crossness which you may read above; and he announced to me that we were Marquis and Marchioness, and that there were eight châteaux and forests, and the hotel in Paris, and many other things. He did not mention the châteaux and the other things, but I have reckoned them all up on my fingers often enough.

"I received the notice of my new dignity but badly. Mathilde, I *do* try to be a good wife to him, and never to be cross to him or give him pain; but you know the state I am in, and I could not help it. I fainted, and I fear very much that I made him a scene on recovering from my faintness. When I came quite to myself and looked up off his shoulder into his dear face, I saw that he was in a very tender and pathetic mood. I struggled up to kiss him, but he anticipated me; and turning from me, he said to some one who stood by, 'It is utterly impossible that she can go to Paris.'

"And Father Martin's voice said, 'It seems totally impossible. What do you think, Madame?'

"I shuddered and clutched Louis tight in my arms, for a very quiet voice—do I rave, then? do I babble? I know what I mean—a *grey* voice, grey, cruel, sharp, keen as the weather from the keen north-east, said,—

"'It is impossible. It would be murder to take her there. She must go to Montauban.'

"I was looking at the grey arched stone vault over my head, for we were in the lower room of the Tour Solidor, and as I heard the voice the grey arches all reeled, rolled, and became a dim mass of grey as I fainted again; for the voice which I had heard was the voice of our mother.

"That foolish Sister Veronica, who says she knows everything about something, says that I can't be too careful about the impressions I receive. Heavens and earth!—what may not happen?—and a marquisate!

"She was gone when I came to myself a second time; there were only Father Martin and Louis. Louis said, 'My love, the country is very disturbed, and I cannot, under present circumstances, take you to Paris. We have many châteaux, but the only one which is safe over our heads is Montauban, to the south in Brittany. My uncle seems to have known that, for he has made it his treasure-house. Will you go there?'

"I said I would go anywhere with him.

"'But I mean without me,' he answered. 'I am a peer of France now, and must take my place. A D'Isigny would scarcely persuade a De Valognes to desert his post at this time?'

"What could I say, dear Mathilde, I do love him so: I never loved him so dearly as I did then; he becomes more and more a necessity to me day by day. Yet I am not all a fool: I am not all frivolous. Ah! I could die for him, or for you, old sister. I was ill: I felt almost as though he was deserting me; yet I knew his truth, and I said, as a D'Isigny should,—'Go, dearest; but come back as soon as you can.' I did well, I think; did I not?

"And he is gone, and I am here at Montauban. I can write little more now. Father Martin brought me here, and stays with me. He is very charming, this Father Martin: he shows one little things which one never saw before. There are no leaves now, and no insects, yet he can show one the swelling bud of the horse-chestnut, and asks me,—'Can I believe that this tar-smeared bud will ever develop into the glorious frond of the full-blown tree?' and I say Yes, I have seen it do so; and he says in reply that I could not take my oath of the fact. And he brings me chrysalises, and laughs at me when I tell him that they will turn to butterflies; in fact, amuses me much by his paradoxes. The post is really going out this time. *Enfin*, it is paradise, and my mother has been to see me. I will tell you all about everything in my next letter. Kiss for me, yourself, Lionel, Mrs. Bone, and also the Rector, if you can reach so high, you little !—I will tell you all in my next letter."

With due deference to the "Memoires," we shall take the liberty of doing that ourselves, having only extracted this last letter from the Valognes' memoirs to illustrate our story, to show the Marquise de Valognes as the affectionate, petulant little creature which she most undoubtedly was. She was vocal on all occasions ; Mathilde was also vocal on most occasions, but silent, or nearly silent, on emergencies.

## CHAPTER XXXV.

### MONTAUBAN.

POOR little Adèle had had a very hard time of it. The Revolutionists had done their revolutionary business in St. Malo in a very disagreeable manner. They had suddenly attacked part of the regiment in which Louis was captain, had crowded it in the narrow streets, had fraternised with some of it, and taken the arms out of the hands of another moiety. There had been nearly half a day of scuffling and crowding from street to street, a great deal of squabbling and speechifying, and a little fighting —a very little fighting. Opposite the north cathedral door the mob had let off their fire-arms, and in doing so had severely wounded the maire, a man of their own party, who was at that moment negotiating with the Bishop of Coutances, who appeared on the side of the troops ; whereupon the regiment "let fly," as De Foe says, and killed their own man, the Bishop of Coutances, stone dead.

After this wonderful passage of arms there was a parley. It was ultimately agreed that no one was bound to agree on any subject under the sun ; that any person who should express any decided opinion on any subject should be considered as no good patriot, and "hors de la loi." The assassination of tyrants was pronounced to be not only legal, but admirable ; the domination of Christian priests was resolved to be abominable ; anyone who said anything against the new doctrine "that every man unattainted of crime, of the age of twenty-one years, should be allowed to think and do exactly as he liked," was declared to be an enemy of the State. These and other vague resolutions were passed very quickly. But the concluding resolution was by no means vague, and I think was the only one which reduced itself to action. It was, "that the Régiment de Morbihan, and the company of the Régiment de Dauphiny, commanded by Captain de Valognes, immediately leave this town of St. Malo;" which that regiment immediately did, saying to itself, "Hch bien, donc!" and also, "Mais c'est incroyable."

There was a great deal of noise over these first passages of the French Revolution, but there was little bloodshed. Both parties were afraid of each other. Neither had got warmed to their work. In their fear, both parties saw that the quarrel was a deadly and a desperate one, and so both parties were afraid. The democracy of France did not as yet know its strength. The wolf and the dog had quarrelled, and the wolf was perfectly ready to kill the dog; but, then, the *master*—the man with the whip? *He* out of the way, it would take three dogs to kill a hungry wolf. However, there was the master with the gun and the whip, and so the regiment of Morbihan was let to march over to St. Servan peaceably.

Adèle, however, was deeply annoyed by the misfortunes of the Morbihan regiment, and thought most decidedly that the main part of their own regiment should have crossed in small boats, under fire, into the narrow streets of St. Malo. She thought but little of the officers of her husband's regiment; nevertheless, they knew perfectly well what they were about. The operation would have been a very difficult one, even if conducted by the *gardes du corps* itself, with all its loyalty, even when disguised in liquor. With a regiment like that of Dauphiny, unpaid, consequently sober, and with no Swiss regiment near, the thing was absolutely impossible. To keep quiet, and to get their men to stay by them until they were paid, was as much as they dared hope for. It is doubtful if even they would have moved on the Revolutionists at La Garaye, had it not been for the influence which a frantic woman always has on men in times of excitement; the frantic woman in this instance being Madame D'Isigny.

Adèle was utterly out of humour with everything. Louis was

exceedingly poor, and she really was leading a life little better than that of a sergeant's wife. She had, since her break with Sir Lionel Somers, taken it into her head to hate the English, call them Orleanists, Palais Royalists—all kinds of names—and gave herself ultra-Royalist airs. It so happened that Lord C——, and his sister, Lady S——, having French connections, had come over here on business, and, as we have seen, put her in the exceedingly bad fit of témper during which she had written the first part of her letter to Mathilde.

Louis had come to her with the news of their splendid succession. She was utterly dazed and stunned by it. The Marquis was not really expected to die. What Adèle said about his dangerous illness she hardly believed in; he had been so ten times before: she only said it in self-assertion against Lady S——. He was a hale old man of sixty, who had had illnesses, of indigestion mainly, and had sometimes been crapulous for days and days after an insular drinking bout with some of his English friends; but that he should die suddenly no one ever dreamt. It was no "insular" brandy drinking which killed him; it was that he overdid himself with too much consideration. Cardinal Leroy, prince of the Holy Roman Church, who was found gasping on his bed the next morning, and praying for wine, said that when he left the Marquis the night before, the Marquis was as sober as himself. Valets might laugh, but the noblesse did not. The Marquis de Valognes had over-excited himself about the state of public affairs.

Adèle had not at first taken in the full magnificence of her new station. She at once began to give herself airs with Lady S—— and Lord C——, and to write to Mathilde a more or less true account of her astonishing good fortune; but she kept her ill temper on. It might suit her to be good-tempered and amiable, but that required consideration. No one better than herself knew the enormous social advantage of getting a name for having a difficult temper. She was not inclined to forego that advantage just at present.

It is so very difficult to decide between two ladies, when they both give an entirely contradictory account of the same fact. We have heard Adèle's account of the same matter, which seems entirely probable; but then, just look at Lady S——, from her diary: "Feb. 18" (1790, of course). "Our silly little new-made Marquise," says *her* diary, "more absurd than ever. Yesterday when her husband brought her news of her astounding good fortune, and told her of the awful death of this wicked old Marquis, whom she had never seen; having no grievance left, she was determined to make a new one; she burst into tears, and walked up and down the caserne, lamenting that her dear old uncle had died without her having been there to smooth his pillow." When ladies disagree on facts, we had better not try to decide between them.

One thing, however, seems to be perfectly certain: that when she had fully realised her splendid inheritance, her temper returned; and she behaved most reasonably and most well. Her devotion to the Marquis (whom we will continue to call Louis de Valognes) was excessive; yet she very nobly, under the circumstances (I do not speak ironically), made no opposition to his going to Paris, and consented to go to Montauban with Father Martin. She cried very bitterly on parting with Louis, but said, "You will not be long, my love; not long." She may have been perverse and foolish, but she was very loveable.

Here, for the sake of telling the story properly, I must call your attention to the parting words between Louis and Father Martin.

"I would sooner she went to Paris with me out of mischief," said Louis. "But it is impossible."

"More the pity, it is impossible," said Father Martin.

"Do not let her get into trouble," said Louis.

"I will not, if I can help it. Is she to admit her mother?"

"How can we stop it?" said Louis.

"I know not how. I wish your wife was farther from her mother-in-law."

"But you," said Louis, "can manage Madame D'Isigny. I have heard you say things to her absolutely terrible."

"And with what result?" asked Father Martin. "What is one's purpose in pouring water on a duck's back? As to *me*, she will listen, but act her own way after all; as regards Adèle, Madame D'Isigny will not even so much as listen. She will play Adèle as a card, mark you. I thank God that Mathilde is safe married in England."

"Not married yet," said Louis.

Adèle had not seen the Revolution as yet. She hated it, as a child hates the pagans, the Roman emperors, inbred sin, or the Jesuits—from hearsay. She knew but little of their purposes, and less as to how they were to be carried out. In her journey to Montauban her knowledge and her hatred were considerably increased.

She was a tolerably good hand at bullying or coaxing, or both, every one whom she met, to let her do exactly as she pleased; and she very soon managed the gentle and tender-hearted Father Martin. He tried hard to prevent her from taking the old Château D'Isigny on their way south to Montauban. He told her that it would shock her; that it was merely a mass of charred ruins; but for some reason she was determined to see it, and prevailed. As usual, Father Martin was right, the effects of the sight upon her were almost disastrous.

They alighted from their coach at the ruined gateway, and walked arm-in-arm through the winding but now neglected shrubberies; Father Martin silent and anxious, and she rallying him and prattling on about their rebuilding it with their money as a surprise to her father, when the king should have stamped out this embroglio. She remembered every step of the way. Here was the place where André and Louis had hidden in black masks, made—do you understand?—of an old *tablier noir* of Madame, their aunt of Dinort (which was droll again, if you thought of it), and had rushed on her and Mathilde as brigands, and made Mathilde cry—the foolish Mathilde. Here again, in this very spot they had played, those four, the story of Job! and André Desilles had been the devil, going up and down the earth growling; and he had played so well that he had frightened Mathilde, and she had run away, "for she has no personal courage, that foolish old Mathilde; and here is the end of the wall by the flower-garden, and we shall see the dear old place again—and—ah, great Lord! you should not have brought me here. You should not have shown me this, you cruel man. I shall die! Mathilde! Mathilde!—*à moi! à moi!* Mathilde! Mathilde!"

She had buried her pretty eyes in Father Martin's cassock, and had clutched his strong arm with her tiny fingers, for they had come suddenly on the old home of her childhood, and she had seen the ruin, and had appreciated it in one instant, in her keen, narrow little brain. Only one stark blackened gable rising from among the scorched trees; and that solitary flame-eaten gable pierced by one half-ruined window—the window of their old nursery, where, years agone, she had prattled, played, and quarrelled with poor old lame Mathilde. She had looked on the Revolution at last.

She lay moaning on Father Martin's cassock. A wolf, disturbed from among the ruins, with arched tail, raised lips, and grinning fangs, fled past them to his lair in the forest; but this she did not see. Father Martin got her away, and by the time they reached the carriage she was quite silent, and sat silent beside him for the rest of the journey—quite silent. Father Martin got thinking somehow of a pretty, charming little kitten he had had once, while studying in the ecclesiastical seminary at Coutances—the nicest little kitten in the world; how the bishop's forester, bringing home a present of quail to his room had brought his dog, which had hunted his kitten into a corner. Why did he think of that expression of utter terror and unutterable hate, which he saw in the face of his dear little kitten just now, with the lovely and loveable little Marquise de Valognes beside him in the carriage? Who shall say?

The glories of Montauban were veiled in night as they approached it. He handed Adèle, the Marquise, out of the carriage; and as he took her up the steps, cast a look right and left at the splendid façade of the almost unequalled building. There was little to be seen except a broken, apparently interminable mass of peaked towers, with blinking stars behind them; there was little to be heard, except the howl of a wolf, far away in the broad forest, with which the seigneur had fenced this home of unutterable selfishness and sin.

Nothing had been changed, for the old Marquis was buried but yesterday. The house was lit and warmed, and everything was prepared for them. The hall, a very noble one of marble, was filled with liveried servants, mostly young men, mostly (one may say with *ex post facto* wisdom) of the *Henriot* type. Silent, obedient, watching. Father Martin shuddered as he looked, and said to himself: "*Here* is the Revolution;" and, for my part, I do not think that the good Father was far wrong.

The person who *ex officio* received Adèle was a very quietly-dressed, lady-like woman, in grey silk, with a few, very few, rather handsome jewels, but who, in mark of her being a menial, wore a cap; which Father Martin recognised as the cap of Coutances; but, as he remarked, worn with a difference. There was a bit of lace about it somewhere, or there was something which a stupid male eye could not detect; but although it was of the same shape as the cap which the Coutances girls wore (and with which, meaning no scandal, Father Martin, when a student, was tolerably familiar), yet it was a very jaunty cap. And the woman again? Father Martin was now an old man, and his ghostly duties had carried him into some very queer places; and whenever he thought of the very queerest places to which he had been called to perform the last offices of his religion, he always thought of a certain square-faced, middle-aged woman, in a cap smarter than anyone else's, however dirty she might be. And here was this same woman, in silk and diamonds now, receiving Adèle with *empressement*, and preparing to conduct Madame la Marquise to her apartment. Was it the *same* woman, or was there a race of them?

If Father Martin had known his Hogarth he would have seen his friend looking out of window on the right-hand side of the street in the "March to Finchley," not to mention elsewhere. Curiously enough, Shakspeare, who got nearly everything, never got her. Poor, foolish, nonsensical old Quickly and she are miles apart. Defoe got her as "Mother Midnight;" as did also Hogarth. Dickens *once*, and only once, in the "Uncommercial Traveller." The least said about her the soonest mended. Nothing on earth is gained by the contemplation of unmeasurable wickedness. Defoe tried, holding up the character in its native wickedness (that is the formula, I believe), and did less than no good at all; merely disgusting the good, who did not want disgusting, and telling the wicked a great deal more than they knew before. I would not have touched on the subject unless I had been in good and pure company. I would have avoided the subject if I could.

Father Martin saw this woman advance to greet Adèle, with a calm stare in her wicked old eyes—a *connoisseur* stare—which made him clench his teeth and clench his hands. He saw his own Adèle, his own little silly ewe lamb, innocent, foolish, loveable, careless, go toiling up the great marble staircase with this woman holding the light for her, and staring down on her as she lighted her. Did he swear?—there are many kinds of swearing; he resolved, which is more to the purpose. He resolved that this wicked household should be broken up the next day. " I have full powers to act from Louis," he thought. " But will they go? I wonder what I had better do?" He had assistance the next day, from a quarter whence he neither desired nor expected assistance.

He was utterly lost in thought, until turning round he found himself face to face with a foolish-looking old major-domo, who seemed as though it would be a cruelty to expect him to be sober, and ridiculous to suppose that he ever had sufficient strength of character to get drunk. The young Mamelukes in embroidered liveries still stood round, and among them Father Martin looked on the face of this half-tipsy old fool as on the face of a friend. The Mamelukes stared at Father Martin, in their way respectfully, as at something they had not seen lately. They had seen many queer things, and expected doubtless to see many more; but the spectacle of a secular priest at Montauban was almost too much for even their highly finished manners.

" Monseigneur L'Évêque " (the major-domo thought he would be on the safe side, though he knew that Father Martin was only a priest) " will be desiring his supper. It is prepared."

" My supper," said Father Martin, recovering himself. " Certainly. Send these young men to bed. You can serve me."

That was impossible. Monsieur the Marquis had given orders that his eminence was to have every attention paid him. There was a supper of nine *plats* ready for Monsieur.

" Put them on all together then, and send these fellows to bed. Wait on me yourself. I want to talk to you. I shall stay here until the supper is on the table. Then come you and serve me; and mind that you are sober."

The major-domo was about as sober, or about as drunk as ever he was, when, having put on the supper, he sent the Mamelukes to bed, he stood behind Father Martin's chair, ready to serve him; but Father Martin, leaning his elbows on the table, left some priceless dish untasted while he thought, " Can I get this kindly-looking tipsy old fellow to talk confidentially with me? I'll try him with sentiment;" and this determination of Father Martin led to a little incident, possibly illustrative of those times.

"My friend," he said, rising from his untasted supper, and confronting him, "I fear this has been a very wicked house?"

The major-domo nodded.

"A *very* wicked house?"

He nodded again, more strongly.

"There are rooms," he said, "which will do very well without airing at the present; of these rooms I hold the keys, which will most probably be better in the custody of Monseigneur the Father Confessor, until the return of Monsieur the Marquis. I will yield them to-night. Monsieur the Marquis is very innocent; he should not have sent Madame here without preparation. Madame is fresh and innocent as the rose."

"My friend," said Martin, "I think you are an honest man. I like your face, and I wish to trust you. Had you ever a sister?"

"I had once," said the major-domo, retreating from him, and growing pale. "But I have none now?"

"Do you remember her when she was young, innocent, gentle?"

"I remember her well. A light-footed, bright, beautiful, angel of a girl, who sang always till the birds in the wood sang in emulation: gentle, innocent, amiable, with a laugh for the rich, and a heart for the poor. Lucille was the pride and the darling of our town: why do you torture me? Is she not gone?"

"I do not wish to torture you," said Father Martin, gently. "I wish to call forth your better and older nature. But I ask you to remember your lost sister as she was, and to think of our poor little Marquise in her place. Would you have had your sister lighted to *her* bedroom by the horrible, hideous, wicked-looking woman who has just done so——"

He was as nearly frightened as ever he was by the effect of his speech. The major-domo, deadly pale, advanced towards him again, pointing one finger at him, and said, with a rapid, hoarse, guttural articulation—horrid to hear—"You are no priest—you are a fiend out of hell. That hideous hag who has just lighted up the pretty bride, IS my sister, the tender, gentle, little sister, in answer to whom the birds sang. He, the late

R

Marquis, who now"—(I will spare my readers)—"*He* made her what she is. Is it a wonder that I made myself what *I* am, and tried to forget it?"

So the major-domo departed like a hot Breton as he was, leaving Father Martin's appetite for the supper of nine *plats*, by no means improved. He had thoroughly roused the old Adam in this Breton's heart now, for he was in most furious rebellion; he only appeared once again that night. He appeared suddenly at the door of the dining-room, and said, "If Monsieur requires nothing more brought, I will retire. There are the keys of which I spoke to Monsieur." He then laid them on the table and departed.

Father Martin took the keys and wandered over the house. Above, on the higher stories, the footmen were wrangling and laughing alternately. The open rooms he left for daylight; but the few, in a very distant wing, which he found locked, he opened with his keys, and examined. Verily here *was* the Revolution.

## CHAPTER XXXVI.

### MEDEA.

IF it could be stayed, even only at the threshing-floor of Araunah! Prayer had done great things in the history of the world; but could prayer change the counsels of the All-wise and All-mighty. He was bound to believe so: he believed that he believed so: and yet this evening his faith had left him utterly; and all that his prayers came to that long and dreadful night, was a wild *ad misericordiam* cry to God not utterly to desert him in the darkness. Father Martin was not the first who cried "Eloi! Eloi! Lama Sabacthani" in gloom of a dark wild evening, rapidly closing into the mirk of an unnatural midnight, which gave promise of no dawn.

He was a man who hated to excite himself and get into an ecstatic state over his religion. No man in this world was a more uncompromising Roman Catholic than he. No man could fight the battle of the doctrines of his church better than he. Yet no one was more furiously opposed to ecstatic religion.  In the lull which came before the end, he took occasion to illustrate this point by an example to Adèle, who required it.

"The night we came to Montauban," he said, "I wrestled all night in prayer; and towards morning I cast myself on my bed, and had a dream, which can perfectly well be accounted for by the state of my brain.  Had I been a fool I should have called it a vision.  I prayed directly and indirectly, to the saints and to the throne (I do not use his words, but an intelligent reader can supply them), until at last I lay on my bed with the crucifix beside me.  Then I thought of all which happened on Calvary, and prayed for the intercession of St. Veronica; and at that moment I believe that I fell asleep.  The last thing which I saw with my waking eyes, was the crucifix beside me; in another moment, St. Veronica, with her handkerchief, was beside me; and she was beautiful to look upon.

"I would have looked after him who was toiling up the hill, but she would not let me, but held the handkerchief in her hand with the divine head upon it, and bade me look.  And I looked and adored.  But while I adored and wept, the head changed into Latin writing, slowly, letter by letter, beginning from the thorn on the extreme left of the crown, and ending to the extreme right of the mouth.  I repeated the words as they appeared; what were they?  The words of the Lord's Prayer —only that; and when the dream ended and I awoke, I was saying, loudly, 'In Secula Seculorum.'  For ever and everlasting, Adèle.  Not for a Revolution; not for a period of time; not for all time; but 'in secula seculorum,' 'for ever and ever' God's Almighty glory, and his eternal justice is to rule the great creation.  I heard the voices of the wicked Mamelukes* laugh-

---

* Expression antedated most probably.  Martin could not have known so much about them as the French did a year or so later; it may as well stand.  It is *extremely* difficult to put a good story together which in any way touches on the past, without making *wilful* errors.  Of course, in the present state of historical knowledge, no novelist of decent repute would dream of writing a tale of the past without being very particular on the score of dates, costumes, and so on.  Pedantry in such a matter as this, however, very often injures a good story.  What would that splendid story, "Kenilworth," have been had not Sir Walter Scott, with a glorious audacity, outrageously violated all chronology.  He makes Amy Robsart

ing overhead; and I said the old prayer again, and found it the best of all. I slept like a child."

They were very fierce in their faith, just now, these priests. So, unluckily for them, were men of the Marat and Carrier school. Who is going to win after eighty years? we have not seen as yet; and with the Emperor on the tight rope between 120,000,000 of Catholics, "sans compter le petit Mortara," and the Revolution, it would be wise to withhold one's opinion for a few weeks.

Father Martin slept soundly after a time, and when he awoke he became aware that there was a woman sitting by his bedside, with her foot in a silver stirrup, netting fishermen's nets. He was not very much surprised; the Revolution was on them, and nobody was likely to be surprised any more. Still he went as far as to say, Ho, Madame!

"Taisez donc," said Madame D'Isigny the Terrible. "I have come to the end of a row, and I must calculate. I drop here forty stitches in the whole length, or is it forty-five? I wish you would wake like another, and not so suddenly."

Father Martin got quietly off the bed and confronted Madame D'Isigny.

"Madame," he said, "will excuse my extreme dishabille. I was tortured with doubts last night about many things, and I did not take off my clothes. Will you give me *congé* to retire and put my dress in order?"

"If I had wanted to see you in fine clothes, I should hardly have invaded your bedroom," said Madame D'Isigny. "Lie down again. I wish to talk to you."

Father Martin looked for his latcheted shoes, put them on, and then sat on the edge of the bed, smoothing his chin, staring straight at Madame D'Isigny, and absolutely silent.

"Which of us is going to speak first?" said Madame D'Isigny.

Certainly not Father Martin. He sat absolutely silent, at the edge of the bed, stroking his chin, and looking fixedly at Madame.

---

appear at the revels at Kenilworth eleven years after the painful and notorious inquest on her dead body at Abingdon (*vide* Pettigrew's Pamphlet). He makes Leicester nod to Shakspeare, and ask him if he has written any more plays? Shakespeare then being twelve years old.

"I suppose I must speak first, then?" said the terrible Madame, after a time.

As there seemed to be no ghost of a doubt about this matter, she spoke.

"This is a very beautiful house here!"

Dead silence from Father Martin. Nothing but the cool, quiet stare. Madame dropped her eyes and went on with her netting.

"It will make a nice house for the young couple, and I shall be near my daughter in the times which are coming. It has all happened very well."

Not a single word from Father Martin's side: he merely sat on the edge of the bed and looked at her. She, on her part, netted faster and faster.

Did he know his woman? He knew his woman. She had put on her sweetest temper and her most charming manners, in order to entrap him, HIM, into a pleasant conversation. He, on the other hand, desired particularly to exasperate her, and to cause her to make a fool of herself; so he sat on the edge of the bed and looked at her.

She netted faster and faster, and tugged harder at her stirrup.

"You wish to exasperate me," she said, growing white with anger. "You wish to exasperate me by keeping silence. You shall not succeed. No!" she went on, rising, rolling up her netting, and casting it to the other end of the room; "you shall not succeed in exasperating me, on your old priestly trick of silence. Speak, and speak to the purpose."

Father Martin, taking up one leg and nursing his foot, spoke at last. He said,—

"I was waiting for Madame to speak to the purpose. When she does, I will answer."

Madame spoke to the purpose—

"I only wanted your help, and you as priest; or, what is the same thing, as time-server; or, what is again the same thing, as coward; or, what is once more one and the same thing, *coquin et misérable;* sit on the edge of your bed, stroking your wicked old shoe, and driving me to madness. You calculated by your silence to drive me into incoherent fury. You have succeeded —but no, my dear, you have not succeeded in your plan. Look, then. I am coherent enough. I want your help. I am quite calm, see you. But this is not, with its present household, quite the place for my tender and innocent Adèle. You must help me to get rid of this household, my dear Father. You must go with me in this."

Father Martin said that Madame now spoke to the purpose, and that he would be most delighted to do so.

"I am calm and sensible, then," she went on. "That netting which I threw; I saw a rat against the door, and I threw it at the rat. They catch rats in nets, do they not? Was it not clever in me to throw the net at the rat?"

Father Martin, I fear very much directed by the devil, said that Madame's courage was only equalled by her dexterity.

"And they catch rats like that now, do they not?" continued Madame D'Isigny.

I regret to say that Father Martin's answer, while he contemplatively stroked his shoe, and was thinking of far other things, was,—

"Certainly, Madame; all the world catches rats in that way now. And the rats caught so, are far superior to those which are reared as standards, even to those planted against north walls."

"You can be like another, you priest," was Madame's sudden and short commentary on Father Martin's wool-gathering. "I could make you say what I chose."

Father Martin, who had been undoubtedly wool-gathering, felt horribly guilty. He had guessed at her next move, and was thinking how to checkmate it, when he made this horrible fiasco about the rats.

"I am not aware, Madame, that I have said anything foolish while speaking of pears."

"*Grand imbécile!* we are speaking of rats; and all the time I watched you, and you were trying to checkmate me. Pick up that netting there, which I have cast to the end of the room, and then come here; listen and obey."

Father Martin picked up the netting, and brought it to her. But she had met her master for all that. He now sat on the edge of his bed again, waiting for her to speak. She spoke.

"I said just now that these——" (I must spare my readers her language; if they want such, let them read the flowers of speech* cast by our young friend Camille Desmoulins on the path of Brissot) ——"that these footmen must be discharged to-morrow. I have no authority here: you have some. Dear Father Martin, are they, or is that woman, fit companions for my daughter?"

Martin agreed at once.

"I," he said at once, "will do that for Madame. I have power to do so from the Marquis. It is an extremely dangerous thing to do, for we shall make deadly enemies of these discharged servants. You are, Madame, the most furious and *emportée* woman I have ever seen in my life; and I love you for this, because you will not, at any risk, see your innocent daughter living here with this horrible *entourage*. I will have these servants dismissed for you, Madame; but under one condition."

Madame was extremely puzzled to think what that condition might be. Her curiosity so far got the better of her self-possession that she stopped her netting, and put her head on one side. Martin gave his condition.

" I will cleanse and purify this house instead of taking, as I could, Adèle out of it, on the simple condition that you do not, when it is silent and quiet, make it the centre of your Royalist plots. Madame, I adjure you, by the God we both adore, not to involve Adèle. Think, Madame, that you are the mother who bore her. Reflect on her facility, her beauty, her frivolity. Remember the time of her babyhood, and for heaven's sake spare her. I know well, Madame, that you are infuriated in the cause of the Royalists: I know well, Madame, that Adèle, since she has seen the ruins of the château, is infuriated against the Revolution. But as a woman, do not implicate her; as a mother, spare her. Listen to me, then, you inexorable woman. Adèle is silly and a coward, and if you play her as a card, she will ruin the game. Your face is hard and cruel, Madame. You propose to play that card. It will be the ruin of many of us if you do. Do you require a martyrdom? Then send for Mathilde. We could trust her."

Medea was down on her knees at his feet in one moment. Her splendid, square, grey head was just opposite to Father

---

* "Histoires des Brissotins." Imprimerie patriotique et républicaine. 1793.

Martin's as she knelt to him. What did she say? Words. Would she sacrifice her daughters? Let Father Martin look her in the face. Her own daughters! Father Martin looked her in the face, and his answer was " Yes." She has the face of a fanatic. *She* would die for either of them; but then she would sacrifice either for her faith.

However she went back to Dinan that very day, explaining that she had only come for a day's visit to her daughter. And in her house in the Rue de Jesouil, she kept silence, making no sign: while Father Martin wondered when she would come back, and on what excuse.

## CHAPTER XXXVII.

MONTAUBAN, WITH A, AS YET DISTANT, VIEW OF NANTES.

ENNYSON, in " In Memoriam," asks, in beautiful rhyme, the question which most Nature lovers have asked themselves, and which children generally ask themselves—" Can one be sorry on a fine day?" The answer which I should be inclined to give is, that it is not very easy. I can perfectly conceive afflictions so very great that one would never be glad again at all. But, short of actual tragedy, I should say that there were few vexations, however great, which could not be to some extent mitigated by weather.

I was with a poet, and a great one, once, and we were in a boat on a cold, steel-gray river, under a cold, motionless, gray sky, with the yellow willow leaves showering upon us; and he was reading. Suddenly he looked up, and said, "This weather is enough to kill one!"—I said "I love gray weather."—"Ah!" he replied, "if it *moves*, I love it, too." He was right; poets *are* right on such subjects: they are our masters there. The glorious, wild motion of a rushing south-westerly gale, even though you cannot see a hundred yards for the rain, excites and rouses one. The dead, dull, leaden gray sky, which one gets in an English autumn, would affect and depress that nearly lowest form of our countrymen, a betting man; not, of course, to the same extent as the gray arch of the guard-rooms at the

Tour Solidor depressed that sensitive little being Adèle, but still to some extent.

If the weather, which means, after all, a change of colouring, can affect a tipsy old vagabond, what can one think of the effect wrought on Adèle by her change of colouring and circumstances? Winter, gray-ribbed stone, and the life of a corporal's wife; then, suddenly, Spring, a marquisate, and Montauban. She gave way utterly and entirely under it. In spite of Louis's absence, which was her only vexation, she told Father Martin that she was the very happiest and luckiest little woman in France, and that she meant to remain so. Let the Revolutionists keep clear of Montauban; she would—I don't know what she would not do. As for Father Martin, what heart had *he* to spoil her gaiety? Why, none at all.

For he could see, wise man, that Adèle was much *better* under these circumstances. I think I know a French friend who would say that Adèle was a being who required light. Father Martin did not put it in this way. His formula was that she was a delicately-organised and very timid little being, and the worst point in her character, a little feline ferocity, never came out until she was frightened. Great, grand Mathilde, he used to say, had neither cowardice nor ferocity; but there were some, and again there were others, children of the good God. And he was glad and pleased to see his lovely little Marquise happy, gay, religious, kind, good-tempered,— drinking in, as it were, the glorious beauty around her. "She must not be frightened," he said; "she will be spoilt, if she is terrified." Whereas her mother, of Dinan, said, "I could scare that little fool into anything I chose." But she only said this to herself; what she did is more to the purpose.

Martin knew perfectly well that there was going to be an end of all things. Many secular priests knew it; one hundred and forty-nine, for instance, at the time of the *Séance du Jeu de Paume* in the June previous. I fancy that few could have known it better than clever, secular priests, who had toiled all their lives among the lower orders in the towns, and who had to answer questions which, with Cardinal Leroy and the late Marquis de Valognes to the fore, could not be answered by any honest man. At all events, Martin believed that the end of things was come as it was: he had looked about to see where his duty lay; he had prayed for direction; and, behold, he found himself sent to Montauban to take care of this very silly little Marquise.

He readily believed that his duty lay here. Certainly, she wanted much taking care of. Honest and pure as she was, she might be the cause of a great deal of mischief—politically. And her mother, a furious Royalist, lived very close by, and had the *entrée:* and Montauban was buried in the depths of a forest. Madame might well make it a place for a Royalist plot, should such a thing become necessary; and Madame was a fool, and would most probably select this most suspected and lonely house as being secret. Did not half France know that it was one of the most notorious abodes of aristocratic rascaldom in the provinces—the only one for miles round in loyal old Brittany. He was evidently at his post here.

And a very pleasant one. It was a beautiful thing to see Adèle's wonder and delight at all the beauties of Montauban, her *own* Montauban. She had seen, hitherto, practically nothing but that wild, triste Sheepsden in England: this place was an absolute paradise. It really was such a place as I believe one cannot see often in France now.

It stood on a slight hill, nearly a hundred feet high, in the middle of the forest, and was approached by four avenues—not regular pleached avenues as one sees in an English park, but more correctly *alleys*, cut in the natural forest, each one of which was perfectly straight, nearly two miles in length, and of level grass. The timber in this forest was not of any great size where the underwood and covert grew thickest; but in other places there were splendid groups of cedars, oaks, and chestnuts of great size and antiquity, with open glades around and under them. Still, from the château, the general effect was of dense, unbroken forest on all sides, with the four great grass rides approaching it. The stables and necessary offices were hidden hard by in the forest, but carefully hidden; there was no farm, no cottage, within two miles; all was careful desolation: "they made a solitude, and called it peace."

The lodges, even, were not allowed to be visible from the château; they were round the corner, and the long-drawn avenue only ended in a screen of woodland. The old Marquis used to declare that no stranger ever rode or drove round the corner into the main avenue, and caught sight of the house for the first time without exclaiming, "*Parbleu!*" or some similar form of exclamation and admiration; and, indeed, no wonder, for it was exceedingly beautiful.

It stood a little above the level forest, all alone, as though upon an altar. Its colour was deep red, of red sandstone, and the roofs were of slate. The sky-line consisted of an infinitude of crowded French-roofed towers, dominated by the vast, soaring, square sheet of slate, pierced with dormers, which capped the principal tower. Dark, warm, rich, lurid, beyond conception: in the distance it seemed of a heavy reddish purple; nearer, with less atmosphere between you and it, more and more of a rich red; and when you had done admiring its colour, you began to see the extreme beauty of the details. The windows were of dark stone, high and narrow, with only one mullion on each, unlike a Tudor house; and when the sun fell on these windows they flamed with glory, and a wizened child might say, "See! the château of Monseigneur burns!" and its mother would say, "Not yet."

The little hill, the Mont Auban, on which the palace, for it was little else, stood, and which was just high enough to enable the château to stand a little above the forest and to catch the sun,—this hill was scarped on all sides into a terraced garden, so that in summer-time, when you got near the castle, you noticed that, although richly coloured when seen from a distance, when you were close it looked almost dull and dingy, by reason of the flowers in which its foundations were set.

There were no glass houses, and so the effect of it was not ruined, as is the effect of most great modern houses in England, by a ghastly inartistic half acre of glass. There was little need of glass so much south, with the warm Atlantic not so far off. There was only the forest, then scarps and terraces of flowers, then a wilderness of roses, which leapt as high as they could along the red walls, and then aloft the solemn towers and pinnacles. There were no fountains; there was no hill sufficiently near to give the requisite pressure of water. The gist of Adèle's first letter from Montauban to Louis was a particular request that he would allow her to have fountains. "I shall scarcely consider myself properly married without fountains," she said. "All the world have them now." Louis wrote back, and gave her *carte blanche* about fountains: "You have but few pleasures, my darling; would I deprive you of one?"—but she never got her fountains for all that. Circumstances occurred; for instance, her mother took to staying there, who, if I may be allowed to say so, was much more likely to assist at fireworks than at waterworks; and to the end the majestic red and purple pile continued to raise its foundations from the blazing beds of flowers, and break the sky-line with its splendid pinnacles, without the indignity of fountains.

The forest around was the great delight of Father Martin. With the exception of the major-domo, he had dismissed all the house servants; but he had made no change among the foresters and gamekeepers. "There must be," he said, "something to attract a landlord to live amongst his tenantry, and nothing attracts him so much as sport. Louis loves it, and I will not remove this source of attraction from him without his express direction." That is the way in which Father Martin practically treated the game laws, which he often furiously denounced, when he was brought *en visage* with them. But, then, this was an exceptional case. In the first place, he found that the foresters and under-foresters were of a class utterly different from those which I have called the Mamelukes. They were, one and all of them, he could see at once, bright-eyed, swift-walking, Welsh-speaking peasants. They did not even understand the language of the Mamelukes; and on meeting Father Martin in the alleys of the forest, dressed as they were in velveteen and gold, they knelt beside the path uncovered. These men were the people of the country—South Bretons.

In the next place, this παράδεισος was a real paradise to Martin. He was a man who passed through the world loving everything but sin; and, wicked man, very often making the best of *that*. But, from his education, he had been forced to love Nature only through books; and, lo! here she was face to face with him, and an old man in green velvet to show her to him. Father Martin, deeply disapproving of the game laws, held over the question of the disforesting of the forest until he should have had time to consult Marquis Louis. On which the reader may moralise.

The oldest forester and Father Martin were at once sworn friends, for the forester was very religious (as, indeed, were the others), and spoke French, which the others did not. He told Martin many things. "This Montauban," said the Breton, "was the only wicked house around; it was the last wicked house southward; but then it was wickeder than hell. The peasants had been true and faithful to the late Marquis, now in glory or soon to be; for he, the forester, had heard that he had left eighty-five thousand livres for masses, which would, no doubt, be sufficient to pull him through, for the late Marquis was a highly-instructed man, and knew the value of a livre like another, nay, better; and his spiritual director had been the Cardinal Leroy, an eminent ecclesiastic, who would, doubtless, give him the best fiscal advice. No doubt, the Marquis was by this time in glory; but the good Father Martin, doubtless, knew best. It was no business of his, and he begged pardon."

Martin turned to him to see if he was mocking. Not in the least.

The forester continued: "The people had been waiting sadly for the new Marquis, and had hoped that he would have come; for they heard that although somewhat tainted with new opinions, he was good. The Marquis not having come, they had been glad that he had sent his bride with such a good father as the one before him. The people thanked the father for getting rid at once of that abomination in the neighbourhood—those accursed Auvergnois."

"What Auvergnois?" asked Martin.

"The household servants, mon père."

"Do they not come from here, then? I thought they were Breton."

The old forester made a demonstration. He sent his three-cornered hat skimming away over the fern, he stamped rapidly with his feet, he spit, he bit his nails, he pulled his hair into wisps, and he spoke.

"These Norman priests! I ask pardon, they know nothing. Allow me, I beseech you, to relieve my mind in private. Do not listen."

"I must beg you not to conduct yourself like a lunatic," said Father Martin, loftily. "They were, at all events, your fellow servants. These are not times in which to enrage yourself unnecessarily."

The old Breton got calm, and begged pardon profusely. "I

was furious because you believed that these Auvergnois were Bretons. Do you not know, then?"

Father Martin did not know; so the old forester told him, which is all I have to say about the matter. It was an ugly story, like many at that time, and like many now; and Martin hated ugly stories—he had had too many in taking confession. He changed the subject.

"I will talk to you again—often—in this beautiful forest, and you shall tell me what the Marquis shall do for the peasantry; and, trust me, he shall do it, old friend, for the Marquis lives but for good. See here, we are through the forest, and there is a hill before us; let us ascend it. 'Montes atque omnes loci desiderati, laudate Dominum.' 'High hills and all pleasant places, praise ye the Lord.'"

They went up together and sat on the top of the hill among some murmuring firs, which reminded Martin of Sheepsden; he was pleased at getting out of the close forest and looking south on an extended horizon.

"The air comes pleasant here. How far one can see! I see village after village, forest, and rolling hills, and then a dull yellow line, with infinity beyond it. What is that yellow line?"

"La Loire, mon père."

"And that white mass? those are ships, I think."

"That is Nantes, my father."

"Ah! dear old Nantes! I was a child at Nantes once. That was before I went to Coutances to study divinity."

They turned, and saw the noble château, glorious with windows blazing fiery in the sunset, dominating the forest.

"It is a splendid sight," said the forester.

"Too splendid," said Martin. "Let us look southward." And so he turned from the flaming castle, and looked once more on the broad, yellow sands of the Loire, in the dim distance. Not for the last time.

## CHAPTER XXXVIII.

### MONTAUBAN, WITH NEWS OF ANDRÉ DESILLES.

HIS forest became his great pleasure; and indeed it was a very pleasant place; for here Nature, in one of her most luxurious, temperate moods, three hundred miles south of Devonshire, had been left utterly to herself. The formation was half limestone and half new red sandstone, and Father Martin, being just enough of a botanist to enjoy it, botanised immensely, and found all kinds of orchises. He backslided worse than this before he finished.

Then Adèle among the flower beds was a sight to see. Here was a thing she thought she could understand and manage, and she became a perfect little Catherine of Russia among the gardeners (Bretons), and ruled her empire of colour and scent most despotically. She made an awful mess of it, and had much better have left the gardeners alone, for they knew their business and she did not. From being ravished with the result of their labours, she began to improve it and try to mend it in a childlike, little way. She would have blowing flowers moved into other places; she would commit all kinds of petty tyrannies, which made the gardeners smile, while they obeyed admiring, and made Father Martin laugh at her, at which she would shake her trowel at him, and laugh again. So perfectly innocent and childish, the feeblest little body, with another still feebler life hanging on hers.

"Why," said Martin once, in one of his very rare outbreaks of solitary anger, "Herod or Marat would spare her; if that woman——" Father Martin said no more, even to himself; he only ground his teeth.

So they spent their time in frivolities—Adèle occasionally quarrelling with Father Martin. Once she penetrated as far into the forest as the home buildings, where she found horses and mules in abundance, and what was still better, cocks and hens. Now the garden was left more to itself, and it was the poultry which came in for her attention. She declared that Martin had known of this beautiful menage so close by in the forest, and had not told her, for his own purposes. Here were horses also—why should they not ride together? Well, it might be better not. But there were ladies' horses, which had been kept in exercise by grooms with horse-rugs. They were the horses of Mademoiselle Minette. Who was Mademoiselle Minette? Father Martin knew, else why did he blush? She had her suspicions, this little person. Who was this Mademoiselle Minette!—that was all *she* asked.

And indeed the good father at this time gave cause for suspicion. Adèle watched his behaviour. What did that man do with himself before *déjeuner*, at eleven o'clock? That was what she wanted to know; and the very moment Louis came back *would* know. Louis should ask him. Why did he always, or very often—they were the same things to Adèle—come in flushed, as if he had been running, and be vague almost to incoherency in his speech? What was this mystery, and why was it reserved from *her*? This man must be watched.

She watched him, and made a great discovery. She saw him coming very rapidly along one of the alleys one morning—along the very avenue which led to the back way; and she planted herself among shrubs, and saw him come by her. It was evident that this wicked old man had committed something. He had only one shoe, no hat, the back of his cassock was plastered with black mud, and there was a great streak of yellow clay right across his tonsure. She was determined to have an explanation of all this. This would never do. The servants would talk; the thing was disreputable. Yes; she must have an explanation.

When Father Martin appeared perfectly dressed at the breakfast-table, radiant, flushed, handsomer than ever, he carried an ornament which Adèle had not noticed as he had passed her hurriedly that morning—he had a black eye.

"My dear Adèle," he broke out, "I have been having such fun."

"So I should conceive, sir, by your personal appearance."

"Yes, but you don't know all. I have been in the forest."

"As you have often been—*botanising*," said Adèle, with killing scorn.

"Exactly. But this morning I have seen what I never hoped to see."

"I hope you may never see it again," said Adèle, demurely pouring out his coffee.

"I hope I shall though," said Father Martin. "I have seen a great boar killed. There is no breach of principle in that, for I wish they were all killed together. It was absolutely glorious."

"For you?"

"Well, not for me, because I am an ecclesiastic, and have been brought up without any physical training; but glorious to those who love it. That is a very foolish head-forester of yours though. He gave me the carbine; and that is a very foolish spiritual director of yours, for he took it. And the boar charged, and I fired, and the boar knocked me down, and the dogs went over me; yet it was glorious for all that. There is too much sugar in this coffee. I have told you of it a hundred times, and still you go on; pour that away, and give me another cup. Will you ever remember?"

She apologised and obeyed quite quietly.

"A priest must be a fool if he cannot manage a woman," said Father Martin to himself. But then all women are not Adèles, my good father.

Things went on pleasantly enough at Montauban with these two for some months, and then more pleasantly still, for Louis, the Marquis, came, and stayed with them for more than three weeks; and while he was there, as was arranged, lo! the young Marquis was born.

It was the oddest baby, the most mournful and melancholy baby ever seen. It submitted with a miserable face to the mistake of having been born, but never protested even by a cry; it gave itself up to a sad melancholy after the first hour. I knew the baby personally (as far as a man in my position may know a Marquis), some fifty years afterwards at Dieppe, when it was younger and slightly more cheerful. At this later time, the time of good Louis Philippe, it was very particular about its little clothes, and used to walk up and down the esplanade, smiling at the sea. It had a tiny little château above the Faubourg de la Barr, with a garden mostly full of poppies, of all varieties of colour. It now lives at Montauban, and is diligent about silk. It grew four pounds and a half the year before last, at a ruinous price, but it thinks that with a change of dynasty it

s

might make it pay. In its political convictions this baby is Legitimist. In its religious views it is Ultramontane : and the last time it was known to weep was at the signature of the September Convention. Perhaps it has laughed since. But every one who ever met it loved it, for it goes about doing good.

No wonder it was a melancholy baby, for over its cradle sat its father, telling nought but disaster, and mourning, and woe. Everything was going utterly wrong, the people really getting more embroiled and more infuriated day by day, in spite of the king's reconciliation ; the present lull being only, as any one might see, temporary. Mirabeau might save us, and would if he could, but bah ! Mirabeau was marked for death ; and after him ruin. Such were the vague, mournful politics which were talked over the baby's cradle ; while Adèle, utterly careless about the whole matter, sat casting beaming looks of love from baby to father and from father to baby.

What did *she* care?—she had those two.

Father Martin was a more intelligent listener.

Louis had left the army, and was busying himself about politics. He expressed himself glad that he had given up his commission in the Régiment du Dauphin,* because the regiment was behaving very badly, and he had quite enough on his hands without making lying promises to men about their pay, which never came for all their lying. This led him to speak of the dearest friend he had in the world—André Desilles.

I will, if you please, tell in my own way, the substance of what Louis told Father Martin concerning this singular young officer.

André, always melancholy, was as a man who had given up hope, and waited for death. He looked old and worn, said Louis, and was more silent and solemn than ever. Louis had

---

\* The word "Dauphiné" was written down before too hurriedly. The Régiment de Dauphiné was placed by me at St. Malo, where I believe it never was. It was diligently misconducting itself at Nismes about the time. (Dampmartin, p. 280.) "Les soldats du Régiment de Dauphiné tenoient depuis peu de jours, de contraindre leurs officiers à se retirer." It is almost impossible to be correct in a romance ; Scott was not. It should have been, Régiment du Dauphin, I think. I know that I was right once, but not having had the honour of being Quarter-Master-General of the French army in 1790, I am no more certain of the fact than the Quarter-Master himself.

taken him to Alexandre Lameth's—had forced him to go there. There had been Bailly, D'Isigny, Barbaroux the beautiful, Lafayette—a pleasant party, airing every kind of opinion. André, who could talk so well, said nothing here, beyond quietly traversing and rendering nearly ridiculous each argument. At the very last, when discussion was ended, he said :—

"And what does your master say to all this?"

"The King?" said Bailly, gently.

"No, M. le Maire—Mirabeau," said André, and politely took his departure with Louis.

"Louis," he said, as he walked homeward through the streets, "I have been making a fool of myself."

"You certainly should not have said what you did say about Mirabeau to M. Bailly. You have made both Lameth and D'Isigny angry."

"Bless them all with their cackle, I was not referring to them," was the very disrespectful reply.

"My dear André——"

"Well then, I beg pardon. I said I had made a fool of myself, and I have made a very great one. I have made a fool of myself about a woman."

Said Louis : "Is it a *tendresse* then, or a *liaison?*"

"*Liaison!*" said André. "Are you mad?"

"I ask pardon," said Louis. "My tongue went too fast. I forgot that you were not as others."

"It did indeed," said André. "I am speaking of Mathilde."

Louis was perfectly silent, which was the best thing he could be.

"I always loved her," continued André, "but I believe I could have forgotten her, at least to some extent, had I not gone to England. Do you remember La Garaye, and that you asked me was there anything between me and her? What did I answer?"

"You said, 'Nothing.'"

"I lied, Louis; I lied horribly. I love her as only a Frenchman can love. She has taken my soul, but I have not hers in exchange. She has taken my soul, and has given it to that accursed Englishman."

The gentle Louis said : "Be calm, my André. See, you will break the arm of your Louis."

"I ask your pardon for hurting you, Louis. I will be calmer; but look at the situation. It was bad that I should love her, it was bad that she should take my soul from me and return nothing; it was worse that she should marry this Englishman as a matter of *convenance*. All this I could have borne. But that she should take my soul and transfer it to this dolt is the thing that is unbearable—for she loves him."

"She loved *me* once," said Louis, very quietly.

"I could have borne it with *you*," said André. "I could have borne it well with you, for you have always been half of my own soul. But he!—that Englishman!—that he should be her husband! Is it not maddening then?"

"But perhaps," said Louis, "they will never be married."

"They may be man and wife now," said André. "D'Isigny will probably give his consent; and as he told me yesterday, with his cursed thin smile, they have probably married without it. It is all over by now, and there is no need to say any more."

"Then there is nothing to be done," said Louis, heartily ashamed of himself.

"One can die, and there are plenty of opportunities," said André. "Once more am I away from my regiment, to hear earlier news from England. You remember my scolding you at St. Malo for neglecting yours. Good. Well, I go back to my regiment to-morrow for the last time."

"I forget where the Régiment du Roi is just now," said Louis.

"At Nanci," said André Desilles.

"Is it any steadier than it was?"

"I can do anything with my own company, in spite of Barbot; so can Peltier and Enjolras with theirs. The other companies are very doubtful; but our men are far better in hand than the Régiment Mestre-de-Camp. And Journiac de St. Meard is in trouble with the Swiss of Château Vieux? But what are the poor devils to do if you will not pay them? However, I will now go back and see what I can do. I wish to heaven that I could get them paid; they would follow me anywhere then."

## CHAPTER XXXIX.

### CORRESPONDENCE.

### The Dowager Lady Somers to M. D'Isigny.

"My Dear Sir,

O youth is given the privilege of pleasure; to a ripe and intellectual manhood such as your own, is given the privilege of social and political ambition; to old age is given the privilege of garrulity. I am going to use my privilege.

"We are much excited here by what we hear from your dear country—France. We are deeply distressed. It seems that you of our order in France are beginning to reap the fruits of a very long course of neglect of your peasantry and your town poor—as you have often pointed out to me."

This was abrupt, but the fact was that Sir Lionel was reading the letter as she wrote it, and stopped this very strenuous old lady from breaking any more windows.

"I, for my part, very much envy you the whirl and bustle of politics in which you seem entirely absorbed. I myself, as the intimate personal friend of Chatham, envy you. But it seems to me that you are looking for a statesman, and are not able to find one. M. Mirabeau, whom I *think* I may call friend, does not seem to understand the situation, and is, in fact, in opposition. M. Necker is a mere banker. What is wanted just now is a minister, who will repress and keep down the mob.

"We are extremely dull here, at Ashurst; and I fear it is duller still at Sheepsden—if you ever, in the whirl of politics, remember such a place. Mathilde, who is as a daughter to me now, finds it, I fear, very dull there. She is utterly alone. When you gave your consent to the alliance between our families I was glad. I am glad no longer. I wish it consummated. There is nothing to prevent it. The poor child is in a false position. You have permitted us to announce the engagement between her and Lionel, and yet he hardly likes to go there. I do earnestly beg that there may be a marriage. There is everything for it, and nothing against it.

"BARBARA SOMERS."

D'Isigny, as was the nature of the man, began just where the old lady left off; and put his spoke in the wheel at once, leaving his garrulity to follow. Do any of my readers know a man who hates having anything *done* unless he does it himself? I know many. It is, however, more an English failing than a French one. But D'Isigny fitted with no party in France; and such decisive power of action as he had was merely physical. If he had been on the spot, with full powers of bullying everybody, he would have forced Sir Lionel to marry Mathilde at the sword's point immediately, would have posted to Lambeth for a special licence, for he dearly loved furious and unnecessary action. But this audacious proposal of having his daughter married to the man of her heart and the man of his choice, without his being present to bully them, was a matter which must be at once put a stop to. He began, as I said, where the old lady left off.

"MADAM,

"With regard to your somewhat extraordinary proposal, that my daughter should consummate a marriage with your son, without the presence of her family, I beg to state that I must give a most *emphatic* refusal.

"I was under the impression hitherto that *the* D'Isignys drew their honours from even a purer source, could such a thing be, than the extremely doubtful one of the Cretin son of David Rizzio, the guitar player."

He revelled over the last paragraph. There were plenty of r's in it, and he burred them. He read it aloud to himself. He thought, should he have to finish Lady Somers face to face, where would he put his emphasis—R-r-izzio or C-r-r-etin? He tried guita-r-r, but that would not do; and Rizzio, as he said it, made a dactyl, whereas Cretin was a good spondee. Cretin was a withering word, and he determined to use it.

"The man was a fool," says the reader. That is just the thing I am trying to prove. At the same time, not altogether such a fool as he looked. Mathilde was not only Mademoiselle D'Isigny of Sheepsden, but she was sister to the Marquise de Valognes, with her immense territories. The consummation of the alliance with Sir Lionel Somers might wait a little. Who could say what might happen in this general overturn?

When he had got so far, he was so extremely pleased with himself that he got to a certain extent civil, and went on.

"Your ladyship is doubtless aware that I have been accustomed to be master in my own house. On this occasion, my dear madam, I must be allowed to use my old privilege, even at the expense of an apparent want of gallantry. It is impossible to say where any of us may find ourselves in a year. Mathilde may be the daughter of a ruined, possibly beheaded outcast. It is better to wait. The Revolutionists have thus early taken the very wise course of ruining the most eminent and to them the most dangerous men, and so my estates in Brittany are laid waste. I am actually at this moment dependent on my wife's estate at Sheepsden for my personal expenditure.

"And again, is this a time for marrying or giving in marriage? You may say that it is right that my daughter should have a protector. She has one in you. Could she have a better one? No, my dear madam; this affair must be delayed.

"I met Brèze the other day, looking older, but well kept. He remembers you, and sends all kinds of compliments. Your old friend Bailly carries himself as well as ever; though not so young as he was, his carriage is still grand and graceful; certainly he stands on the finest leg I have ever seen. The King gets fat and sleepy, the Queen as radiant and brisk as ever. A sad thing about the little Dauphin, was it not? He was always a puling child, and *on dit* that they exhibited calomel when he had the catarrh on him," etc., etc., etc.

Let the reader fill up this fiddle-faddle for himself. Lady Somers never read it fairly through. While D'Isigny was flattering himself that he had shown the old lady the perfect determination of his character, and then had charmed her into good humour by his fashionable and political babble, Lady Somers was rubbing her mittens together, and was saying to her son :—

"That future father-in-law of yours is a very remarkable man."

Sir Lionel expressed a somewhat doubtful assent.

"It is all very well for you to be doubtful, but I tell you that he is a very remarkable man indeed. He is by far the vainest, shallowest, and emptiest person whom I have ever met in the whole course of my life."

"My dearest mother!"

"My dearest son! I am very old, and not very wise, but he has written me the shallowest, falsest, flimsiest letter which I have ever received in my lifetime. Read it for yourself, and judge. When you, or I, or Mathilde write a letter with a purpose in it, we state that purpose: he never states it. His purpose is delay; why, I cannot conceive, because Mathilde is not likely to meet again with such a *parti* as you. He could not say so. Just examine that letter as a curiosity. Why, the man did not know what he was going to say when he began writing it. And then, when he thinks that he has thoroughly deceived and dazzled me, he tries to come over me with his Brèzes and Baillys. It is absolutely impossible that Brèze, who is, I believe, Lord Chamberlain, or something of that sort, could ever have heard of me in his life. As for Bailly and his legs, I don't know his legs, because I never set eyes on them. That is the oldest trick known in society, that of trying to flatter a person by pretending to bring messages from eminent people whom they have never seen. And for him to try such a very old trick on such a very old woman as I am! Why, it is monstrous! He is not truthful, that man."

"My dear mother, I should have said that he was the soul of truth."

"He will not be to any one who will allow him to bully them," was all the answer Sir Lionel could get from his mother.

This letter came on Sunday morning.

"I shall not go to church this morning, my dear. I could not communicate after that letter. Stay you at home also, my dear, and read me the service."

Sir Lionel got his father's prayer-book, and pushed a chair opposite to his mother. He then found her her own prayer-book.

"Shall I ring for the servants," he said.

"No," she said; "you and I alone. And I am getting blind, and the print of this book is too small: and I am getting deaf, and cannot hear you where you sit; so come and sit on this stool at my feet, and I can look over your shoulder."

So Sir Lionel sat down before his mother, and leaned his head against her knee, while he read the Litany to her, as was his custom on the mornings when she could not go to church.

"There is nothing left," said the old lady at last, "but to wait. I should say no more. Submit."

## CHAPTER XL.

### NANCI.

SO they were all scattered and separated one from another, wondering were they ever to be united again. Each, however, had some hope, some pleasure. Adèle had her baby and her castle, Mathilde had her Lionel, D'Isigny had his politics, De Valognes his society. One only of the whole group was utterly and entirely alone, perfectly without any hope: it was André Desilles.

There had been misunderstandings, and things had gone wrong, and he was the victim. He quietly returned to his duty and his barracks.

The old regimental life was so thoroughly distasteful to him now. He had loved his regiment, his duty, and his men; but all was now a wearisome and to him an ignoble complication, difficulty upon difficulty, and among the whole of the Régiment du Roi there was scarce any one whom he could call a real, true friend, beside Peltier, and the other two.

He was very popular among the officers. He was a gentleman, a kind-hearted man, a man whom every one in their hearts respected and deferred to before his face; behind his back, however, all the officers, from Colonel Denoue downwards, would regret that André Desilles, thorough *bon homme* that he was, was to some extent infected with the new ideas.

A very young nobleman, the last joined officer of this most unlucky regiment, said one evening, as André Desilles left the mess-table,—

"I don't like that man. He wears no moustaches, and his heart is with the people."

Denoue was on him at once.

"Captain Desilles, sir, is the finest officer I have. If the worst comes, I trust to his gentle influence with the men, which he has so long exercised, to prevent a catastrophe. If we had all been Desilles, sir, we should have rendered revolution both unnecessary and impossible." And there was a general murmur of applause all round the table, for a bold and generous sentiment is sure to catch a Frenchman's heart.

This was all very well, but it was weary work. Though he was respected by the officers and trusted by the men, not only of the Régiment du Roi, but also by the Château Vieux Swiss, and the Mestre-de-Camp dragoons, he was utterly alone. He would have liked peace, this poor fellow; here was none: he would have liked action; here was none either. Nothing but a ceaseless, miserable, ignoble wrangle about money, in which his order was most distinctly in the wrong; and he standing between officers and men, in the thankless office of a peacemaker.

He grew sick at heart when he began to examine the regimental accounts, and to find out, what he had long suspected, that the men had been grossly and systematically cheated, and that their case was one which could only be put right by prompt acknowledgement and restitution on the part of the officers. Acknowledgement and restitution! The officers were a set of high-bred, high-fed nobles, confident in their ignorance, of victory, who hated their men.

"I have done as you asked me," he said to Denoue, in secret conclave, "and the men are in the right. To declare this at this moment would be, you say, ruin. I do not believe it. By paying these men, and by pacifying them, we could make them follow us to the devil."

"What is the sum?" asked Denoue.

"I make out 180,000 livres.* Barbot will not make it much less."

"This Barbot is at the head of those who demand accounts, is he not?" said Denoue.

* The men said 1,000,000 livres more in the last twenty years. Who shall decide now?

"He is that man," said Desilles. "He is very ignorant, very ferocious, but at the same time very shrewd. And he has always checkmated my influence among the men, for he hates me; why, I cannot conceive, but he hates me."

"Give him his yellow ticket, and send him marching," said Denoue.

"I prefer having the most dangerous man in the regiment under my own eye," said André.

"What shall you propose, *enfin?*" said Denoue.

"Restitution," said André.

"But we shall have to borrow the money from the municipality," said Denoue.

"I would lend it myself, were it not for my sisters. Nay, I will lend 50,000 livres as it is."

"But it is such a precedent," said Denoue. "We shall have Mestre-de-Camp, and even Château Vieux, up in arms at once."

"Let us do *right*, and put ourselves in the keeping of the honour of Frenchmen," was the answer of André Desilles.

Denoue drummed on the table, and whistled.

"This," he very sensibly remarked, "will be the devil."

It was the month of August when Sergeant-Major Barbot demanded the accounts. It must have been a strange scene. The état-major was on one side of the table in the caserne, and on the other Sergeant Barbot and the men. Behind the état-major stood André Desilles, calm and majestic, the only man among the crowd of officers which backed him who had his lip shaved —a fact which possibly did him more good with the men than a hundred protestations. His great soul recoiled from his position. He had to confess immense injustice and wrong, and was put forward as the best-trusted of the officers, to offer a tardy and utterly incomplete restitution.

There was a great squabbling, of course, over the books. The état-major, however, with all his vast experience in the peculation of soldiers' pay, was no match at all for the cunning and brutal Barbot, backed and prompted as he was by a keen young lawyer from Dauphiné. Matters went worse and worse against the officers: the men's case was too good. At last André Desilles had to come forward and make the, to him, sickening confession that the officers allowed the men's claims, and would pay 175,000 livres, which they would borrow from the municipality.

Denoue's voice was heard over the half-murmur, half-cheer, which followed this announcement.

"Captain André Desilles lends 50,000 livres of this money out of his own pocket, without security, and without hope of payment."

The murmurs swelled into a cheer, the cheer into a roar. Barbot found himself pushed half across the table by the white-coated soldiers from behind, who pushed forwards, stretching out their hands to André Desilles. They were excitable, these rebels, and cried out, "Bon Desilles! Bon Capitaine!" Some of them, "Ami du peuple!" which did him no good among his brother officers. They behaved badly, this Régiment du Roi; but what did they want? Only to be treated as men and not as dogs, and to have their wages paid.

When Barbot had recovered his equilibrium after the *culbute* he had suffered from the white coats behind, he handed the books back to the état-major, and looked round him before speaking.

And indeed, if one may pause, on a strange sight. On the one side of the table were the officers, defiant and humiliated; on the other side the soldiers, defiant and triumphant: officers and soldiers separated in thought, habit, and manner of life, by the longitude of the earth. Now, the other day I happened to be walking about among a French regiment, and I witnessed the scandalous fact of the officers talking familiarly with the men. I saw more than this. I saw the colonel himself, in his shirt-sleeves, leaning out of window in a by-street, and talking to a sergeant. I could bring witnesses to prove that fact; quite sufficient in number to hang that colonel, if treating your men familiarly were a capital offence. Yet they say that the French army is not the worst in Europe. And any state of things is better than that at Nanci in August, 1790.

Barbot, the head and front of the mutiny, looked at the soldiers behind him and the officers in front, and saw only André Desilles standing between the two parties, and Barbot hated him with a hatred which would have disgraced Collot d'Herbois. He spoke to him.

"We are deeply obliged to Captain Desilles for what he has

done for us. He loves the people, this Captain Desilles, my comrades. Has he not made up the deficiencies of his brother aristocrats out of his own pocket? But he is patriot, this Captain Desilles. He loves the daughter of D'Isigny the Breton. He loves Mathilde D'Isigny; and she, as all the world knows, is the bosom-friend of that king and emperor among patriots, Jean Paul Marat. Ah! he is good patriot, this man. See how he blushes."

There was a horrible dexterity in this blow which made André reel. He turned to Denoue and said,—

"Let me go out. I have done this shameful business for you; let me go to my quarters. Why is everything to fall on me? What have I done that God should visit me so hardly?" And the commandant made room for the young man with bowed head.

Denoue was perfectly right in his view as to what would happen after this concession. The regiments Mestre-de-Camp and the Swiss Château Vieux were up at once. I cannot think that it is my place to follow out in a mere story the details of this most miserable and unhappy squabble at Nanci further than the exigencies of a tolerably told story require. I will do so as briefly as possible. But I may be allowed to say, that whenever I have puzzled out a piece of history for myself, and go to either Gibbon or Carlyle for confirmation, I find them not only absolutely correct, but I find myself referred to other authorities which I had never consulted. Writing to general readers, this seems worth while to say. There are, I believe, no critics alive now who can correct Gibbon or Carlyle with regard to accuracy.

I think, then, that I would rather pass over the miserable squabble about the arrears of pay and so on, and attend principally to our old friend, André Desilles.

André Desilles had so much on his hands for the next few days, that he had but little time to brood over the words of Barbot. A deep and growing anxiety had begun to possess him. The men were different to what they had been before, in spite of their short-lived enthusiasm towards him; and he began to see more and more clearly that the whole matter was resolving itself into a duel between the two coolest and soundest heads on each side: that is to say, between himself on the part of the officers, and Barbot on the part of the men.

They had been on scarcely concealed terms of hatred and suspicion for more than two years now, and André had always believed that he had taken the measure of his man. He found that he had not done so. This elephantine Titus Oates of a man had a brain which, if as small in proportion to his bulk as the elephant's, was of equally high quality. The brutal Barbot, he began to see, was a man who knew well what he wanted, and would not be turned from the thing he wanted except by death. To him was opposed André Desilles, with his hands tied, backed by a mass of violent, feather-brained aristocrats who distrusted him, and with the consciousness that his cause was bad. Barbot looked at Captain Desilles as almost a conquered man.

The cavalry regiment Mestre-de-Camp, and the Swiss Regiment Château Vieux, rose at once, demanded accounts, and the officers of the Swiss regiment were so incautious as to give the strap to the two soldiers who came to negotiate. The other three regiments made heroes of these two Swiss, and the quarrel assumed quite a new phase. The men in these two regiments beat their officers, and the Swiss regiment extorted from them 24,000 livres, and the cavalry regiment 27,000 livres, as a provisional instalment of their just demands. There was a distinct panic among the officers of all ranks, and among them all André Desilles was known as being the only one of any talent whatever who had in any degree the confidence of the men.

They looked to him for impossibility. He told them so. "I am only one," he said. "Why have you not been as I have been? Do you think that in my single person I am capable of saving you from reaping the fruits of your own actions? 'Arrest Sergeant Barbot, you say.' I doubt if it would be possible: you would only make a martyr of him. Leave him to me: I will do all I can—by my life I will;" and they were forced to be content.

The Régiment du Roi continued now, having seen the success of the other regiments, to demand a rectification of their accounts. At the instigation of Barbot, a detachment of them carried away the military chest to their quarters: by the persuasion of André Desilles they brought it back again next day. The duel between these two singularly different men had now fairly begun: both had thrown away the scabbard: the Lafayettcist and Hebertist stood face to face, without any disguise whatever; and between them, for them to act on, and turn one way or another, a mass of men; honest fellows enough; who had but little will of their own, and would rather be loyal than not.

André's hands were much strengthened all this time by the National Guard, who respected him. These men seem to have behaved very well indeed. Before the arrival of the decree of the National Assembly against the mutineers, they had persuaded the three regiments to submission; and all seemed as if it would go smoothly. The arrest of the eight soldiers of du Roi, when sent as deputies to Paris to explain their grievances, made things worse again, but the National Guard were in favour of order.

Then came Malseigne, blundering and scolding, scolding among others André Desilles for truckling to the men's demands. When dismissed from his scolding, André could not help a secret smile at the utter defiance of Château Vieux for this gentleman, in spite of their favourite, Journiac de St. Méard.

If one dared laugh in the middle of such a miserable business, one would laugh at the troubles of this most unfortunate M. Malseigne. What unutterable confusion a bull-headed man of the "Plunger" order can make, we have seen once or twice in our own times; but never better than here. He undid all that little which André Desilles had been able to do, and did worse mischief still. His troubles are told by Mr. Carlyle with a wit after which my feeble efforts would look poorer than poor. Only, if I may dare say so, Mr. Carlyle has strangely enough missed a little of the humour of the situation. The sudden arrival of Desmottes, aide-de-camp of Lafayette, at Nanci, was such a characteristic instance of Lafayette's fussiness, that I wonder it escaped him.

André had done his best; he could do no more. Malseigne had turned the officers, except Peltier, Enjolras, and Cassaignac, against him, as having tampered with the men, and he was now all alone. Denoue turned against him now, as much as his good heart would allow him. He had few friends, except among his men: he spent the next few days among them.

"Help us, and we will submit. Why are they not all like

you?" was what the younger men said, pitifully. "What have we done that we are to be cheated and treated like dogs? We are not disloyal." And the elder ones said, "Monsieur le Capitaine means well, but we must be paid, and we must have promotion from the ranks. There is not a man in this regiment who would not follow monsieur to the world's end; but look at the others."

He said to one old moustache, " I am, to tell you the truth, my friend, somewhat tired of my life. I thought I lived only for good, yet see I cannot do any. Is not that strange again?"

"You should declare for the Revolution," said the old private. "All things will come right after the Revolution. You are good boy, you. You could do anything with the men if it were not for—ah! voilà Monsieur Barbot."

In fact Barbot was everywhere. André cared less about this now; for such powers of doing good, and of mending matters, had been taken from him. He thought himself beaten, although he was *not* beaten; for the good which he did in the Régiment du Roi remained. " La loi! la loi! " they cried in the agony of the struggle. I have got somehow to love that regiment, and to connect its virtues with André Desilles.

Malseigne, it is known, found the claims of the soldiers of the Château Vieux so exceedingly sound, that he had nothing to do but to scold them for insubordination. They tried to confine him to their barracks; he cut his way out, and the two other regiments, acted on by André Desilles, gave him a guard of honour. Nevertheless the shrewd Swiss insisted on being paid without abatement, and Malseigne had nothing for it but to scold, and scold, and order them to Sarre Louis, whither they apparently declined to go.

At this point in stepped Desmottes, ordering the National Guard to assemble, for they knew not what: the confusion was beyond a vilified and snubbed André Desilles *now*. He sat and walked, thoughtful, during these few days, very grave and very quiet, for he had got a letter from Adèle, which made him think and think again. His work, which was still diligently done, was done as it were with a wise instinct; for he was saying to himself all the time, first "yes," then "no," then "impossible."

Malseigne made his bolt to Luneville, pursued by a troop of

Mestre-de-Camp. He arrived at Luneville in time to save himself. He sent a troop of still loyal carbineers against the troop of Mestre-de-Camp. 3000 men started from Nanci, marching on Luneville at this intelligence; but *les esprits conciliants interviennent*, and Malseigne gave his parole to return to Nanci on condition of safe guard. He broke it in trying to bolt once more, and was brought to Nanci, now infuriated by rumours of being sold to Austria, a prisoner.

And meanwhile the active André Desilles was paralysed. What could have paralysed him now, at this supreme moment? What could have made him disregardful of the impending civil war? The insolence of Malseigne? hardly. The cold looks of his brother officers? still less: he could give scorn for scorn with any man. Dread of Barbot? not that assuredly, for he was in the barracks with his men, and as they showed at the last, they were as much under his influence as he could ever hope them to be—only insisting on their rights. He stayed with his men, and he talked to them, and Barbot saw his influence growing, and made his determination accordingly; but with regard to external matters, André Desilles moved no more than the humblest lieutenant.

What was this letter from Adèle which kept him from his duty? Well, it was merely a letter full of babble and foolishness, written for no particular purpose, during the idleness of Montauban. She had the habit, as many idle women have, of writing letters about nothing; of keeping up her correspondence. She made it a rule to write a letter a day—in these days of cheap postage the rule is five, or thereabouts—and one day she had no one to write to, and thought that she would write to André at Nanci. She didn't like him, but she might as well let him know how fine she had got to be, for he had always made a pretence of thinking her a silly little thing.

Her intention was innocent enough. She wrote him a fiddle-faddle letter, describing Montauban, and abusing the Revolution. But on looking over it again, she said to herself: "What will he care for all this gossip? He will only laugh at me, and he shall not laugh." So she, out of her own head, put in this postscript:—

"You know, of course, that Mathilde is engaged to Sir Lionel Somers. This is an arrangement which I regret extremely. It

T

is quite impossible that it can come to anything, or even that it can last long. They are utterly unsuited for one another. Is it true that she has engaged herself to him in mere spite, because you would not say the necessary words, while you had the opportunity so long in England? *I* think so. You are too precise. André; get *congé*, and go back to England and try again—if you think it worth trying."

"As wicked a little lie as ever was told!" says the better informed reader. Yet it had the effect of paralysing André, by making him turn over in his mind, "Is it true? is it false? It might be true, even in spite of what Barbot had shown him." And he stood by his men and talked to them, while the fierce storm of misunderstanding raged outside. And the men listened to him. For there was a brightness in his eyes, and a briskness in his carriage, which told among the young men, and will tell among young men until love is dead. "The captain has good news of Mademoiselle," they said among one another. Who Mademoiselle was they knew not; but with their keen French intellects they knew whence came that light in his eyes. "La loi, Capitaine!" was their cry to him; and he answered, "You shall have it."

This miserable, disgraceful business over, he would go to England once more, and for the last time, see how matters stood. And he was dreaming about Sheepsden, about how he would come round the corner of the old screen and confront Mathilde, when Captain Peltier came hurriedly in, and aroused him.

"Desilles, for God's sake get to your men, and keep them quiet. Bouillé is within a mile of the gates."

"Do you mean to say he is advancing?" said André, all abroad for a moment.

"He is *here*," said Peltier. "Are you mad? You to whom we trusted so much. Have you not heard the *générale*? Do you not know that Malseigne and Denoue have been sent to him as he ordered, and that he refuses to treat with our men as being rebels? Do you know this?"

"I have done my regimental duties, and was resting," said André.

"Sleeping, you mean," said Peltier. "What were you dreaming about?"

"I was dreaming of Sheepsden," said André. "But I will come."

"Of Sheepsden?" said Peltier. "What is that?"

"The place where I would be," said André Desilles; "but I will come with you, and see what I can do. I think my men will be quiet."

He caught up his sword, and ran with Peltier to the Gate Stainville; all the furious puzzled crowd gave way for him. He understood the situation little better than they did.

The Gate de Stainville is a large triumphal arch, very like the Marble Arch at Hyde Park, but of inferior pretensions. On the town side, from which André and Peltier advanced, there was a great and confused gathering. There were National Guards, women, and children, soldiers of the Régiment du Roi, and of the other two regiments, Sergeant Barbot, and, worse than all, an eighteen-pound cannon, loaded with grape shot. On the other side of the gate was Bouillé, who, having sent in his ultimatum, was advancing. A Swiss of the Château Vieux was advancing towards the cannon, flickering the linstock to and fro in his hand to make it burn up.

"I am awakened too late," cried André Desilles, leaping orward and hurling the tall Swiss with the glowing fuse heavily on to the ground. "My friends, listen!" he shouted, standing between the cannon and the crowd. "These men who come are your friends, are your brothers. They are sent by the National Assembly. Regiment of the King, are you going to disgrace yourselves thus?"

There was a low, furious growling at these words. Peltier, Enjolras, and Cassaignac, men who were his comrades, and who loved him, threw themselves upon him, and dragged him from the cannon; but he broke from them, and stood now between the deadly mouth of the gun and the advance guard of Bouillé.

Scarcely any one telling the story of the Revolution has passed by that solitary figure in front of the cannon—that solitary figure in the white uniform, which should live for ever in the memories of men. He stood alone between the ranked enemies, with his arms stretched out, like a tall white cross, under the shadow of the gate, as if to catch the deadly *mitraille* from the cannon; and some heard him say, "Yesterday I had a new life given me, and I will give it to-day for France. It is well that one man should die for the people. Listen," he shouted, in a voice clear and loud as a trumpet; "if it is only for one moment, listen——"

Who among the sons of Cain, cursed of God, did that? Barbot? if not by his hand, by his instigation. There were four reports of musketry, and André Desilles, standing there like a great white cross, with outspread arms sank on his knees and bowed his head in death.*

In the horrible confusion and slaughter which followed in one instant, Peltier, Enjolras, and Cassaignac got his body, and carried it into a neighbouring house. They noticed that the face of the dead man was very quiet and calm. Enjolras said, "He had good news from his lady-love, for he told me as much. Thou, Peltier, must break it to her." Peltier said, "I do not know who she is, but I believe it is one of D'Isigny's daughters." Cassaignac said, "Which of them, for I know them both; and one of them has married Louis de Valognes, and the other is a cripple. He would not love either a cripple or a married woman; therefore, oh Peltier, thou art wrong." So André carried his secret with him to the grave.

"Let us kiss him for the last time," said Cassaignac the Catholic. "How quiet he looks! He is in purgatory now. But I have money, and he shall have masses."

"He is in Heaven among God's angels, Catholic though he was," said Peltier the Huguenot.

---

* With regard to the death of André Desilles, every authority which I know is against me in a trifling particular, except the text of the Tableaux Historiques. The St. Malo picture represents him as sitting on the touch-hole of the gun. The *picture* in the Tableaux Historiques corresponds with the last. Mr. Carlyle, quoting apparently "Deux Amis," gives the same account of the matter, but then the letter-press of the Tableaux Historiques is utterly different :—" Il s'échappe des bras de ses amis (Châteaux Vieux Swiss, with oaths and menaces, says Mr. Carlyle), s'élance de nouveau *entre la porte et l'avant garde de M. Bouillé.*" My opinion is, that Desilles (or to be more correct, Desille) was shot by the imaginary Barbot and his fellow conspirators, when he was in *front* of the cannon, between the cannon and Bouillé's advanced guard. Nevertheless, if Mr. Carlyle thinks differently, one may be pretty sure that I am wrong. The extraordinary vagueness of M. Thiers is—well, is instructive.

"He is merely dead," said Enjolras the Voltairean. "Your superstitions are not half so beautiful as mine. I am the only one of the three who dare say he is at rest."

## CHAPTER XLI.

### MADAME APPEARS IN STRANGE COMPANY.

O every one seemed likely to have his own way. There had never been but one disturbing cause— the *incompris* André Desilles ; and he was dead, and out of the way. If he had never (been reported to have) said those words about Mathilde's ugliness, things might have been otherwise.

But André Desilles was what is called a square man, and would not fit into a round hole ; and he was dead on the stones of Nanci, and there was an end of him. And Adèle cried over the quiet, melancholy baby for one whole September afternoon, for she had a very tender little heart ; and she told the melancholy baby that she had always told him what would come of this odious, this wicked, Revolution (which she had not, by-the-bye), and the baby screwed its face into the ghost of a giggle. And she went sadly among her flowers for nearly a day.

Sir Lionel Somers, coming softly, as was his custom, into the great room at Sheepsden, saw Mathilde staring out of window towards the south-east.

He came up and kissed her hair ; and she turned a perfectly white face towards him, in which there was an expression of ghastly wonder and terror. "Lionel," she said, quietly, "they have killed André. The soldiers have shot him stark dead upon the stones at Nanci. Old André ! I cannot understand it. Will you stay by me and bear with me? for I feel as if all the world were gone from me but you ; and there is no church here."

So the interest of our story concentrates now, I hope naturally, upon the two sisters, and, to some extent, on the two houses in which they lived so entirely separated from one another.

Montauban, now utterly destroyed as an evil and unbearable thing, was a typical place—a place so remarkable as to be almost worth recalling again. Approaching it from almost any quarter, you passed through miserable villages, the foreheads of whose inhabitants were stamped not so much with the seal of Revolution as with the blood-red Cain-mark of Jacquerie. Read Arthur Young, and see how much they will bear. The approaches to Montauban were an exception in Brittany, where the peasants had still so much faith in landlord and priest as to be ready to die for them, would they only lead.

Passing these miserable villages you rose to the level of the great forest, and looked upon an ocean of trees, an apparently level ocean, from the diametrical centre of which, on the only mound in that great wooded plateau, rose the castle, dominating the highest tree: a lurid mass of crimson and purple, many-peaked, fantastic, with one great tower of flat slate standing high aloft above the others. It looked like a vast red ship at anchor in and above an endless ocean of green forest. Was it beautiful? It was beautiful beyond measure, with the beauty of Jezebel. Peasants and travellers sometimes saw it aloft from afar, like the evil wild sunset of a day grown hopeless, of a day so hopeless that men turned in despair to the very night itself, hoping only for what weather the morrow's sun would bring. The interior of this beautiful domain had been, hitherto, nameless wickedness; outside, a desolate Paradise of boars, wolves, and stags, as far as the eye could reach. The inside of it abomination, the outside of it desolation. If ever a place had reached the requirements of the abomination of desolation, it was Montauban.

And here had come two of the gentlest, most innocent, souls ever born into the world, and had taken possession of it—Adèle and Father Martin. To them this wicked place was an Eden of perfect purity and beauty. There was no evil for *them*. Some souls can make an Eden in a reformatory. I learnt that fact twenty-five years ago, when I first saw the late Miss Neave (now, I fear, forgotten with her work), among the fallen and refractory girls at Manor House.

So Father Martin and Adèle, and the very melancholy baby, lived in the red castle, and for music heard the wolves howl at night; with the marks of the *tapage* of the now-banished Mamelukes all around them, and the ghosts of old iniquities rustling in every corridor.

Wipe the palette of these chromes and vermilions, and let us have some grey. Enough of Montauban for the present. Let us breathe without four miles of a dense forest all round us. Let us see where the other sister was. Let us have a look at Sheepsden.

How brisk and nimble the south-west wind comes here then! Take off your hat and sit on the close turf, and drink it in like the best of all good champagne. And you shall have music with your wine. If you do not believe me, listen. What is that sound like the low rushing of innumerable violins up to a great passage? That is the wind amidst the grass and among the fir trees, high over head. What is that strange, booming, subdued harmony, which comes in so well, as though of the wind-instruments supporting the sibilant rush of the violins? That is the lowing and the bleating of the cattle and the sheep. What is that magnificent golden staccato which comes in and subdues and harmonises with everything else? That is the sound of the minster bells at Stourminster Osborne rung by our young men. They are in for a grandsire triple, and will do it under the hour; such wonderful young men are ours. Music? You shall have music enough here, if you will listen to it,—better than Brittany bagpipes.

Scenery again. Is not this better, and better used, than the dull, everlasting woodlands of Brittany? In all Brittany is there one grand chalk down so fine as this, hurling itself down suddenly into the level of the valley, and so wonderfully well utilised; from the summit, where the short, sweet thymy sward is nibbled by the sheep, down to the rich base, where it subsides into the cattle-bearing meadows? No forest here nearer than Cranborne or the New Forest. The peasants in these parts would not stand wolves and wild boars; and let that matter be understood very early and with singular emphasis. Gilbert White tells us that a lord in his parts tried to introduce them, near about this time, "but the people rose on them and destroyed them." It seems, sometimes, a pity that the French people should not have made their will known sooner. But this was their *first* Revolution; ours was over and gone one hundred and fifty years. And so it was a pleasanter thing to live at grey dim Sheepsden, among the elms, below the fir trees, than it was to live at the dark red Montauban, rising, as if on an altar, above the level forest.

Although one would much rather have been at Sheepsden in those times, yet action was all at Montauban. The reader may say that both places were equally dull; that Sir Lionel and Mathilde, philandering — almost platonically— at Sheepsden, were scarcely less dull than Adèle and Father Martin philandering—quite platonically—at Montauban. To which I answer, by no means. At Sheepsden there was no Madame D'Isigny; now, on the other hand, at Montauban there was.

She had got in there. Father Martin knew that she would, and wondered how; and she did. Though he knew that she would, he wondered how she would do it; and as time went on, and she made no sign, but lived in her old house in the Rue de Jesouil, at Dinan, apparently quite contented, this very foolish priest began to think that Medea was going to keep her word, and was not going to involve Adèle in any of her very dangerous political schemes.

Foolish priest! Did he not know that there comes a time in every house when something happens with which the priest has nothing to do at all—when he is of less importance, and of less authority, than the dirtiest old charwoman who has had a family; a time when he is put out of court as an inexpert, and has to get his meals as he may; and when some member of his flock is certain to rise from her knees, in the middle of prayers or mass, and leave the room hurriedly on a false, or purely fictitious, alarm from the *nursery?* Where is your priest at such a time? Nowhere. Father Martin had not calculated on this; but, on the other hand, Madame had.

The melancholy baby fell ill, and they sent for the doctor. Now it will raise your opinion of Madame's power of conspiracy when I tell you that she had brought up one of the discharged Mamelukes to do her bidding, paying him nearly enough to keep his fellows, for the mere purpose of watching the only available doctor's house for her. The messenger arrived from Montauban at one o'clock in the day. By ten o'clock at night this exemplary young man was before Madame D'Isigny's door, in the cross street above the Jesouil gate, at Dinan, rather drunk, but remembering his message.

No one answered his knocks, and there was no bell. He at

last bethought himself of opening the door, and did so, shutting it behind him, in terror of the anger of the terrible lady who was somewhere within.

It was so dead, so silent, so cold, and so dark, that it appalled him, drunk as he was. He groped his way along a slippery, slimy passage, paved with slate, until he tumbled against some stone stairs, up which he went, and arrived at a long, dark corridor, through the window at the end of which corridor the moon seemed to have bent down to have a sly look at him; after which she disappeared. This exemplary young Mameluke began to think that he had been having more to drink than was good for him lately, which was indeed the fact, and was inclined to call out; but was only deterred from fear of the terrible Madame appearing. He opened very gently, according to his training, door after door along this corridor, and looked into the rooms. Four of these rooms in succession were dark and silent, which frightened him; the fifth, which was lit up, he opened with more confidence, but very quietly.

A very beautiful girl was lying in bed, asleep. She had been reading in bed, and had left her lamp burning, so that its light was shed upon her face. Her right arm had pulled the clothes up on to her throat, her left arm lay bare over the coverlet, with the book she had been reading fallen idly from her hand. Her cheek was pressed on to the pillow, and over the pillow lay her hair, spread out like the seaweed on the rocks at St. Malo. Our tipsy Mameluke shut *this* door pretty quickly. It is difficult to brutalise a man before he is one-and-twenty. He closed the door in terror, and stood once more in the dark corridor.

The young man passed along the passage until he came to the window at the end, through which the moon had looked at him, and then he perceived that the keyhole of the door to the left of him was illuminated, and he heard voices.

He listened, as his nature directed him, but although he could hear every word, he could not understand much. There were, he guessed, four people in the room, and they were speaking of numbers—51, 52, 53, 54, were the first numbers he heard. Each number was read out by a rather pleasant female voice; and after each number there was discussion. Fifty-one and fifty-two seemed, to this rapidly sobering young man, to pass without challenge; fifty-three, however, was most strongly objected to by two out of the four voices. Fifty-three, it seemed to the young man, must be a terrible fellow. Hearing the catalogue of fifty-three's crimes, our young Mameluke began to feel himself rather a respectable and virtuous youth.

The way in which this fifty-three, nameless for evermore, was denounced by the two dissentient voices, made our young man very much inclined to bolt. There was nothing which fifty-three had not done. The loudest of the denunciatory voices summed up his crimes. Friend of Lafayette; friend of Mirabeau; friend—would Madame pardon him—of D'Isigny; lover—would Madame once again pardon him, these were not times for hiding truth—of a young lady who was the open and avowed friend of the devil Marat.

The second denunciatory voice took up the tale, but very shortly. This gentleman shortly said that unless fifty-three was removed from the roll, he would blow his brains out with a pistol.

"You heat yourselves unnecessarily, you two," said the strong voice of Madame D'Isigny. "Fifty-three is removed from the list. In fact, he is dead, and has saved us all trouble. He struck out for the law at last, and the men of his regiment killed him. He was worth the whole lot of you put together. And Marat again! Why do you call Marat a devil? I talked with him the other day, and thought him rather a good fellow. He wants to hang us and our party up in a row; and we, on the other hand, want to hang him and his party up in a row. It is equal, is it not? I rather like your Marat; he speaks out and says what he wants."

There was a dead silence after this very terrible speech. No one seemed inclined to say a word. The roll of numbers was read on, until there was a violent hitch at fifty-nine and sixty. Over these two numbers there was battle royal; on the one side Madame, on the other the four voices. The argument was so fierce and so loud that its purport could not be gathered by the listener; but Madame's voice was the loudest and most determined of all the voices, and in the end prevailed. The first coherent thing said about these two numbers was in the voice of Madame herself.

"You are all imbeciles about these two men. You say they are tainted with the new opinions; it is true. You say they are fools; also true. But they are both thoroughly frightened at the Revolution, and will stay in heart with us, while at the same time they will keep up social communications with, at all events, the Girondists, and will do us infinite service. Why fifty-nine, my husband, visits Marat; and sixty is a fool who has married my daughter. I tell you that we must keep these two with us."

The gentleman who had proposed to blow his brains out, asked whether, as Madame was so resolute in retaining her husband's name on the list, it would not be better to utilise him in some way. Could they not, for instance, get M. D'Isigny to act as their agent in buying up Marat. Marat was a most notoriously needy man, and a very dangerous man. Madame's husband was a friend of his; was it not possible that she could use her influence on her husband to bring about the negociation.

Madame's answer was, "No. I am not afraid of my husband or of anything else, as the world most notoriously knows; but I should hardly like to face him with such an iniquitous proposition. Again, you people are, as I have often told you, silly, and know nothing. You could as little bribe Marat as you could get D'Isigny to take your bribe to him. 'Every man has his price,' some one said. I tell you they lie, and are fools. A fanatic has no price. You do not know a fanatic: look at me then and see one; and the madman Marat is another. We have no price. We are *enragés*."

All the numbers up to 72 seemed to go right to this listening and somewhat crapulous groom. There was a hitch and a discussion at this number, however, which he only partly heard, as he became painfully aware that some one was trying the front door as he had done, and that his time was short, unless he wished to be caught listening.

This discussion was not so loud as the others. Madame had bullied the rest of the conspirators so thoroughly. "I tell you," she said, "that I expect a summons which will call me to Montauban; and once in that house, let those who would turn me out, try. My daughter Adèle is foolish, and I can mould her. The priest will be with us in the end, or die. Hark! some one knocks!"

In fact it was the case. The young man, hearing a belated conspirator come blundering up the stone staircase in the dark, clicking his sword against the stone walls, began to reflect that if he was caught listening there, his life was not worth, in time two minutes, in money not a livre and a half (reducible in the present French currency to one franc and eighty to eighty-five centimes); so he knocked.

Madame was deaf to the first knock, but our young man was so painfully alive to the fact of a bloodthirsty aristocrat with a sword, blundering through the darkness towards him, that he knocked again almost furiously. The advancing aristocrat cried out, "Qui vive?" and Madame cried out, "Entrez." The young man accepted Madame's invitation, and went in.

Of course there was no one but Madame, and she had on a silver stirrup, and was netting fishermen's nets. The young man was not wise, but having been listening for nearly an hour outside the door, the behaviour of Madame did seem to him a little overdone. Even in his benighted mind there arose a dim consciousness that Madame was overdoing it, and that he could have done it better himself. He could hear the other conspirators squabbling in fierce whispers in the next room perfectly plain; and here was Madame netting away, in spectacles, and not making very good weather of *that* as a sailor might say. Our young man had no objection to a farce, but he liked it done well. He liked a tone of probability about it. There was no probability here.

All embarrassment was saved in his case, for the latest conspirator blundered over him as he stood in the doorway, and shot him into the middle of the room. The Mameluke, turning to offer a mild remonstrance, perceived at once that the belated royalist was deeply disguised in liquor.

Madame pointed out the fact to this belated aristocrat in that extremely emphatic language which I have previously noticed as being a *specialité* of hers. The language was too emphatic for reproduction, and the aristocrat resented it. After balancing himself carefully, he informed Madame, who was perfectly unconcerned, that it was foreign to his nature to resent an insult from a lady, and then retired, revenging himself by swearing awfully along the corridor. Madame heard him fall down stairs with perfect equanimity, and silently turned her stony gaze on the terror-stricken Mameluke.

He delivered his message under the influence of that Gorgon

stare. The son and heir of the house of De Valognes was dangerously ill.

"I am *en route* for Montauban, you people," he heard her say. "Don't make greater imbeciles of yourselves than you can help without me. We shall none of us meet very likely for a long time, for once in that house, in the midst of that loyal population, I shall remain. And you will send no more communications to me, without my orders. There are snakes in the grass. Just come into the front room again for a moment. There is a young man there whose portrait I want taken."

The young man heard a trampling of feet and a rattling of swords, and a moment afterwards the whole of these very dangerous *Vendean* conspirators were before him, looking at him. What little nerve he had left was gone, as they say, through the heels of his boots, by now; he was simply desperate. Fourteen gentlemen of the class whose desperate mettle he knew, having lived among such for good or for evil all his life. And these fourteen terrible gentlemen calmly fixed their twenty-eight eyes on him with a view to future recognition. Marat would have shaken his tawny hair, stretched out his ten fingers, and given them utter defiance; Danton would have hurled some of his terrible words at their heads; Robespierre would have—I do not know what Robespierre would have done —even Lewes could hardly say. But the wild young Mameluke, a parasite on their tree, was simply stricken with terror at the dreadful array of fourteen of the order of which he had been taught to dread and had learned to hate, standing before him with their eyes on his face. And besides there was Madame D'Isigny smiling carelessly upon him.

These particular fourteen were a set; Mameluke knew them all save two; and those two stood in front of the others.

Madame D'Isigny said, "I have trusted and paid this young man, Messieurs. You will remember him again."

A very young gentleman among the crowd suddenly said, "It becomes then a question whether or no the highest and purest morality does not dictate his death. Madame's indiscretion is enormous. I do not see how we can save ourselves and the cause without the death of this young man."

The terrified Mameluke cast his eyes on the two men who stood in advance of the rest, in utter despair. He saw that they were laughing at this bloodthirsty nonsense, and took heart at once. A valet is as used to judge men by their appearance as another, and he looked at these two with wonder, with the more wonder because one of them, the one who stood in advance of the other, was not a gentleman, but a young man, a little over twenty-five, who seemed half-sailor, half-peasant. Yet the magnificent gentleman who stood rather behind this peasant, and kept his arm affectionately on his shoulder, was, from his appearance, a gentleman of the first water; and they were both, evidently, in some way or another, men of mark. Indeed they were. The sailor-peasant who stood nearest to him, was Charette; the nobleman who had his arm in the French way round his neck, was Henri de la Rochejacquelein—names, like Danton's, "not unknown in the Revolution."

"Stop that nonsense, De Morbihan," said La Rochejacquelein, after he and Charette had had their laugh together. "We have no intention of murdering the young man. You disgrace the King. He gets his dismissal from Madame."

"Swear him," said De Morbihan, coming forward.

"Nonsense!" said Charette. "What would be the use of that? What is his oath worth until he understands the question? Let me speak to him. Look at me, young man."

The young man looked at the sailor, and felt that he would rather have looked at a pleasanter face. It was determined, it was calm; but there was a twinkle of ferocity about the eyes, which he did not like at all.

"If you hold your tongue, you are safe. If you speak, you die: whether you are in Brittany, in Paris, in London, you die. You would ask, are we assassins, then? We answer, not as yet. Do not force us to become so. Your life is in your own hands, and not in ours. To keep it safe you had better join us."

The young man thought so, also; but at that moment Charette was thrust aside by Madame D'Isigny, who said:

"Leave him, Charette; he is under my care. Go, at once, to Montauban, and tell Father Martin that I am coming."

"Madame, I am afraid of the forest alone."

"Believe that Captain Charette the Sailor is behind you, my friend, and you will not fear the wolves. Go now, swiftly and straight, and remember that I am following. I also dread the forest, and so may require some of these gentlemen to follow me. Let us find you there, my good young man, with your message safely delivered when I arrive, or some of my escort may take it into their heads to look after you as they return."

## CHAPTER XLII.

### MADAME'S PLOT PROSPERS.

ATHER MARTIN summoned the major-domo. He was walking quickly up and down the room in a state of comical confusion and ill-temper. "Madame the mother of the Marquise is coming," he said.

"Does Madame stay long?" asked the major-domo.

"Yes; in permanence," snapped Father Martin. "I have tried hard to keep her from getting her foot into the house; but she has got it in, in spite of me, and she will take it out again no more. No more!"

"What rooms shall I prepare for Madame?"

"Those in the extreme end of the east wing, or the west wing, or in the attics, or anywhere, where the clack of her tongue may not be heard by passers-by."

"Will the east wing do, M. le Curé?"

"If it is out of the way, it will."

"It is retired. Does Madame expect guests?"

"I suppose so. Women seldom talk their own nonsense without listeners."

"Will Madame receive many?"

"Yes; all the fools in Brittany," said Father Martin testily.

So Madame arrived, and nursed the melancholy baby. I dare say her presence had something to do with the extraordinary complacent misery of that child. Possibly, also, the expression of Father Martin's face reflected itself in some way on the baby's; for Father Martin's expression of face was extremely melancholy. For Madame's messenger, the Mameluke, like a loose-mouthed young Auvergnois, finding himself under the protection of a tight-mouthed, determined Breton-Norman, like Father Martin, had not only given Madame's message, but had told Father Martin every detail of the extraordinary circumstances under which it was sent. He looked over his shoulder once or twice, to see if Charette was behind him; but the instinct of gabble was too strong for him, and he told Father Martin everything, from beginning to end. He saw that the château was to be made the centre of a great Royalist plot; and he groaned hopelessly.

Madame did her duty as a mother by Adèle and the baby, and then retired into her rooms again. "In the present state of politics," she said, "she did not wish to speak too much to her daughter on any subject which would be likely to agitate her; she confessed that she herself felt strongly on politics,—an old woman might without offence. Her daughter's husband had taken up, to a certain extent, with the new ideas. Nothing was more wicked than to cast any word between man and wife which would lessen their respect for one another. Therefore, she felt it her duty to see as little of Adèle as possible. Yet she had her sentiments as a mother, and only asked to see her daughter once a day, if Father Martin did not object. The good father would allow for her weakness towards her own daughter. The good father (she never could keep that forked snake's tongue of hers between her teeth long together) knew nothing of these things. He was too righteous, too far removed from human passions to appreciate the revivified *storge* which came upon a mother when her daughter first gave her rank as a grandmother. The good father, in his perfect righteousness, would forgive a poor, sinful, old woman for taking an interest in her own daughter. Might she see her own daughter once a day? How long might she stay? And, oh! might she go to mass?

I don't know what Father Martin was going to say when she said this. What he said was, "Madame, you may go to"—(she says he made a pause here, he said he did nothing of the kind) —"mass as often as you like."

Father Martin rather astonished the old major-domo after this. The major-domo was giving the good father his dinner on a Friday—the very day of this conversation—and his dinner consisted of trout—a *consommé*, or something of that sort—I do not understand gastric matters. I doubt there was meat in the gravy of it, and that the good father was committing venial sin in eating it; but that was the cook's fault, for no one was more particular than Father Martin in observing the rules of his Church; and the old servants loved him so well that they deluded him out of his fasts. However, he left his trout untasted, and, after a long silence, rose up, and walked to and fro. Then he turned suddenly on the major-domo, pointing his finger at him, and said:

"You can manage them if they don't take to lying; but when they take to lying persistently, what are you to do? You can't tell them of it, you know."

And the major-domo, without the wildest idea of what Father Martin spoke about, said promptly, with the well-trained dexterity of an old servant, and he a Frenchman: "Such a course would be wrong in two ways: in the first, it would be impolitic; in the second, ungentlemanlike."

Father Martin looked at him with wonder and astonishment.

"Do you mean to say that you understand my allusion?"

"Not at all, M. l'Abbé, but it is necessary for a servant to give a polite answer."

"Do you know, my dear friend, that you are very little removed from a foolish person?" said Father Martin.

"It is most likely, M. l'Abbé. For my part, I quite believe it."

---

## CHAPTER XLIII.

### AN ACCOUNT OF THE PIETY AND VIRTUE OF MADAME D'ISIGNY.

MADAME D'ISIGNY being thus established at Montauban, beyond Father Martin's powers of removal, months and months went on, and she only sat netting fishermen's nets, being profoundly affectionate to Adèle, and profoundly deferential to Father Martin.

She profited deeply by this good man's ministrations. She had been, and she confessed it, exasperated by her husband's incessant contradiction into a state of fury; but that, she told Father Martin, was all passed, and she forgave him. Would it not be possible, she asked him, to bring about a reconciliation? She for one was ready?

Father Martin would be delighted to undertake the negociation. Whereupon Madame dissolved into tears, and blessed him.

Next, it appeared that her religious state was all wrong together, and required seeing to. She never, she said, would have got into her late state of fury if she had had the benefit of *his* offices. Would he direct her? To which Martin replied that he should be most happy to do so.

"I will show you your duties, Madame, in a perfectly plain manner. It will be better for all who are connected with you if you will follow them. I direct you therefore this night to meditate on the patriarch Abraham, who represents hospitality, in order that you may not abuse that of your noble and good son-in-law, by ruining his very foolish wife. I also direct you to pray to the Virgin, who represents the piety of a mother towards her child. I will also to-morrow, Madame, preach in the chapel to these Bretons, and I will illustrate and expose the later and spurious legend of St. Elizabeth, of Thuringia—the legend of the loaves and the roses, Madame; the legend which makes the good God himself back up a lie by a miracle; a thing which he never did yet, Madame, and never will."

Father Martin was not a woman's priest, as I have remarked before.

In spite of such very *prononcé* spiritual directions as these, Madame believed she was humbugging him. I rather begin to believe that a thorough-going conspirator will believe anything —even that every needy rascal, to whom he unfolds his plans, will not sell him for a gallon of beer; else why did that celebrated "party leader," Catiline, go down to the house on a certain occasion? The Philistine Cicero is generally too strong for the Samson of conspiracy; for conspiracy generally ends in the breaking of shop windows, and the world hates that just now, as much as it does the devil.

Madame D'Isigny would have deceived a younger priest; she only puzzled him, without for a moment putting him off his guard. "What an awful fool that woman is!" he said. "Does she believe that I can forget that eight months ago she was the most furious woman in France? Does she conceive me to be a man deprived of memory? Does she think that this continued quiescence on her part will lull *me* to sleep? She evidently does, and is therefore mad. I wish to heaven she would make her next move, I am sick of this."

Madame, however, continued in a state of the most masterly inactivity. She knew that her work was being done better elsewhere, and that her *rôle* was to wait. She knew, although she had no precise intelligence, that the great Vendée earthquake was getting ready its forces; the great earthquake which was now preparing its vast sea-wave in the south-west; that great earthquake-wave which was to burst at its northern point against the granite rocks of Mont Dol, and then recede, leaving greater ruin in its track than did the earthquake-wave described by Darwin at Concepcion. She knew all that, and sat contented, believing that she was humbugging Father Martin, and believing that the majority of the down-trodden masses of France would rise as one man, *on the side* of their oppressors. For what will not conspirators believe? Alas! our late police reports will tell you.

She sat there, netting nets, in 1792, at nearly the furthest point northward which the wave of reaction ever reached. The wave rose, burst, and retreated; and four years afterwards, a person, different from her, Carrier, long-faced, lanthorn-jawed lawyer of Auvergne, was at the southern point of its retreat at Nantes.

But she made no sign for months and months. She was a terrible woman, more terrible than Medea, and there was something to Father Martin perfectly awful in her quiescence. He knew her, no man better. He had a sharp, keen tongue, and more brains than she. He had managed her and bullied her in old times; now he was utterly powerless. If she had gone on her old plan of violent objurgation, he could have done something, but now in her silent mood he could do nothing. She was so dreadfully *good*. The contemplation of this phase in her behaviour exasperates me, after eighty years, into the vulgarism of saying that butter would not melt in her mouth. Conceive, then, the effect which her inactivity must have had on a warm-hearted and warm-spoken man like Father Martin. If he smote her on the right cheek she immediately turned the other; and when he smote her on that cheek, as I regret to say he always did, she turned the original cheek again, with a charming smile.

"I can do nothing on earth with your mother," he said, testily, one day to Adèle, when they were walking together among the empty flower-beds, for time had gone on. "I can do nothing with her at all."

"She is converted," said Adèle. "It is you who have converted her, you good man. How good she is—how amiable. How wicked I must have been ever to have hated her."

Martin was too good a man to sow seeds of discord, or even to give a caution between mother and child. He said nothing now; but when he was gone to his room, he said to himself, "I wonder when she will show her hand, and how she will show it."

She only continued her devotions, and the house went on much as ever. There were two or three visits from Louis, and two or three letters from her father and from Sheepsden, that was all. Martin went out about the forest, and through the forest, to the poor people, generally accompanied by the oldest forester.

One morning as he was starting he said to his companion: "Who is that young man who bowed to me just now? Have I not seen his face before?"

The forester replied: "C'est l'Auvergnois de Madame D'Isigny."

"The what?" said Father Martin, stopping abruptly.

The old forester, with all the pleasure which a servant feels in exciting your curiosity and astonishment, gladly enlarged upon his text.

"The Auvergnois, one of those whom the good father had so rightly discharged, and whom Madame had taken back into her service. Was Monsieur not aware?"

"Why!" said Martin, stopping still; "she *asked* me to discharge them."

"That is very possible, yet she has taken one of them back. It was he who took the account of my Lord the Count's illness to Dinan, and brought her here."

## CHAPTER XLIV.

### IN WHICH MADAME BECOMES ONCE MORE ENRAGED.

NE day, Adèle and Father Martin, standing on the terrace and looking along the northward avenue, saw, in the extreme distance, above a mile away, a group dressed in black, which puzzled them still more and more as they very slowly approached. When they were close enough to them, they made them out to be a company of nine nuns.

"What can be the meaning of this?" asked Martin. And Adèle said, "Can it be my aunt?"

It was indeed. Saint Catherine's had escaped for a longer time than its Superior had expected, but a revolutionary band had remembered it at last, and swarmed in suddenly at primes. Sister Priscilla, trying to save the pix, was killed by a young man, and was in glory, for which they gave thanks. Sister Priscilla had been apt to be contradictory and use strenuous language with regard to trifling backslidings of other sisters, but they had loved her almost the best of all. The convent was burnt, and they were left so utterly helpless that it had been two days before sisters Veronica and Acquila, who were very strong, had been able to get the grave of sister Priscilla deep enough. After they had buried her, they sleeping in the forest, (which was bad for sister Anne's rheumatism,) they were about to prepare themselves for death, having nothing to eat, when the Superior, directed of God, bethought herself of her niece's château of Montauban, feeling assured that they would find a welcome there. So they had started, singing hymns and offices for the comfort of sister Pavida, who was afraid of wolves, and screamed out when she saw a squirrel or hare; and had come very slowly, in consequence of sister Podagra's corns, originally inflicted on her for inattention in chapel, and not subsequently mitigated by frequent prayers, although there had been no visible backsliding on her part. They had avoided Dinan, as being dangerous, and had got the route from godly peasants, one of whom had given them bread and honey and milk, and had let them sleep in his barn : for him they would pray. And so they had arrived.

Here they stood, this jetsam from the mad sea of revolution, cast on *this* strange shore,—women whose lives had been given to God and to good works. Old enough, some of them, to be grandmothers ; simple in the ways of the world as babies ; utterly helpless, yet perfectly brave, with a bravery beyond that of a soldier : for they could die, these silly women, without fear ; for what was death but the gate of glory ? There they stood, possibly to some eyes ridiculous, not to mine : their dress was unbecoming and their shoes were large ; they were none of them in the least degree beautiful. Sister Podagra had got her shoes off and was openly attending to her corns ; sister Pavida, having got over her terror of wolves, was staring her eyes out in wondering admiration of Adèle's beautiful clothes and jewels ; other sisters were looking in wonder at the splendid jagged façade of the castle, others at the beauty of the flowers. They were dressed in clothes, purposely made ridiculously distinctive by the founder of their order, and even these clothes were muddy and out of order : they looked, on the whole, absurd, and their belief was in many respects childishly superstitious ; yet they knew how to die, these silly women, as well as the best brandy-primed Marseillais of them all. I cannot laugh at these women. I know their ignorance like another, but I would make a deeper reverence to any one of them than ever I would do to a duchess.

I believe that Father Martin thought as I think about them —he was not a man to express his opinions strongly ; but the spectacle of these poor brave draggled nuns took effect in the light, sensitive, kind little heart of Adèle in a moment. She left the comparative degree of existence (she had abandoned the positive to that slow Mathilde years ago) and went in for superlatives. The sack of St. Catherine's was the wickedest thing done since the murder of the Innocents by Herod. Her aunt had always been the best loved friend that she had, and she would spill her life's blood on her own hearth sooner than allow these miserable revolutionists to invade her sanctuary. That was her dear old friend, sister Pavida. She must have *her* room, because she was always nervous. Sister Podagra was in trouble with her corns as usual : she must have her feet in warm water instantly. There was that old sister Veronica, who had frightened her so about baby. In short, her kind little heart had something for each. And so the handsome little Marquise, with her pretty bright-coloured clothes, and her jewels, swept the herd of clumsily shod old nuns into the château before her, giving her arm to sister Podagra in the rear. And when she had got them in, she did with them as she liked.

Perhaps it was a pretty picture to see this beautiful little creature in pink and jewels bustling about among these foolish dull-clad old nuns, attending to their wants. Perhaps it was a pretty thing to see her lay the baby in sister Veronica's lap and say, " Now, you will believe, you foolish old woman." Perhaps it was pretty to see the nuns, set in a row on chairs, served with the best of everything by Adèle's new staff of Breton footmen. I cannot certainly say what is pretty, but this has struck me as being so.

When Adèle had seen to their wants and had made them comfortable, she stood in the middle of them beaming with pleasure. They were safe *here* at all events. Suddenly she said, " Where is sister Priscilla, have you left her behind ? "

Sister Veronica, the out-spoken sister, said, " Sister Priscilla, who was very strong and resolute, fought with a young man for the pix containing the holy body, and what is more, the ring of St. Catherine, with which "—(I cannot go on. Romish legends go too far for me). " It was our only relic, and we placed it in the pix surreptitiously, thinking to keep it safe. And she fought this young man for the pix, and he killed her."

" Is sister Priscilla murdered ? " cried Adèle.

" Yes ; the young man killed her for the sake of the pix : and we had much trouble in burying her ; for our best spade got burnt in the fire, and we were two days in doing it, or we should have been here before."

Adèle put her pretty hands over her shell-like ears. The flood of the Revolution was all around her, and the tide seemed rising to her feet.

Meanwhile, Mademoiselle D'Isigny, the Lady Superior, who, though in many ways as simple as the others, was in some sort a woman of the world, was staying behind her nuns and talking to Father Martin.

"Is it true that my brother has taken to the new ideas?"

"He has no ideas, he is utterly adrift."

"Will they try to kill us?"

"Unless the south-west keeps quiet, certainly."

"Is this place safe?" she asked.

"Most dangerous. It is too far north. And I have no ultimate hope from the south," said he.

"One will have to die, then?"

"One will have to die."

"It matters not much, one has nothing to live for."

"One has much to live for," said Martin; "one has to live for a purified France. But, then, they will not let us live; it is their policy. Do you know that Madame, your sister-in-law, is here?"

"One has been terrified by so much that one is not even afraid of her. We must meet, I suppose; let us meet quickly."

"You will find her changed. What her reception of you may be I cannot at all undertake to say. I think it will be an agreeable one."

It *was* a most agreeable one for all parties: there was no ostentation about it whatever. Was it possible that Madame D'Isigny began to see that she had overacted her part with regard to Father Martin, and was determined not to repeat her mistakes; that is most probable. There was certainly no attempt whatever to overact it in the case of her sister-in-law. The poor draggled old nun, who had been frightened beyond terror,—who, in the last terrible passage of her life, having had the responsibility of seven others weaker than herself thrust upon her, and who, in consequence of this feeling of responsibility—of having to care for others who could not care for themselves,—had risen to heroism; this old woman was afraid of nothing now, not even of the terrible Madame D'Isigny. The bitterness of death was passed with *her*.

She was shown by Father Martin into a long, large, dim drawing-room, filled with *bric-à-brac*, and beautiful fiddle-faddle expensive tomfooleries of all kinds: astonishing to her, for she had looked on the Revolution, and had believed that all such things had come to an end. The deep carpet on which she walked made no echo from her clumsy shoes. She saw in a distant window illuminated by the last gleam of a wild sunset a figure, which sat at work: it was that of the awful Madame D'Isigny. She rose, tall, gaunt, and graceful, and came towards her. She kissed her and said quietly,—

"We old women are being driven south rapidly, and to the south is the sea. Our time is not long. Let us try to love one another; to forgive and to forget."

Kindness opened the floodgates of the Lady Superior's heart at once. She was in tears directly; and Martin saw at once that his influence was gone, and that any warnings he might address to the Lady Superior about her sister-in-law were worse than useless. He let it go; saying that it was in God's hands, and so these two excellent women began unconsciously to labour as hard at the digging of Mathilde's grave, as ever the two strong sisters had to dig the grave of the martyred sister Priscilla.

"You have now looked on the Revolution yourself, my dear," said D'Isigny's wife to D'Isigny's sister when the poor old nun had got her cold feet on the fender, and was having weak negus. "You have seen some of its earlier results. Do you now blame me for my fury against it?"

The Lady Superior was obliged to say "No."

"I *am* furious," said Madame D'Isigny. "But I can be sufficiently calm and gentle at times. I can be calm and gentle with you in your adversity, although you remember my behaviour to you in your prosperity. Sister, the men are all half-hearted. It is left to weak women to stop this Revolution. I calculate on your assistance. Your sanctity and goodness are known even here. Among these peasants we must utilise it, as I intend to utilise my daughter's beauty and amiability. Sister, it lies with us to stop this wicked flood of atheism and disloyalty which men call the Revolution."

"But I doubt there will be more bloodshed, sister," said the poor Lady Superior.

"I hope sô," said Madame D'Isigny, rising. "Sister Priscilla's death is not avenged yet. We will have masses for her—bah! I forget the details in my growing fury. Come to bed. We will talk of it again."

She put the old woman tenderly to bed, and staid with her a long time—to give Father Martin time to go to bed. He, on the other hand, did nothing of the kind, but waited with his door ajar, knowing that she must pass it.

He heard her coming, and stood out into the passage to stop her. He saw advancing towards him a tall woman in a grey cloak, with a lamp held close before her face. Tall, dim, colourless, inexorable. In her steady, pitiless gait he saw the as yet unorganised reaction which was to destroy them; in her splendid beauty he saw the matrix of the beauty of her two daughters; in her terribly set face he saw the only woman who had used the weapons of the precisionist D'Isigny against himself, and had beaten him with them. She was as terrible as Medea; yet he was not in the least afraid of her. He put himself in her path, and told her to stop.

She thrust out her breast, and looked on him.

"Out of my way, priest!" she said. "I am not in the humour for priests. I am *enragée*."

"It matters little to me, Madame, whether you are sane or insane. I intend to be heard, and I will be heard. I always knew you to be ferocious, but I liked you better in your worst old moods of ferocity than I do now, when you are cowardly and deceitful."

"How dare you use such words to me!"

"How dare I? To whom do you talk? Do you not know that you are making a tool of our imbecile little Marquise, and that equally imbecile old nun, to forward your reactionary plots?"

"I know it well. I use them. And why not? I use them, and I mean to use them. Do you then declare for the Revolution?"

"By no means, Madame."

"Then hold your tongue. I don't say get out of my way, because I wish to pour a little more scorn over your head before I have done with you. I have kept quiet too long. Vesuvius was quiet three thousand years, and then it destroyed Pompeii. I have tried to be good, but I can't. I could go in for Maratism, but this twopenny Girondism has maddened me again. I come of the nation which has conquered India, and I am, as my nation sometimes is, in a dangerous mood. You are going on to object to my making this house the stronghold of a Loyalist plot. I am going to do so."

"Will you not think of the danger to your own daughter,

Madame?" said Father Martin, suddenly altering his tone to about an octave lower. "Will you not consider that this is a suspected house, and that it is the very worst place in which to concoct a reactionist plot?"

"My own daughter must take her own chance. I fancy that I am as good a judge of these matters as you are. Still, understand this for the future, that I am once more enraged, and leave me alone."

## CHAPTER XLV.

### PARIS.

FATHER MARTIN soon wrote to Louis.

"MY DEAR LOUIS,—

"There are only two men in the world, I believe, who can keep any given woman out of mischief,—her husband and her priest.* The priest can generally do it, if the woman is fool enough; when he fails he must call in the husband.

"I wish you would come here, and come at once. There will be heads falling if you do not. Your mother-in-law is here. She has taken full possession of the place, and every one here is entirely under her influence, with the exception of myself. Your aunt, who has brought her nuns here for refuge, is utterly under her finger. Adèle adores her, and is so entirely her slave that she attributes any little warnings which I have dared to give her against her mother to jealousy. Yesterday, on my praying her to be cautious, and not to believe all her mother said about the chances of Royalist success, she broke out on me and accused me of making mischief between mother and child.

"My influence with your wife is gone since the arrival of your mother-in-law. How much you may yourself possess, I have no means of knowing. But, for heaven's sake, come.

"I imagine that there are two things which you would ask me. The first, Why do I not use my old influence over Madame D'Isigny?

"My answer is, that it is utterly gone. I am not more afraid

* I beg to state that these atrocious sentiments are not *mine*.

of her than I ever was; indeed, dear Louis, I think that I have no more fear of anything than had my own André—son of my heart!—my child in God!—my beloved—taken to heaven like Elijah—whom I shall meet. *N'importe.* I have no fear of anything, but this woman fights me on equal terms. She does not beat me, but she is no longer afraid of me, and will no longer obey me. To her fury I give back calm scorn; it is all I have to give, but it is useless. I am absolutely powerless with her. She has said many times that she and Marat represent the fury of the Revolution, and upon my honour she is perfectly right. She has passed miles beyond the point which I would allow myself to pass in any cause. I would stop short and testify to my cause by martyrdom (a dangerously powerful testimony, as those who know history can tell you), long before I would dream of casting myself into the headlong blind stupid fury of a Jacquerie or of a Stuart reaction. I have lost all hold over the woman. As for Adèle, she dare not say that her life is her own. I am quite powerless.

"The other question which I should think you would put to me is this, What are they doing, these women of ours? I do not know. I do not believe they entirely know themselves. But one thing I am sure of; every revolutionary committee for miles round does. I am loyal and Christian, I need hardly say; but this castle of yours is too far north for either loyalty or Christianity. We are a mere outpost. Madame was playing this game, with her usual courage, at Dinan, even further north, but has removed her implements of conspiracy to this place. I cannot sleep for mysterious whistlings under my window. One of those most unhappy Auvergnois, whom your mother-in-law has taken back into favour (not, I think, knowing who he is), is Mercury to the whole business. The others, whom I discharged with your consent, are mainly, as far as I can understand, revolutionary. What the awful danger may be of a band of Mamelukes, brought up in the contempt of God and in every form of luxury and vice, and then turned loose, I leave you to decide; and this young Mameluke, whom Madame has in her pay, almost certainly betrays us to his brothers.

"Again, I am told nothing. Last night I went into the library late to get my Anselm's 'Meditations' with Fénelon's autograph annotations. You knew it and loved it in old times—no, I forgot—it was André who knew and loved it. I beg pardon; and lo! after I opened the door, there was what the South American Spaniards call an estampedo. That very hare-brained young man, La Rochejacquelein, was winding your mother-in-law's string, and a common sailor, or, to be more correct, a sea-captain, a man miles removed from a gentleman, was being shown pictures by Adèle in a book. The name of the sailor, I afterwards learned, is Charette. And I don't like the looks of him: his face seems to me both cruel and mean.

"'He is on our side,' you say, 'and thine is only a priest's judgment.' It is possible: nevertheless, *you come here, and come quickly.*"

No doubt Louis would have come quickly enough, but unfortunately the arrests had begun, and Louis was safe in the *Conciergerie*. So he was saved the pain of reading this letter, and continued bowing among his brother aristocrats, believing that his wife was sufficiently far south-westward to be safe. But the letter was, I need not say, read by others, and a revolutionary cordon was placed round Montauban at once. I will not insult the reader's reason by pointing out the small fact that the Mameluke in the pay of the infuriated Madame D'Isigny, carried every item of news to his four brothers and his twelve cousins. I can only reiterate with every feeling of reverence the words of our Litany—" From all sedition, privy conspiracy, and rebellion, Good Lord, deliver us."

That nest of loyalist conspiracy at Montauban was considered by the Revolutionists too good a one to be disturbed. "A hen always lays in the same place," says Desmoulins (who, judging from his writings, had a somewhat powerful tongue inside that loose and rather worthless mouth of his); "wait till the eggs are all laid, and then take them." Madame D'Isigny went on, and believed that her plot was hidden in darkness; while Father Martin, whose tongue was tied, saw her own Mameluke trying not to laugh in her face.

Mirabeau was dead and buried, but there was no king to send for D'Isigny: "Tant pis pour lui," some one old friend D'Isigny was reduced to walking and stalking up and down Paris, and to proving to every one who allowed himself to be button-holed, that all this might have been prevented, that he was the only person who could have prevented it, and that it was only the Queen's party which had prevented his being sent for at Mirabeau's death. A great many people believed him: reiterated assertion is about the most powerful weapon I know of. But Louis de Valognes got thrown into prison, and things otherwise went wrong, or at least not as he thought they would go; and he began to feel that he could not make head or tail of it.

Whether his head carried him, or whether his legs carried him, I do not know, but he went one afternoon to the Rue Jacquerie. He had been warned that it was dangerous, but what cared he? The people swarmed in the street as before, but looked more savage, more furious. Yet they knew him. They were to wade knee-deep in blood directly, but they knew him and let him pass. And he walked on, utterly unconscious of the sympathy which these people, now utterly maddened people, felt for him. At one point there was nearly an end of him. A wild-looking young man, exasperated beyond bearing by his clothes, his beauty, his cleanliness, his air of command, who knows, ran out to attack him. And two women ran out and cast themselves on the young man, holding him. "You shall not touch him," said the women. "He is an aristocrat, but he is the man who took up the dead child and kissed it." And so D'Isigny passed on, with his head in the air, and his hand on his sword, totally unconscious that the one little touch of ordinary human love which he had shown here a year ago, had saved his life now. For there was no accord between classes, or there would hardly have been *such* a Revolution.

The streets, as in his former visit, grew more and more empty as they got narrower. D'Isigny had learnt the habits of the man with whom he wished to speak, and stood quietly in the middle of the street. It was getting dusk, cockshot time as they would have said at Sheepsden, the time when nocturnal birds, such as the woodcock, "shoot," or fly wildly round before beginning their night's work. D'Isigny had calculated "cockshot" well, for here was his woodcock.

Fluttering swiftly and untidily along the middle of the street came the awful Marat.* He was not ill-dressed, for his sister,

* What *was* the personal appearance of this most extraordinary and mysterious person? The "David" portrait (?) we most of us know. It is that of a bold, wild, rather noble-looking person, the sort of man any one would

the neat Swiss woman, whom Lord Houghton knew, did all that she could to prevent his lapsing into the utter squalor which his mistress would have permitted. He wore tight-fitting breeches, grey stockings, and tied shoes; his legs and feet were well shaped, and well clothed, but his upper garments were distinctly Bedlamite.

He wore a loose redingote buttoned across his throat, but nowhere else, over which flowed and waved in the wind a large white scarf; he was bare-headed, for he held his hat in his hand, and as he advanced gesticulated with his two arms wildly, talking to himself the while, sometimes in accents of persuasion, sometimes of furious denunciation. And as he came fluttering on his way to his club, lo, there was D'Isigny, calm, clean, perfectly dressed, who stood at the corner, leaning against the wall, who stopped Marat by the mere force of his eye, some would say; by the mere power of his clothes and looks, I should say. Marat was, however, aware of a "foreign substance," and came up to D'Isigny.

"You are D'Isigny the Breton?" he said.

"I am. Your people have arrested my son-in-law, and he is in the *Conciergerie*."

"Is your daughter Mathilde married, then?" said Marat.

"She is not. I speak of the husband of my daughter Adèle: the Marquis de Valognes."

"An aristocrat?"

give his hand to, with a powerful jaw, a broad good-natured expression, and a noble curling head of hair. Look upon this picture, and on this. Look on the Duplessis-Bertaux portrait; only do not look at it too soon before going to bed, lest you should have the nightmare. The Duplessis-Bertaux portrait is that, not of a man, but of a nameless *Thing*: a horror —a thing, if possible, to be forgotten. I have always had an intense curiosity about this man, but I fear it will never be gratified. These two, the best authenticated portraits of him, I believe, are utterly dissimilar. There is a wax-work of him as he lay dead in his bath, which is shown at Madame Tussaud's in Baker-street, claiming to have been done by order of the Directory, and to be authentic, as, I believe, is the case. This again is immeasurably hideous; from the internal evidence one would say that there was little doubt of the correctness of *this* portrait. It was done, I believe, by the late Madame Tussaud's father, and he would hardly have invented the missing teeth. With regard to Marat himself, I fear he was a worthless, bloodthirsty vagabond. His dress, *en passant*, I have partly taken from Duplessis-Bertaux's small drawing of his coronation.

"A marquis is generally an aristocrat," said D'Isigny.

"Huruges is not, but I will not argue," said Marat. "What do you wish me to do, then?"

"To have my son-in-law set free."

"I fear I have not the power," said Marat, standing with his toes pointed inward, and his nervous lean thighs showing through his breeches, before the solemn D'Isigny, who towered above him in height, and whose figure was thoroughly draped. "I fear I cannot do that for you. I will do everything I can, but not that. Besides, he is better where he is than loose. Let him stay. Is your daughter Mathilde here?"

"She is in England."

"Keep her there. No man can serve his own brother in these times. I must die, I know that; but I can die without murmur if I see some others dead before I go. And I am not all wolf. I am so far developed that there is a little of the dog in me; excuse me, I am a comparative anatomist by profession. I am so far civilised from my original wolfishness, that I can be doglike to you and to yours. I will bark, and if needs were, bite for her. As for your Marquis, let him stay in the *Conciergerie;* he is safe enough there; but don't, in Heaven's name, let your daughter Mathilde set foot in France. She is too outspoken. Why, she spoke out for me when you all loathed and hated me."

"M. Marat, you are not all unkind," said D'Isigny, feeling the same sort of strange attraction to the man which the French population did.

"I am not all unkind," said Marat. "I love the people too well to be all unkind. I am furious, and I am wicked, and I am cruel. But, D'Isigny, our case is good."

"Your case is terribly good; but your means, my good sir."

Marat laughed; but was serious again at once. "Never mind my means. Give this message to your daughter Mathilde. Tell her that she has nearly made me love Christianity. By the bye, does your other daughter live at a place called Montauban? Is she the Marquise de Valognes who lives *there?*"

"Certainly," said D'Isigny.

"Send her away directly. *Stay;* I will watch matters for

you. Yes; let things go as they are. I can remember old kindness. Will you trust me?"

"I will, M. Marat," said D'Isigny. "Where are you going to-night?"

"I am going," said Marat, "to meet all the furies of hell. I am going to the club of the Cordeliers. Now, you sleek man, you pious man, you man with the well-shaven, beautifully-made face, and the perfectly-made clothes, who is the most blood-thirsty devil of the whole of us at the Jacobins?"

"You are," said D'Isigny, quietly.

"I am only the dog who bites and tears," said Marat; "but who is the sly cat? That cat—that devil, Maximilian Robespierre. I would destroy you, for you are dangerous; but I will spare you and yours for the sake of your daughter Mathilde. If Robespierre had a hundred daughters, each one a hundred times better than yours, I would not spare him. Cat! Devil! I go to the Cordeliers. Remember what I have told you about your daughter. I will do all I can. We can spare fools, such as you and your daughter Adèle; but thoroughly virtuous and uncompromising people, like your wife and your daughter Mathilde, must die. People like yourself and your daughter Adèle are not very dangerous to the Revolution. We would keep you alive as an example. But people like your wife and your daughter Mathilde are too good to be allowed to live. They must die. I don't want any good examples on the other side. The man Roland's wife, also, is offensively virtuous. I distrust her. Now attend to me," continued he. "The Revolution will begin in bloodshed and wickedness; but will end, I believe, in good. Such people as you and your daughter Adèle I can save more easily than such noble warriors as your wife and your daughter Mathilde, *if I choose*. We are going to have the Revolution; it is your order that has made it necessary. You stand there, smiling at me with those cursed thin lips of yours; but what I say is true, in spite of your shallow smile. You will go down like corn before us; but I want to spare your daughter. I might as well talk to the fountain in the Place de la Révolution. Remember what I have said about your wife, for whom, they say, you don't care much; and remember, again, about Mathilde. Do not let her come to France."

So he went, fluttering like a great bat—fluttering, with outstretched arms, under his dark redingote. And D'Isigny, who might have taken his warning, stood like a well-dressed pump at the corner of the street; and, after long cogitations, came to the conclusion that Marat was a lunatic. As if any one had ever doubted the fact.

In Paris, at that time, there was a little club within a club. It was a sort of Whig club, because it was called the Henri Quatre. The members of it were mainly aristocratic Feuillans and Girondists; but as exclusive as the Traveller's or White's. At this club you might air the most outrageous Voltaireism, but you must have your four generations of nobility. Of course, D'Isigny belonged to it. He went to it the same evening, after his interview with Marat; and he told old Count Gobemouche, with whom he dined, that Marat was mad.

## CHAPTER XLVI.

### IPHIGENIA IN TAURIS.

THERE is no doubt that Marat was mad, though there was a certain method in his madness; but things at this time hitched, and when things hitch there is apt to be a catastrophe. The hitch was the arrest of Louis de Valognes. Louis de Valognes was in the *Conciergerie*, and just at that time five hundred Marats could not have got him out of it. So the foolish woman's plot at Montauban, the consequences of which were to fall on utterly innocent shoulders, went on.

It was all very well for Father Martin to beg them to be cautious. They had all that apeiric courage which women have who have never known danger,—the courage of women who have been kept from danger by the men whom the rules of society have set to guard them, and who fancy that they can face danger as well without as with their male protectors. Madame D'Isigny (who scarcely came under this category, however) declared herself to be in a state of rebellion, and defied Father Martin, and invented a sentence of "brave words" for him. She said that he only wanted courage to declare for the Revolution, which words, being long and apparently meaning something, had a great effect on Adèle, who reproduced them by saying that "Father Martin, though strangely positive on some matters, seemed to be making up his mind about this wicked Revolution, and was a long time doing it." Even that poor, gentle, kindly old nun, D'Isigny's sister, picked up a stone, about as hard as a boiled turnip, and slung it at Father Martin's head. She said that he was obviously bent on Gallicising the Church, and that it never would do. In short, three foolish women, one of them clever and furious, were too much for this good priest, and beat him.

He asked them to let him come into their counsels. No. He argued with them, and showed them that their cause was the same as his own; but they would not trust him. Lastly, he earnestly begged and prayed of them not to be so ridiculously mysterious; and told them that with their everlasting midnight messengers they were ruining both the cause and themselves— rousing the suspicions of every disaffected person in the country. They paid no attention to him. They had a nice little conspiracy, and they meant to enjoy it. Father Martin's power was gone; the arch-rebel, Madame D'Isigny, had fairly beaten him, and he looked for—nay, prayed for—the arrival of the master of the house, the sole man who had power to say, "I will have this thing done, and I will have this other thing *not* done."

My friend Martin was not a man who would give up the prerogative which his Church gives a priest; but then he was a wise priest. His most important ally was always the *master* of the house. He was not, as I have said before, a *woman's* priest. He used to say in convivial times that the only perfect constitution was the British: that the House of Commons represented the male bread-winning element, and the throne the female. "Then, don't you see, if the throne rebels, as it often does, the House of Commons can stop supplies, and refuse to pay even the milliner's bills. So *my* ally in every house is the master. The priest is the House of Lords, the moderator. My true ally is the Commons, or purse-holder."

Now in this case there was the throne in flat rebellion, and the House of Commons, represented by Louis de Valognes, not forthcoming. Father Martin was fairly beaten.

The gay and bright Louis de Valognes was in the *Conciergerie*. The Revolution had come home to *him*, among others.

I wish to touch as lightly as possible on the mere facts of the politics of that year, having before me the example of almost the most splendid novel ever written—in which one gets almost wearied with unfamiliar politics.

D'Isigny, stalking up and down Paris, and saying the first thing which came into his head, got himself somehow informed that Louis de Valognes was arrested; and having seen Marat and dined with Gobemouche, thought that he might as well go and see Louis.

He was arrested. All the world was arrested now. A man of his (D'Isigny's) eminence would be pretty sure to be arrested soon. But he must in common decency go and see him; and so he stalked off to the *Conciergerie* and banged the door with his cane, to the unutterable astonishment of the National Guard sentries and the strange loafing patriots around.

The wicket was opened by a slovenly gentleman, who did not seem to appreciate M. D'Isigny's appearance in any way. D'Isigny thought him an objectionable-looking person; but this person evidently thought him more than objectionable. For D'Isigny was far too neat, too clean, and too ornamental for the present phase of French thought.

"I wish to see the *ci-devant soi-disant* De Valognes," said D'Isigny, thinking that he had said enough of revolutionary slang to admit him to the Jacobins, at least.

The untidy patriot would not have anything to do with him at all.

D'Isigny had thrown his sixpence of revolutionary jargon to the man, and the man refused to give any change whatever.

"Where is the citizen's order, then?"

"One may see one's own son-in-law, one might suppose?" said D'Isigny.

"Not at all," said the patriot gate-keeper, looking *past* D'Isigny.

D'Isigny heard a thin but singularly clear voice at his right elbow, which said,—

"The virtues of D'Isigny, the Breton, are well known to the Revolution. He is not patriot, this D'Isigny; but he is virtuous, and the Revolution is virtue. Let him pass, good patriot; let him pass. The more that I have followed him here to speak to him."

Dare I? Well, I will try; I can but fail. I have looked at the face so long, that at least I may *speak*.

D'Isigny, standing in the shadow of the door, saw before him, in the sunlight, a small man, with a flat chest, who looked up at him with an expression of calmness, which seemed like a caricature of quietness itself. This small, thin, weak little man, was handsome enough, though all the lower part of his face advanced towards you. Marat would have said, that with his advancing jaw and his receding forehead, his face was feline.\* He was nicely, neatly dressed, this little man; and over his close-cut hair he wore a white wig with a tail, and over his white wig a delicately-set-on three-cornered cocked hat. He looked up with that set, inexorable smile on D'Isigny, and D'Isigny scowled down upon him. D'Isigny was as neat, as well made, as the little man. He could have broken this little smiling man in halves by mere physical strength, but he looked down on him with a mixture of hatred and respect.

D'Isigny was a man not without genius or passion. He looked once again at this little feeble man, dressed so well, with the protruding jaw, and the well-put-on clothes; and he said,—

"M. Robespierre, you will destroy us, as we would destroy you; but let us meet first. If you have power here, let me see my son-in-law."

"What do you talk of?" said Robespierre, taking his arm. "Why do you speak of destroying? Why do you talk to me, a lawyer who lost his judgeship for refusing to register an edict of destroying?"

"You can be like another," thought D'Isigny. "Still you do hate bloodshed. I wish you could speak the truth."

There was of course no difficulty about D'Isigny passing where he would, now. Robespierre and he talked for a considerable time, a conversation one need scarcely reproduce, as Robespierre was trying to find out what was in D'Isigny, and D'Isigny was trying to find out what was in Robespierre, a thing which has puzzled better men than himself. When they parted at the end of a corridor, they had formed an opinion of one another. Robespierre said, "That Breton hog (I use the

---

\* Where has one read of this singular hatred of Marat and Robespierre? I cannot quote just now, but it was in some place of respectability, otherwise I should not have dared to use it.

word in the Indian sense, he said 'sanglier,' not 'cochon') has nothing in his head; he is not worth troubling oneself with, though I do him the justice to think him as honest as myself." D'Isigny said, "That man has sense, and would be easily won."

A very beautiful picture was painted last year, with the title, 'Summoning of the Prisoners in the *Bastille.*" The Bastille was down two years before that began. It was into the great hall of the *Conciergerie* that D'Isigny carried his splendidly-set-on head, like the sail of a ship. It was in the great hall of the *Conciergerie* where he saw the crowd of the aristocrats whom he had once called his friends. It was in the hall of the *Conciergerie* where he heard "great people," according to his measure of greatness, say, with their well-trained drawing-room voices, very low : " This is D'Isigny, the Breton, the turncoat, the traitor, the friend of Marat. Do not speak to him."

He was not prepared for this at all. He was still less prepared for *this.* The Marquis de Mont Aigu was very old and very infirm. He was also very virtuous, had given his life to the poor, but he held notions about the way in which the nation was to be governed, which did not fit with the new ones; and so here he was in the *Conciergerie*, with gold spectacles, rambling about among the others, and giving them examples of his kindly, Christian, gentlemanlike babble.

He was the father, the papa, of these poor souls in the *Conciergerie.* He was passing from group to group, and encouraging all. D'Isigny, coming on and seeing that no one would speak to him, caught this old gentleman just as he was crossing the hall.

The old gentleman was nearly blind. D'Isigny put his two hands in his and kissed him. The old gentleman shook them warmly. "Are you, then, just arrested?" he said. "I cannot see you; but I feel the long, thin hands of a gentleman. But what is your name?"

" D'Isigny."

The old fellow dropped his hands and turned away. "I cannot speak to you," he said, "you are the friend of Marat. It is necessary sometimes that a French gentleman, however old, should speak as his forefathers spoke. You are strong, your family was always an athletic family. My family is, on the other hand, one nearly worn out, and become effete by war. I believe that I am the first male representative of my family who has exhibited virtue; and it falls upon me to tell you that you have betrayed your order, and that you are looked upon among us as a traitor."

"Call back that last word."

"I fear that I cannot do so. But do not resent it here. I will totter up to you pistol in hand, following the wicked old traditions of our order, if I ever get free from the clutches of your friends."

D'Isigny was deeply shocked. From the old gentleman who had used these awful words to him there was no appeal of any sort or kind. And was not the old gentleman's accusation true —had he *not* betrayed his order?

He looked upon the calm, pale, scornful faces which surrounded him in every direction, and they all said "Yes." He never forgot those faces. Precisionist as he was, with a well-regulated mind, he never forgot them. All those scornful eyes, without scarcely any exception, were closed in death within a year; and he told the Rector early one morning, after a wild, nearly mad, walk over the downs above Sheepsden, that they alone would be enough to scare him from heaven; even if it were not for another one, which never left his eyes, waking or sleeping.

But among the scornful, angry faces, pale in the gloom of the *Conciergerie*, waiting for their doom, there was one which was neither scornful nor angry. Louis de Valognes came towards him and embraced him, saying: "My dear father, I am so glad to see you."

D'Isigny was by this time—with one of those rapid Celt-Norman transitions of feeling which we calmer English notice in the Irish—in a state of white fury; but he was perfectly calm. In the presence of the row after row of doomed faces, he kissed his son-in-law (the old Duchesse de Marechaussé said that he bit him), and looked round defiantly, saying: "I am glad that there is one at least who has not the impudence to despise me."

"My dear father," said Louis, "these good souls are irritated, do not mind them." And then, wishing to avoid painful subjects, said: "My dear father, how did you gain the *entrée*, now so difficult with men so well known for correct opinions as yourself?"

"I got the *entrée*, sir," said D'Isigny, "from M. Robespierre. His influence was sufficiently great to get me in, sir; but apparently not sufficiently great to save me from gross insult after I *had* got in. M. Robespierre seems to me to be a thorough gentleman in all essentials. For his origin he is not to blame. I like M. Robespierre, and intend to cultivate his acquaintance. He seems to me well read and intelligent, more intelligent than many who would vilipend him. To you, Louis, my son-in-law, I have only to put this question—Why did you summon me here to be insulted?"

Louis was not discursive. He saw that D'Isigny was angry, and utterly unreasonable. He said rapidly:

"I have a letter from Martin. He says that your wife and mine are getting up a Royalist plot at Montauban, which will ruin us all. You have no influence over your wife, I know. I have over mine; but then I am prisoner, and you are still free. Stop the plot by your influence over your daughter, my wife. Stop it in some way. Your influence over Adèle is still as great as my own; she is more afraid of you than she is of me. I know that you are afraid of approaching your very terrible wife; but you can surely do *this*. For the sake of your own head do it. If I was not a prisoner I could do it to-morrow. Now go; the people here are infuriated towards you."

D'Isigny carried his clean cut, scornful face out through the faces which were to fall in saw-dust, without another word. He acted according to his lights; but they were dim. Instead of going to Montauban, and facing his wife and daughter, he having, as he conceived, *thought* through the matter, sent a letter to England; and this was the letter:—

"MY DEAR MATHILDE,

"Your sister is, as usual, making a fool of herself. She has, with the encouragement of your mother, declared for the Ultra-Royalists.

"I told you once that I should call on you to sacrifice yourself. You promised that you would do so. The time has come.

"Come instantly, by way of Poole, to St. Malo, from thence to Montauban. For me I am too busied by politics to attend to your sister's frivolities. Go and see after her.

"You may be respectful or not to your mother. It is too bad

of her to have led such an utter idiot as your sister into such a complication.

"Remember your promise to me. You said once, if you remember, that I could depend on you. How is your lover? Come instantly, and bring him if you choose."

"D'Isigny."

The thin-faced, handsome man who wrote this letter, read it through once or twice before he sent it. He had got it into his handsome, foolish head that he was wanted in Paris, and that Mathilde could manage her sister. So, looking at it once or twice, he sent it.

The warning which Marat had given him so often was thought over by him. But Marat was only a lunatic and a vagabond. Still he might have listened. D'Isigny never listened. Had he listened he would have appreciated the awful danger in which he was leading Mathilde.

## CHAPTER XLVII.

### THE JOURNEY.

"IN the ordinary state of affairs, such a course as you propose would be utterly inadmissible," said old Lady Somers to her son Lionel. "Still, under the circumstances, I really cannot advise one way or another," which meant that she held a rather strong opinion on the subject.

"Do tell us what we ought to do," said Sir Lionel. "Her name is as precious to me as it is to you."

"Well," said Lady Somers, "having thought it all over, and understanding that Mrs. Bone and the groom William are going also, and considering the way in which all the old rules for our guidance are being swept away, I really think you had better go. It is out of course; but I believe that if your father was alive he would agree."

The rector spoke out more roundly.

"My dear Lionel," he said, "for heaven's sake, don't let your mother, by any of her old-world crotchets, dissuade you from doing the duty which is most natural and proper to you, of all men. Hang etiquette, Lionel! I know there is a ridiculous notion that a man may not travel with his *fiancée*; but if you are not to be allowed to defend her through the very serious dangers of her journey, who is to be allowed? She has quite determined to go, then?"

She had. As in the case of the storm, during which I first introduced her to you, she had begun by protesting to Mrs. Bone, that she wouldn't go, and couldn't go, and that her father was mad. But she had ended, as she always did, by gently scolding herself into perfect acquiescence. Sir Lionel, riding over furiously, after she had sent her father's letter to him, hoped to find her in flat rebellion. But by that time she had gone through all the mental (doubtless, illogical) phases which were necessary to her in forming a resolution, and he found her as immoveable as a rock.

"You are risking your own life and my happiness," was one of his best arguments.

"But I promised him," was her reply.

"Your father is utterly inexcusable!" was one of his wild exclamations.

"It is possible," she said. "But I promised him in this room before I promised you; and I will not go from my word."

"I may come with you, then?"

"*You* would never leave me *now?*" was all she said, with the most perfectly innocent wonder. "Come with me? Why, how could I go without you, after the words you have said to me so often? I should die without you now, I think. I have only you, Lionel."

"Let us go, then," said Sir Lionel; "and we will face the world, the flesh, and the devil: Madame D'Isigny, Leroy, and Marat; all together."

"Be gentle to my Marat, mind you. I tell you, as a secret, Lionel, that Marat will do us no harm. I cannot tell you why; but I know it."

"Do not mention the dog's name, Mathilde."

"I will not again. But, if everything goes wrong, find the dog, at all risks. He will bark for *me*."

"If you have determined to go, then, we had better go before" —he was going to say before a certain place gets hotter, but, as a gentleman, he only said,—" before affairs get more hopelessly confused."

Well, and so she started in the early days of July. Sir Lionel, of course, could not possibly have anything to do with the business officially, but drove his curricle down to Poole, and made preparations for her on board the little brig which was to carry them to St. Malo. Mathilde was carried away somewhat triumphantly in Lady Somers' coach, with four horses, and postilions in crimson jackets, with four grooms outriding, two before and two behind. Mrs. Bone, got up in the last style of fashion, was sitting beside Mathilde. Mrs. Bone had a shortish dress on and silk stockings; she had also an idiotic bonnet and a blue veil. William the Silent sat on the box, entirely enjoying the expedition, dressed very much as grooms are dressed now, a dress which has not developed like others. Mrs. Bone insisted on keeping her head out of the carriage window. When she was remonstrated with by Mathilde for doing this, she said she did it to let her veil blow. Perhaps one of those kind critics who tell us that we were "evidently thinking" about something of which we were not thinking in the least, and very probably never thought about, will explain Mrs. Bone's reason for putting her head out of the carriage window.

If you will use your memory, and think of the person who in any of your doubtlessly numerous voyages was more sea-sick than any one else, you will find yourself able to conceive the state of Mathilde during their voyage; if you will go further and use your imagination, if you will try to fancy a person about nine times more sea-sick than any one you ever saw, you will arrive at Mrs. Bone. Before they had passed Swanage, Mrs. Bone was in a state of fatuous imbecility. Mathilde was idiotic with sea-sickness, but Mrs. Bone beat her hollow. She had superadded to her imbecility a kind of penitential delirium, during which she told Mathilde the whole old story of Adèle's correspondence with Louis de Valognes, and also told her three or four early love passages of her own, confiding to her the reason why she had not married several eligible young men. Mathilde, finding her necessity greater than her own, attended to her, and advised her to be ill like another, as she herself had been. Mrs. Bone said that she would gladly be ill if she could, even only to oblige Mademoiselle. Mathilde, however, at intervals of sickness attended to her, and they were all put ashore, utterly stupid, at the Dinan gate of St. Malo.

They were too stupid with their voyage to notice anything, or they might have noticed that they were received by National Guards. William the Silent was the first person to land. "Name, then," were the first words he heard from a sergeant of the National Guard, who stood before him bare-headed, holding papers in his hands, with a face and head which was wonderfully like Matthew Prior's and Napoleon Buonaparte's. "Your name, then?" he said to our stupid groom, in English.

"William Dickson."

"Your position?"

William could not understand what he meant, and looked back to see if Sir Lionel was coming.

"You need not look for assistance to your confederates," said Prior Buonaparte. "I only ask what is your position."

An old man with a grey unshaven beard spoke out.

"He is only the jockey of Mathilde, the daughter of D'Isigny the Breton."

"He may pass."

Next came Mathilde and Mrs. Bone, with the passport. It was scarcely *visé*, they were let to pass on through the narrow wicket into the narrow gloomy street, and the wicket was shut to behind her.

"Where is Sir Lionel?" she cried, suddenly.

"He is arrested," said one of the guards; "and is in the guard-house. You must come and see after your baggage to-morrow."

"Why is he arrested?"

"Who can tell?" said the man, shrugging his shoulders as if to dismiss the subject, as so far beyond hope of solution as to be uninteresting; and Mathilde stood alone among the idlers in the street, scared, and yet with the responsibility of the two others upon her. The old apple-women, who had come inside the gate because the barrier was closed, began to jeer at her.

"Send for thy mother, thou lame daughter of D'Isigny," said one.

"Thou and thy jockey, indeed!" said another.

"Get mademoiselle a cabriolet, that she may drive to her father's château," cried another, amidst laughter.

"Or to her aunt's convent at Dinort," said another.

"Or to La Garaye," yelled the oldest of them all.

Mathilde had stood steadily looking at them all this time, utterly speechless; but regarding them with a scorn which grew and grew till it burnt like a clear fire. All this time her bust seemed to expand, and her imperial crest to grow higher, and her magical beauty to grow more splendid in her wordless contempt. They could feel it, these women, for were they not French?—it scorched them like flame; their jeers became inarticulate mouthings.

"She has her father's accursed beauty," cried one; and this so exasperated the oldest crone of the lot that, hooking her withered old fingers, she made towards Mathilde, and in her fury, fell headlong.

As the others were raising her, Mathilde turned slowly and majestically through a somewhat admiring crowd, who made way for her.

"Those D'Isignys carry their heads well," said one.

"They must come off," said another. "They must die."

"They know how," said another. "They can die like Desilles."

## CHAPTER XLVIII.

### THE LAST OF ST. MALO

MATHILDE had not much trouble. She was at old St. Malo, and knew every house in the town; and indeed there were many poor shipwrights' and fishermen's wives, both in that quarter next the Sille, and in St. Servan, who knew her also through her good works. The tenants of her father's houses were a little shy towards her, for there were arrears of rent; and unless history lies, there was a general disinclination through France for those few years to the paying of rent. The first on whom she called began to talk about repairs; and had no room for her, most unfortunately, at that particular time. The second could have taken her in, but had no room for her servants; but learning that Mademoiselle's main object was merely to hire a carriage, grew over-pressingly polite, and reminded her of her

father's tenant and friend, Laroche, the post-master, who would doubtless serve her. This gentleman was so exceedingly delighted at her having said nothing about the rent, that he insisted on accompanying her down the street in a scull-cap, dressing-gown, and slippers, to show her a house which she knew perfectly well—quite as well as he did. "Hola, hi! M. Laroche," he cried, when he was opposite to it, "here is an old friend, indeed!" And when Laroche came out, he kissed his hand to Mademoiselle, and skipped gracefully back again.

Laroche came out, and looked at them,—a square-looking old man, whom Adèle and she had always disliked, because he was very abrupt and cross with them. Mathilde said,—

"How do you do, M. Laroche?"

He replied, "Now what the devil brings *you* here?"

"I am only come for a carriage, M. Laroche. I suppose you will let me have one?"

"I suppose I had better. You want an airing; a drive along the Dol road. Yes, I will give you a carriage."

"I want to go——"

"S——! You are going to Dol, do you hear? You are on your first stage to Paris to your father?"

"Certainly, M. Laroche," said Mathilde with tact.

"When do you wish to start?"

"I would gladly start to-night, but I had better start now. We are very tired, and have eaten nothing, and would gladly rest till night. But the Malouins have grown wicked. They have not only arrested my English friend, but they have insulted me. I had nothing to give them but scorn, and I gave them that until it maddened them."

"Come in to Madame Laroche: rest, and make yourselves at home," promptly replied Laroche.

Mathilde walked in, head in air, and paid her compliments to Madame Laroche, whom she had known all her life. Madame Laroche never rose to receive her, but took great pains in threading her needle, saying to a beetle-browed young woman who was in the room,—

"These people must eat: they cannot starve. If I undergo suspicion they cannot starve. What is there in the house for dinner?"

"There is ham and salad, as Madame well knows."

"Can the daughter of the *ci-devant* D'Isigny, the Breton, eat that?" asked Madame Laroche.

Mathilde, seeing Madame's intention, said, eagerly,—

"No, madame; if madame will allow me to say so. We have been very sea-sick, and are faint from want. Madame, if we could only have a little cold chicken, we would depart at once, and trouble no one."

Madame took out of her pocket, after long fumbling, an *écu*, and said to the beetle-browed young woman,—

"Go and buy her one, if there be one in this grass-eating town. We owe her father money, and she shall not starve."

The young woman departed, with a curiously disagreeable look, and as soon as she was gone Madame Laroche, who had been looking steadily at William, pointed her finger at him, pointed to the door, and then put her hand against her ear, as if listening. William did not understand her, and stared stupidly.

But Mrs. Bone did. She quietly opened the door with her right hand and listened, then she turned and nodded to Madame Laroche. This piece of really fine dexterity on the part of Mrs. Bone confirmed William in his foregone conclusion that she was the cleverest of the lot. To his dying day he used to tell that story, as proving how much cleverer women are than men.

The instant after Mrs. Bone had raised her head, Madame Laroche was on Mathilde's neck.

"My well-beloved," she said, "what madness is this? Why have you come here? And why, of all houses, did you come to this? Do you know that we are suspected? Do you know that Laroche is a violent Royalist, and that you could not possibly have come to a worse house?"

"I know nothing of these things," said Mathilde, simply. "I only know that I always believed M. Laroche to be a very good man; but he was always *difficile* with us, and so I disliked to come here. M. Benger brought us."

I will not reproduce the strong language which Madame Laroche used with regard to M. Benger.

"He used to receive your father's rents, and claims lien on them now. He would ruin us, as he will. We shall be interrogated to-morrow morning for your being here. We talk republicanism to save ourselves, but they know us, and we are ruined."

"I will write to my father on this," said Mathilde.

"*That* is no use. Our time is short, my well-beloved; she will be back with the chicken in a moment. See here: where are you going with your carriage? Speak low: she may be near."

"To Montauban."

"Do not go there. It is surrounded by a cordon of patriots. Go to Paris to your father. Go and live in the ruins of your father's château. Go and live among the wolves at La Garaye. Go anywhere but *there*."

"But, dear Madame, you so kind. I promised my father. I must go; and therefore I go. Can you tell me why they have arrested Sir Lionel Somers, my friend?"

"Hush! Here she comes," said Madame Laroche. And the beetle-browed young lady came in with the chicken, accompanied by M. Laroche.

It was not a very pleasant dinner. They all sat down together, and William sat next the young woman, to whom he showed, in his insular way, an extreme repugnance; for which he accounted, when Mrs. Bone taxed him with it afterwards, by saying "that he see at once that she warn't no good." What was wanted at this banquet more than anything else, probably, was reticence of speech, in consequence of the presence of the young woman; which material Mathilde of course supplied, by a petulant objurgation of the authorities who had arrested Sir Lionel Somers, of the miserable deterioration of the once good St. Malouins, by a burst of extreme anger at hearing of the captivity of the King, and by many other extreme indiscretions, which drove her host and hostess nearly mad with fear. She entirely, in her strange way, counterbalanced these indiscretions by saying that she should write to her friend, M. Marat, to-morrow, for *he* could know nothing of such things.

"You know M. Marat, then, Mademoiselle?" said Laroche, almost eagerly.

"Oh, yes," said Mathilde. "He and I are very old friends. He is very fond of me, and I of him, though I have often been scolded for liking him."

"He is a good patriot, Mademoiselle," said Laroche.

"Yes. He, like myself, loves the people. He is a good patriot, though strange in his ways. I also am strange in my ways. I think that all those who love the people are."

"Mademoiselle actually knows the patriot Marat, then?" growled the beetle-browed young woman.

"Bless you, who better? Why, I nursed him when he was ill in England, and had not one friend, and no money but what my father gave him."

"That is indeed true," said Laroche. And the young woman rose and left the room.

"You are safe enough now," said Laroche. "They will see you through, these precious patriots, now that they know you are friend of Judas Iscariot. Are you going to Montauban?"

"Yes; I am going to see to my sister."

"Get her away from there, and bring her here to one of your father's houses. She is in great danger. Among the Malouins, and with your friendship for Marat, you may save her. Mind what I say; I dare say no more. Now, wait quietly for your carriage, and commit no more indiscretions."

Late in the evening the carriage was waiting on the quay, and her lighter luggage had been passed and fetched; so she went out. There was a very curious crowd assembled round it, prominent among which was the very advanced patriot with whom we made acquaintance two years or more ago. He was dirtier than before, but much the same. The respectable man whom we called the Girondist was there also, but was not in any great request.

"Here she comes," said the advanced patriot. "This is the daughter of D'Isigny the Breton, now at last a patriot, the friend of the amiable Marat. See her, and respect her. She is the nurse of Marat, and the friend of the people. Know her again."

If her mother could only have heard them!

She was as safe among them as if she had been in the Tower of London; for by all I can gather, the power of that wonderful Marat had travelled even as far westward as this. Another thing made her safe. D'Isigny was a Breton, and they attended to what he did in Paris. Malouin patriots had brought or sent word that D'Isigny had been seen in communication with Marat on distinctly two occasions, and in most friendly talk with

Robespierre on certainly one; they also knew that he had been grossly insulted in the Conciergerie by the aristocrats. D'Isigny was turning to the people, said the men patriots; the women would not believe a word of it. Had it not been for these facts, I fear that Mathilde would never have been allowed to go on to Montauban.

When Mrs. Bone had got hoisted in, and William was on the box, M. Laroche said to the postilion,—

"Dol."

"Not at all," said Mathilde, very loudly; "I do not want to go to that dirty old place at all. You and your Dols again. I want to go to Montauban, the seat of my brother-in-law, the Marquis de Valognes. He must go first to Dinan, where he must change horses, and then by Vasansdire and Vaurien southward to Montauban, the only decent house left in the country, as it seems to me. It is one thing for these patriots to have burnt my father's château, though they might have spared *that*, I think, but it is quite another for them to have burnt La Garaye; that has ruined their cause for ever. I am to be driven to Montauban."

Rather too emphatic a young lady to be trusted to her own guidance in France in 1792. But she was quite safe. The advanced patriots rather liked temper and emphasis: and Marat's name would have carried her through anything.

Said one, "She is aristocrat at heart still."

Said another, "She never was aristocrat. I know that her father, before he came to the people, set her penances for talking the merest pure patriotism."

Said the first, "There are to be arrests made at Montauban soon: that pear is ripe."

Said the second, "It is true; but it is in the circle of Rennes. It is no business of ours."

Said another, "But she is good patriot, though extremely indiscreet. Would it not be as well to send to the Rennes committee, and tell them that this woman is good patriot?"

Another said, "The Rennes men are but half-hearted dogs; they are not with the people or with the Revolution."

"But the woman will be arrested," said the first speaker.

"Let her be arrested," said our original advanced patriot, who had cursed André Desilles. "She is safer in arrest, for she is very indiscreet. She is a good woman, but she is better in prison than out of it. If she is arrested by the Rennes or central committee, we can act then. Leave it alone."

And so they did not send any one even to answer for Mathilde's identity.

## CHAPTER XLIX.

### MA SŒUR.

RS. BONE went to sleep habitually in positions which would have appeared, to any one not so used to her as Mathilde, to be impossible. On this night's journey she surpassed herself. She seemed to slumber most peacefully when going at full speed over a paved road, while all Mathilde's teeth were chattering in her head, and she was holding on by the seat; on the other hand, when the carriage entered the turf avenue of Montauban, near the middle of the night, and began to roll nearly in dead silence over the grass, Mrs. Bone woke up and got very lively, waking up Mathilde, who was now dozing off. At the same time William leant back into the carriage and said:

"We are near the castle, mademoiselle; if you stand up you can see it."

So she stood up and looked at it. Styx and Cocytus! what an awful place! She shuddered, and laid her hand on the young man's shoulder.

They had come up the eastern avenue, and the moon was westering and sinking behind the fantastic pinnacles; the whole building which rose above their path and barred it, was as black as a hearse; and crowning the catafalque, rushed up the great dominant slate-roofed tower, between them and such dim light as there was in heaven. Mathilde shuddered and sat down once more.

They were not expected, and the household was in bed. William's ring at the bell broke the midnight silence, and set a wolf, which was prowling among the gaudy flower-beds in the darkness, howling. He was answered by others in the forest, until night was hideous. Mrs. Bone clutched hold of Mathilde, saying:

"The dogs are howling, my dear, and there is death in the house."

Mathilde said, quietly: "It is only the wolves," which by no means reassured Mrs. Bone.

At last there appeared lights, travelling from window to window, as if through long corridors; and, after a long parley, the door was opened by a hastily-dressed footman, and they were received by the old major-domo and another.

"Tell Madame la Marquise that her sister is come," said Mathilde; "and take us to a room with a fire. Is Father Martin here? If he is, awake him; and tell him I am here."

The old major-domo despatched one young man to arouse the necessary servants, and another to put in motion the extremely elaborate machinery necessary for awakening the Marquise. Meanwhile, he himself attended on our somewhat dazed and scared party, and showed them into a drawing-room, which opened into another drawing-room, and then into a picture-gallery, and then into a banqueting-hall, and then into Lord knows what; but which had an ort of fire still burning in one of its grates.

The major-domo excused himself while he made up the fire and lighted wax-candles.

"Mademoiselle had not been expected. He hoped that Mademoiselle would not complain to La Marquise, or still worse to her mother, for her reception. The necessary women would be with her immediately; the necessary young men would be aroused. He hoped, nay, he felt sure, that Mademoiselle would send in her complaint through Father Martin."

"I have no complaint," she said, in French, somewhat wearily. "Bone," she added in English, "I should go mad in this house."

Mrs. Bone submitted that she had hardly been in it long enough to know her own mind, and that *she* thought it beautiful.

"I daresay you do," said Mathilde; "but then I don't. Satin-seated chairs, wolves in the flower-garden, and the peasantry starving, don't happen to suit me. Well, we are all as God made us. I like fine things as well as another, Bone. Let you and I look at these, for they say that there are none such in the world. Adèle will be cross at my coming, and will not come down to-night. Take that candle, and let us look at these fine things until they give us supper, or show us our beds. William, you stay exactly where you are, and don't move your feet; you should not have come on these Turkey carpets at all with your boots."

William said that he thought so himself; and asked whether he had not better go into the passage, as he called the marble corridor.

"Well," said Mathilde, "you will hurt the carpet by walking over it, but as you can't stand where you are for ever, and must go out some time or another, you had better go out at once." So William went.

Mathilde and Mrs. Bone, rambling through a wilderness of luxury greater than Blenheim or Chatsworth, must have seen something worth seeing. Mrs. Bone highly approved of it, and said it was " Noble," as indeed it was, in a way, but had remarks to make about the state of the fire-grates, and of the droppings of wax-candles on priceless carpets; during which she alluded to certain imaginary idle sluts and husseys. Mathilde, whose whole heart was waiting for her sister, was querulous and anxious.

"I have no patience with this wicked old uncle of Louis', Bone. He has out-Heroded Herod in his extravagance. Just look at the suite of this ante-room, will you? Just look at this sofa, will you?"

Mrs. Bone did, but did not seem to be any the wiser.

"It is all tent-stitch Gobelin, and he has worked it up into furniture. I never heard of such a thing in my life; and you complain of your Revolution!"

Mrs. Bone had not done so, but she thought that the suite of rooms was very beautiful. And so she went on holding a candle before Mathilde from one room to another, in one of the most splendid houses in France or in Europe.

"Beautiful; yes," said Mathilde. "The devil is handsome. It does not suit me. It is all dark and cold to me."

Dark and cold no longer: for stupid old Bone, rambling with Mathilde among a wilderness of sofas, satin and other, had said, " here is somebody; " and she had held her light towards that somebody. And who was that somebody? A little creature more beautiful than morn, just roused from her innocent bed, with her bright hair all abroad, dressed in loose, flowing white.

And this little creature suddenly cast herself into the arms of Mathilde, and laid the glory of her hair across Mathilde's broad bosom; and Adèle said only—"Ma sœur! ma sœur!"

And Mathilde said—" Ma bien aimée! ma bien aimée! how did I ever do without you?"

## CHAPTER L.

### THE LAST NIGHT.

"I THOUGHT you loved me no longer," said Mathilde, turning up the beautiful face towards hers, and gazing down upon it.

"You speak false!" replied Adèle, looking up. "You know very well that you never thought anything of the sort, you dear old foolish; and that very foolish old Bone, who traitorously used to carry my love-letters to Louis. For you two to come here in the dead of night, like revolutionists! We believed that it was an arrest. My dearly beloved, come to the light and the warmth, and let me love you."

The two sisters wandered back through the long rooms towards the one where the fire was burning and the supper was preparing, with their heads close together. What did they say? Very little, or nothing. They were content without speech, those two. And when they came into the lighted room, lo! there was Father Martin, with his back against the mantelpiece, looking at him. Mathilde had the pretty head upon her bosom, and had her left hand twined among the curls which crowned it; but she had a right hand ready to stretch out to Father Martin, and he took the long white fingers in his hand, and put them to his lips.

"I am in my old home now, Father," said Adèle, quietly. "I am safe here—I want no mother now. She was always my real mother."

"I am content to die if you will only speak to me like that," said Mathilde. "Father Martin, how do you do?"

"A great deal better than I deserve, my dear. I have been staying here in idleness and luxury, waiting for your arrival, when I ought to have been at Nantes. My father is dead, and

I heard of his death before his illness, or I should have been away before; but he being dead, I, not having been able to see him alive, have left details to my sister. I have delayed on here because mine was the only sound head in this house. I go to-morrow, because, in consequence of your arrival, I can leave another sound head here to manage matters."

"Don't be an old disagreeable," said Adèle, looking up from Mathilde's bosom.

"I am speaking to your sister, not to you," said Father Martin. "There are no servants present at this moment, and our good Bone does not understand French; my time to-morrow morning will be short, and so I will speak now. Your mother has made this the most suspicious house in the country, the centre of a reactionary plot, the details of which are in possession of every revolutionist for miles around. The revolutionists are merely waiting until the pear is ripe, and then they will pluck it. The plot has been betrayed four times over; any one but a foolish person would have known it. Your mother has risked all our lives, if she has not lost them. I might have stayed here a little longer, but I go to my sister, and to arrest. I go to-morrow, and leave all this folly in your hands to manage. If you can manage your mother, it is more than I can. What is the matter now?"

Adèle had taken her head from Mathilde's bosom; Mathilde had straitened herself, and was looking over Father Martin's shoulder, with terror in her eyes. Mrs. Bone had plunged herself into the lowest depth of inane and imbecile terror; for Madame D'Isigny had slid in and had placed herself behind Father Martin; and all gaunt and grey, listening to every word he said, awful, magnificent, and terrible.

Martin, following the direction of the eyes, turned round and saw her. He burst out laughing.

"Madame," he said, "you play this trick too often. You do it well, this *coup de théâtre*, but you do it too often? Can you understand me when I say that you do it too often? Can you understand me when I say that you make yourself ridiculous?"

Madame could understand being ridiculous to *him;* but her object just now was her daughter Mathilde. She stood like a tall, grey pillar, staring straight at her, and took no more notice of Martin's words than if a dog had barked.

He went on explaining the utter hopelessness of the plot of Montauban, and she waited in firm contemptuous silence until he had done. She would not speak, and she beat him by that manœuvre, as he well knew.

"God help them all," he said, as he went away. "I can do nothing more." And so he went to his bed.

Madame, after he was gone, sat down and spoke. "A good man," she said, "a pure, true-hearted, noble man, who gives example to us all; but too cautious. He cannot see that we must risk all, or perish. A good man! My dear Mathilde, come here and kiss your old, cruel, fierce mother, who loves you well, and who is risking her life for king and for church."

Mathilde approached her mother deliberately, and when she stooped over her did a somewhat odd thing—but she *was* odd. She took her mother's face in her two hands and looked into it. Then she stooped and kissed her, and said: "You are not cruel, you have a good face, mother. I will help you in this matter, for I am sworn to my father about it; but we must both try to save Adèle."

Madame D'Isigny immediately rose. "You have looked at me," she said, "let me look at you." Mathilde at once found her mother's powerful hands laid on her two shoulders, and her mother's strange square face, now perfectly quiet, peering down into hers. She looked steadily into that dreaded face, to see if the inspection was satisfactory; but the face showed no sign. She only said, "There is power there, my child. I wish we had known one another sooner. It was your father's fault. We will make acquaintance now."

Alas, no, Madame.

A white-capped nurse came in, and said that M. le Vicomte was awake; and Adèle said, "*Now*, my sweetest Mathilde, you shall see baby."

Mathilde, full of eagerness, curiosity, and tenderness, went and saw the melancholy baby, and *believed* in him: a thing she had scarcely done before, for some things are so passing experience to some minds, that they are scarcely really believed in until seen. She had got, through the force of her intellect, to understand and believe that Adèle was a marchioness with £30,000 a year, velvet-piled carpets, tent-stitch Gobelins tapestry worked up into furniture, and the De Valognes emeralds; but that Adèle had actually had a live baby had been hitherto unrealised. There he was, though, with his quaint, little, peaked face on his pillow. And so Mathilde and Adèle went to bed together for the last time, with the melancholy baby between them.

"My sister," said Mathilde, once in the night, "I wish to sleep that I may rise to see Father Martin before he starts for Nantes. But I cannot."

"Let us wake and talk, then," said Adèle. "It is only the wolves in the forest: you will soon be used to them here. Mathilde, I will try to make you happy here; I think that I am wiser and better than I was. Have you quite forgiven me all my old petulence?"

"I never had any to forgive, crown and object of my life. Why ask such a question to-night? Hark at the wolves again!"

## CHAPTER LI.

### À LA LOIRE.

"LET us get up and walk with him a little way," said Mathilde to Adèle. "I should like to see the last of him."

"The last of him!" said Adèle; "he returns as soon as he has administered his father's affairs. He is only going to Nantes to help his sister. But we will see him off."

So in the early clear morning, they rose to get him his coffee, and see him on his way. He chanted primes for the Breton household in the chapel, and then over his coffee with them he discoursed pleasantly of many things.

"My sweet Adèle, be as cautious as you can, and listen to your old Mathilde. No one loves you better than she; and has she not come to see you, and thereby got Sir Lionel arrested? Listen to her."

"I care for no one any longer now that she is here," replied Adèle, nodding her head very rapidly. "And when Lionel comes we shall be stronger still. They will not detain him long."

"Oh, no," said Mathilde; "it is only some informality in his papers, and you will soon be back, you know."

"Well, my children, I cannot say. I go from this dangerously-marked house, to a still more dangerous town. It is totally impossible for any man to say one word about his movements in these times. The committee of Nantes are notoriously enraged, and there is very little doubt that I shall be arrested."

They both began to weep.

"But my hands are so clean. They can scarcely put the banishment in force together against *me*, one would think. I wish your mother had been more cautious. Keep cheerful hearts, my daughters, watching and praying. Arise and let us walk; I have far to go, and will walk to avoid suspicion."

They partly dried their tears and went with him. Strange figures to our eyes now, with scanty gowns scarcely big enough in the skirt to let their feet move freely, large hat-bonnets and scarves: figures which would be laughed at now by the mob; and yet inside those clothes were two women much the same as we have all of us known in our own experience, but tuned, by the necessities of the times, as it were, to concert pitch.

They went fluttering in these, to us, quaint garments down the long south ride, one on each side of Father Martin; the rabbits, the hares, and the pheasants ran across their path, and Father Martin jocularly reminded Adèle of his first backslidings, with regard to the game so many months ago now, and of her perfectly unfounded suspicions of him. But his jocularity fell dead, for Adèle only took his arm, and looked up in his face with an expression slightly more miserable than that of her own baby; and she could look so intensely miserable, poor little thing, that no man except her father ever made her look so twice. They went along under the springy, thymy turf, between the walls of forest and copse, more silently after this; and at last arrived at the little hill from which Father Martin had looked on the Loire with the old forester, and they sat down among the breezy trees and talked awhile, until he arose and said that it was time to start southward.

Before them lay the deeply-wooded country, beyond it the dimly-seen sand-banks of the Loire, and beyond the Loire, creeping steadily up against the fitful summer wind from the north, great Alp-like thunder-clouds. Mathilde broke into one of those, for her rare, fits of emotion, which though much less loud than those of Adèle, were so much more powerful—nay, even terrible. Her great chest shook with emotion, and her face was tortured, yet she was tearless. Poor Adèle broke into wild wailing, foolishly asking them both to forgive her, all, everything, she knew not what. There was a fluttering in the nerves of Father Martin's face for one instant, and then it was gone. His religion had trained him well. He lightly laid his hand on each of their shoulders, and said :

"What mean ye to weep and break my heart? for I am ready not to be bound only, but to die at Jerusalem for the name of the Lord Jesus."

And they had only to say, seeing that he would not be persuaded, "The will of the Lord be done."

And so he blessed them, and left them aloft among the trees on the breezy knoll, and went south towards the sand-banks of the Loire, and towards the great thunder-pile which was rising from beyond it.

They heard him singing as he went, as he was wont to do as he walked, and singing well. Not a chant, but a kind of tune like some of those very strange single time German waltzes, which are so strangely sad and wild, and of which Strauss was master. I know what he sang, though they did not :—

> "Urbs Syon, inclyta turris, et edita littore tuto,
> Te peto, te colo, te flagro, colo, canto, saluto :
> Nec meritis peto ; nam meritis meto morte perire :
> Nec reticens tego, quod meritis ego filius iræ."

And so singing

> "Oh, mea spes, mea, tu Syon Aurea, clarior auro,
> Agmine splendida, stans duce florida perpete lauro,"

he disappeared into the wood, and was gone.

Let me borrow some more glorious words, they are so infinitely finer than any which I can give you.

"And they wept sore. Sorrowing most of all for the words which he spake, that they should see his face no more."

What words kept ringing in Mathilde's ears as she walked beside weeping Adèle up the grass ride ! There was the flaming red and purple château towering above the trees, straight before her. Why did she keep thinking of a wild wet day among the dim English downs, with a ringing English hymn, contending with the dull fury of the English weather? What were the place and time which she was trying to recall? She saw it in a moment: it was the little chapel under the down, on the day when Lionel came to her. And what were the words which were trying to force themselves on her memory? The words came also: they were the words which Evan, the dissenter, had preached on that very day.

"I will lay my soul bare before you. I find no assurance in the Book that those who have loved here will meet in glory; and what is glory to me without the beloved of my heart?"

So she quoted it from memory. And during what came to her, this was the bitterest thing she had to suffer, the thought that they would not meet after. "I would die for them, but shall we meet again?"

## CHAPTER LII.

### THE THUNDERBOLT.

ATHER MARTIN was a shrewd man, and knew that the house was suspected and watched; but he little dreamt how near the pear was ripe. The house was a mere mousetrap; the very first attempt at *movement* in it made the revolutionary tribunal act at once. The state of "preternatural suspicion," as Mr. Carlyle calls it, in which France, particularly at the edge of reactionary Brittany, was then, was quite enough to make his open departure into a *casus belli*. He would have staid on had he known the state of matters outside the forest, but he did not; or at least did not appreciate it fully. He little thought that by his innocent departure he brought down ruin.

The old simile of the little bird flying from the edge of the avalanche, and bringing it crashing down, is somewhat worn, but it must serve yet once more.

The crash might have been *delayed*, of that there is little doubt, but that the bolt was ready to hurl is perfectly indubitable, and that their policy was perfectly prepared was also indubitable. Their plan was not badly conceived. They had no wish to *break up* Montauban, it was far too warm a nest of royalism to be broken up yet. But one thing had been seen by the Central Committee in Paris. Louis de Valognes was safe in their hands; but his wife was still at Montauban, doubtless communicating with her husband by secret means, and her husband had free communication with other Royalists in the prison, who had communication with the frontier in spite of all their efforts. Brittany was most dangerous, and must be watched. Montauban was the very hot-bed of royalism, presided over by the notoriously infuriated Madame D'Isigny. And so it just happened, if you will think it over, that our poor little Adèle was looked on by them as one of the principal sources of communication between Brittany and Coblenz.

They, therefore, wanted *her*. Montauban, Madame D'Isigny, La Rochejacquelin, Charette, might *wait*. They wanted this poor little Marquise of ours, whom they suspected of being, quite wrongfully but most naturally, one of the most important of the carrier-pigeons between Brittany and Coblenz,—they wanted her, I say, under lock and key.

The order of the mother society to her daughter ran somewhat like this:—"On the first sign of movement at Montauban, arrest Madame *soi disant* de Valognes. She can bring her child and one attendant. Treat her justly, for she is perhaps innocent. She goes to the Abbaye, and not to her husband."

Adèle had very little idea of her importance. She went to bed with her baby the night after Father Martin's departure quite comfortably. Mathilde also, sleeping in her own room this night, went up to it, but instead of going to bed, followed an evil old habit of hers, of sitting up in her room, and gossiping with Mrs. Bone about the pigs and the poultry, and the corn and the turnips, across the water there at Sheepsden. Bone to-night added her mite to the entertainments by speculating as to whether or not they had hung Sir Lionel yet, or whether he would be, as she put it, "remanded."

"You stupid old Bone," she said. "He is only detained about his papers: he will be here to-morrow at latest."

William the Silent, after vilipending his bed as being French, got into it, and slept the sleep of the just in three minutes.

The Lady Superior, who had knocked up an impromptu dormitory in a disused gallery, declaring that after so many years she could not sleep without company, was sleeping among her nuns, or rather at one end of them, for she had taken the bed next the door, in the draught, as a sheepdog's duty over nine ugly old women. There had been a few alarms of wolves from Sister Pavida, and Sister Podagra's corns had made her more querulous than usual; but they were all asleep in a row now, snorting like pigs; and the Lady Superior was just beginning to tune up herself.

Who are these two? Who is this terrible inexorable-looking woman, with her stern face looking *at* her glass, but not into it: with her long grey hair all about her shoulders? Beautiful and awful! That is Madame D'Isigny. Who is this beautiful, bright-haired girl who is combing that hair? That is Madame's innocent little maid: the girl whom the tipsy young Mameluke saw asleep and fled before. Madame liked pretty things about her.

As the hair-dressing went on Madame looked into the glass, to see the beautiful face of her little maid: and she said, suddenly,—

"I was handsomer once than you ever will be; but he never loved me."

The French girl said, as a French girl would, not having any idea of whom she spoke,—

"He had no taste, Madame."

"I don't know. It is a pity we never agreed, for I think I loved him. I was very beautiful; but I never had the beauty of Mathilde."

"Mademoiselle's figure——" began the girl.

"Silence, imbecile. If she had been bent double, her beauty would have been as much higher than mine, as mine was than yours, Bambino. There is a beauty of soul, child; and you have none."

As this was rather a civil speech, considering who spoke it, the girl left well alone and combed.

Who is this who knocks suddenly at Madame's door, and without waiting for "*Entrez*," comes in at all hazards? It is the handsome young Mameluke, pale and terrified, who says,—

"Madame, the revolutionists are coming to make arrest."

"What circle?" said Madame D'Isigny.

"The central, acting from Nantes."

"How many do they want?"

"Only the Marquise. I have it all from my brother. The others are to be left for the present."

"How far are they off?"

"Ten minutes, Madame; I have run hard."

"Here is a diamond for you, boy; you can live on the sale of it till you are hung. You have done well, boy. Girl, tie up my hair. Quick! The fools, they do not know one of us from the other. I will beat them yet. Mathilde shall go; and we will be with La Rochejacquelin before they find out their mistake. Quick, girl!"

Mathilde had said: "It is perfectly ridiculous, and totally impossible. I will have no hand in the buying of any more meal at retail prices. Poor folks' pigs pay, while our pork costs ninepence a pound."

And Bone was saying: "Now perhaps, Mademoiselle, you will believe me another time——" when in swiftly stalked greyheaded Medea, with all the fury and wrath of the French Revolution close behind her.

"Mathilde! Mathilde!" she said. "The dogs are coming to arrest Adèle. You have told me that you vowed yourself to your father to assist us. For God's sake help us now."

"What is it necessary that I should do, mother?"

"Personate her. They do not know one of us from the other. By the time they find out their mistake, Brittany will have marched on Paris, and La Vendée will be up in a month with real France at its back. They want only *her*. I will get her out of the way. If she had *only* courage, she might go herself and be safe. But she is a coward and would betray. Her nerve gives way, yours does not. Go for her."

"Of course," said Mathilde. "Keep her out of the way, and leave the rest to me. Bone, go and call William."

The Guards gave good notice of their arrival by arousing the wolves. Short as the time was, they were ready for them. They had only to beat once at the great door, when it was swung open, and the somewhat startled Guards saw a long drawn corridor, dimly lighted and filled with statuary, in front of which stood Mathilde, old Bone, and William, all alone.

"In the name of the King,"* said the foremost man, "I demand the body of the daughter of D'Isigny the Breton."

"I am she," said Mathilde.

"He has two daughters. Are you the one which was married to the *ci-devant* Marquis de Valognes?"

Gleams, shall we call them, of old tendresses from Louis de Valognes, false but very sweet; a glimpse of an English ford in May time, when she had died one of her many deaths, came swiftly across Mathilde's soul, as she told the great lie from which she never departed.

"I am."

---

## CHAPTER LIII.

### THE JOURNEY.

ATHILDE, when she began to reflect on her position, had not the slightest fear or anxiety for herself, and indeed, to tell the truth, but very little for Adèle; for as she was personating her, there was very little chance of her being molested, and their mother, so skilled in politics, would doubtless take care of her. There was danger, no doubt; but if you came to that, there was danger in a common summer thunder-storm. She was arrested. Well! but that, although uncommon in England, was common enough in France, even in old times: as for now, it was always so now. And so she jingled away in the rattling old carriage, which they had brought for her, pretty well without anxiety. She would do more than this for Adèle: and so she fell quietly asleep, until awakened by the light of the morning.

She looked round her then to see how things were. She saw through the glass windows, first of all, William, asleep on the box beside the driver; and then two men, evidently mounted foot soldiers, in blue uniforms, with those tall "bearskins," or, as they are now irreverently called, "Busbies," and those long

---

* I think so; but it must have been nearly the last time it was said.— H. K.

gaiters, which were very soon afterwards disagreeably known, not only over the continent of Europe as far as Moscow, but even on one occasion in Ireland, and on one in South Wales. "These," she said to herself, "are your new National Guards." Putting her head out of window to see how many there were coming behind, she found her face so close to another of them, who rode by the wheel, that she nodded and smiled to him, and said,—

"*Bon jour*, Monsieur. It is a beautiful morning."

He also raised his hat and bowed, and, riding up to the window, asked if he could do anything for Madame.

"There was nothing at present," said Mathilde; "but when there was she would trouble Monsieur."*

So with a nod to Monsieur, she sat back in the carriage, almost delighted to find herself among Frenchmen again.

This pleasure grew greater soon. There was a stoppage, and she asked her new friend, who was before the carriage window, what it was. He said they were resting the horses before pulling the carriage up the hill. Mathilde said, "Ask the gentleman in command whether I may walk up. Tell him that I am lame, and would not run away from such good company if I could. Ask him, for I love the morning."

The sergeant in command was at the window, and had let down the steps in a moment: and behold, not only he, but the whole escort of five were dismounted, leading their horses. Why? Not on account of the hill, by any means: only because the old rules of French politeness forbid a man to sit on horseback while a lady in company was on foot. Our fathers taught us this same rule, but I don't see any evidence that our last batch of young gentlemen ever heard of it.

William also descended from his box and joined Mathilde, walking a little after her, and talking to her. The escort of revolutionists drew away immediately.

* Citoyen and Citoyenne and "Tu-toyer-ing" only began in Paris about the middle of August. The old chivalric form of speech was as yet kept up. A connection of mine, a rector, on the borders of Somersetshire but in Devon, once told me that he had to compose a squabble between two Devonshire women. Lady No. 1, had, it appeared, *abused* Lady No. 2. "What did she say to you?" asked the rector. "She thee'd and thou'd me," said Lady No. 2. The rector had to point out how much better it was for Christian people to live together in unity, and not use injurious epithets such as these on every trifling occasion.

z

"My dear William," said Mathilde, "they will not leave us alone beyond the top of the hill, and I want to impress one thing on you very much. We are in France, and France is different from England."

William nodded and smiled. He quite understood *that*.

"In France we pride ourselves on our politeness; and politeness is only good-humour and kindliness reduced to practice. Now you, so good-humoured and so kind, will you not also be polite?"

William the Silent understood her perfectly, but had only time to nod, when it was, "*Montez, s'il vous plait*, Madame," and on they jingled again.

William remembered his rôle well. He had not for some little time a chance of showing his good-will, however.

At last they stopped for breakfast, at a very little inn; and William waited on Mathilde while she took her meal at a table apart from the soldiers. On going out to start, he found the sergeant in command kicking his horse in the stomach. He got Mathilde to ask the reason.

The reply was scarcely a practical one, though delivered with great politeness. The horse, it appeared, was an Austrian Feuillant Emigré, descendant of that Judas Iscariot—Nero-Foulon, Frederique of Prussia, *soi-disant* le Grand; and he had gone lame, as they always did. And, indeed, when they started the horse was certainly too lame to go.

William called out and stopped the cavalcade, and, getting down, went to the sergeant's horse, and taking up its near fore foot, showed them a large stone in it. Taking another stone from the road, he knocked it out, to their wonder and admiration.

They were only mounted foot soldiers, who could just, and no more, sit on their horses. Was it admiration for his dexterity, or for his good faith, which made them trust him? Probably some little of both. But it helped to make their strange, long journey pleasant.

As for Mathilde, she would make anything pleasant; and now, among her beloved French people, she won their hearts utterly. Her tongue, so long debarred from its natural language, poured out, almost unceasingly, a little crystal rivulet of good-humour and kindness, at which everyone drank by the way as she went.

Adèle, who was a giving soul, had thought in the night during which they slept together of what she should give Mathilde in the morning for a present: and she had thought of Lady Somers missal with the Byzantine filigree binding, and the piece of the true cross: so that when Mathilde had awakened later, and Adèle had got up, she had found it on her pillow with a note. It made the way to Paris short for her. I never read a missal, and never mean to, so I do not know what is inside one; but there was, I daresay, something in it which pleased Mathilde better than the Ferdinand and Isabella illuminations; and when she had done with that, she looked at the almost unequalled illuminations; and when she had looked at some of them, she closed the book and looked at the splendid exterior with loving admiration. She was well amused,

"Will Madame be pleased to alight?" "Certainly. Madame supposed they were going to change horses?"

The man in command said that the diligence went from here to Falaise. It rested, therefore, with Madame whether she would post or go by diligence; but, if she posted, it would be at her own expense. Mathilde said that certainly she would post; she was well supplied with money; and asked, would her present escort go with her?

The present escort was to go all the way, it appeared, whether by digilence or post. "That is good," said Mathilde; "it would be a pity to part just as we have got to be good friends. What, on earth, are we to do at Falaise? Where are you taking me to, then?"

That was a question for which there was no answer; so Mathilde went up the stairs of the hotel where they stayed, and, while dinner was getting ready, looked out of window.

William was in the room when she left the window, helping, or pretending to help, in laying the cloth. "William," she said, in English, "do you know where they are taking us? Look here."

William came and looked out of window, and saw a broad market-place, with a fountain in the centre; beyond, pleached alleys of lime-trees, and on a rocky elevation, among the lime-trees, a splendid ruined keep; beyond which again, a river snarled at the bottom of a deep glen. William looked at it all, and said nothing, seeing he had nothing to say.

"Do you not see that they have brought us to *Vire*, and that they speak of Falaise? Is it possible that they are going to take us to *Paris?* I know this place; it is the centre of the *bocage.* Why do they keep this route to the north of Maine, when it lay through Alençon? Do they think that Maine will rise with Bretagne? If they only take us to Paris, we shall do well; for my father is there."

And then she laughed at herself for supposing that William could understand her; and when she had eaten her supper, and the man in command had come in and said that it was time to start, she, in a pleasant humorous way, told him of the absurd mistake she had made in discoursing the route with her English servant, who thought that France adjoined China. So humorously did she tell the story of her consulting with William about the Normandy roads, that she quite threw the good patriot off his guard.

She concluded by chattering, "It is well for you on horseback not to care for roads, but it is otherwise to me inside the carriage. From here to Falaise I can sleep; but from Falaise to Bernay the Seven Sleepers would each awake one another. It was the corvée of the Marquis d'Evreux, one of you revolutionists. And from Bernay to Evreux is not much better."

The man said that the roads there were not so good, but that they would go slowly.

"It *is* to Paris, then?" said Mathilde, looking straight at him. And the man looked somewhat like a fool. He got out of his position, smiling, like a Frenchman, by saying, "Madame's sagacity has triumphed. It *is* to Paris."

The conversations she held with these men during the walks up hill were, like herself, odd. No one ever joined in them except the young man whom she had first made acquaintance with, and the commandant of the little escort.

"Now, what do you propose, you people?" she said. "What is to be the end of your precious Revolution?"

All kinds of things. Mr. Thackeray says, in the "Rose and the Ring," "Here a pretty game may be played by each child saying what it would like best for dinner."

"Those are all very good objects, with the exception of the destruction of religion, in which I cannot sympathise, as a religionist myself. But if you cannot get them without taking a poor innocent soul, like myself, to Paris and to prison, I doubt if you will ever get them at all. What has the King been doing, that he is in prison?"

I do not know what the King had not done. I agree, with many others, that he had done nothing; but they said that he had done all manner of things.

"Don't believe a word of it," said Mathilde, in English, to William. "I do not believe one word of it," she repeated in French. "He says himself that he never meant to cross the frontiers."

"But he evidently meant to do so, Madame," said the commandant.

"The best thing he could do," said Mathilde. "I know I have been stupid in ever crossing them. There, put down the steps, you good man, and let me get into the carriage. Why did you not let him go, you people? Why did you not hang Drouet? I have only half heard of this before. It seems to me that you have all made great fools of yourselves. You will have Europe on you. Are you prepared for a coalesced Europe?"

So vaguely, and, as she thought truly, poor old Mathilde, with more or less light, and more or less correctness; and so they rumbled on to Paris.

At last there came a separation. This very strange company had toiled up many hills, and toiled down many hills, on their very strange journey; but, by the time they had all grown fond of her, and by the time that the first young man, to whom she had spoken, had got that strange gnawing at the heart for her which men call love;—by the time they had all got sentimental over her, and one at least, was head over heels in love with her; —to the last hill of all, and Paris beyond.

This sentimental young man got a few precious moments alone with her as they walked. He said, "We are about to part, Mademoiselle."

"More's the pity. I have got so fond of you all; and you like me, too! What a pity you should talk such nonsense as you do! I never, in all my life, saw a kinder lot of men; and I like you the best of all. Why do you not give up this ultra-revolutionary nonsense?"

Words! words! They were not spoken in idleness, these

words of Mathilde; but he gave up the Revolution, and lost his head over them, as he had lost his heart to her.

"If Mademoiselle were to command," he said, "I would throw the Revolution to the winds."

"Who am I to command?" said Mathilde. "I only wish you to leave off talking nonsense; moreover, you have called me Mademoiselle twice, when you should have called me Madame, which is not good manners."

"Mademoiselle, I know you," he said: "you are the eldest daughter of D'Isigny. You are not the Marquise de Valognes at all. You are Mademoiselle D'Isigny. I have your secret."

"Then, if you are a gentleman, as you seem to be, you will keep it," she replied. And, indeed, that was all that this sentimental, though ill-considered young Republican ever got for his devotion. Poor boy! let him go away into night. He was not the first moth scorched in the flame of that strange, odd beauty, which had attracted the douce Sir Joshua himself; nor, indeed, was he the last. Every man who had a chance of seeing her— and they were very few—fell in love with her, save two. Dandy de Valognes and William the servant. To the dandy she was old Mathilde, with one shoulder lower than the other; to the hind she was simply Mademoiselle, a kind young lady, daughter of the French gentleman whose wages he took, and who had killed the mad dog. *He* had no idea whether she was ugly or pretty; it never entered into his head to think about it.

## CHAPTER LIV.

### THE ABBAYE.

HE journey came to an end on a hot July afternoon. The sergeant in command came to the door of the carriage, and said that they were arrived, and Mathilde got out. "What place is this?" she asked.

"I deeply regret to say, Madame, that this is the Abbaye."

"It is all equal," said Mathilde.

"You will acquit us of having done our duty, Madame."

"My dear friends, I am so sorry to part with you. We have had a pleasant journey, all of us: have we not? Please to try and think kindly of me ; and do not forget your religion, you ; and do not speak so about the King ; it is not good."

She looked up at the façade of the building for a moment, and then went on to the wicket, but not alone. One young man of the escort was left to hold some of the horses, and rambling citizens held the others. The whole of her guard crowded round her, and went with her across the crowded *trottoir* to the wicket of the Abbaye.

"You will allow us to see you safely housed, Madame," said the sergeant. "I can manage matters better than you."

"Certainly," said Mathilde ; and the sergeant beat upon the door.

It was opened by a rather nice-looking old man, who said,—

"A prisoner ?"

"Yes," said the sergeant. "Now, to the bureau, quickly !"

"Are any more of you coming in?" asked the old man, for the whole escort thronged in.

"Patriots have *entrée* here," replied the sergeant. "Be silent, thou old man ; to the bureau."

The bureau was a very nasty little office at the end of a long, dark passage, of which William took stock as he went, with some dim idea of the way *back*. In it sat a pale young man, of feeble aspect, who was boiling haricots over a slow fire, and trying them with a fork.

"Bureau !" shouted the commandant, and the young man upset his pot of haricots on the fire, and put it out.

"Imbecile ; here is a prisoner," said the commander ; and the young man opened a door, and cried out, also, "Prisoner." Whereupon, there appeared, quite leisurely, three men in red caps : one only wore breeches, the other two had trousers ; but all three wore short jackets. One seated himself at the desk, and took out his pen ; the other two amused themselves by watching the party, and spitting.

"Now," said the man at the desk, "what is it ?"

"Madame la Marquise de Valognes."

"We know of no Marquise," said the patriot at the desk ; "what is the woman's name ?"

"You know, like another fool," said the sergeant, "with thine argot, thou. Mathilde de Valognes, then."

"We know of no ' de's,' " said the man with the pen.

"Mathilde D'Isigny, then, thou difficile imbecile."

"That is her maiden name. What is the family name of her husband?"

"Then you know, you," said the irritated sergeant; and the rest of the escort said—"He knows, this one, and he plays the fool with us. These Parisian tinkers and tailors, they make fools of us."

"Ne dites pas d'injures," said the man with the pen. "You provincial patriots require castigation. Where is your warrant? Give it up."

"We provincials!—you Parisians!" cried the sergeant, white with fury. "Have we come here to be insulted, coquin?"

"Vous injuriez la nation, vous injuriez les tribunaux," said the patriot with the pen.

"What does it matter to us, thou brandy-drinking dog, whom we insult, or what tribunals we insult? We are men of action, we. We are for the frontier against coalesced kings. Thou sittest here brandy sodden, to judge better than thyself. My warrant runs, Adèle Carillon, and I give it to thee. Is that correct, Madame la Marquise?"

"It is perfectly correct," said Mathilde, looking full in the face of the young man, who knew her secret. He bowed his head.

She bade an affectionate farewell to her guard all round, and gave William instructions as to where he should find her father, and tell him in secret the great fact that it was she who was arrested, and not her sister; and then she passed up some broad stone steps, wondering whither.

"I have then given up my two prisoners, and require receipt," said the sergeant.

"Two prisoners?" said the man; "there is but one."

"This young man," said the sergeant, thrusting William forward, "is another."

"You have no warrant. We have enough and to spare."

"I have lost the warrant," said the sergeant.

"Then he must go free, this young man," said the man at the desk; adding "coquin to you!"

The escort crowded round William, and the spokesmen were the sergeant and the young man who loved her better than the rest. They urged on William that he should not leave her, that he should follow her. That she was utterly unprotected and alone; that the prisons, some said, were scarcely safe even now. That he had taken her father's wages for many years. "That surely, in the name of God" (these were the words of the young man whose head had got turned by Mathilde), "there was some manhood left in the nation of Cromwell, and that surely he would never desert one he seemed to love so well." To all of which passionate appeal William turned a perfectly deaf ear, for the simple reason that it was addressed to him in French, of which, in spite of his opportunities at Sheepsden, he understood scarcely a word.

French gesticulation, however, did what the French language could never have done. William was utterly puzzled. He did not know what he had got to do. The young man with his head turned solved his doubts for him. He came up to him and touched him on the breast; then he pointed along the black passage which led towards the street; then he pointed to the better lit staircase up which Mathilde had gone. William understood them now. He pointed towards the stairs, and patted the young man on the shoulder.

They crowded round him, and would have kissed him had he allowed it: and so they went back to the Bureau. The sergeant spoke:

"I have lost my warrant for this young man, but I accuse him."

"Of what then?"

"Of conspiring with emigrants; of being friend of André Desilles—the murderer, of Nanci. You knew André Desilles?" he said, turning to William.

"Bon, bon," said William, not uninstructed.

"You know also M. de Valognes?"

"Bon, bon," said William.

"That is enough, I suppose," said the sergeant.

And the man sulkily acquiesced, saying; "If he is a friend of the murderer's, of Nanci, he will find a friend of his upstairs," —as was, curiously enough, the case; for history helps fiction in the strangest manner sometimes, whereas I never heard of fiction helping history.

## CHAPTER LV.

#### WILLIAM'S WATCH.

"ANOTHER prisoner," said a pleasant voice, as she reached the top of the stairs, and paused for breath. "You are welcome, Mademoiselle."

"Madame, if you please," said Mathilde; "Marquise de Valognes, at your service."

It was a pleasant-looking abbé who had spoken to her, and she gave him his smile back again. "Why, then," he said, "there is here an old friend of your husband's, and a dear friend and comrade of your cousin's, André Desilles; the man who was with him at Nanci. M. Journiac de St. Meard, here is the wife of your old friend Louis de Valognes."

St. Meard knew better, but he held his tongue and welcomed her, and the others drew away, and left them to talk.

"Your secret is safe with me, my dear Mademoiselle D'Isigny. I see at a glance that you are following out the object of your life, and taking care of a sister who is not very well able to take care of herself. Your secret is perfectly safe with me."

Mathilde looked at him and saw that it was. A kind, frank, honest soldier, and moreover a gentleman.

"There is no one here who is likely to know you, except myself, you have been so long in England; and since your sister has come here she has been buried at Montauban, helping your good mother to dig our graves. Come, tell me what I can do for you?"

"I thank you very much," said Mathilde; "there was a little malle——"

But she had no need to go on, for turning she found William beside her, silent, with the little malle before his feet.

"How did *you* get in?" she asked eagerly.

"The light dragoons" (William had a cousin in the 14th, and so considered that all soldiers who rode a-horseback in blue were light dragoons) "got me took up to mind you. Where be I to put this?"

Mathilde's face grew flaming crimson for one instant; but wisely considering that this was not the time either for sentiment or thanks, and that she must keep her wits about her, said, after a pause, to Journiac de St. Meard,—

"This is my father's groom, and the poor lad has conspired with the National Guards to get himself arrested and attend on me. M. de St. Meard, for the love of old days and old faces, will you help us, for we are very helpless?"

"With my life," said Meard. "I speak some English, and will go with him. Go to the ladies; there they sit at that end of the hall. Tell me one thing more: they have taken your money from you, of course?"

"No. I have a very large sum on me now."

"That is very strange. Did they not search you?"

"No. The escort which brought me from Brittany quarrelled with and frightened the jailors; and while they quarrelled, I came upstairs."

"Give me all your money instantly; when they remember it, they will search you, while they will never search me."

Mathilde handed him secretly a heavy bag of mixed guineas and louis, with a nod of thanks, and went slowly towards the end of the corridor where the ladies were sitting all alone; for this was the time of day when the gentlemen were supposed to be on their farms, or at the chase, or riding on horseback, or driving, or promenading; the time of day when the ladies had always been left to themselves. So, although farms, horses, promenades, and carriages were gone for ever, they kept up the old fiction, and the men kept at one end of the room until the dinner hour; and having paused a certain time, after their dinner of carrion, they then rejoined the ladies.

"They have learnt nothing, and forgotten nothing," said some one of the Bourbons; which can be said no longer about one of them at least.

This being the hour before dinner, the ladies were in imagination in their drawing-rooms, tittle-tattling; Mathilde approached them quite unconcerned. With one single exception, they none of them took any notice of her at all. She had never been presented at court, and it was said that her husband's opinions were, to say the least of it, odd. But out of the corners of their eyes they watched to see what the old Duchesse de la Pierre Cassée would do, and abided their time.

The old gray-headed Duchesse rose and went towards her.

"My love," she said, "we have heard your name, and we welcome you to our drawing-room. The Abbé Secard is confined to his room upstairs with chagrin about events. I represent him."

"You are very kind to me, Madame la Duchesse," said Mathilde; "but people *are* kind, at least to me. Will these ladies receive me?"

They would receive her now: there was no appeal from the Duchesse. She was presented to one after another; they each one, as she was presented, raised herself a little, bowed, smiled, and then sat down again. But Mathilde was presented and accredited at the Court of Death.

A great many of these ladies sat on a long stone bench which ran along the wall; others sat on chairs and rude benches opposite to them. The Duchesse was one of the latter, and made Mathilde sit beside her. She took up her work, and said to her,—

"How do you like our drawing-room, my love?"

"It is a very nasty place, indeed," said Mathilde. "Don't talk to me for a few minutes, for I want to look at these others. Will they be kind to me?"

"They will be very kind, my love."

"Then it matters to me nothing at all, the rest," said Mathilde, and looked principally at the row who sat against the wall, and to her they seemed as if they went in pairs. For one of the highest attributes of man is, that he is *not* truly gregarious, like the beasts, but is capable of rising to the height of selecting one poor mortal, as ignorant and feeble as himself, for whom he will, if needs were, *die*.

The first pair she noticed were possibly the strangest. A big, fat, cross-looking woman about fifty-five, with ringlets, was sitting beside a lean little nervous woman, who was knitting. The fat and vulgar-looking woman sat with her hands upon her stomach, staring at Mathilde. The lean little woman beside her knitted on, and looked at nothing, but through sheer imbecility dropped stitches. When she did so, she handed her knitting-pins to the fat woman, who patiently took them up, and handed the apparatus to her again. After which, she crossed her hands on her stomach, and stared at Mathilde.

Mathilde managed to ask the Duchesse who was this fat, vulgar woman.

"She is the Comtesse d'Aurilliac. Her husband has 200,000 livres a year, and she has been used to all luxuries, yet she is here and does not murmur. The lean lady who sits beside her is her sister, Mademoiselle de Hautent. She has been in the cloister all her life, and would be utterly lost without her sister."

This pleased Mathilde, seeing these two ugly, stupid, commonplace old women sticking to one another so well. But she had genius, this old Mathilde, and she loved beauty dearly; and so the next pair she looked at pleased her better still. Her heart leaped out towards the next pair which she noticed, for in them she saw Adèle and herself; and as she looked on these two, her purpose got fixed.

Against the whitewashed wall sat a girl with a square, fine face, of great beauty and power, who was sewing; in her lap lay the head of her sister, a golden heap of splendid beauty. The younger sister lay there utterly wearied, utterly idle, and petulant in her idleness; playing at times with the string of her sister's apron, at times with the hands which sewed so diligently; at times sighing in her *ennui*, at times rolling her restless head into some new position. Mathilde watched this pair with intense eagerness. They suited her. The younger sister was only another Adèle, and she thought how Adèle would have been in the same situation but for her; but then *without* her. She listened to their conversation.

The younger sister said, "This is so triste and dull, that I shall die if I stay here: and I have nothing to amuse me, nothing whatever. I wish that I had brought my squirrel now, but they said we were to go back again directly."

Mathilde saw the elder sister sew faster, but say nothing whatever. *She* understood her.

"That foolish, giddy Contine will forget to feed him, and he is petulant if he is not fed. Sister, do you know what I wish?"

"No, dearest."

"I wish I had flowers. My garden will be half ruined when we get back, for I took it so entirely in hand myself that none of our gardeners dare meddle with it. And those balsams should be in their largest pots by now; they will not show beside Faustine de la Rivière's. Thou art weeping now, sister, for thy tears fall on my face. Have *I* made thee weep?"

Mathilde sat as rigid as a stone listening to this, drinking it in, every word. The elder sister, with whom she was deep in friendship that night, told her the bitter truth. Their château was burnt, their estate was ruined; their father and mother in the *Conciergerie;* their servants dispersed or faithless; the wolf in their garden, the hare upon their hearthstone. But she had kept it all to herself, and had flattered her giddy sister with the hope of a speedy return to what was gone for ever.

"How could I tell her, Mathilde? How could I tell her? She was the little singing-bird in our house. Would you have me stop her singing for ever?"

Mathilde did not answer directly, but told the eldest sister *her* secret.

"Thou happy woman, if I could have done *that* for her I should have been content."

Hot times these, by all accounts!

"Where do you sleep?" said the elder sister. "Sleep with us. Marie, thou sleepest already, but must awake, for I am not strong enough to carry thee."

"I do not know where I sleep," said Mathilde; "but I have friends here. Journiac de St. Meard and my servant are arranging for me."

"Your servant?" said the elder sister.

"Yes, my dear, one of our English servants, who has managed to arrange with the National Guard to denounce him and get him arrested, that he may take care of me. He and Meard will provide, I doubt not. Meard is the old friend of my cousin, André Desilles, and knows me well. Why are they all standing up?"

"It is the Abbé Secard," said the elder sister. And Mathilde, who knew who he was, stood up also, with her hand on the elder sister's shoulder.

The noble and gentle old man came bowing and smiling about among the ex-courtiers, making straight for Mathilde.

"Madame la Marquise," he said, "I fear you do not like the Abbaye."

"Monsieur l'Abbé," said Mathilde, putting her strong arm

over the elder sister's neck, " I love, above all things, to be near God: and I think that I am not far from him while I am near her, and near you."

"You will be nearer to him soon," said the old man, and passed on.

And lo ! William following her in top boots, and saying,—

"Your room is ready, Miss; you will excuse my showing it to you. It is not fine, but it is private."

St. Meard had given up his room to her, and William and he had been toiling ever since they came in at getting it ready for her. This she never knew.

She said to the two sisters,—

"Where do you sleep ?"

"With the others," they both said.

"Come and sleep with me. I have a room to myself. We shall have privacy, we three."

"But our bedding !" said the elder sister.

"William will remove it."

William would remove any amount of bedding; but, unluckily, could not go among the ladies.

Mathilde dashed at the Duchesse de la Pierre Cassée, who turned up trumps at once; and French ladies not being as particular as English ladies, William was allowed to fetch away the bedding of the two sisters, and carry it in triumph to Mathilde's room, lately that of Journiac de St. Meard.

"Never saw anything like *this*," said William to Mathilde, as he brought the things in. "Why all the ladies are going to bed, on the stone floor, in a row. If my opinion was asked about this business, I should say straight out that I didn't think much of it. What have they all been up to? It don't seem to me that they have been doing anything particular. However, I am no judge. There is one gentleman in the place, at all events; and I have been used to gentlemen."

William was perfectly right about there being one gentleman in the place. There were probably many others, but this gentleman spoke English in a limited manner, and so William understood him and respected him, Frenchman as he was. William's gentleman was Journiac de St. Meard.

Ask William to define a gentleman, and he would have asked

you to explain what "define" meant. But he knew one when he saw one, as our people do. William must naturally have been utterly ignorant of pedigrees. A man's father might have been a tinker, for all he knew or cared; and yet he knew a gentleman when he saw one, and respected him, and would follow him. Let me, therefore, define a gentleman, as William and I understand the term.

A gentleman is a man, sufficiently well educated for the duties he has to perform, and who thinks of the interest of others before he thinks of his own. And, moreover, my gentlemen must not be lazy, but must try, with such powers as God has given him, to set an example, and show what a very valuable person a *gentleman* is.

The lower orders in England, in this revolutionary time, believe in their gentlemen, in spite of their faults. That, I think, is not yet changed by horse-racing and Hay-marketing, for our agricultural people are long-suffering. I cannot say how deep the poison has gone. I speak merely of 1792,* and of William the Silent, who, finding a gentleman in Journiac de St. Meard, followed him like a dog.

From the outside world there could come no word. The past was past, and one had to force one's soul into a perfectly new and strange present; with new petty dull cares, and new anxieties. She was content, she had been born to endure.

No word? Well, only one, and that with the greatest difficulty. One day, a week after she had been there, there was a disturbance at the lodge of the Abbaye, and William, who happened to be near with Journiac de St. Meard, listened to it. It was nearly a disturbance.

From five-and-twenty to thirty National Guards were demanding to see a prisoner. They had forced their way in, and were

* For the small country gentry in those days may have been one 'thing or another; no better, possibly, than they need have been. But the labourer was, at all events, by every testimony, better off. And again, there was not that extreme contrast between classes which there is now, and which might become dangerous. The extreme ends of the social system are in the agricultural districts diverging further and further every day. What is the reason of it? Easily told. *Luxury.* And Mr. Fawcett, the last epitomist of political economy, seems to clearly prove the fact (as I understand him), that every hundred pounds spent in luxury represents a sheer loss of thirty per cent. on capital.

thronging the vestibule. The wicket was shut behind them, and they were practically in possession of the place, which fact made the four men at the bureau, if not civil, at least acquiescent. William at once recognised the voice of the sergeant in command who had brought them from Brittany, and of the young man "with his head turned." William told this to St. Meard, and he replied, "Be silent, this means something."

It seemed to mean a furious quarrel. When they came up, the Brittany sergeant had the young guard by the collar, and was confronting the three advanced patriots in the bureau; and the three patriots seemed to be getting the worst of it.

"None of the prisoners can be seen," said the patriot.

"I tell thee that this young man stole this silver watch from the young man of England called William, on our journey from Brittany; and that his conscience having pricked him, he desires to give it back."

"Give it to me then, and I will give it to him."

"Who would trust *thee* with a watch? Who art thou, then?" said the sergeant. At which the guards, "patrollotism," as Mr. Carlyle calls them, laughed in an offensive manner, and made the patriot furious.

"Who art thou, then? A Lafayettist and a murderer."

"He is an aristocrat, this one," said the sergeant, turning to his backers, who laughed again. "He talks of Lafayette. We true patriots only know of Sieur Motier. They may well talk of plots in the prisons, which are dangerous to be left behind by real patriots going to the frontier against Brunswick. They may well speak of them. This man has called Motier the murderer as Lafayette. He is an aristocrat."

"Messieurs," said the frightened patriot.

"Messieurs, again," said the sergeant. "This man is an aristocrat, and in a post of importance also. Here is a truer patriot than he. Citizen Journiac, thou of the Château Vieux, formerly royalist, thou at least are not a sneaking dog; take this watch from us, and give it to the English young man, William. We can trust thee. Thou dog of a Sansculotte aristocrat, with thy Lafayettes and thy monsieurs, let us out. We are for the frontiers."

Which the advanced patriot did with the greatest pleasure.

"These men," said Journiac to William, in English, "have

smuggled in some intelligence to Mademoiselle D'Isigny in this watch. Walk swiftly up the stairs behind me, so as to hide me."

They were not up ten steps before the men in the bureau were after them. Journiac turned at once.

"The watch," said the foremost. "Give it up."

"I will do nothing of the kind," said Journiac. "William, back me up. I will not part with the watch!"

They were half way up the stairs, and the odds were four to two. William, though strong, was not dexterous; and the Frenchmen were both strong and dexterous. William was rapidly overpowered, while Journiac de St. Meard, after a feeble resistance, dropped the watch, and fairly ran away upstairs.

William, as soon as he was released, followed him, a little sulkily, thinking that Sir Lionel Somers, or the Rector, would have made a better fight of it; and when he came to him in the large room, said so.

Said Journiac, "My dear child, the great fault of you English is stupidity. I knew there was a letter in that watch; and I knew that they knew it also. If I had given up the watch without a struggle, they as Frenchmen would have known that the letter was on my person; that is why I deluded them by struggling. While you covered my retreat, I put the letter in my pocket; Mademoiselle D'Isigny has it now; they will be here to search me for it, the idiots, directly. Here they are."

"We have reason to believe, citizen Journiac, that there was a letter contained in the watch we took from you. We require to search you."

"There is no need, citizens," said Journiac. "I have outwitted you. There is such a letter. It has been handed to and read by the person to whom it was addressed. Do you want to see it?"

The jailors thought so.

"Mademoiselle D'Isigny," said Journiac, advancing towards her, "these good people wish to see the letter which you received from your father through my hands. I think you had better show it to them."

The puzzled patriots read as follows:—

"I know all. You have done well, and have kept your old promise to me. The blessing of God be on your head for what you have done. Good daughter; good sister; good woman. Madame la Terrible is here with me. Keep your secret. There is not the least danger. In case of a trial, I should appeal to your friend, Marat. Keep your secret as you promised. I dare say no more."

They were puzzled, but she was contented. She knew what she had got to do until further orders; and many a puzzled woman goes rambling up and down the earth for direction, from Moravian parson to Romish priest, with the same object to this day. She had got her direction from one who had never failed her, and she followed his directions.

## CHAPTER LVI.

### THE PRISON MICE.

ITH the exception of this one letter from her father, the silence was unbroken. No news ever reached her from without. Ill-guarded as the prisons were, it was extremely difficult to get news into them. News did get into the Abbaye, or rather rumour, with regard to which St. Meard told her that he hardly believed one word.

He was her constant friend and companion; he went about for her like a dog; he talked with her about André Desilles, Louis de Valognes, and all the old times, till he really made her happy. She told him the state of affairs between Sir Lionel Somers and herself, and he comforted her about him, laughing her fears to scorn. He had only been arrested for his papers, he said, and would be in Paris immediately. She also was as good as a naturalised British subject, and Sir Lionel would no doubt demand, in case of emergency, her release from the British Ambassador. There was really nothing to trouble oneself about.

It was a pity he fell in love with her. But he did, like the others. Mathilde said that, in case of any disagreement, she should appeal to her old friend M. Marat; and remained tranquil.

As for her, she made a world—a very little one, certainly—wherever she went; and she made a little world now. Her world consisted of the two sisters who lived with her, and who suited her utterly. The elder sister, she said, was herself, but more beautiful and more courageous: the younger sister was Adèle, but even more beautiful and very much more helpless. She told all this to Journiac de St. Meard, who understood her; and also, in her odd way, to William, who understood her also.

The elder sister implored her not to let the younger one know of the ruin which had befallen their house; and Mathilde only said,—

"My love, I must judge for myself—people do not die of ill news."

But the younger sister got in her fits of *ennui*, from laying her bright head on her sister's lap, to lay it on Mathilde's; and she said once, in the time which passed,—

"I am *ennuyée*, thou crooked old, who hobblest in thy walk, and hast the face of an angel. Tell me a tale. My squirrel is dead in his cage, my bird is dead on his perch, and our father and mother have forgotten us and left us here. Therefore tell me a tale, thou old."

It was not much in our downright Mathilde's line, but she struck off at once, thinking that she saw her way to good. I doubt that she was darning her own stockings, when she told her first story to the glorious beauty who was lying in her lap.

Mathilde, as a precise religionist, only could tell a "bon Dieu" story. She did not wish to begin in this fashion with the girl, and so she told her the least "bon Dieu" story she knew—a Teutonic story; will you find me its equal? Such English as know it, call it the story of "Dick and Doll."

"Dick and Doll got on very well until they got married, but after that they quarrelled so dreadfully that they agreed to part for ever; and so Dick went east and Doll went west, and they were to meet never more.

"Dick made a terrible mess of it, but Doll made a worse. Every misfortune which could happen to man, happened to Dick. As for Doll, as the weaker vessel, she was worse off than Dick.

"But the earth being round—if one person walks east and the other west, they will be sure to meet. So Dick, in the midday midnight of the antipodes, heard Doll blundering along among the thickets.

"'Is that you, Doll?' he said.

"And she said, 'Is that you, Dick?'

"And they both agreed that they had made fools of themselves, and went quietly home together, to part never more."

That was Mathilde's first story to the golden head in the Abbaye.

"That is a curious story, you quaint woman," said golden hair. "But I do not believe it. I shall quarrel with him when I am married, but he will never leave me; and if he leaves me, why, instead of going away from him, I should run after him, and kneel at his feet. She was an imbecile, that Doll of yours. Suppose they had missed one another in the dark. Thou hast a lover thyself; wouldst thou not follow him?"

So Mathilde's first story was utterly unsuccessful in bringing the poor girl to a sense of her position. She merely turned her from thinking about her squirrel and her canary to thinking about her lover. Where he was, what he was doing, whether her father would let them marry as soon as they went home, and so on. She was more hopeless than Adèle, for Adèle had seen the black walls of her father's château, and had looked on the Revolution. This poor child had not.

Mathilde, watching the face of her good friend Journiac de St. Meard, saw it grow more anxious day by day. She asked him at last, "Was there news?"

"There is no news, but only a steadily growing terror among the best informed. There is nothing tangible. Have you really interest with Marat?"

"He would do anything for me," said Mathilde. "But do you see, representing as I do my sister here, I cannot move in any way. And besides, I have promised my father."

"But your sister is two hundred miles away."

"On the discovery of their mistake she would be at once arrested. I shall do nothing without orders from my father."

"He will be puzzled to get his orders to you. The wicket is swarming with patriots inside. There is frightful mischief abroad of some kind. As for me, I am a dead man."

"What makes you think so?" said Mathilde.

"Talk in English," he replied; "and, William, you come here and listen. You remember the affair of Nanci, when our André Desilles was shot."

"Could one forget," said Mathilde.

"Who shot him?"

"Who can say?"

"I can—I had it from some of my poor Château Vieux,—Sergeant Barbot. Ha! William, your eyes brighten. You know him then. *Ten minutes ago that man was in the bureau downstairs.* He has come after me."

"But," said Mathilde, "you behaved so gently there. It is quite as likely that he is come after me, or after William. He hates us both, I know."

William practically suggested that he had come after all three; which was probably the truth.

"But what can he do, sir?"

"Nothing which I am aware of," said Journiac de St. Meard. "But it means mischief. My dear Mademoiselle Mathilde, we know nothing and fear everything. For my part, from all I can gather, I fear the very worst."

Mathilde pondered with herself after this, as to how she was to renew her effort to make the pretty child—the younger sister—understand her situation. She thought she would try another story; and this one was, as was generally the case with her efforts, a worse attempt than the first. She was not the first one who tried her hand at symbolic fiction and failed. Yet she did her best. The next time the poor innocent thing laid her head in Mathilde's lap, and asked for a story, she was ready.

"Whenever the Bon Dieu walks out in his garden, which is Paradise, you know, he gathers flowers, in the cool of the day; and he always gathers the newest; for there are hundreds of new flowers blooming in his garden, every day, for all eternity.

"And once, I do not say whether in the past or the future, as the Bon Dieu walked in the garden with Mary, lo! there were two new lilies blowing. One was a golden martagan, and the other was pure and white as are the lilies of the blessed Saint Joseph.

"And Mary speaking, said: 'Here is one of his true lilies, and I will gather it and put it in my bosom.'

"And the Bon Dieu said: 'And I will take this golden-headed martagan.'

"And Mary said to the white lily: 'My child, thou art paler than Joseph's palest lilies; why is it, then?'

"And the lily said: 'Because my sister, the golden martagan is angry with me here in Paradise, that I kept things from her.'

"And the Bon Dieu said to the golden-headed martagan: 'My child, thou art redder than the passionate rose, and thy petals are curled back as if in anger. Why is this, my beautiful lily? Here there is only to be peace, calm, and love for evermore.'

"And the golden martagan answered the Bon Dieu, and she said: 'I am angry with my sister that she kept things from me. The people down there have burnt our castle, have killed my squirrel, have ruined my flowers, have put in prison my father and mother, and she kept it all from me, through her love for me and her anxiety to spare me pain, until we came here, where mourning is forbidden for ever, and tears washed from all eyes. So I am angry with my sister because she did not let me mourn for my mother.'

"Then Mary beckoned to them, and they came to a rose tree, on which was a white rose and a red. And the white lily and the golden lily knew the roses, and laughed with joy, for they were their father and mother. And the Bon Dieu and Mary gathered them and tied them with the two lilies, and carried them, smiling, up and up——"

"Whither?" said the beautiful girl on Mathilde's lap.

"Whither?" said Mathilde, after a pause. And then after a longer pause, she broke out suddenly, quickly, and almost incoherently, as she sometimes, though very seldom, did:—

"Martin! Lionel! Father! Adèle! is it to be never more? Why do you leave me here alone?"

You see that the foolish girl had worked herself into a state bordering on the hysterical, in pondering over the chances of seeing those she loved very deeply, again, and in telling this foolish story. As her father often told her, she had a very ill-regulated mind. I think, myself, that she is to be pitied more than blamed.

She had, however, done what she intended to do, as was usual with her; but also, as usual, in a somewhat too emphatic way. The poor beauty's head lay on her lap, very silent, and very pale.

"What do you think of that story, my love?" said Mathilde.

"I understand it," was all the girl said.

The fat and vulgar Comtesse D'Aurilliac had her eye on these two. She left her thin sister of the cloister, and sailed towards them.

"Is Mademoiselle ill?" she asked.

"No," said the girl, quietly. "I have only heard news."

"From whence, then? And you, Madame La Marquise," to Mathilde, "you made a sudden exclamation just now, and invoked names. Is there anything imminent? For I have neglected my religion,—I,—and would be glad to be ready."

"The news I have told is old news, Madame D'Aurilliac," said Mathilde. And the Comtesse D'Aurilliac waddled back to her sister, and having seen to her knitting, sat down again with her hands on her fat stomach and villipended the community.

But the girl said not one word. Henceforth she was nearly dumb, but perfectly obedient.

The elder sister stopped Mathilde as they were going to bed, and said, "Have you told her?"

"Yes, in a way."

"How does she stand it?"

"I do not know; she will not speak."

When they were all in bed, and the light put out, the voice of the younger sister was heard.

"Mathilde, thou knowest. Are our father and mother dead?"

"I think not," said Mathilde.

"But about me, the poor, red martagan," whined the girl. "Mary may surely pluck me as a white lily, and not as a red. For I have no anger towards my sister because she in her love kept from me the ruin of our house, which thou hast told."

Enough of this you say, and I say "enough" also. Yet you must please to remember that I am doing a task to the best of my ability. And I think that if you will, in imagination, surround yourself with an *entourage* of pious and half-pious

Roman Catholic women, in a time of Revolution, you will arrive very much at the above results. These results may be good, bad, or indifferent, according to the reader's opinion, but I think that they would be very much like these.

Until the end, the poor girl remained silent. She took Mathilde's foolish allegory for the truth; and until the time when Journiac de St. Meard went on an errand of inquiry down the stairs and found that she and her sister were gone, she spoke no more. Once or twice she talked about her squirrel, and regretted his neglect; but of coherent talk there was none to be got from her. The wave of the Revolution had burst over her and stunned her. It was well for Mathilde and her sister that it was so. They had something weaker than themselves to protect.

William the Silent, with his rat-catching cunning, caught a little mouse, which in its hunger he tamed, and gave to the bright-headed beauty. And it pleased her, and she lay on the stone bench, with her head now on her sister's lap, now on Mathilde's, playing with her little mouse, until Paris was in white hot wrath, and Brunswick over the frontiers.

## CHAPTER LVII.

### "BUT DANTON HE HAS SLEPT."

HE weather was as white and hot, and fierce, as were the Parisians, and the smell which Mr. Dickens, in his "Tale of Two Cities," calls "the smell of imprisoned sleep," was hot and heavy. Yet there came no change. The elder sister sewed, and the younger sister played with her mouse. The Comtesse D'Aurilliac sat and glowered with her hands on her stomach, from time to time patiently taking up the stitches in her sister's knitting. The men of the imprisoned party were as polite, and the main part of the women as frivolous as ever; but there was no sign of a change.

Prisoners behind narrow-barred windows in a street, have little opportunity for seeing the thunderstorm, which is to crash into their prison and burst their bonds, thrust up its cumulus above the horizon.

These poor people in the Abbaye did not really *believe* that anything violent or sudden would happen. They certainly said all day that their lives were in danger, and that they would lay them down at any moment; but few of them actually believed it. I should fancy (who can know?) that the only man in the Abbaye who knew the danger, was Journiac de St. Meard, who had looked on the Revolution, and had wept in his French way over the stark body of André Desilles.

Then came a day as all days come—a day which makes itself a day for a whole life. The boat goes down the river, and a dripping, frightened man comes back and tells of the disaster. The horse goes out, and there comes back a terrified groom. The carriage goes out, and the footman comes back white with horror. These supreme days come in the midst of the most carefully-tended luxuriousness, in accidents, in paralytic strokes, and such matters. Death marches in, triumphant over Luxury at all times.

If in times of perfect luxury and perfect peace such days come on us suddenly and swiftly, ruining or altering the current of lives, it is not to be thought violent or extraordinary that such a day should come upon our three watchers in prison, in a time of Revolution.

There are, I think, few of our readers who have not seen such a day: a day when death or extreme danger comes to the door, and when it is necessary not only to think but to act. The supreme day came to Journiac de St. Meard, to Mathilde, and to William, in this manner.

At twelve o'clock Mathilde was sitting in the little room which she possessed with the two sisters, when Journiac de St. Meard, with William the Silent, came to the door and called her out. When she went out to them they motioned to her and shut the door behind her. When she looked on their faces she saw danger if not disaster. She was used to men, and she knew the look which comes on the face of brave men when there is danger abroad. They were both, Frenchman and Englishman, perfectly calm, but very pale. St. Meard had his hand on the shoulder of the English groom, and was the spokesman.

"Mademoiselle Mathilde, there is serious trouble."

"I read that in your faces. Can you trust me with the extent of it?"

"Can you trust yourself to our guidance?"

"Most heartily," said Mathilde. "I always want guidance, you know."

"Then come with us," said St. Meard. And Mathilde went quietly and willingly.

They took her up a corridor to a bench at the end; and they all three sat down in a row.

"Well," said Mathilde, "I am going to be perfectly obedient, and perfectly submissive, for I know you two, and you are good. How much are you going to tell me?"

"Not much. This much, however. There is being made a partition of prisoners, and there should be no confusion."

"You mean, I see, that the two sisters are to be removed; and that you think that I had better not take leave of them."

"That is the case exactly," said St. Meard. "Do not trouble yourself to take leave of them. They are going to liberty. Do not take leave of them."

"Why?" said Mathilde.

Of all the whys ever uttered, this must have been one of the most difficult to answer. St. Meard only said,—

"You will meet them again; and your seeing them now would give rise to complications."

And Mathilde said,—

"I am content, as I always was. I trust you two."

And after that she sat on the stone bench and talked, first only *causeries*.

"I hope that that foolish and fat old Comtesse d'Aurilliac will be put in the same prison with her good sister. That old woman of the cloister, her sister, would die if she were separated from her now. I hope, also, that they will not separate my two sisters, for they are as necessary to one another as are those two old women. For me, with my secret kept, *I* am safe. I hold but one life in my hands, for Lionel will mourn, but will not die."

William went away, and she was left alone, sitting wearily on the stone bench, with Journiac de St. Meard walking up and down before her.

"St. Meard," she said, boldly, "I see two things, very plainly."

"And what are those, Mademoiselle?"

"I see first," said she, "that you admire me—that you love me!"

"It is true."

"I love you also. I love you very deeply. But that part of a woman's heart which is given to sentimental love will never be yours. It is given to an Englishman, Sir Lionel Somers, quite beyond recall."

He bowed and said,—

"I always supposed this. I was prepared for it. Yet I may minister to you?"

She said only, "Yes."

"May I ask," said St. Meard, "what is the second thing which you have seen in my face?"

"Death!" she said. "I have looked on death more than once, and I saw it in your eyes when you brought me here to this stone bench: and I saw it in the eyes of my poor old groom, William. Tell me, are my pretty sisters killed?"

Such a dreadfully downright woman, this Mathilde of ours, forcing even Journiac to lie: for he said,—

"I suspect that they have been ordered to the *Conciergerie*."

William came back, and told her that she could go to her room again now. And she went to her room; but the sisters were not there.

And she never saw them again—nevermore! "Shall we meet the loved ones in a future state?" Mathilde's friend, the primitive Methodist, Evans, doubted on the subject!

## CHAPTER LVIII.

### ADIEU.

ILLIAM and St Meard had been, with a crowd of other prisoners, looking out of-the window at the often described September assassinations: about which we will say as little as possible. I would not have wished to come to them, but the St. Malo story brings me here, and I must go on. These two strangely-contrasted men—the dandy brave French soldier and the stolid English groom—had been watching this horrible affair from the same window.

The women had been kept from that window; but the men had crowded round it, and had watched one fall after another. There had been a strange discussion among them as to how they should act when their turn came. It was agreed, after the witnessing of many examples, that the difficulty of dying was only increased by trying to defend your head, and that the best way was to walk slowly, and put your hands behind your back.*

"You see Barbot, down there?" said St. Meard.

William saw him, and saw something else also. Saw, for instance, that the assassins, backed by a very slight crowd, were mainly on the right of the door; and that on the left of the door there were comparatively few of them. He saw also that the door was in the extreme left of the building, and that from time to time people came round the corner of the building, under the pepper-box turret, and either ran swiftly across the street, or turned back with shrieks (perhaps Dr. Moore was one of them). He pointed this out to St. Meard, and asked him if there was a "right of way" round the corner.

When St. Meard understood him he answered, "Yes. That he knew the place well. It was the *Allée des pas perdus*, and at the end were two turnings; to the right you found yourself in the *cul-de-sac* of the *Allée d'Enfer*, to the left you went straight into the *Rue de la Bonne Garde*." Which William remembered.

This young man also remembered about a certain rowing or scolding which he had got from D'Isigny one time. There had been a prize-fight in the Stour Valley, and that good-for-nothing old Martin, the poacher, had tempted William from his allegiance to go and see it. This prize-fight had ended suddenly and fatally by a blow on the jugular vein; at which D'Isigny

---

* Text to "Tableaux Historiques," tableau soixante-deuxième, confirmed again by Lamartine. Lamartine's "History of the Girondists" may be vague, foolish, and bombastic in part; but for mere *causeries* about the Revolution and revolutionary characters, there is, as far as I am aware, no book like his. For his authorities I am not, of course, answerable. He is an historian and a statesman; I am a writer of fiction, as correct as I can make it. Yet M. Lamartine must have talked familiarly, at a mature age, with many of the men concerned in these affairs; and, considering the position he once held, must know as much about them as another. He is certainly as correct as Thiers. "Enfin."

had rejoiced, because it had not only enabled him to point his moral against William more venomously, but had enabled him to bully Mathilde as an open encourager of assassins, instancing old Martin and Marat as two cases in point. This prize-fight came into William's head now; but he said nothing.

After a time they went back to Mathilde's door. They knocked; she told them in a calm, clear voice to come in. She had just risen from her knees, and had Lady Somers' missal before her.

"My dear friends," she said, "will they come for me to-night? Do you think I might go to bed?"

St. Meard, seeing her noble and beautiful face set so coolly and so calmly, took a sudden resolution, like a Frenchman.

"Mademoiselle, no!"

"May I know what is happening?"

"Mademoiselle, yes. They are assassinating the prisoners. I have some dim hopes that I can plead successfully for my life, in consequence of my behaviour at Nanci when your cousin, André Desilles, was killed. This young man, from his absolute innocence, may escape; but it is doubtful. You, in your assumed character as Marquise de Valognes, must inevitably die."

"I promised my father that I would die mute, and I will die mute," said Mathilde.

"Mademoiselle, listen to me again. I am Provençal, and one of the jailors is my friend, for I speak his language. I know more than another. I know this. Danton and the secret Committee of the Commune have, through Marat, been removing prisoners to save them from this danger. You have not been removed, because Marat thinks that you are your sister; Marat has saved many on his own responsibility, and even now, if you declare yourself, he could save you.\* You are provided with witnesses to your identity. This young man, myself, and my Provençal, who would swear, if I told him, that the devil went to mass and drunk nothing stronger than holy water. We would answer for the fact that you are not the Marquise de Valognes, who is suspected of being carrier-pigeon between Brittany and

---

\* This mercy of Marat's, individually rests, as far as I am concerned, on the authority of Lamartine. I believe in it myself.

Coblentz, but her innocent sister, who has been living quietly in England."

"That is all very well," said Mathilde; "but you do not consider my sister."

"She is perfectly safe," said St. Meard.

"Indeed, she is not. I came here to France to fulfil a promise to my father, and I shall fulfil it."

St. Meard knelt at her feet.

"I implore you, Mademoiselle, to listen to reason."

"You have no right to kneel to me, M. St. Meard. I am *fiancée* to Sir Lionel Somers."

"I will betray you," said St. Meard, rising furiously.

"You will not do so. In the first place, you gave me your honour as a gentleman that you would do nothing of the kind: in the second place, no one would believe you."

He argued again and again, and William in his way argued also. But she said, first and last, "You weary me, you two. I promised my father." And so after a time they sat still, and saw her pray.

At last she said, "Here they come;" and they came. The door was partly open, and the first person who entered was a large dog,\* who went to the water pitcher, and lapped. Then came four men in slouched hats (like broad-leaved wide-awakes), and then a neat man in breeches and a cutaway coat, and the cocked hat with which we are all familiar in the pictures of Napoleon.†

"The woman calling herself the Marquise de Valognes?" said the well-dressed man.

"I am she," said old Mathilde.

"Follow."

And she followed, and St. Meard and William followed also; but on the stairs there was a difficulty. Mathilde turned to St. Meard.

---

\* Tableaux Historiques, *passim*.

† Official dress makes sudden and singular pauses. Look at our own court dress. Look at our own evening dress. Look at the dress of the first costumed reception of the Directory, which is that of Louis Quatorze. "Sartor Resartus" with a vengeance! The imperially beautiful dress of the first Napoleon at his coronation seems to have been a creation of French genius. In my ignorance I know of no precedent for it.

"This missal," she said; "may he have it, to give to my sister?"

"It is a case for the tribunal," said the well-dressed man; "we know of no missals."

The night was late when they got downstairs into the main passage or hall which led to the street. What need is there to describe it here? You may see the scene for yourselves in many books, among others in Knight's "Popular History of England." A table with ruffians, guards with pikes, brandy-bottles on the side-table. The president, the awful "man in gray," who strangely turns out to be no other than our old acquaintance "Huissier" Maillard, interrogated her.

"You are the *soi-disante* Marquise de Valognes?"

"I am the *soi-disante* Marquise de Valognes," she answered, firmly; and thought, "I shall not die with a lie on my lips, after all."

"You are accused of plotting at that hell on earth, Montauban, against the nation. You are accused of carrying news from Brittany to Coblentz. There is enough against you to destroy a hundred, for the nation is angry. It is accused against you that you, your lover, the Englishman there, and that she-wolf, your mother, have been conspiring with *émigrés* at Coblentz. What have you to say?"

"That you lie," said Mathilde, pale with fury and scorn.

They told her to stand back, and she turned towards William, and slightly shivered, for William had done a strange thing, to her inexplicable. I beg your pardon for telling you these things, but I have begun, and must perforce finish.

William stood before her, with nothing on him but his breeches, his stockings, and his shirt. A loose-mouthed patriot, Jean Bon, who had once guided her father to Marat, remarked,—

"Le citoyen se dérobe."

"Malbrook s'en va-t-en guerre," said Mathilde, which did her no good.

"William," she said, "why have you taken off your clothes?"

"It is so hard to die like this."

"I have died before now," she said, and turned to the table, for they called her.

"À La Force!"

"I am the friend of the people: I am the friend of Marat; but I cannot make my case good, and so——see, you men, I forgive you all."

"I will compromise you by no messages," said Mathilde to St. Meard; "but if you live to see any one whom I loved, tell them I love them still."

So she went down the steps, carrying her missal, and entering the dark passage was lost to sight.

St. Meard was at William's shoulder as she went. William was for following her, but St. Meard pointed out to him the utter uselessness of the attempt.

"They have spared many," he said. "They will surely spare her. Reassure yourself."

"I shall bolt," said William. "I believe that I can get away by the left; they will not harm her, and if I can get hold of her father and Marat, we shall, as you say, be safe. Will they kill me?"

"I should think that you would be condemned. I fancy you have no chance."

"Then good-bye, sir, and many thanks for kindnesses past. There is my name."

William silently stepped up to the table. Of the "pleadings" he understood not one word. He was accused of being the lover of Mathilde, but he knew nothing of what they said, and cared less. He understood in some measure the words they said to him, for they were the same as they had said to Mathilde—"À La Force!" He turned to follow her down the steps.

The winner of some great boat-races who had the reputation of being a cool and rapid starter, once told me that he frequently felt so nervous before the start, that he feared to fall out of his boat, but that the instant his body began to move his terror was gone. It was so with William; he had been trembling slightly, but the instant he turned from the table his terror was gone.

He was by no means an athlete, only an ordinarily well-made young man of active habit and great physical courage; but now he possessed the concentrated fury and the concentrated strength of ten men. As he stepped swiftly, lightly, and silently as a leopard down the steps towards the passage, he felt the muscles of his arms tighten and harden under the excitement. With a bound like a young lion he was out into the light, and made his dash towards the left.

His old friend Barbot had heard that he was coming, and begged his fellow-conspirators to leave this young man to him. When William bounded out so swiftly, he was before him with upraised bludgeon, but it never descended on William's head. Nerved by despair and hope, with immense dexterity and vigour William dashed at Barbot, and struck him with all his force a round-handed blow under his right ear; he stumbled over him as he fell, and cried, in his agony, "Dear God!" But his legs kept under him, and before the astonished assassins could close upon him, he had sped away into the darkness of the summer night.

Journiac de St. Meard's agony and acquittal are matters of history. His escort of three bringing him out of the door, were attracted by a group bending over something which lay close to the threshold. "What is it, then?" they asked. "It is the patriot Barbot," they said. "He has been struck by the *coup de poing* of a young Englishman, and he is dead."

"And the young man?" asked St. Meard.

"He has escaped," they said.

"And saved my life," thought he. "I would not have given much for it if Barbot had not been killed. My friends," he said aloud, "lead me, for I am going to shut my eyes. One lies here, I doubt, whom I loved."

And so they led him with his eyes shut, and when he was released he said good-night, and walked away, thinking of André Desilles, Mathilde, and of many things.

## CHAPTER LIX.

### MADAME'S JOURNEY.

DÈLE was quietly spinning out her life with her aunt, the Lady Superior, the nuns, and the baby, at Montauban. There was little danger there; the peasants around were Loyal, not to say dangerous to the Revolution. The commune of Paris believed they had got her, and would probably leave matters quiet: and so Madame D'Isigny had followed Mathilde to Paris.

"I will see," she said to the Lady Superior, "if I can do anything with that husband of mine. He is *répandu* with many of these revolutionists. You and Adèle are far too contemptible and insignificant to be troubled, now they believe they have got the Marquise——I beg your pardon, sister; I cannot always control my tongue."

The Lady Superior begged she would not mention it.

"You are kind and good now: let your tongue march, my dear."

"And I am doing no good here," said Madame, after a pause. "I am only bringing danger on the house. I shall go to Paris, and act with my husband. I shall do more there than here."

"Into the lion's jaws, my sister."

"Yes. I do not want to be caught like a rat in a hole. There are many as declared as I in Paris. I can make my tongue heard in Paris, if the worst comes to the worst. And it is a sharp one, as thou knowest, my kind and good sister."

The Lady Superior wept feebly—the recollections of a dreadful day at La Garaye came upon her.

"Yes, I will go. Though Mathilde is perfectly safe, for Marat would risk his life for her, yet my good husband, your good brother, is such an extremely wrong-headed fool that he may disarrange matters. Charette will see to you; you will do very well. Mathilde is the finest member of this family, and wants a better head than her father's to see to her."

"And oh!" said the Lady Superior, "if such a thing could occur, as a reconciliation between you and my brother, I would pray——"

"The imbecility of you women of the cloister is one of the things which is ruining Christianity," said Madame. "Get up, and do not be foolish. If I meant to murder him I should not go to Paris to seek him. Get up."

So she departed for Paris "to seek him," revolving many things by the way.

What a handsome young fellow he was when he first came courting her, thirty years ago, in the old youthful days. There was a high-toned precision in his very gallantry, which had taken her fancy at once. Barbara Morley, now Lady Somers, would have had him, though she was ten years older than he, being thirty, if she was a day; but she could not. Yes; he was a generous young fellow then; what a pity they had quarrelled.

"Why had they quarrelled?" Madame asked herself. They were too much alike. Neither would yield, she thought. She was furious, he inexorably and detestably calm. "If he had yielded on any one occasion, we might have done well; but I saw my intellect to be superior to his, and he never yielded once. If he had done it only once! Isidore, there are worse men than you. Why had not I called him Isidore sooner? I suppose because he never would call *me* by my Christian name. The inexorable!

"If he would yield to me now, in any one point. Let me tell myself the truth, as I have always told it to others; for I am getting old, and am weary of isolation. If I could get him and Mathilde, Adèle might have her De Valognes, my sister-in-law her nuns, Father Martin his psalm-singing; but I should be content.

"I wonder if I can win him back? He is a dangerous and *difficile* man, and must make the first advance. I shall be old and all alone soon: Adèle and his sister, the nun, are absolutely intolerable. And I have my temper more under control."

At this point the carriage stopped, and the door was opened.

"Madame will alight," said a man with a grey moustache, in a rather dirty blue uniform.

"And why, then, inconceivable pig?" said Madame, suddenly infuriated at having her more sentimental meditations interrupted. "Do ladies of my position alight to the bidding of such as you?"

"Fortunately or unfortunately, yes, Madame. I must inspect your papers."

"They are signed by one of you," said Madame, in a loud voice. "By old Hebert,* Maire of Dinan; a rascal whom I have fought for twenty long years for giving short weights to the poor, but whom I have never yet got convicted, in consequence of the unutterable cowardice of the territorial aristocracy. This rascal, short-weight épicier, has turned to the Revolution now. He has signed my papers. They are good enough, I should think, to let a lady pass such as you."

The grey moustache did not laugh outwardly, but Madame must alight.

She alighted with a vengeance.

"Now, then," she said, in English.

"What is the object of Madame's journey to Paris?"

"Is it in the slightest degree likely that I should tell you the truth?"

"Most unlikely, Madame; but it is one of the questions which we are obliged to ask."

"Which shows the outrageous imbecility of the whole affair," said she. "See, I will tell you the truth, then, you. I go to Paris to assist in a royalist plot; what do you think of that?"

"That Madame amuses herself. Madame is patriot, by her denunciation of the Maire of Dinan."

"A better patriot than you."

"Madame can proceed."

"Thank you much," said Madame, *in English, sotto voce.* "I should like to have seen the man of you who could have stopped me. I would have had Charette on you in twenty-four hours. What place is this then?"

"Alençon."

When she was safely in her carriage again, she pondered.

"Alençon! I must keep my temper in better order. I have been near ruin—I am out of my bounds. Alas! my poor tongue, it has never done any good."

"This," as she thought herself, "does not look like a reconciliation with D'Isigny. Yet," she thought once more, during the last stage into Paris, "I am after all a little afraid of him, and

* Not *the* Hebert.

I am not afraid of these dogs. That may make me keep my tongue in order towards *him.*" And so she went on.

Now what was D'Isigny doing?

I cannot say that D'Isigny was a conspirator on either side. No decent conspirator would have had anything to do with him. To be a conspirator you must learn the art of lying with a clear bold brow and an honest eye. Now D'Isigny had a clear bold brow and an honest eye (which eye, however, refused to meet yours, if he did not like the look of you, like many another honest man's), but in the habit of lying he was as deficient as his wife. In consequence of which inability for verbal lying, D'Isigny's contribution to the great French Revolution was his going up and down Paris fuming and contradicting, offending all, conciliating none, and doing nothing.

Lady Somers once said that he was false. So he was; for he trimmed from day to day; and he ordered Mathilde, his daughter and slave, to continue a deceit which he in his own person would have repudiated. Again, as in the old case at Sheepsden, with Sir Lionel Somers, he would adopt a lie for a time, though he would never originate one.

And his wife, the fury, so singularly like him in her morality, but miles above him in intellect and in determination, was coming after him through the long dull roads.

I know of what I speak, when I say that the fury of that woman arose mainly from love, balked at all points by his inexorable stupid severity; one touch of tenderness even now would do what five-and-twenty years had not done. But was it not too late!

D'Isigny had a flat in the Rue St. Germain, room after room; in one of which he used to sit fiddling and fribbling over his papers; writing speeches to which the Assembly never listened, as he was invariably coughed out of the tribune by right and left. Robespierre was in the same predicament at the very same time, and D'Isigny and he laid their heads together over it. It was apparent to both dog and cat that the country was going to the Devil.

D'Isigny, sitting up late one night over his papers, and wondering at intervals how Louis de Valognes got on in the Conciergerie, and how Mathilde, soi-disant for the nonce Marquise de Valognes, got on in the Abbaye, when his room door was opened, and his wife, unseen for so many years, came in.

He was up to the occasion. He was up to the point of all occasions, though never to their preparation. "I salute you, Madame," he said.

"I also salute you, Monsieur," said Madame. "As there has been no formal separation between us, I ask your hospitality."

"It is granted with the deepest pleasure, Madame."

"That is kind, at all events," said Madame, looking keenly at him. "We can never live together, you know, because we don't suit one another. But we will part friends."

"I have never been unfriendly to Madame."

"Foolish man," thought Madame. "One trifle of tenderness would have made me follow you to the world's end and send all my principles to the deuce. Though I am fifty I can appreciate beauty and manhood, and you are very handsome, my dear—handsomer than ever. I'll have you back; but you must *come*, not be fetched."

But he would neither come nor be fetched. French politeness is a very fine thing for concealing sentiment, but not always so fine for announcing it.

So these two actually lived together again, but in a way in which only French people can live. They were both getting old, and both getting weary of isolation. They both in their inmost secret hearts desired to be one again. But that devil which we call by so many names, Pride, Jealousy, Temper; but whose real name is Self, had a stronger hold in the heart of the precise, self-contemplating D'Isigny, than he had in the wild, fierce, furious, and yet affectionate woman, who had once been his wife.

On the other hand Madame said to herself, "He must speak first: it is always so. He may sulk and sulk yet again, but I will make him speak at last."

A difficult task, Madame, which with a lady of your very short patience might never have been accomplished at all. D'Isigny was not a likely man to make advances: you two might have gone to your graves, saying, like the guards of the two great nations at Fontenoy, "Fire first."*

---

\* Which it seems is an outrageous falsehood. What with "Vengeurs," and certain other stories, some of them Crimean, the unfortunate taxpayer is uncertain if he even gets his *glory* for his money.

Yet she made advances; all women do. The world would be a howling wilderness if they did not. They were of a peculiar nature, as was natural in such a woman. Will the reader grant one more vulgarity, and allow me to say that "the grey mare was the best horse," and that she was determined to show it.

"I suppose, Monsieur," she said the first morning, "that occupying the same suite of rooms, it would be as well if we took our meals together?"

D'Isigny would be charmed.

"Again," said Madame, "economy will be necessary. We are just now poor, and women understand economy better than men, who live in politics and in life. Economy is the duty and honour of a woman. Will you let your wife undertake the management of the household?"

"Madame, you do me honour."

"That was kindly said," she replied. "You must know, and I will confess, that it is entirely owing to my extreme political opinions, that we *are* poor. It was through me that your Brittany estates were ruined."

"Madame," said D'Isigny, like a gentleman, "you seem to forget that my present revenue is drawn, almost illegally, from *your* estates in Dorsetshire."

Madame said that she had never thought of it; and she told him afterwards again that she really never had.

Still no angel came down to trouble these strange waters of Bethesda. The pool remained perfectly dull and level, with English oil and French polish (I am afraid this is dreadfully "vulgar" again). Yet these two people were drawing together. The angel had not come yet, and when he came he was a singular one.

If I have done my task so well as to make you know D'Isigny, you will know that he would have died sooner than have fired first. Madame said to herself, "I shall have to do it all."

They got now into the habit of sitting opposite one another in the evening, before the fire. One evening he asked her if it would amuse her to be read to. She was charmed. He read to her from Boileau. Madame thought the poem interesting, and was obliged. When he had finished it, she asked him if she might arrange his papers.

He was highly flattered. She arranged them, and asked leave to read some of them, at which he was again flattered. They now began to talk for the first time about the Revolution, and for the first time in their lives to agree about anything. They agreed that the Revolution would not do, and must be put a stop to immediately, at all hazards.

He yielded so far as to say that he, in his love for the lower orders, had truckled to it too far. Madame, on her part, said that her love for the people, always notorious, remained undiminished. "I also am notorious in England for my democracy in social matters," said Monsieur. "I also am notorious in the same way," said Madame. "Every one knows it," said Monsieur. "I have had the honour to address remonstrances to Madame on what I then called the extravagance of her charity. Madame will acknowledge that."

Madame acknowledged it, and shook her grey old head. "It was but too true, and Monsieur had reason."

Still there was nothing which brought out one atom of the tenderness which was in both their hearts after their long isolation. There was nothing between them but that wretched, false, oily French politeness. The pool of Bethesda was not troubled.

"Monsieur," she said one evening, "I take the liberty to note that your shirt collar is frayed. Will you allow me to superintend your wardrobe?"

Monsieur was deeply obliged. Getting nearer and nearer. Nothing now left but two proudly defiant Lucifers, too proud to speak, too cowardly to speak, the interdependent love; the love of the old; stronger, some say, than the boy and girl, bride and bridegroom love; which was in their hearts.

So the two inexorably rigid and handsome faces shared their fireside together again. Monsieur D'Isigny read aloud to her a great deal, from books containing the most beautiful sentiments, Fénelon, for instance. But, seeing that even Madame's solid face expressed *ennui*, he read her Shakespeare in English. They were both good at Shakespeare, and so Madame stood it better; she knew his text, and was not so much bored as with Fénelon. Nay, he went further afield for her, and Bowdlerised "Rabelais" to the extent of reading the trial before Pantagruel for her. Madame liked that better than anything, but went to the extent of telling him bluntly that she knew it by heart.

Nearer and nearer.

Their servant went out to one of the innumerable feasts which were beginning then ; to which one I do not commit myself, because it would be a weariness to the flesh to look it up. She went to this feast, and came home drunk. Whereupon she was most promptly packed away by Madame D'Isigny.

"We can get on together," she said to her husband. "I am now more quick, more self-helpful than you."

D'Isigny agreed.

"They are getting more brutal and defiant than ever, these people," said she. "Is Mathilde safe?"

"Safe enough," he said ; "why, Marat would take her place to-morrow."

"It is well, then. You know more of these people than do I. Yet it seems to me hard that she should be there while we are here."

"It *is* hard, wife," said D'Isigny ; "but she is safe there. St. Meard is with her. Think of De Valognes, think of the king."

Madame had apparently thought of them before, for she said, "Mathilde's is a more valuable life than any ; you are perfectly sure that she is safe?"

"She is perfectly safe. I could arouse Marat in a moment."

And Madame said : "Enfin, I suppose you are right. Yet there are two whom we love dearly in the prisons, and if you have truckled to or made acquaintance with this double-dyed, God-forgotten, accursed spawn of Satan, Marat, it would be as well if you utilised him, and use his infernal influence to save our beloved ones. A thousand pardons, Monsieur. You know my tongue of old."

"It is equal, Madame. I think that they are perfectly safe. And please to remember how utterly suspect you are yourself. Remember that any communication between yourself, just arrived from Montauban, and either Louis de Valognes, or Mathilde, would assuredly render me suspect. Remember who you are, and what you have been doing ; and forbear. My truckling to Marat, as you so kindly put it just now, has, at all events, enabled you to live a fortnight in Paris without arrest. Taisez-vous, Madame."

And, said Madame to herself, "You are no fool, you. I used to think that you were."

There is one phase of politics, which they call in the United States (as I am informed) Lobbying. I only half know what the phrase means; but I wholly know that D'Isigny would have been a great Lobbyist. This phase of politics was called, unless I am deceived (when there *were* any politics in these distracted islands) button-holding. D'Isigny was a master of it. Few Feuillants or Girondists came into the lobbies of the Assembly without being button-holed by D'Isigny. Adèle says, in her memoirs, that he button-holed Louvet, and said, "It is for you to answer Danton." "How, then?" said Louvet. "I speak not." Whereupon, says Adèle, her father gave Louvet his snuff-box, and said, "Sneeze continually, it would spoil the periods of Demosthenes." But that is only what Adèle said.

Lobbies and passages are notoriously draughty, and gentlemen of nearly sixty who loiter in them are extremely apt to get Rheumatism. Consequently, D'Isigny, continually dawdling in these lobbies of the Assembly, got one evening, late in August, a nip of Lumbago across the lower part of his very stiff and upright back, which made him say a very dreadful word, never heard among gentlemen, but which begins with *s*, several times on his way home. And he had to go to bed, and Madame in white jacket nursed him, kindly and tenderly.

Nearer and nearer. Yet the great word unspoken. Was it likely to be spoken under such circumstances? An elderly man with Rheumatism, and an old woman nursing him. *Sentimental* love must have long been dead between those two. *Storge*, concentrated on the same object, might unite them once more.

Would M. and Madame D'Isigny ever have been united without disaster? I decline to express an opinion. He could not go to the Assembly, but lay in his bed, rubbing his back with opodeldoc. She fluttered about the rooms in her camisole and assisted him, congratulating herself and him, that they could get on without a tipsy maid. "Oh, heavens! had there been but a maid who went into the street and brought news, she might have lived drunk, died drunk, and be buried drunk." This was Madame's language afterwards.

Opodeldoc and tisane: and the fire in the stove to be kept

up, and no servant to bring the wood. "You will be cold, Monsieur, my husband," she said; "I will put some of my not numerous petticoats over you." So she talked walking up and down the room.

Merciful heavens, spare us! and save us from dying of sheer terror, like dogs! What figure is this, standing bold and horrible in the lamplight, which makes the infuriated and dauntless Madame D'Isigny cower down into the bed beside her husband, and which makes D'Isigny rise, with his arm around his wife's neck, to confront it? What figure is this, then, that strikes terror into the hearts of those who had never known terror before, and, divided for so many years, now felt their hearts beating one against the other? Who was this ghost?

William the Silent. William, the English groom, standing there before them in the lamplight, in shirt, breeches, and stockings. Handsome, in the defiant, triumphant fury of his look, yet saying words which made him hideous and horrible.

"Monsieur, they are murdering the prisoners. I have escaped by running; but they have murdered Mademoiselle Mathilde."

## CHAPTER LX.

### TOGETHER ONCE MORE.

REIGN OF TERROR! Yes, it had fairly begun. William saw nearly the first of it; for retiring, after they had asked him a few questions, into the anteroom, he in a few minutes saw M. and Madame D'Isigny come swiftly forth. Both tall, majestic, and handsome, beyond most of their fellow men and women now, yet with a look in their grey and smitten faces as though something too horrible for human speech had looked upon them, and turned them into stone.

They had said to one another as it were but one word; and that was "Marat." So they never stopped, either to notice him, or to interrogate him; but passed swiftly on down the stairs, into the street.

"Do you believe it?" asked D'Isigny, as they walked rapidly.

"There can be no doubt, from what your man said," replied Madame. "But it is Marat's work, and he will be hiding at home. Let us confront him; and, if it is true, you have your sword, and can kill him. Our only hope lies with Marat. There is a wild chance that your man is wrong. Keep your sword up under your redingote, or we shall be stopped."

"Yours is the best head, Marie," said D'Isigny.

"But a poor one, if it has brought us to this, Isidore."

"The fault was mine," said he.

"Nay, it was mine," she answered.

"You are generous, Marie."

"We can be generous to those we love, Isidore."

D'Isigny's hand felt out in the dark for hers, and it was done: henceforth these twain were one. Mutually fearing, mutually respecting one another, from this moment, until death, there was no cloud between those two.

Even in this night of horrors unutterable, the spectacle of two such imperial grey figures walking swiftly, attracted attention. Most people knew by this time what was being done, and spoke in whispers, lurking at street corners. The Parisian people were not yet used to blood; they were not yet trained to the pitch of howling round Bailly in his death agony for hours.

"These people are terrified at what their agents are doing, my beloved," said D'Isigny.

And Madame pretended that she had not heard him, and made him call her his "beloved" once more.

"They will be educated soon, Isidore," she answered.

There were very few crowds in the more open streets. There were many National Guards, who were half-hearted. Moreover, Roland was expected to act (and, in my opinion, had he had the courage of a *man*, not of a *suicide*, might have acted). The thing was being done by a small, but very powerful and concentrated minority. The Parisians knew this well, and, without a leader, were afraid to act. That they disapproved of it, is proved by their verdict on the matter when they began to free themselves from this terribly powerful clique under Tallien, and got themselves contented, after seventy years, with the present state of things. I do not believe that the French are more cruel than ourselves; but the Gualches had already invented the art of insurrection, the finishing details of which are given us by M. Victor Hugo in "Les Misérables;" and so they kept the broader streets clear, for fear of artillery.

So M. and Madame D'Isigny were only looked at, until they came to the narrow street, which we have known before as the Rue Jacquerie.

Here there was a dense crowd, nearly closing up the street.

"Isidore," said Madame, "we shall be assassinated; but let us die together."

D'Isigny knew better. He put his arm round her waist, and still walking quickly, cried out in a loud voice, which might be heard from one end of the street to the other,—

"Room, Citizens, for ci-devant D'Isigny, the Breton, known here before, who goes under emergency to visit the Citoyen Marat."

They parted at once, these people; and Madame said directly, "He has gone home."

And more than one in the crowd said, "Make way. This is D'Isigny, the Breton, who nursed the dead child, and who loved and supported Marat when he was deserted of God."

There was no difficulty in getting to Marat's door. There were plenty of assistant hands to batter at it, for every one was puzzled, and no one understood thoroughly what was going on.

It was opened by Madame Delit, sister of Marat, who had her child with her. "He has laid down to sleep," she said. "He must not be disturbed." D'Isigny, whom she remembered, promptly put her aside, and slipping in with Madame D'Isigny closed the door behind him, and passed quickly upstairs, into the room we have seen before, and to the bed we have seen before.

Upon it lay a tangled heap of grey clothes, from the upper part of which came a bare lean arm, the hand of which was twined into the coarse wavy curls of what looked like a human head. Marat, on this night of unutterable horrors, had thrown himself on his bed in his clothes, and, like Danton, had slept. There was no face to be seen; it was under the arm. D'Isigny was approaching the bed, when Madame, quietly, but with decisive strength, anticipated him, and going up to the bed said, with a loud clear voice,—

"Marat, awake!"

The grey heap of clothes moved, and from under the naked

arm there came a face, which looked on that of Madame D'Isigny with that dull stupidity and look of inquiry, which I suppose all men have when they first awaken.

I cannot describe that face; but I can describe the effect of it, however.

As it moved from under the naked arm and disclosed itself, D'Isigny, who had seen it before, drew back and turned away. Madame drew up her crest like a rattlesnake, prepared to strike, and confronted it. Not only with courageous defiance, but with furious words, words which I am loth to use, but which, considering the period, the people concerned, and the situation, I am compelled to use.

"Marat, thou dog, thou hast died in thy sleep, and hast awakened in hell. I, the other fury of the Revolution, demand to know what thou hast done with my daughter, Mathilde?"

The heap of grey clothes, with the face among them, was sitting on the side of the bed directly.

"It is not hell; and thou art distracted," said Marat. "I know of but one Mathilde, and she is safe in Brittany. And who art thou, thou grey fury?"

"I am Madame D'Isigny. My daughter, Mathilde, has been murdered by your orders. I ordered her to personate her sister, the Marquise de Valognes, and our groom says that she has been murdered; perhaps it is not so. Say it is not so!"

"You mean," said Marat, "that you sent Mathilde to Paris to personate her sister?"

"That is the case, man!"

"Oh, you incredible lunatics! In what prison was she?"

"In the Abbaye."

"Why she nursed me and tended me when I was penniless and alone. Why, I could have saved her. Why, I liberated eight, four days ago, in addition to Danton's list, from the same prison. I saw in the list of the imprisoned, Marquise de Valognes, whom I remember as a foolish girl who insulted me, and all the time through your silly deceit it was my own Mathilde, for whom I would have died. Come quickly, there is yet some glimmer of hope. Quick! quick! Are you made of stone?"

Marat, descending the staircase, fluttered swiftly in his grey clothes along the street before them like a bat before two herons. Not a soul spoke to any of the three, for they knew Marat well, and guessed what was going on. The conscience of the Rue de Jacquerie was troubled, and it was a little afraid of its idol. The idol also had signs by which it made the worshippers understand that this was not the hour of sacrifice or prayerful flattery.

The streets grew more and more solitary as they grew broader, and the tall, strong couple had a difficulty sometimes in keeping pace with the figure which passed so rapidly on before them under the lanthorns, casting on the wall and pavement a hundred flickering shadows, more goblin-like than itself. At last, in the distance, at the end of a street, they saw a tall narrow building of many storeys, with two little turrets at each corner, in front of which there was a small crowd with flambeaux, the light of which lit up every angle in the building from the lower side. There was rapid occasional movement in the crowd, but very little noise, and neither of our friends at first understood what was going on, until Marat stopped and said, holding up his arm:

"This is the work of your order. It is possible that I may have to ask you to look on it: but will spare you if I can. Stay here, I will return immediately."

Time, in their terror for what was so dear for them, had become dead. The courage of both failed. D'Isigny, with the instinct of a gentleman, stood between his wife and what was going on under the flambeaux, but indeed she was as well able to bear it as he. Earth seemed gone from them, and the only link between them and *hope* was the wolf whose maddened head conceived the iniquity. In their rapidly vanishing hope, they almost loved him.

He was quickly back with five men: and they knew the fearful truth with certainty.

"We are too late here," said Marat: and paused, even he.

They were dumb with horror and grief, and said nothing. For the time, Marat was time and the world to them, and they hung upon his gasping lips.

"It may not be too late elsewhere, for another purpose," he said, very quietly. "Go with these five men. Each one of them has the power of an emperor or a king to-night, for he is patriot. You are safe with them. I, Marat, say so."

"Will you not go with us, M. Marat?" asked Madame D'Isigny.

"Fools, conspirators of the salon, how fit are you for revolution. Why, if my beloved sister lay dead upon the stones before me, I could think, I could act. You stand like frightened sheep before the vengeance of the people for their unutterable wrongs. Listen, and understand. Had not the people demanded my life I would have laid it down for her who is lost through an unhappy mistake. I will make some amends, for you, in your way, were kind to me. I have been late at the Abbaye, and must fly to the Conciergerie. If, in consequence of your incredible imbecility, I have not been able to save your daughter Mathilde, there is yet a wild chance that I may save your son-in-law, De Valognes."

He passed swiftly from their sight into the darkness, and they saw him no more.

The five men hurried them away.

"There is barely time," one said, "we must be very quick. You know me, D'Isigny, I am Jean Bon, who first brought you to Marat's house."

"I know you," said D'Isigny, "and I will reward you."

"I want no money. We take only the wages of the Commune.* We are enragés, and aristocrat money would burn our hands. I want swift walking, though. Can your wife walk swiftly, or shall we leave her?"

Madame could walk as fast as any of them, and proved it. Once more time was in abeyance, even now that hope was gone. The streets grew narrow, and once more again broad, and upon the night air were borne whisperings of trees and faint scents of the country, carried from a distance in the fresh wind of the coming summer morn. At last, in a square place, among larger streets, they came on another group of flambeaux, and were stopped again.

Jean Bon went on, "I knew her well," he said, "I saw her in the Abbaye." And they let him go, and after a time he came back again.

"We are too late here again," he said, in a whisper.

---

\* It is a singular fact, attested by, I believe, every one, that as far as could be ascertained, hardly any robbery was committed.

"What place is that?" said Madame, pointing to the flambeaux.

"The opening which the secret committee of the Commune caused to be made in the catacombs," whispered Jean Bon to Madame, for D'Isigny was spent and dumb.

"Shall we have no relics of her, then?" asked her mother.

"Her good works," said Jean Bon, "and this. They found it on her bosom. We do not steal, and the Commune would have got it. But I had it given up directly when I told them that her mother had come even here to seek her."

She took what he gave her mechanically, and they were escorted home, knowing nothing and caring nothing about their own fate. The lamp in D'Isigny's room was still burning when they got home, and D'Isigny cast himself on his bed. Madame came to him.

"This is all we have left of her," said she, and showed him what Jean Bon had given her.

Old Lady Somers' missal, with the Ferdinand and Isabella illumination, and the silver filigree Byzantine binding, with the piece of the true cross set in it. On one leaf, which opened easiest to D'Isigny's hand, as being the most used, there was an illumination in red, which the patient monk who had done the beautiful work had never contemplated; though unconsciously, he in his way, by his idea of making an ideal lazy Heaven in this world, had helped that state of affairs which set, centuries afterwards, the broad red stain across his lilies and his ivy leaves.

## CHAPTER LXI.

### CONCIERGERIE.

POOR LOUIS DE VALOGNES: thinner and more beautiful ghost of my favourite Havelock, Willoughby, Desilles. Do you care for him? Where was he? And how did he fare?

With less determination, with less character, with less intense religionism than General Havelock or Lieutenant Willoughby, he was still bon Chrétien; and with less of all three attributes than I picture to myself in André Desilles, he was yet a very valuable man. Had there been a large majority of such men in France as he or the Lameths—nay, even as the Polignacs —there might have been no Revolution ; for good or for evil, as the reader thinks.

Life had been intensely dear and sweet on the whole to Louis de Valognes. To ornamental men of personal beauty, used to admiration and kindliness from their fellows, of good health, good conscience, good manners, a real love of their kind, and sufficient real earnestness of purpose to make them well thought of among the very best and highest of their acquaintances, life is generally very precious. Louis de Valognes had all these qualifications for an entire enjoyment of life even when he was a cadet. Superadded to all these things now he had a splendid estate, a beautiful wife loved beyond measure, and a position such as would be envied by most men in Europe.

And it was all gone from him utterly. The pleasant, smiling Atlantic of prestige, love, wealth, society, had sunk from below his feet, as the sea had sunk from the feet of him and André Desilles on the first day when you saw them sitting together on the rocks at St. Malo. Of his deeply-loved wife he had seen but little ; of his child the melancholy baby still less. He was a very affectionate man, and had always had some one on whom to lavish his affection. Now he was all alone ; for the people with whom he was confined did not suit him, and indeed he scarcely suited them, for the son-in-law of the traitor and trimmer D'Isigny, friend of Marat, could scarcely be popular among them ; and again he thought them for the most part frivolous, vain, and shallow, with all their courage.

"These people," he said to himself once bitterly, while eating his own heart in his bitter disappointment, " are ready to die decently, yet a good number of them never managed to live decently. Old Cardinal Leroy has sufficient personal courage to prevent him making a scene on the scaffold ; I never heard of any one who did, except Lady Salisbury, and she only did it through an excess of personal courage. These people, who one half of them have neglected every duty, now take credit for courage. Bah !

" And their manners," he growled on in his sour mood, " they are no better than mine : their tittle-tattles about precedence are to me insupportable now that hell has broken loose. Why if that old fool, De Barsac, happened to be sleeping with his wife when the last trump sounded, he would hold a polite argument with her as to which of them etiquette required to get out of bed first.

"I am sick of the whole thing. I want my liberty and my wife. The worst of it is that these Parisians seem to have arrested all the fools to keep me company, and to leave all the clever men walking free. I suppose it will be the turn of the clever men next."

Poor Louis. Life so dear, and yet at the price so worthless. He moped alone, and hungered in his heart for one look of Adèle. The look she had when she came towards him with her mouth slightly curled up at the corners, and when her eyebrows followed the motion of her mouth: the look that told him that he was loved above all things on earth, and most things in heaven.

Where was she? In prison or saved? How far would these revolutionists dare to go? Not to the extent of death, surely? And so the poor innocent kindly lad sat and ate his heart alone! for the frivolity, the snuff-boxing, the badinage, of the ghosts down-stairs were as insufferable for him to see as it is for me or you to read of.

On the afternoon of the night in which Mathilde was lost, he became aware that the prisoners were being sent into the street, and were being murdered. The man who told him was a young man, like himself, with a wife, who had sympathised with him, and who had sources of information.

"Are they killing all?" said Louis.

"I think so. Danton, I know, sent out lists, which were supplemented by Marat. The people on those lists were those we saw removed yesterday. You and I, you see, were not removed."

Death, then: and without even one last kiss from Adèle. It was come to this.

Through long hours he sat and brooded in his window on the stairs, and heard one after another go down. He tried to prepare himself to die, but life was too sweet, and he could not do it. So far from getting into a frame of mind fit to meet his God, he got into a frame of mind more fit to meet the Devil. "Oh for a knife, that I might give an account of even one."

It was towards the dawning of the summer morning when he

was summoned. Five men came to summon him, and he saw them go into the dog-hole where he had slept.

"What is your errand for?" he cried.

"Ci-devant De Valognes," cried one, in reality Jean Bon, friend of Marat.

"I am he."

"Come down, then," said Jean Bon, taking him by the arm, and whispering to him, "Be discreet."

This whisper was overheard, by at least one of the five, who at once spoke out.

"Jean Bon, thou art a dog, a traitor, and a liar; and Marat is not all the world."

So Louis went to his hopeless death down the stairs, Jean Bon holding him by the arm. He would have bolted had he not known what was going on outside; but he only prayed, and found that, in the last agony, the power of prayer had come.

A smell of brandy and tobacco, and he was in a lighted room, with six men, in a row, on one side of it, and he himself, with his five guides, on the other.

Once more Jean Bon whispered, "Be discreet!" but he did not understand, and yet was discreet; believing that his death was three minutes off.

"Who is this man?" said the president of the tribunal.

"Ci-devant Louis de Valognes," replied Jean Bon.

"His crime?"

"None. I, Jean Bon, known as a patriot, declare that there is nothing against this man. This man is an aristocrat by birth; he has married into his order. Well, then; he married the daughter of D'Isigny, the Breton, friend of Marat; and is brother-in-law to Mathilde, the friend and nurse of Marat, when he had no friends. This man is innocent."

"It seems to me," said the president, rather promptly, "that this man is perfectly innocent. Are there any specific charges against him?"

"He is an aristocrat," cried the patriot who had quarrelled with Jean Bon on the stairs. "He was friend of the Murderer of Nanci, whose funeral obsequies were performed on the Champ de Mars, with those of his fellow murderers, by Lafayette and Bailly."

"My dear friend," said the president, "I am an aristocrat

myself; as is St. Huruges. For André Desilles, you must be in a state of distraction—he was killed in trying to save life. Is that all against him?"

It appeared so.

"Dismiss him with 'Vive la Nation,' then, and, Jean Bon, keep close to him."

Jean Bon kept close to him, and said, "Shut your eyes, for you have been near death, and you tremble."

Louis shut his eyes, but did not keep them shut, for he opened them too soon, and saw before him a handsome young man, with outspread arms, lying, as if crucified, on the pavement. After this he closed them again, and, led by Jean Bon, passed on in safety.

## CHAPTER LXII.

### THE ALTAR.

'ISIGNY threw himself on his bed when they got home, and lay there, saying not one word. Madame, saying not one word either, paced up and down the room with her hands beside her. Each one was thinking that there might be terrible recriminations on either side, yet both were quite unwilling to begin them. There was nothing now left to either of them but the other; a new-born love, the love of the old for the old, was nascent between them. Both of them dreaded its disturbance. So Madame, walking up and down the room, kept saying, "It was my fault for using Adèle's house as a rendezvous for the followers of Charette and Larochejaquelein." And D'Isigny lay on the bed in dumb grief, saying to himself, "It was my fault for telling her to continue her falsehood." So these two were silent: each refusing to speak, each ready to yield.

There opened the door, and there came in a ghost. It was the ghost of Louis de Valognes.

"I have been saved," he said, "and I know all. We will mourn together, for we are all three guilty of her death. I have had my share in it, as I had in the death of my André Desilles. It was I by my cowardly deceit who kept her from André until it was too late. You, sir, by your extreme precisianism, made me fear you, and drove us all into deceit ; and you, Madame, who could have saved all this misery, separated yourself from your family by your violence. Are we not all three to blame, I ask ? "

The answer was a mournful " Yes."

In a subdued and humble frame of mind, and in a low voice, they discussed details which Shakespeare, with his bold, clear, decisive drawing, might handle, but which I, wanting his art, must leave alone, from sheer inability to do so without offending the great " Ars Poetica " canon, in which I believe. They talked long, and then Louis went out to arouse William and get further facts.

It was nine o'clock in the morning, and broad glorious day, when Louis went out to him. The first thing which Louis saw was a wild, dirty-looking man in the further doorway, who pointed with his finger to something in a corner close to Louis's feet, nodded, and then vanished. This was the very last of Jean Bon.

Louis turned towards the corner indicated by Jean Bon, and grew terrified for a moment. On the floor in that corner lay William the Silent, of whom no one had thought, on his back, just as he had cast himself down after his fearful swift struggle for life. He lay on the floor with his arms stretched out, so awfully like the figure which Louis had seen on the pavement in front of the Conciergerie, that he dreaded to approach him.

Overpowered with sleep he lay there, not dead, not likely to die : only lying in the happy death of sleep, just as he had cast himself down. He had nothing on him but the clothes in which he escaped, his breeches, stockings, and shirt. His shirt was open at the breast, and on the centre of his breast lay a letter. Louis, bending over him, took the letter from his breast, putting his hand on the left side of it. William's heart was going as steadily, and as well, as his brother's did when he stood with his thumb on the touch-hole of the thirty-eight pounder, and after the first horrible and glorious two hours of Trafalgar.

He was easy about William, but he took the letter from his unconscious chest, and went back to M. and Madame D'Isigny, saying in his pretty French way : " Here is an offering which I have stolen from the highest of all altars, the bare breast of a thoroughly noble person. May we hear its contents?"

D'Isigny read it to them at once.

"I believe that I am traitor for what I do, yet I have consulted Camille Desmoulins and Barbaroux; and they say that I am right.

"My heart is grieved. It was the stupidity of you and your wife which caused the mischief. I will make what amends I can to you. If you have a heart as good as a dog's, you will see that it was not my fault. The nation is beginning its vengeance, for many things. A time will come when the civilised world will sum up, in retirement, the case between us and between you; and mark me, the balance of atrocities will be against you aristocrats; or the world is delivered to the devil: a thing I do not believe.

"With regard to your order, we mean to slay, and slay, and slay. Your order has courage, brains, very often high virtue. These three things oppose our views, and we mean to put an end to them by death. If your order had been less dangerous, you might have lived: as it is, you must die.

"As for you and yours, I, who hold really the reins, tell you that you are free. You are perfectly safe, for the present. But not always. There is a cat scrambling up by dirty gutter-holes to the roof of power, who would ruin me as certainly as he would ruin you.

"I have immense power now, and I have no mercy except towards a few. I have mercy towards you, for *her* sake. And I tell you that my power may increase or decrease. Barbaroux's (my old pupil's) beautiful face, and Verniaud's more beautiful tongue, may destroy me, and would never spare you. It is all a throw of the dice. I will protect you as long as I can; but how long will that be? Danton only truly stays by me, for Camille Desmoulins has partly gone from me. Those two men are human; I and the Cat Robespierre are beyond the pale of humanity.

"Get away quickly, sell up all you have and retire to England. I will protect your retreat. This is the last mercy which I can show.

"MARAT."

## CHAPTER LXIII.

### SHEEPSDEN ONCE MORE.

HE old house once more, but in more quiet times. The golden autumn had faded from his brighter glories, until only a few fluttering yellow and red leaves were wasting on the trees. November was dying into December; the wild spring winds and rains under which I had first to introduce Sheepsden to you, had blown themselves into quiescence, and all was still.

Yet Sheepsden in a way was more lively and more pleasant than it had ever been before, for there were more people there. They were none of them cheerful, for the shadow of the great disaster had not yet passed away; they were all subdued, and still the mere number of them brightened up Sheepsden, for there were assembled there nearly all the people of our story, inside the screen. The French party had returned, and had quietly asked the English party to a supper: Mrs. Bone, William, and the Rector's and Sir Lionel's men were waiting; and the guests were all speaking in a very subdued tone, so that it was difficult for one pair of speakers to hear what the other said, or for the general company to hear what any particular pair of speakers said. Madame D'Isigny sat at the head of the table, and Monsieur fronted her. They were almost absolutely silent.

The Rector, sitting between the Marquis de Valognes and Sir Lionel Somers, happened to talk to the former first.

"I have not realised it yet," said he, "what actually became of her. Where was she buried?"

"In the Catacombs, which the Secret Committee of the Commune had opened five days before."

"It seems incredible," said the Rector.

"It would not be so to you if you had been where I have," said Louis.

The Rector had scarcely realised it as yet. He said:

"I am sorry to hear that Madame la Marquise, whom I used to call Adèle, is so ill as to be unable to appear at table."

"It is merely the case of a supplementary heir," said the Marquis de Valognes.

So the Rector turned to Sir Lionel,—

"Lionel," he said, "there is another saint in glory, for a friend of yours, Evans, is dead."

"Ah! So I should have expected, his death has been near for two years. I am not sorry, Rector; how can I be? When did he die?"

"On the first of September."

"Then Mathilde and he will actually meet," said Sir Lionel. "How passing strange. My time will not come yet, and when it does they will have wandered so far into the maze of paradise that I shall not be able to overtake them, and even if I could I should not know them for the glory which would be in their faces. Will they wait for me, those two, do you think, Rector?"

The theology of Oxford offered no answer to this singular question; but as a man of the world the Rector found a lame answer for him.

"Lionel, my boy, you must not brood and get fanciful."

"I will not," said Sir Lionel. "I have no such intention. There is surely nothing fanciful in hoping that I may see Mathilde and Evans again, and in company, for they were twin souls. Are the Revelations fanciful?"

"Lionel," said the Rector, "you should remember how very little is revealed about the future of the blest."

"I know," said Sir Lionel, "and I know what I mean also. What has become of Evans' widow? because she must be handsomely provided for."

"She was in deep poverty and ill health, but she is well provided for now."

"By whom?" he asked.

"By your mother."

"No!" he said. "That is very beautiful. Mother," he said to Lady Somers, who was sitting solemnly beside her old schoolfellow, Madame D'Isigny, "the Rector and I have been speaking of Mrs. Evans, and I give you my thanks."

"And I give you my blessing, my son," replied the old lady, turning to Madame D'Isigny.

"My dear friend," she continued, "whatever could have made me dislike you?"

"My furious ill temper," said Madame the Terrible, "and moreover the failure in winning my husband's love. Yet you never saw my temper at its best. Sister dear," she said, "was I not terrible at my worst? Do you remember the day at La Garaye?"

A bland, timid, and pale old lady, who sat on the other side of Lady Somers, in a religious dress, raised her head and said,—

"Yes, sister, I remember it. You were angry with us, but you saved our lives by your courage."

"You were the Lady Superior of Dinort,\* Madame," said Lady Somers. "My heart burned when I heard of your splendid heroism. Your nuns are here, Madame, I understand."

"They are at Lulworth with the Welds," answered our old friend, the Lady Superior of Dinort, Lady Visitor of La Garaye. "They will be provided for among the Catholic English families in various ways. For me, I stay with my brother, and go and see them sometimes."

Said Mrs. Bone to William,—

"So this is your going abroad."

Said William to Mrs. Bone,—

"You are always right; that's just it."

Said Martin the Poacher, who had looked in, hearing that the gentlefolks were going to meet at supper, on the chance of a feed, to William in the scullery,—

"They're carrying on fine games, they French."

And William said,—

"Fine games, indeed."

And Martin said,—

"And so you circumvented of the hull lot. I'd never have give you credit for it, but you done it. Your uncle Bob, I'd have backed he."

And William said,—

"I seen it was all over with her, God bless her, and I see

---

\* To save my readers trouble, Dinort is a perfectly fictitious place. Montauban, chosen for the sounding beauty of its name, is of course also fictitious. Vasansdire and Vaurien speak for themselves. All my other localisms—(is there such a word?)—are I think correct.

nothing but cutting and running, and I cut and run according. As for games, they are always up to all manner of games, they French."

"I knows 'em, they allus were, and they allus 'ool," said old Martin. And I am inclined to agree with him.

## CHAPTER LXIV.

A CHAPTER WHICH I HOPE THE READER WILL BE SORRY TO READ, FOR IT IS THE LAST.

IR LIONEL SOMERS married his mother after all, as the valley had before accused him of doing. At least he married no one else until four years after her death. Whom he married one may have forgotten or not have cared, but there was an heir to Ashurst born in the early part of this century, who still sits in the House of Lords.

In the awful storm, which followed the retreat of those with whom I have made you acquainted from France, not one of them moved in the French Revolution. D'Isigny was declared *emigré* and his estates confiscated, leaving him utterly dependent on his furious, now tamed wife, which was not a bad thing for him.

Strangely enough Louis de Valognes was never declared *emigré*. Some estates of his were confiscated and taken possession of by several laws, passed in the turmoil which followed, yet he was never declared *emigré*. The melancholy baby, whom I knew at Dieppe when he was sixty, was not without means. Under the Tallien reaction, and under the Buonaparte reaction, Louis might have recovered the main of his estates, but lacked the cash required in a civilised country to get himself quite righted.

For the rest of him, he would not stand Tallien ; and Adèle would, of course, have died sooner than speak to the Cabarus ; or, indeed, to Madame Buonaparte in the disreputable days, while she still rode with the Cabarus in the Bois de Boulogne, on a white horse, and while Napoleon was on his fool's errand in Egypt. On the receipt of the news of The Nile she said that she had always, from the first, said that this would be the end of it. But no living soul had ever heard her say so; and besides, it was not the end of it at all, only the beginning.

When Napoleon, however, was well seated, Louis, hungering after his old trade, offered his services; and Adèle, now that Cabarus was not received, was content to make her bow before the heretofore disreputable Josephine. Louis got employment, and rose high; though he never was Marshal. The melancholy baby early in life turned Legitimist in politics, and Ultramontane in religion, which, as Mrs. Bone would say, "vexed his pa." Exeant.

William the Silent married Mrs. Bone. That is to say, he never married her in the way of taking her to Church; seeing that she was old enough to be his grandmother, it would have been strange if he had. But he gave up his life to her first, and to the D'Isignys afterwards. Audrey, his sweetheart, being desirous of a wedded life, married the rising young sweep from Stourminster-Osborne, and William did not care a bit. So time went on; the Revolution blazed up, died into Tallienism, Buonapartism, while the war blazed on steadily, getting in its heat from red to white: until—until—it was all over. Nothing left but the command of the seas (now lost), 840 million of debt, and a tradition of great deeds sufficient to keep any nation alive for a century.

So I have accounted for every one of my characters. You shake your head, and say that there is still one, of whom I have given no account. Why, I gave the last account of this man when I first made acquaintance with you. You desire more. Well then.

It was during the peace of Amiens that Madame and Monsieur D'Isigny were walking through their estate at Sheepsden together. They had walked down to the ford, where Louis de Valognes had met Adèle in the old times, and D'Isigny had said, "I hate the place: it was partly the cause of all the mischief." And Madame had said, "Isidore, let us walk aloft on the Down;" and they had gone up, and rambled along the road which came from Christchurch, when they saw a young priest coming swiftly along the road towards them.

He stopped, of course, and spoke. "I seek the house of M. D'Isigny of Brittany. Kind sir, can you guide me?"

"I am D'Isigny, the Breton."

"I have a message for you from the dead," said the priest. "I am for Lulworth, but have made the detour. In the black darkness of worse than death I have kept to my purpose, and so see it is executed at last."

D'Isigny took a brown soiled letter from him, and opened it: there were but few words in it; but there was a curl of grey-black hair in it which he knew, and which made him put his hand to his head and moan aloud.

Madame picked up the letter, and knew the curl of hair as well as he. The letter was very short; she read it aloud.

"I dread committing any one, but I have been two years in prison now, and they say that this Carrier who has come down has no mercy. It is equal. I fear not dashing at the gate of glory. Yet the others. You, to whom this is written, be careful of Mathilde, for she knows how to die too well. This young priest, to whom I give this, is strong and athletic, and is going to try to escape. You see that I can say no more."

As they walked, the young priest told them how the end had come. This young priest was a Jesuit (forgive me, my readers), and had been selected by the order for missionary work, in consequence of being singularly athletic and powerful. Arrested on his way to Brest, en route for Pondicherry, he had been sent to Nantes, where he had lain two years, with our old friend Father Martin. At the end of it, when Carrier came, they had expected the Fusillade, but were spared that: then they heard of the Noyade, and prepared.

"I, being a good swimmer," said the athletic young Jesuit, "determined to try for life, knowing that, if I could dive half way across the river, the peasants on the other side would save me. Father Martin gave me his blessing, and this; and when it came to my turn, I kept so long under water, that you see I have brought it to you at last."

"What was he doing when you saw him last?" said Madame.

"Standing and chanting, trying to encourage the others to chant. Yet he was the only one who sang."

"What did he chant?" asked Madame. "Was it a Psalm?"

"No," said the Jesuit; "he chanted from the Revelations, pointing it himself."

"'And I heard a great voice out of Heaven, saying, Behold, the tabernacle of God is with men, and He will dwell with them, and they shall be His people, and God himself shall be with them, and be their God.

"'And God shall wipe away all tears from their eyes, and there shall be no more death, neither sorrow, nor crying, neither shall there be any more pain. *For the former things are passed away.*'"

With this last and greatest chant of Father Martin's I must bid you adieu, my reader. Let me hope that I have left you something to think about.

Truly, indeed, the former things are passed away.

THE END.

www.ingramcontent.com/pod-product-compliance
Lightning Source LLC
Chambersburg PA
CBHW022114290426
44112CB00008B/675